TACKLE CRAFT

TACKLE CRAFT

BY C. BOYD PFEIFFER

fully illustrated

CROWN PUBLISHERS, INC., NEW YORK
Distributed to the sporting goods trade by Stoeger Industries

Library of Congress Catalog Card Number: 73-82959

Manufactured in the United States of America
Published simultaneously in Canada by General Publishing Company Limited
Designed by Shari de Miskey

All photos by the Author

First paperback printing, August, 1975

ACKNOWLEDGMENTS

〜 BOOKS ARE ONLY RARELY THE WORK OF A SINGLE MIND. THIS BOOK IS
no exception. For twenty-five years I have been experimenting with making fishing tackle, and I have personally made and used all the items mentioned in these
pages.

Along the way I have learned of new ways of building tackle and new items
of tackle that can be built at home, and I have picked up other tackle-making tips
from countless friends, casual acquaintances, and fellow fishermen.

In spite of the paucity of literature on tackle-making, books, articles, and
pamphlets have also added to my knowledge of the craft. For all this a general
debt of gratitude is owed and gratefully acknowledged.

Many companies—manufacturers, retailers, mail order supply houses, and
others—have kindly helped with this book by supplying catalogs and information
about their wares. Thus, thanks must go to

Ace Cast Metal Products Company
Anglers Pro Shop
Best Bet Lures
Brookstone Company
Cabela's, Inc.
Sewell N. Dunton and Son, Inc.
Easy Molds, Inc.
Fairfield Sporting Goods Company
Fireside Angler, Inc.
Fish-It
Fishin' World
Gladding–South Bend Tackle Company
E. Hille
H & L Distributing Co., Inc.
Horrocks-Ibbotson Company
H. L. Leonard Rod Company
Lure-Craft

Midland Tackle Company
O. Mustad and Son (USA), Inc.
The Orvis Company
Ottawa Supply Company
Phillipson Rod Company
Reading Instrument Company
Reinke Brothers
Santee Lure and Tackle Company
Shoff's Sporting Goods
Tack-L-Tyers
Tackle-Craft
Tackle Shop
Thomas and Thomas
Toledo Manufacturing Company
Varmac Manufacturing Company, Inc.
Weber Tackle Company
Erwin Weller Company

In addition, many companies and their personnel went far beyond their duty in answering my requests for information or in supplying materials, line drawings, or size charts for the Appendix, and other special help that has added greatly to this book.

Thus, very special thanks must go to the following for their interest, enthusiasm, and help:

Allan Manufacturing Company and especially Bert Kaplan, for materials and permission to use size charts from their catalog.

Ament Mold Company and Paul Ament, who supplied much material for photos used in the chapter on making bucktails and jigs.

Aspen Lures and Tom Kassler, for supplying both materials and thoughts on making spinners and spoons.

Bead Chain Tackle Company and Richard H. MacDonald, for materials and permission to use size charts of their products.

Berkley and Company and Bob Koepp, for material for photos.

Gene Bullard Custom Rods and Gene Bullard, for alerting me to a new type of English ceramic guide that should now be on the market.

Carver Plastisols, Inc., for materials for photos.

Lew Childre and Sanders, Inc., and Ted French, for material for photos.

DDD Tackle, Inc., and Dick Savage, for allowing me much time to photograph his surgical tube lures and manufacturing techniques and for his many thoughts on tackle-making

Featherweight Products and Ralph Brinkerhoff for photos and permission to use many size charts from their catalog.

Fenwick/Sevenstrand Tackle Manufacturing Company along with Phil Clock and Dave Myers, for materials for photos.

Finnysports and Al Daly for size charts used in the Appendix.

Gudebrod Brothers Silk Company, Inc., and Fred Hooven, for materials for photos and size charts used in the Appendix.

Herter's, Inc., and especially George Leonard Herter, for materials for photos and kind permission to use a chart of fly rod grips from his book *Professional Glass and Split-Bamboo Rod Building Manual and Manufacturer's Guide.*

Ike's Fly Shop and the advice and enthusiasm of John Pinto.

Joe's Custom Rods and Joe Armold for materials for photos used in the book.

Lectrochem Company Inc. for materials used in photos.

Limit Manufacturing Corporation for materials used in photos in the book.

Luhr Jensen and Sons and Dan Stair for materials used in photos.

Lure Kits and Norm Bartlett for materials used in the book.

M-F Manufacturing Co., Inc. for materials for photos.

Maumelle Plastics Company and Henry Cooper for materials for photos.

Mildrum Manufacturing Company and Ted Benson for materials and size charts used in the Appendix.

Netcraft Company and H. T. Ludgate for photos, materials for photos and copies of his books *Popular Netcraft* and *Tackle Tricks with Wire.*

Palmer Manufacturing Company for materials for photos.

Reed Tackle and R. J. Reidmiller, for kind permission to use rod-guide-spacing charts from his catalog.

Rodmaker's Supply Catalog and Walt Edmondson, for help and advice.

Sampo, Inc., for permission to use size and charts from their catalog of products.

Santee Lure and Tackle Co., for materials for photos.

L. S. Starrett for permission to use metric-English equivalent charts found in the Appendix.

Stembridge Products, Inc., and Stan Herdlein for materials for photos.

Super-Sport and Bob Riker for materials for photos.

The Worth Company and Robert Worth and Dave Meyers for materials and size charts from their catalog.

Wright and McGill Company for permission to use size charts of their hooks from their catalog.

In addition, many individuals have helped in many ways. Special thanks must go to Chuck Edghill of Baltimore, Maryland, for his comments and photographic models of aluminum bucktail molds; to Dick Enger of Livonia, Michigan, editor of the rod-building booklet published by the Michigan Fly Fishing Club; to Dick Blauvelt of White Marsh, Maryland, for his help with ice-fishing equipment; to Mrs. Kitty Lourie of Buxton, North Carolina, for her comments on her electric rod winder; to Frank Woolner, editor of *Salt Water Sportsman* magazine, for permission to include his method of glass rod repair; to Steve Hines and Lefty Kreh for their hints on plastic rod cases; and to a host of other friends, acquaintances, fellow outdoor writers, and fishing companions who have helped in many ways, both great and small. For all of this a debt of gratitude is owed and gratefully acknowledged. Special thanks must go to Paul Jorgensen, a good friend and excellent fly tyer, for his help in learning about making several types of fiberglass ferrules for fishing rods.

But particular attention must be singled out to several who have helped directly with the completion of this book. In chronological order of help rendered, deep thanks and appreciation are extended to each of the following:

Irv Swope, a constant fishing companion and good friend, assisted by reading the rough copy of each chapter and supplied much in the way of constructive criticism, tips, comments, and ideas. As a retired engineer, part-time tackle-tinkerer, and full-time perfectionist and fisherman, he is ably suited for such a task.

My father, Curt Pfeiffer, while not a fisherman, nonetheless took endless hours to pose under hot floodlights and in often awkward positions for many of the photos in the book. He also helped during a final proofreading of the manuscript.

My wife, Jackie, deserves special recognition for her understanding during my long absences from more domestic tasks while writing and in long photographing sessions. And as an excellent secretary, she not only typed the entire book, but also corrected my too many typographical errors in the original copy. As such she was my harshest critic as well as a constant inspiration.

And finally, Nick Lyons, editor extraordinaire, waited patiently and I am sure with some misgivings while the book deadline passed and the manuscript and photo package grew three times larger than its originally intended size.

C. Boyd Pfeiffer

NOTE TO THE READER

This book on tackle craft is as complete as I can make it; I have tried to include all the types of tackle that can easily be made in any home workshop. Obviously, there are probably some special methods of tackle-making, and even some special tackle items, with which I am not familiar.

While I will be unable to enter into extensive correspondence with readers, I would be delighted to hear of and to acknowledge new and different items of tackle or methods of making tackle. Readers may contact me through the publisher.

C. Boyd Pfeiffer

CAUTION

I have made every effort to describe tackle-making methods that are not only easy, but safe. Familiarity with tools is important in any craft, and certainly no less so in making fishing tackle. In the making of some tackle, such as the molding of lead sinkers, bucktails, tin squids, and plastic lures, improper technique may prove extremely dangerous, so I have taken care to describe methods of tackle-building that are completely safe, and to warn the reader clearly of possible dangerous practices.

However, neither the author nor the publisher can assume responsibility for any damages or injuries resulting from the construction, molding, repair, or formation of tackle described in this book.

INTRODUCTION

Making Fishing Tackle Is A Satisfying Hobby. It Gives You something constructive to do during the "off" months when the weather is too cold for serious fishing, or when the seasons are closed. It can become as detailed and complex as you want, or can remain simple, involving only a small cash outlay for materials and utilizing, for the most part, tools found in any home workshop.

There has been a tremendous hiatus in the appearance of books dealing with the making of fishing tackle. The several books that have dealt with this subject in the past are incomplete or out-of-date because of the introduction of new techniques and materials. The molding of soft plastic lures, such as the popular plastic worm, and the use of two-piece plug parts are relatively new and are not, to my knowledge, included in any book dealing with the making of fishing tackle.

By contrast the fly tyer and bug builder has a vast supply of books at his disposal. My library contains thirty-eight books dealing exclusively with flies and fly-tying, and this is by no means a complete collection of books on the art. Thus, flies, bass bugs, and similar lures tied by means of a fly-tying vise and tools will not be dealt with in this volume. The excellent publications already available would make any such addition superfluous.

The rod builder does have a few volumes to choose from, but for the most part these are older or out-of-print books that deal mainly with the construction of split-bamboo rods. When these books do deal with glass rods, it is generally with earlier types of fiberglass rods, and they do not take into account the multiplicity of rod blanks and accessories available from many outlets today. Thus, building of modern fiberglass rods is included in this book.

Perhaps you have considered making your own lures and fishing tackle in the past, but have never actually tried it. The most frequent complaint is that it will require too many tools or more-than-average manual skill. Nothing is further from the truth! With only two pairs of pliers, you can make any of the standard spinners on the market, in addition to originating any new designs that you would like to try. And the pliers are only needed to form an eye in the spinner wire, and to wrap this eye after the hook is added to the spinner.

Without *any* tools except the proper molds, you may make any of the new soft plastic lures. Plastic worms, plastic plugs, crayfish, hellgrammite, and minnow imitations can be made with molds that are readily available.

With only a pair of wire cutters and a small file (and again the proper mold) you can make any type of bucktail, jig, sinker, or saltwater squid. The wire cutters are needed only to cut away the excess lead from the pouring spout of the mold, and the file to remove any excess metal or "flash" from along the seam of the mold.

Rods may be built or rewrapped without any tools at all. Only the rod parts, some glue, a spool of thread, and varnish are needed for an expert job.

The degree of skill needed for making fishing tackle varies with the type of tackle being made and the degree of perfection required in the lure or piece of tackle. You'll need more skill to carve your own wood plugs (not necessary, since plastic or lathed wood plug blanks are readily available) or make your own molds. But anything in this book may be made with ease by anyone who can hammer a nail, put a screw in the wall for a spice rack, or repair a lamp.

Cost is another reason why it is advantageous to make your own equipment. For example, most spinners cost between 65 and 85 cents retail. Identical copies of these same popular spinners may be made in only a few minutes' time and at a cost of less than 19 cents each. Other lures are proportionately cheap to make and require comparably little time.

Aside from basic economy, there are two far more important reasons for making lures. First, having the parts readily available to make favorite lures, you will be likely to make a number of those that prove effective, and also to make up a small variety of other types of lures that may also be effective. Thus, at the same time the danger of running out of the one effective lure while on a fishing trip is reduced and the possibility of having a variety of lures for different situations is increased. A second and more important reason is that you will fish more effectively. How? By subconsciously knowing that you are using a lure (say a spinner) that costs 19 cents rather than 75 or 85 cents, you will fish in snaggy, rock- and stump-strewn water that you might otherwise pass up for fear of losing an expensive lure; these places are where the fish are most likely to hide and those most likely to be passed over by other fishermen. I firmly believe that this fact, together with your natural tendency to experiment in making lures, will in a short time make you a better and more accomplished fisherman.

I have mentioned that the experimental or custom-made lures and tackle are another important reason for making your own fishing tackle. These custom lures or tackle accessories are costly or unobtainable any other way. Also, by making your own lures and accessories, you can—if you desire—make them of finer quality materials and with finer workmanship than those obtainable on the open market.

Not the least of considerations is the pure pleasure of making a lure or piece of fishing tackle, and satisfaction that comes from doing a good job. The culmination of this chain of events—and of course the real reason for doing it— is the thrill of hooking and landing a fish on a homemade plug or bucktail (and perhaps also with a rod custom-built by you, to your particular wants and needs.)

A final reason why you should seriously consider making your own fishing tackle is the possibility of eventually realizing some profit from selling your lures, rods, or other home-built equipment. This is a distinct possibility if you manufacture a lure that works well in your area and is difficult or impossible to obtain otherwise, if you come up with a new effective design, or if you build a rod that is ideally suited to the type of fishing done in your locality. For example, in my section of the country, tackle tinkerers sell shad darts (a specialized type of tapered jig used for hickory and American shad) all along the roads leading to the Susquehanna and Potomac rivers each spring. These lures are molded, tied, and painted each winter to be ready for the early-spring rush of shad fishermen, in about the middle of April. Mostly, these are one-man operations and the lures are sold only at one or two roadside stands, but there are several small companies that do a wholesale business and provide a number of tackle stores, riverside lunch stands, and boat liveries in these areas.

Please note that I am not advocating this as an ultimate reason for making fishing tackle. I do not make it for profit myself, and know very few of a vast army of tackle tinkerers that do. As a "sure" business proposition, it is definitely open to question. On a large scale, it will involve expensive machine tools such as lathes, drill presses, and spray painters that must be amortized against your time and profit. Any business operation like this also involves licenses, patents, or copyrights for new lure designs, business records, and the ultimate income tax form for small businesses—all of which are well beyond the scope and intent of this book.

This book is meant to increase your personal pleasure—pleasure in making tackle, in having something to do in the off-months, and in increasing your skill as an angler. I hope that you will have as much enjoyment in reading it as I have in preparing it, and more important, that you will have as much fun making your own fishing tackle as I have making mine.

CONTENTS

1

TOOLS AND MATERIALS

∿ PROPER TOOLS ARE THE KEY TO DOING ANY JOB WELL. A REPAIRMAN who comes to your house to fix a dishwasher, TV, oven, or hot water heater always has his well-equipped tool box; a carpenter or cabinetmaker could not begin constructing anything without the proper tools. By the same token, the tackle tinkerer must have the proper tools to construct the fishing equipment that he wishes to make. Fortunately, the basic tools needed for making most fishing tackle are not expensive or hard to get. In all likelihood, you already have a number of these tools, and can improvise others.

Nor is it necessary to collect or buy all the tools listed here before you begin making fishing tackle and lures; you may be interested in only two or three types of lures or accessories and will not need the tools required for others. Each chapter of this book lists both the minimally required tools and those tools that are not required but will make the job easier. If you plan to make all the equipment listed in this book, you will ultimately need or want all the basic tools listed—otherwise, look over the chapters of interest before heading to the hardware store.

Bench or Work Table. You will need a place to work and to hold tools, materials, and finished products. This can be as simple as a small TV tray to hold the parts and a few pliers if you are only making spinners; on the other hand, a sturdy workshop bench will be needed if you plan to saw out wood plugs and make gaffs, tackle boxes, and other major equipment. In some cases, as in molding plastic lures, lead sinkers, and jigs, you may not be able to work where you wish but may have to work in the kitchen where you will have access to heat. Here, a small square of thin plywood, masonite, or other scrap material will give you a place to work, will catch any spilled metal or plastic, and will save the kitchen counter surface from scarring. If you are unwelcome in the

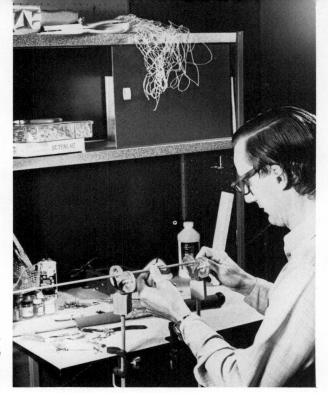

Small self-contained work-bench and bench sets like this one are fine work areas. Here, the author wraps a rod.

kitchen as a tackle tinkerer, use a propane torch or stove in your workshop, and do your molding there.

I use several types of workbench depending upon the type of tackle I am making. A large—8 foot by 3 foot—sturdy wood workbench serves as a general work area for all types of tackle tinkering. A small pegboard workshop unit with built-in shelves and storage space is ideal for small jobs such as winding rods, wrapping tails on bucktail lures, assembling spinners, and similar tasks. When a fly-tying vise, rod winder, wire wrapper, or similar tool must be mounted, the thin one-inch-thick bench top is best.

Vise. A machinist's vise, secured to your bench or clamped to your working table (be sure to protect the table finish first), will be needed to hold wood for cutting it down to plug size, heavy sheet metal when cutting out spoons, and do-it-yourself aluminum for making tackle accessories. It is best to buy or make wood or composition faces for the vise jaws so as not to scar any work clamped in the vise. Commercial faces are available with a soft metal back and soft but sturdy plastic face and cut to be folded around the vise jaws.

Larger vises bolt through the workbench for a permanent attachment; smaller clamp-on vises are also available.

Lighting. Proper lighting over any work area is essential. Without it, doing good work is impossible. I use a 4-foot-long utility-type double-tube fluorescent lighting fixture over my 8-foot workbench. This throws broad, even light, and sells for less than $15.

Even something this sophisticated is not necessary. On a small workbench, a gooseneck lamp with a 60-watt bulb is often adequate. The small high-intensity lamps are also good, as are fluorescent desk and drawing-board lamps.

Large workbenches are also helpful, especially for hammering spoons and pouring bucktails. All these tools are not necessary for making the items in this book. However, some arrangement of storage or hanging (such as the pegboard shown here) will be needed.

A good machinist's vise is necessary for some heavier tackle-building tasks, such as making wood plugs, spoons, gaffs, etc.

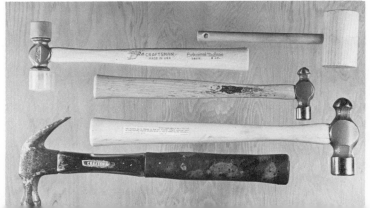

Hammers useful in tackle building. Top to bottom: wood mallet, nylon-rubber-faced hammer, two ball peen hammers, carpenter's hammer.

Hammers. Hammers are not needed for most of the delicate work of lure and tackle making, but if you plan to make your own spoons, you will need two types of hammers. A soft face (plastic or hard rubber) hammer is needed to form the spoon after it has been cut out; a wood mallet works equally well and is sometimes better for forming large spoons because of the large surface area of the mallet. A ball peen hammer will be needed if you plan to make a hammered finish on any of your spoons.

Saws. Saws are generally not needed in making lures but you will need one to cut out blanks of wood for plugs if you do not buy the blocks or the pre-formed plugs that are available. Carpenter, coping, back, and keyhole saws will all work adequately. A hacksaw is necessary for cutting out spoons from heavy sheet metal, and it can also be used for cutting large chunks of lead or tin down to fit in a ladle or melting pot, or for cutting the excess lead from the sprue hole of a lure or sinker. For this latter job, however, a pair of wire cutters will do just as well.

Drills. An electric or hand drill is useful for drilling the holes in spoons or spinner parts, drilling pilot holes in plugs for screw eyes and hook hangers, and also for making molds. An electric drill with a variable speed control is best since it will allow you to use the fast speed on metal and hard wood, and the lower speed on plastics (so as not to burn them). If you have an electric drill without a speed control, and you plan to make a lot of plastic plugs, you may want to add a small cheap hand drill to your tool kit, for working with plastics. Twist drills will be needed, of course—the high speed type being required for the fast electric drills. For most jobs, the smaller size twist drill bits between $1/32$ and $1/8$ inch, will be most useful. One-quarter-inch electric drills are available for less than $10.

Pliers. Several types of pliers will be needed, and these will be among your most useful tools. Large combination pliers are used to hold plugs, spoons, and spinners while you're adding split rings or other parts that are hard to handle. When opened wide, they're also good for handling hot molds and the flat open-face molds. But in general, smaller pliers are best for most tackle-making jobs. A small pair of round-nose pliers is needed to form eyes in both ends of a spinner. These pliers have round, tapered jaws to allow any size eye to be formed in the wire.

Sometimes sets of pliers and wire cutters can be found in hardware, electronic, or hobby shops. I recommend a set that includes one each of the following: diagonal wire cutters, end-cutting wire cutters, tapered round-nose pliers, long-nose pliers, and flat-nose pliers. All of these are between 4 and 5 inches long and very handy for the tackle tinkerer. If you do not get a set like this it will be necessary to have a pair of wire cutters to cut spinner wire and to trim lead from sinkers and jigs. Diagonal pliers cut closer and give a neater finished appearance.

The Bernard "Sportmate" pliers will be particularly handy in a number of tackle-making procedures. The parallel-acting jaws hold nuts securely and open them without damaging them, and the compound-acting cutters cut wire, screw eyes, hook shanks, and similar hard metal handily.

Saws used in tackle building. Top to bottom: small jeweler's saw, keyhole wood saw, hacksaw.

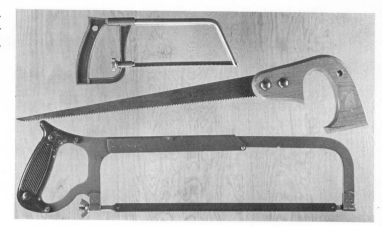

Pliers useful in tackle building. Top to bottom: chain-nose pliers with wire cutters, small chain-nose pliers (left), square-nose pliers (right), round-nose pliers (left), side-cutting wire cutters (right), Bernard Sportmate fisherman's pliers (left), Worth split-ring pliers (right).

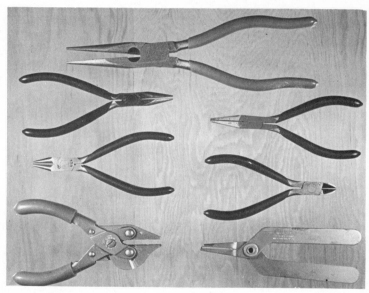

Sheet metal cutters. Left, small duck-billed tin snips; right, top to bottom, straight-cutting, left-cutting, and right-cutting compound leverage aviation snips.

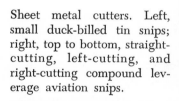

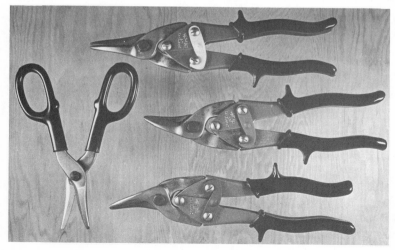

Metal Snips. Snips will be necessary only if you plan to make your spoons from sheet metal or if you make tackle accessories (tackle boxes) that have sheet metal in some part of them. If the metal you have to cut is thin (under 20 gauge) regular duck-bill snips will work fine. For cutting out spoons, however, you will need the sturdier leverage of aviation snips. Unfortunately, to be able to make all types of cuts, you will need three of these—one to cut straight and one each to cut right- and left-hand curves. A good set will cost about $15 and unless you are planning to make a great number of spoons or cut a great deal of heavy metal, it is usually uneconomical to buy them. If you are an addicted tackle tinkerer or have designs for yet untried spoons, you may well want a set anyway. Cheaper compound leverage pliers that will cut straight, left and right, are available for about $5.

Files. Several files will be needed for a variety of tackle-making operations. Coarse flat files can be used for shaping spoons, roughing-out wood plugs, filing points on gaffs, and similar tasks; medium files give a smoother finish in the same operations, and can also be used for the preliminary shaping of rod grips; fine files can be used to cut the flash off of jigs and lead sinkers, making and finishing molds, sharpening hooks, and filing down guide feet for a smooth fit on the rod blank. I have a set of a dozen of these that includes flat, triangular, round, half-round, oval, knife, and other shapes. This set has proved to be very handy for all types of tackle jobs. If you want to make your own rods you will also want a round or rat-tail file; with this you can easily ream out the cork rings when making up a rod grip to fit the rings exactly to the diameter of the rod blank.

Wood rasps are handy for roughing out rod grips and wood plugs. One rasp is sufficient for most tackle jobs. If you plan to work extensively on tackle, you may want to consider owning special files for use on special materials. All-purpose files will do the job, but since they are not specifically designed for use on lead, aluminum, or brass, they tend to foul when used on one or more of those metals. Special files with teeth that will not clog up when used on these metals are available.

Whatever files you use, be sure to buy a file cleaner. These are small, flat cleaners with very short, tempered bristles for cleaning particles from file teeth.

Soldering Iron. A soldering iron will be most useful in making spoons, and some specialized lures in which spoon and spinner blades are used. A soldering iron with a small tip, of the type used for radio and electronics work, will be best. Hooks can be soldered to spoons and spinner blades to make small ice-fishing and crappie lures, and blades can be weighted with solder if you wish to experiment with the action of a lure or make it heavier.

Miscellaneous Tools. In addition to the basic tools, you will need a number of miscellaneous tools, and may want some others that will also prove very useful: an ice pick or awl will be useful to locate center holes for drilling and to scratch lure dimensions on both wood and metal lures. For hard metal a center punch will be needed to make a small round hole prior to drilling, so that your drill will not slip. A reamer will be useful to enlarge a hole in a spoon, spinner

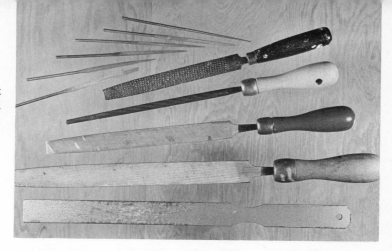

Files. Top to bottom: six small jeweler's files, wood rasp, rattail file, fine flat file, coarse flat file, abrasive bar.

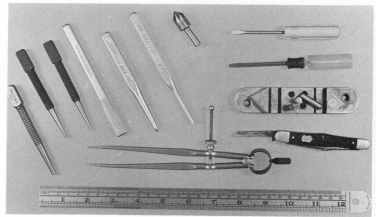

Miscellaneous tools used in tackle building. Clockwise from twelve o'clock: countersink, two small screwdrivers, wire bender, pocket knife, calipers, metal rule, three nail sets, chisel, and two punches.

blade, or plug lip. A sharp knife will come in handy for a number of tasks and is a real necessity if you plan to carve out your own plugs; a whittler's pocketknife will prove best. Scissors will serve to make templates for your lures, unless you plan to make a number of the same type of lure. Then a thin sheetmetal template, cut with metal snips, will be better.

You'll need dividers, or inside and outside calipers to transfer lure measurements from a drawing or a template to the actual material to be used in its construction. Calipers will also be far better than a metal ruler for checking the measurements of partially finished plugs and spoons and accessories. A metal ruler will be best for all other measurements, however, since it will retain its accuracy far longer than a ruler of any other material.

If you're planning to make a great many spoons from scratch, a small anvil and a wood block with depressions will be needed for the preliminary shaping of the lure. Anvils can sometimes be purchased from hardware stores for a few dollars, or even found in second-hand stores. You'll need a ladle and meltpot to make your own lead jigs, bucktails, and sinkers. An ingot mold to hold your excess melted lead will also be useful. Check with your plumber or with a plumber's supply house for these tools.

A wire former of some type will make constructing wire leaders and wire rigs faster and easier. If the wire is heavy and hard to bend, the wire former will also save wear and tear on your round-nose pliers. One of the easiest ways to make wire leaders and other wire rigs is to use wire such as Sevenstrand and

Safety equipment is extremely important in tackle building. Heavy gloves are necessary for bucktail and sinker molding, a face mask for painting, and goggles for painting, drilling, hammering, and cutting.

to make the wire loops using the sleeves designed to crimp and hold the wire loops in place. You'll need the special wire-crimping pliers, since regular pliers will not crimp the sleeve properly to hold the wire loop.

Power Tools. Whatever power tools you have will probably prove helpful in making tackle. The advantages of an electric drill were mentioned earlier; a wood lathe will make the task of cutting out wood plugs easier and faster than by any other method, and the results will be more uniform. Using a drill press, you can plan your tackle making on an assembly-line basis. Electric routers and similar hobby tools will prove handy for a number of operations, including cleaning lead lures and sinkers, shining spoons and spinner parts, carving plug blanks with popping discs and eye sockets. These are definitely not *necessary* tools but will make your tackle craft easier, particularly if you are making a great variety or number of tackle accessories and lures. If you do not have these tools, do not go out and buy them unless you can justify the expense for other interests, hobbies, or household chores as well.

Safety Equipment. Some basic safety equipment is a must in tackle building, especially when you are using power tools. Drilling and sawing operations frequently throw off small bits of wood and metal; wear safety goggles during these operations. It's also wise to wear safety goggles while cutting spinner shafts, cutting and making wire leaders and riggings, and cutting and hammering out spoon blades. Safety goggles are inexpensive (about $2). If there is a question in any operation as to whether to wear them, the answer is to put them on.

When molding bucktails and sinkers, it's a good idea to wear heavy work gloves or, better yet, asbestos welders' gloves. If you carefully follow the directions in Chapters 3 and 4 the molten lead will seldom, if ever, spill. (In fifteen years of molding sinkers and bucktails, I have never had such a spill.) Even if it does, it is unlikely that it will spill on your hands, but the added protection of gloves is definitely worthwhile. The ladles and molds themselves become hot and the gloves protect your hands from them as well.

Since spray paints are recommended extensively for the finishing of lures, it's worthwhile to invest in a small breathing mask, with removable filters. Most of the excess spray paint can be trapped by using a "painting box," as outlined in Chapter 12. It's also important to have adequate ventilation and preferably, an exhaust fan. These precautions are also relevant to the molding of soft plastic lures, since the fumes of any burned plastic can be somewhat toxic.

This may sound like a large quantity of tools, but remember it will allow you to construct a tremendous variety of tackle accessories and lures. The tools—either necessary or useful—for any given tackle-making task are relatively few. In fact, the lures discussed in the next four chapters can be made with only two pairs of pliers, a small file, a little paint and a few brushes, and the necessary parts and molds for the lead and soft plastic lures.

2

SPINNERS

*TOOLS • SPINNER PARTS • STEPS IN BUILDING A
SPINNER • SPINNER VARIATIONS •
SPINNER COSTS • SPINNER KITS*

BASIC TOOLS	HELPFUL TOOLS
Needle-nose (chain-nose) pliers with side cutters	Small round-nose pliers Diagonal wire cutters or Bernard Sportmate pliers Wire former (commercial or home-made)

SPINNERS FIRST BECAME POPULAR WHEN SPINNING TACKLE WAS introduced to this country. And their popularity is well founded. Spinners—in all their variety of colors, styles, sizes, shapes, and finishes—are one of the best of lures for almost all types of freshwater game fish. Unfortunately, these small hunks of metal are also expensive. And to be fished well, they must often be fished deep. This means more fish, but it means more lost lures as well, as the treble hooks of the spinners catch easily on underwater snags and stumps.

By making your own spinners you can reduce a substantial part of the cost of your terminal tackle, and as a result find yourself fishing more effectively, since your concern over losing spinners will be markedly lessened.

TOOLS

Many anglers avoid tinkering with spinners because of a false notion of either the complexity of making them or the tools required for the job. Many people think that a complex wire former—selling at slightly under $20—is required to bend and form the eyes on the spinner shafts. Few of us fish so

10

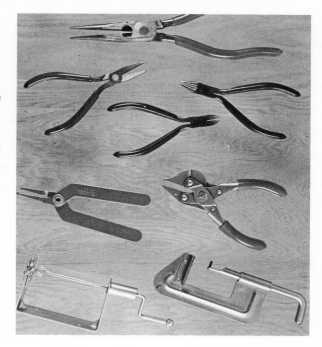

Tools for making spinners. Top to bottom: chain-nose pliers with wire cutters, flat-nose and round-nose pliers, wire cutters, Worth split-ring pliers and Bernard Sportmate pliers, Netcraft wire former (left), Worth wire former (right). All that is absolutely needed for most spinners is the pair of pliers shown on top.

much as to be able to afford expensive equipment to make only one type of lure. Actually, the only tool needed is a pair of needle-nose pliers with built-in wire cutters. (However, there are several smaller and less expensive ($1.50 to $7.00) wire formers for forming eyes in spinner shafts and making other bends.)

The singular disadvantage of needle-nose pliers, however, is that the two jaws are not round, but half round, making it impossible to get a completely round eye in spinner shafts. For this reason round-nose pliers and wire cutters are preferable, although spinners can be made without these if you already have needle-nose pliers. Many fishermen have Bernard Sportmate pliers—compound-leverage pliers with wire cutters—in their tackle boxes. These are far easier to use than normal wire cutters for cutting the hard piano wire used in spinner shafts. The Worth Company offers a pair of split-ring pliers (retail at $1) that are useful in a number of tackle operations, including making spinners, spoons, leaders, plugs, and wire tackle items. A small tooth on the end of one jaw opens split rings of all sizes easily to allow hooks, spinner blades, spoons, and other tackle parts to be added easily.

SPINNER PARTS

The basic part of the spinner is the shaft, usually made of straightened piano wire. An eye is formed in the wire at each end, one for attaching the line and the other holding the hook, usually a treble hook. The blade, with a hole in one end, is designed to rotate or spin around the shaft, thus giving the spinner its name. But to spin properly it must be attached to the shaft by a clevis, a small U-shaped piece of metal with a hole through each end of the U. The spinner blade swings from the bend of the U, and the spinner shaft goes through the small holes at the end of the U. The body of the spinner also fits on the shaft. Bodies are formed of beads, solid-formed bodies, or a combination of both. Most lures are designed so that the body added to the rest of the lure will bring the total weight of the lure up to a standard casting weight of $\frac{1}{16}$ ounce, $\frac{1}{8}$ ounce, and so forth. The hook-end eye in the shaft contains the treble hook. Sometimes the shank of the treble hook will contain a colored piece of tubing or will be wrapped with feathers as a further attraction.

While this is the basic design, there are innumerable variations for all of the parts. Even the shafts come in several basic styles; wrapped eyes, swivel eyes, spring closure eyes used with a coil spring lock, self lock-snap eyes. The first two are eyes to which line is tied, with the lure built on the shaft progressing toward the treble hook step-by-step. The second two are used as eyes at the hook-end of a spinner when it is desirable to be able to change the hook or make other attachments.

The most basic of these shaft designs, for the standard spinner, is the one with a wrapped eye already formed on one end of the shaft. However, one of the most common problems in fishing spinners is the twist that they tend to put in the line. The shaft containing the barrel and loop eye of a barrel swivel at one end alleviates this problem, since essentially, a swivel is built into the shaft of the completed spinner. These naturally cost a little more than normal shafts but still retail in quantity for only 2 to 5 cents each.

Parts needed for making spinners. Clockwise from twelve o'clock: blades, bodies, split rings and clevises, shafts, hooks, and beads.

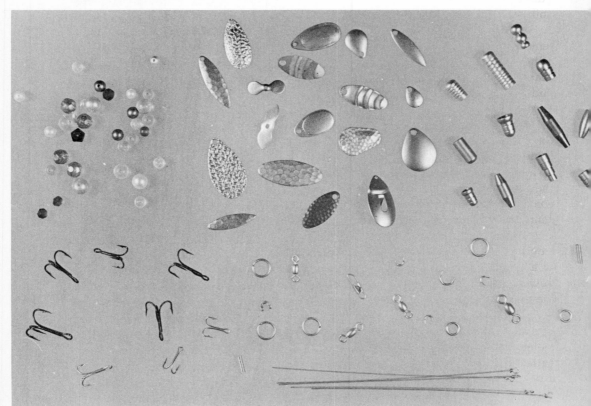

The spring-closure eye-shaft is commonly found on the commercially made "June Bug" spinner. The fourth type of shaft has a small hook on the end of the eyed portion of the shaft. This is usually described in catalogs as a "self lock-snap type" shaft. This type of shaft makes it easy to change hooks and doesn't require the coil-spring fastener, as does the previous style. And both of these latter types retail at about the same prices as the wrapped-eye shaft.

In addition, Finnysports has a "speed shaft" for which they have applied for patent rights. This speed shaft makes it easy to place hooks on the spinner, as well as to change them if desired. Essentially, it incorporates a split ring as a shaft extension. It is designed to be used as the hook-end eye, so that the spinner is built up toward the line-end eye.

All these shafts come in lengths from 3½ to 9 inches. Most are of 0.024 diameter wire, but the longer lengths are of 0.030 diameter wire. In lots of 100, which is the best way to buy them, the wrapped eye shaft in a 5-inch length costs just 1½ to 2 cents each. Short lengths of wire will be a little cheaper, and longer lengths a little more expensive. If you plan to fish your spinner in salt or brackish water, you should get stainless steel wire; these will cost about 50 percent more than regular shafts.

Wire can also be ordered in straight lengths, if you wish to do all the work yourself. Music wire, stainless steel wire, and spring-tempered brass are all available, in both coils and straightened lengths. Coils are difficult to work with since the wire cannot be completely straightened satisfactorily by the home craftsman. However, if you are making spreaders or other types of rigs (discussed in Chapter 10) where perfectly straight wire is unnecessary, these coils will do fine.

Be sure to order the type of shaft that suits your fishing best, and in a length long enough to build the largest spinner that you plan to make, usually either the 3½ or 5 inch length. To determine the optimum length, measure the shaft length of your longest spinner (or the longest that you intend to make), and add approximately one inch for easy formation of the eye with needle-nose or round-nose pliers.

Clevises are needed, also in lots of 100, since each shaft must have a clevis for the attachment of the spinner blade. They come in three types—folded, stamped, and wire. Folded clevises are stamped out of sheet metal in the form of an O and then folded over to a U shape with holes formed by the fold of the metal at the upper part of the U shape for the shaft to run through. They come in several sizes, and are listed in current catalogs at approximately 30 cents to 50 cents per 100.

Personally, I don't like folded clevises since I feel that the broad folded clevis presents too much resistance in the water to allow for the rapid spinning of a good spinner. Some anglers and tackle makers prefer the folded clevises, however, and many commercial spinner manufacturers use them, including the maker of the renowned Mepps spinners.

The stamped clevis is made from an I-shaped piece of metal with a hole at each end. They are then bent into a U shape so that the thin edge of the metal cuts the water for freer spinning. The wire clevis is made of round wire flattened at both ends, with holes punched through the flattened portion. This type is actually the best for spinners but also the most expensive, at 50 to 75

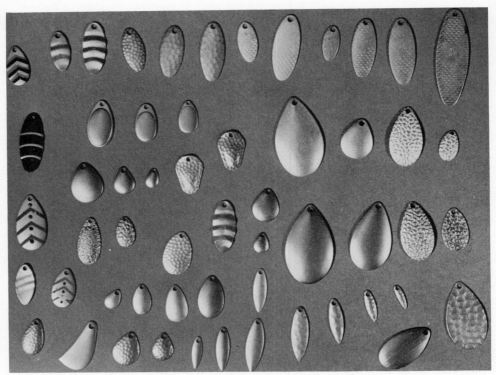

Some of the vast varieties of spinner blades that are available to the tackle tinkerer.

cents per 100. All of these types of clevises are available in either a brass or nickel plate finish.

Blades are available in such a bewildering variety of styles, shapes, finishes, and sizes that an orderly description is all but impossible. The standard spinner blades, such as the Colorado, Indiana, Willow Leaf, and June Bug, are all available in up to eight different finishes in three different materials—copper, brass, and nickel. A hammered blade is also available in either nickel or brass. The smaller blades cost 25 cents per dozen; the larger sizes running approximately 75 cents per dozen. Slight changes in shape and style have resulted in new, lesser-known styles like the Bear Valley, Deschutes, Coast Special, Wide Willow Leaf, and Smith River. Most of these are heavier blades and have been highly polished with jeweler's rouge for a mirrorlike brilliance. The quality and weight of these blades shows up in the price since they retail at 12 to 20 cents each.

The more typical blades found on most spinning lures, however, are types known as French Spinner Blades, Swedish Swing Blades, and Corrugated Spinner Blades. They come in four to five sizes each and in the three basic finishes of nickel, brass, and copper. They vary in price from 35 cents per dozen in the smaller sizes to 85 cents per dozen in the larger blade sizes. Blades can also be ordered in quantities of 25, 100, or for that matter, 1,000; the greater the quantity, the cheaper the cost of each individual blade. However, a dozen each of the most popular styles, sizes, and finishes should be enough to allow for the greatest variety of blades at a given amount of money for most anglers.

The body of a spinner can be made of beads, as in the well-known C. P.

Swing, or of solid lead or brass, as in the popular Mepps. Beads come in an even greater variety than blades; some look like leftovers from a bead chain key ring, while others would be at home in a Tiffany display case. They come in basic round, oval, and teardrop shapes; some of them come in as many as ten different sizes from $\frac{1}{12}$ to $\frac{3}{5}$ inch, and in color they can vie with an artist's palette: pink, fire red, chartreuse, nickel, yellow fluorescent, blue fluorescent, aqua, and pearl are all available as well as the standard colors of black, white, red, and yellow, though not all colors are availabe in every shape and style. Glass, aluminum, plastic, solid brass, and hollow metal have all been used to make beads. Some of the most exotic types have hammered or faceted surfaces, and one type even has rhinestone inserts. Others contain specks of silver foil or swirls of color within the bead. Besides the standard shapes mentioned above, there are also flat bead "bracelets" and glass spacers which will allow you to make an almost infinite variety of bead body styles. In addition to beads available from the regular fishing tackle supply houses, art supply stores and craft and hobby shops frequently carry plastic, glass, and metal beads that can be readily adapted by the fishermen for spinners.

Prices for beads vary as much as the styles and colors. Since anywhere from 5 to 8 beads are needed in an average bead body, they should be bought in lots of 100, although they can be had in lots of 12, 25, 1,000, and 5,000 as well. Some of the plastic beads with colored stripes sell for as little as $1.50 and $3.00 per 100, and at the other end of the scale, beads cut from semi-precious stones can cost 50 cents each, even though it is doubtful that fish find them any more attractive than cheap plastic ones.

The solid spinner bodies come in bullet, bell, torpedo, teardrop, and joined bead shapes and a number of variations of each. Made primarily of brass, they can also be obtained in a nickel finish, and painted lead alloy bodies are available in a variety of colors. In price they average from 50 cents to $2 per dozen, depending upon the size, finish, and complexity of the body shape. The different weight and size bodies make it possible to build a lure of optimum casting size and weight.

In one sense, hooks are the most important part of the lure, since this is what will come in contact with and hold your fish. Bronze Mustad or Eagle Claw treble hooks of excellent quality cost about 50 cents a dozen in the sizes needed for spinners. Some fishermen, particularly those on the West Coast, prefer a single Siwash Salmon hook on the eye of the spinner shaft. These hooks come with a soft open eye so that the lower eye on the spinner shaft can be formed and the hook added later, its eye then closed with a pair of pliers. West Coast anglers feel that this type of hook on a spinner will snag less on the bottom and will hook most game fish better. It costs about the same as the standard treble hooks.

An attractive lure can be made by dressing up the treble hook with a small piece of plastic tubing or bits of colored strips of plastic. The plastic tubing in red, yellow, orange, and other colors must be cut in short ($\frac{1}{2}$") lengths, so as to fit the treble hook, and leave the hook eye clear to swing freely. Soft plastic tubing costs about 5 cents per foot (20 cents for fluorescent tubing) in the catalogs and might be even cheaper at a local plastics dealer. (One foot of tubing will be enough for about two dozen lures.) Tail tags are

Beads for spinners are available from tackle supply shops, but many, such as these shown here, can be obtained from hobby and craft departments. They come in many sizes, colors, and finishes.

sometimes placed on the eye of the shaft along with the hook. These tiny pieces of plastic are fishtail shaped or round, with a hole at one end for attaching to the spinner shaft. They come in bright fluorescent colors as well as red, silver, and gold, and vary in price from 10 to 50 cents per 25.

STEPS IN BUILDING A SPINNER

While the listing of all these spinner parts in a catalog can sometimes be confusing, the construction of a spinner is simplicity itself. Take, for example, a standard spinner, such as one with a brass Swedish swing blade and a body of brass beads. First, pick a shaft of the "wrapped eye" type about 5 inches long, for ease of handling. The wrapped eye will be the "line end" eye of the lure. Now, take a stamped or wire clevis and put it through the hole in the blade of the brass Swedish swing blade. (It is a good idea here to remember to use as small a clevis as possible in all spinners; the small clevis will spin better and start easier than those in the larger sizes. However, in no case should the clevis be so small as to permit the spinner blade to bind against it or the spinner shaft.)

Now hold the blade with the clevis through the hole and put the spinner shaft through the holes in the clevis. Check *now* to be sure that the concave side of the blade is next to the spinner shaft when the blade hangs against the lower part of the shaft. If the blade is on backwards (convex part toward the shaft), take the shaft out of the clevis and run it through the holes again, in the opposite direction.

Next, put the body on the shaft, which in this case is made of several sizes of brass beads. Select a small brass bead first to go next to the clevis and also to serve as a "bearing" so that the spinner will rotate easily. (If a solid body rather than beads is used in the spinner, be sure to place a spinner bearing or two between the clevis and the spinner body. This provides a frictionless surface so that the spinner blade will spin freely.) The rest of the body is built up first of successively larger, then smaller beads to give an overall cigar tapered shape. The total length of the bead body should be such that it will end just above the end of the spinner blade hanging down from

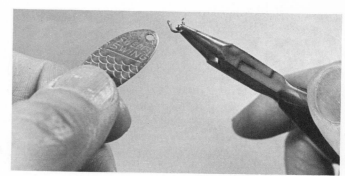

Attaching the clevis to the hole in the spinner blade.

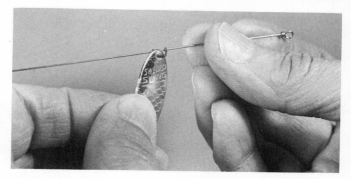

Sliding the spinner shaft through the two holes in the end of the clevis. Make sure that the spinner blade is properly oriented on the shaft.

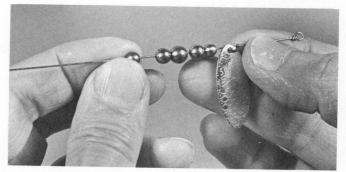

Beads or the body is added to the shaft below the clevis.

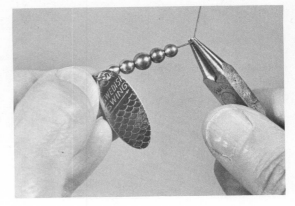

Once the body is added, the spinner shaft is bent at right angles about ⅜ inch below the body or last bead.

the clevis. The size and number of the beads will determine the actual length of body that should be used with each size blade. Beneath the last bead, leave about ⅜ inch clearance. This ⅜ inch clearance is important, since without it the parts of the spinner may bind between the two eyes once the spinner is completed.

Now bend the spinner shaft sharply with the needle-nose or round-nose pliers, bending the part of the shaft containing the spinner parts. Still holding the shaft between the plier jaws, take the other end of the shaft and bend it 360 degrees around one plier jaw to make a complete eye in the wire.

If you want attractor tubing on the hook, or a tail tag, or the hook dressed with feathers, now is the time to add it. To add attractor tubing, cut a ½ inch length of the tube and place it on the hook shank. To dress the hook with feathers or fur, tie it on using fly-tying methods or the methods described for finishing a bucktail (Chapter 3).

Now hold the eye of the shaft and the eye of the hook together securely with pliers and then, being careful of the hook, wrap the wire tightly around the shaft of the spinner. If this loose end of the wire is long enough, the operation can be done by hand, otherwise another pair of pliers will be needed. Make several turns of the wire to hold it securely and then clip off the excess wire with wire cutters.

> CAUTION: When cutting off this surplus wire, hold the wire over a waste basket and "aim" the wire toward the bottom since the cut portion will otherwise fly off dangerously. When completed, you will have an imitation of a well-known spinner that is effective for trout, crappies, bass, pike, and other game fish.

Sometimes, after completing a spinner, you will find that the blade will not work or spin as expected. It may be that not enough clearance remains between the two eyes on the shaft and that the spinner parts are pinched together, preventing any movement of the parts. If too small a clevis is used the blade may bind against the wire shaft.

It's best, of course, to check carefully to be sure that these faults are corrected *before* the second eye is wrapped, and the lure is completed; but if your spinners do have this defect, there is a corrective: squeeze the clevis *lightly* between pliers, to give the parts additional play on the spinner shaft, or to give the blade more play on the clevis. Generally, the two ends of the clevis can be squeezed

After the spinner shaft is bent at right angles, an eye is formed in the shaft for hook attachment.

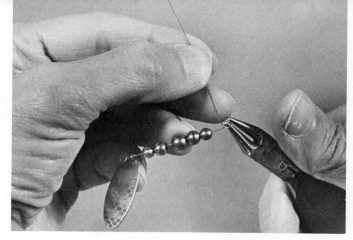

Short lengths of red attractor tubing can be added to the treble hook before the spinner is completed.

The treble hook is slipped onto the unwrapped eye of the spinner shaft.

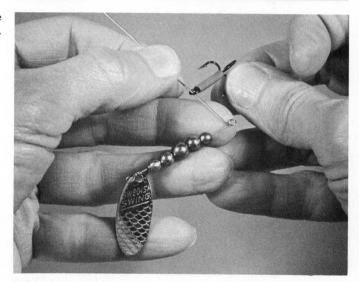

Once the treble hook is in place, wrap the end of the wire around the main spinner shaft several times.

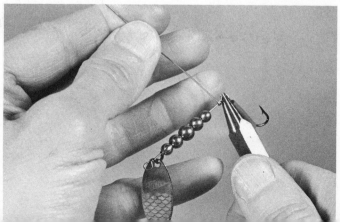

together to about half the normal spread without adversely affecting the clevis action; squeezed too much, the clevis will bind on the shaft or blade, and ruin the spinner. This procedure will work only with stamped or wire clevises—not with folded clevises.

Sometimes even with the right size clevis, and enough play in the shaft of the spinner, the spinner will still not work properly in the water. Check to see if a small wire clevis has been used; a large stamped clevis, particularly on a small spinner, can create too much water resistance for the blade to spin properly.

Also, the clevis resting directly on a spinner body can sometimes catch on a rough spot, preventing the blade from turning. To prevent this from occurring,

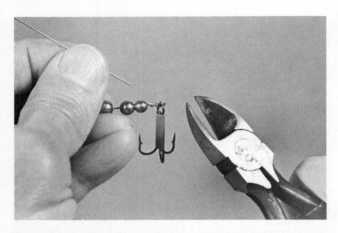

Once the eye is wrapped, clip the excess wire. CAUTION: Be sure to hold the wire while it is being clipped so it will not fly off dangerously.

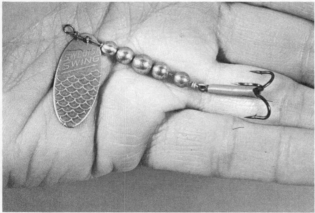

Typical spinner completed.

Common defects in making spinners include a poorly wrapped eye that can bind a clevis (upper right), and using a clevis too small for the blade so that the blade will bind against the spinner shaft (lower left).

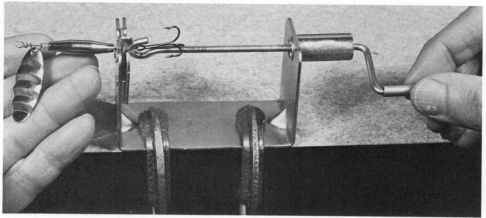

Wire formers such as this Netcraft tool can form uniformly wrapped eyes simply and easily.

Using a Worth wire-wrapping tool to form a spinner shaft eye.

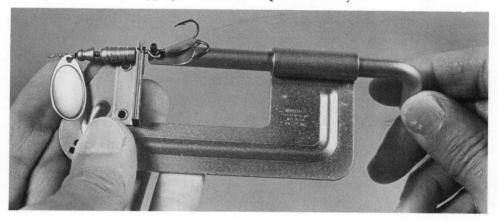

use one or more small beads between the clevis and the body. Very small bearing beads called "unies" are made especially for this.

Spinners, even those commercially made, are noted for their line-twisting characteristics. This is especially a problem with small 2-, 4-, and 6-pound-test lines, and lines that are especially soft, an otherwise desirable characteristic. To prevent excessive twisting, use spinner shafts with the built-in swivels or add a swivel to the top (line-end) eye. The technique used is the same as adding the hook to the lower (hook-end) eye. Another solution is to make the spinner shaft longer than normal, bending the shaft ½ inch from the line eye, so that the eye is offset at an angle from the rest of the body. Thus the pull of the line is not on the same plane with the twist of the spinner blade, reducing line-twist problems.

It's possible to build the spinner in reverse order, starting by forming an eye, adding the hook, then the body and the clevis and blade, and finally wrapping the upper eye. This is commonly done with the French type of spinner, to give a neater appearance to the finished lure. Instead of forming a wrapped eye, bend the lower (hook) eye so that a short length of the shaft is bent around parallel to the main shaft.

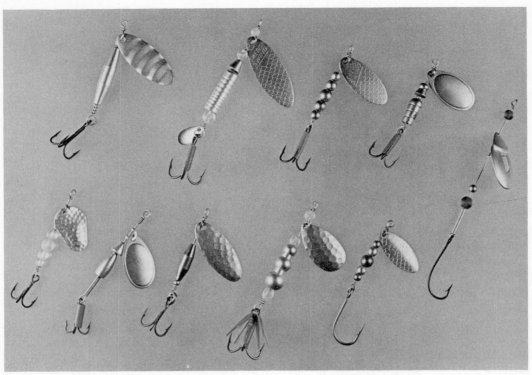

Typical homemade spinners in a variety of blade, body, and hook styles.

Methods of making spinners to minimize the tendency to twist line. Top row, swivels added to or built into the eye end of the shaft. Bottom row, spinners with blades and/ or spinner shafts at an angle from the main body to minimize twist.

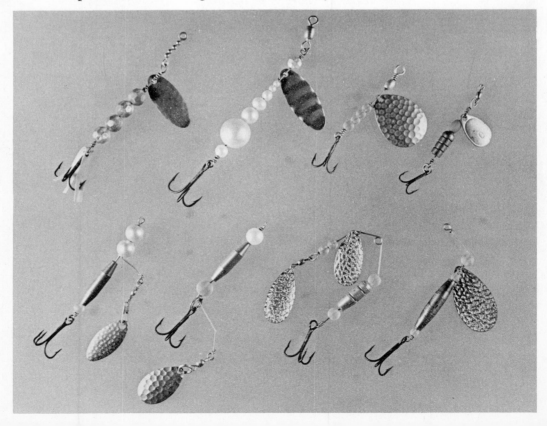

To make this type of eye correctly, the wire must be "kinked" at an angle at either side of the completed eye. Otherwise, there will only be a 180 degree bend in the wire, with the parallel shafts apart rather than close together, as in a true eye.

Slide the hook on, then slide the body over both parallel shafts. The short end of the shaft should extend out from the top of the body. Bend this over sharply, and clip it off short. Add another body, a bearing bead, then the clevis and blade, finishing with a wrapped eye at the top. This is how the Mepps spinner is made.

The same method of forming an eye with parallel shaft is used with a spring when it is desirable to be able to change the hook arrangement. This is commonly seen on June Bug and Willow Leaf spinners, often used in bait fishing. The technique of making the spinner is the same as with the French spinner, except that a short length of spring is added to the lower shaft to lock the hook in place. Finish the lure with the rest of the body and blades. Before wrapping the top eye, make sure that there is enough clearance to slide the spring up to permit removal of the hook.

SPINNER VARIATIONS

There are endless variations in making spinners, considering the vast number of parts available, and experimentation is frequently fruitful. Spinners can be made with double blades, mixed solid bodies and beads, blades hanging from the hook eye as well as the shaft, spinner blades riding on extensions built out from the main shaft, and "safety pin" spinners in which the body and hook are on one side of the V-shaped shaft, the spinner blade on the other, the line tied at the apex of the V.

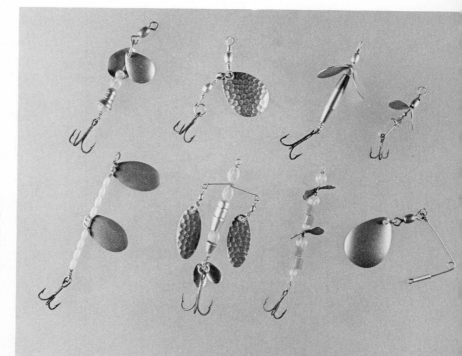

Variations of spinners can include double blade, propeller blade, tandem blade, and an attachment to be added to a jig to make a spinner bait.

Propeller blades are also effective. In fact, some of the earliest spinners in existence, made for use with equally early casting tackle, were of this type. When spinning tackle became popular in this country, Devon-type spinners, with a solid body and revolving propeller on a central shaft also proved to be effective lures, although they are seldom seen today. It is possible to make double-propeller spinners, with the two props on the same shaft, separated by several beads. While most propeller blades are available with only one direction of blade pitch, it is advantageous to bend one of the props to a reverse pitch so that the two blades spin in opposite directions. This will minimize, if not eliminate, any twist.

Sometimes the water resistance on the forward blade of a double blade spinner will cause the rear spinner to bind. If this happens, drop a small ball of solder on the shaft ahead of the second spinner blade so that the bearing body or beads will not press on the rear clevis and cause it to bind. For this same reason, spinners are seldom built with the body ahead of the blade when they are all on the same shaft.

SPINNER COSTS

What does a spinner cost the tackle tinkerer to make? It is surprisingly inexpensive. The Swedish spinner mentioned above, based on parts bought in small quantities, costs something like this:

APPROXIMATE 1973 COSTS

shaft	$1.65/100	or	$0.0165 each
clevis	.50/100	or	.0050 each
#2 blade	.40/12	or	.0330 each
⅛" bead	1.40/100	or	.0280 (2)
⁵⁄₃₂" bead	1.80/100	or	.0360 (2)
³⁄₁₆" bead	1.90/100	or	.0190 each
#8 hook	.60/12	or	.0500 each
½" length tubing	.06/ft.	or	.0025 each
		TOTAL	$0.1900 for the completed lure

With a few minutes' time and for 19 cents, you have a spinner that would cost approximately 80 cents to buy on the retail market. Of course, this is figured on an approximate cost and a piecemeal basis, and you must buy the parts in quantities listed to get the lure at the above-mentioned price. What does it cost to buy enough materials to get started in spinner making? Well, this varies from angler to angler, depending upon how many lures you plan to make and the type and variety wanted. Figured out on a basis of the lure mentioned above, it will be something like this:

100 shafts	$ 1.65	
100 clevises	.50	
3 dozen blades	1.25	(one dozen each of sizes 1, 2, and 3)
300 beads	5.00	(100 each of sizes ⅛″, 5⁄32″, and 3⁄16″)
3 dozen hooks	1.80	(one dozen each in sizes 12, 10, and 8 to match the blade sizes)
2 ft. attractor tubing	.12	
TOTAL	$10.32	

For less than $10.50, you have enough parts for three dozen lures, with shafts, clevises, and beads left over for the next batch. That same $10.50 will buy you only about one dozen of the same type of lure on the retail market.

You can, of course, reduce the price of making spinners even further by buying the parts in greater quantities. But this is only advantageous for the incurable angler or for fishing clubs that might want to mass-produce lures. This way the lures—or lure parts—can be distributed to the participating members as a club service or sold to build the club treasury.

There is another way the cost can be reduced, but only with additional work. You can make your own blades and mold your own spinner bodies, and avoid entirely buying them from the tackle supplier. Making blades is much the same as making spoons in cutting out sheet metal and forming the cut blade into the proper curve. Since it is so similar to making spoons, the techniques are covered in Chapter 6. You can't make beads but you can mold bodies out of lead and then paint them before adding them to the spinner. Special molds are available for this purpose; the techniques are discussed in Chapter 4. Both these "money-saving" devices are time-consuming, however, and in addition require additional tools and materials not listed in this chapter. Making your spinners from scratch this way is worthwhile and necessary if you are making a new type of blade, or body, or experimenting with a radically new design. Otherwise, it can hardly be recommended.

SPINNER KITS

For those who would rather skip the step of figuring out all the necessary components needed in making up a set of lures, there are kits available that contain everything needed to make spinning lures. The Worth Company has a "Lure Making Kit" that contains a wire former (to make eyes in the spinner shafts), along with blades, hooks, bodies, wire shafts, snaps and swivels, beads and other parts. It makes 25 or more spinning lures. It sells for about $10 or less, includes complete instructions on using the wire former, and makes it easy to get started in spinner making.

Aspen Lures has several spinning lure kits and these kits also include everything needed to make spinners. Several different Aspen kits are available; one is a super spinning kit to make 24 spinners of several styles, and there are also kits to make spinners of only one style. Kits for French spinners, Colorado blade spinners, Bear Valley blade spinners, Indiana blade spinners, and propellor spinners are available. While they're called kits, these are actually the components for a complete lure in a variety of sizes and finishes. They are sold as "single" lure kits, although more of a saving can be realized by buying them in lots of a dozen. Current prices for the single lure parts kits range from 13 to 25 cents each and $1.40 to $2.60 per dozen, depending of course on the style, size, and finish of the lure. Refills of specific parts for both kits are available from both Aspen and Worth as well as from local tackle stores and mail-order companies that carry other spinning lure components.

One advantage of a kit like this is pointed out by Aspen Lure Company president, Tom Kassler: "There are a good many catalogs offering component parts, but in order to assemble a lure from these catalogs a person must buy 100 bodies, 1,000 clevises, and so forth, so that the average fisherman does not bother to make his own lures."

I can't help but agree with Tom, yet it is a shame that more anglers don't make spinners. Spinners have a well-deserved reputation as fish catchers, and they are easy to make, either with a kit or by using component parts, at substantial savings over almost identical commercially manufactured lures.

Kits for making spinners. Left top, a kit of miscellaneous parts from Netcraft; left bottom, individually packed spinner kits from Aspen Lures; a kit from the Worth Company.

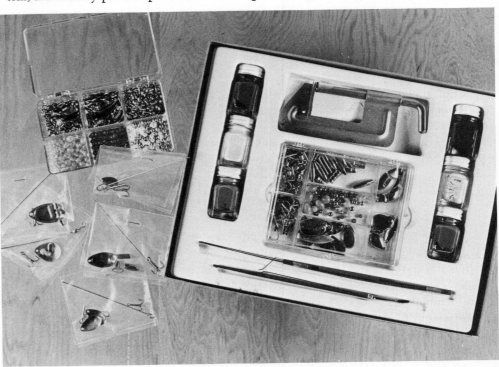

3
BUCKTAILS AND JIGS

TYPES OF MOLDS · BUCKTAIL HOOKS · SOURCES OF LEAD · HEAT SOURCES · MOLDING TECHNIQUES · MOLDING STEPS · FINISHING MOLDED BUCKTAILS · WRAPPING TAILS ON LEAD HEADS · JIG AND BUCKTAIL KITS · COST OF BUCKTAILS

BASIC TOOLS	HELPFUL TOOLS
Old cooking pot	Plumber's melting pot
Cheap gravy ladle or large serving spoon	Plumber's ladle
Bucktail molds	Wire cutters
Fly-tying vise, machinist vise, or C-clamp	Ingot molds
Hot pads, gloves, and safety goggles	Heavy pliers
File	

∾ IF ASKED TO PICK ONE LURE FOR ALL TYPES OF FISHING, MANY EXPERT anglers would pick the lead-headed jig or bucktail. Time and experience have proved that this lure, in all its variations, can effectively imitate saltwater bait fish, eels, squid, and freshwater minnows and hellgrammites.

Commercial bucktails and jigs come in tiny $\frac{1}{64}$ ounce sizes, and giants that weight 6 ounces or more. While all these lures are basically the same, those fished in saltwater are generally called bucktails; those in freshwater, jigs. Essentially, all of them are lead-headed lures, with a hook molded into the head and a skirt of some type.

Tools and materials used by Dick Savage of Severna Park, Maryland, to make bucktails: a self-heating electric ladle, a low melting alloy, home-made plaster bucktail molds, heavy gloves, pliers, and a fluorocarbon lubricant for easy release of the bucktails from the mold. The lubricant is sprayed on the mold before use.

Skirts or tails on these simple lures vary from bucktail (hence the name) to other furs, feathers, polypropylene rope frayed out, fine strands of nylon, marabou, and more recently, vinyl tails that have only to be slipped in place.

Each type has a different name in different parts of the country or for use in fishing for different species. Banjo-eye bucktails, for example, are used for striped bass along the mid-Atlantic Coast. Crappie killers are small, $\frac{1}{64}$ to $\frac{3}{8}$ ounce, ballhead jigs with a chenille body and marabou tail, and have earned their reputation on freshwater crappies, although they are good for other game fish as well. Shad darts are small, slant-faced, tapered jigs. Each year they take thousands of white and hickory shad in the mid-Atlantic area.

Bucktails range in price from 10 cents each (for the little bulk-packed jigs) up to $2.75 or more for large saltwater sizes. Yet these same lures can be made easily for only a few pennies each.

All it takes to make any number of lead heads is the proper mold, a few hooks, some lead, and an old file. To finish a head as a bucktail takes only the tail material, thread, paint, and a vise for clamping the hook in place while tying on the tail material.

The supplies mentioned above will serve as a bare minimum; a ladle and special melting pot are better for melting lead than old soup ladles and cooking pots sometimes used for the same purpose. Also, wire cutters are handy for removing the lead "sprue" still attached to the head from the molten lead poured through the sprue hole, or gate, of the mold.

TYPES OF MOLDS

Commercially available molds are usually two-piece, made of aluminum, with one or more lure cavities. These cavities form the lure when molten lead is poured into the mold cavity through a tapered opening, called a sprue hole, gate, or down-gate.

There are two classes of molds—those for the fisherman and those for the small commercial operation. The latter can be bought and used by the average fisherman, but usually are not since they are single-cavity molds, designed for production use with lead melting ovens. They are also several times more costly than the regular molds, which retail from $2 to $5. They are precision molds, however, and make lure heads with no flash. (Flash is the molder's term for excess metal that leaks from the mold where the two mold halves join. It must

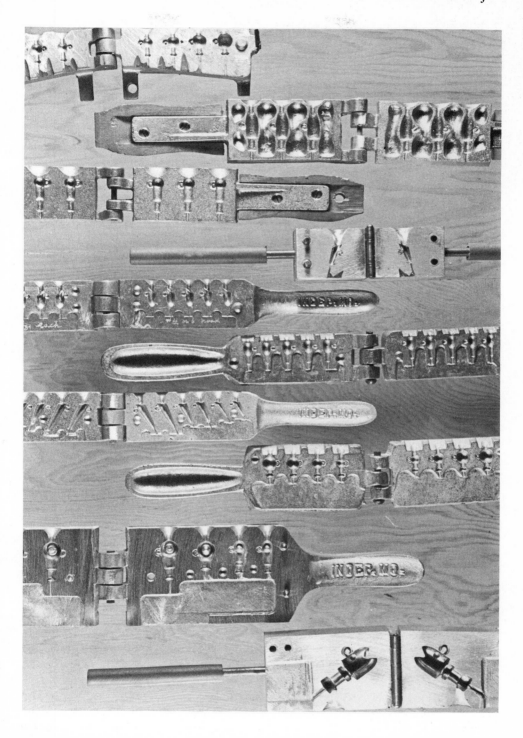

Typical bucktail molds. Top to bottom: ball-head mold, bullet-head mold, banjo-eye head mold, professional single-cavity shad dart mold, multiple-cavity shad dart mold, doll fly mold, shad dart mold, ball head mold, banjo-eye bucktail mold, and professional single-cavity trolling bucktail mold.

be filed off the lure heads to make top-grade, perfect bucktails.)

Regular molds are not precision machined, but are good enough for any angler to make excellent lures. The number of cavities varies from two to eight. Some molds make identical lures while others mold one or two each of several different-size bucktail heads.

Pinned molds are the least expensive, but also the most difficult to work with. They must be clamped together with C-clamps, or otherwise held together securely each time a lure is molded. They are made in two separate halves with a pin on one side of each mold half, which fits into a socket on the other half as the mold is closed. This holds the two sides in place for proper register of the finished lure. To their advantage, they generally form very good lures with little flash.

While these molds are somewhat inconvenient to use, they are inexpensive and do make lures just as well as any other type of mold. But the clamping and unclamping of the mold is time-consuming, and makes it difficult to turn out a number of lures quickly. One way to speed up the operation when using pinned molds is to use a pair of woodworkers' spring-loaded gluing clamps to hold the halves together.

There is another type of mold that has two clamps, one on each mold half, so that after being placed together, the clamps lock the mold closed. Otherwise these are just like the molds mentioned above.

Hinged and handled molds are the easiest to use, since the handle on each mold half makes it easy to hold the mold together while pouring. The only slight disadvantage here is that for good castings, the mold must be hot, and the handles can quickly get uncomfortably hot. Actually this disadvantage exists more on paper than in reality, since all of the molds will get hot in use, and in fact, for best results, they should be preheated before using.

For safe operation of any lead molding, have at hand several hot pads, asbestos hot plates, and asbestos or kitchen padded gloves. Herter's molds are supplied with wood grips on the handles that make them easy to work with. Some hinged molds come without handles, and this type of mold always has either a clamp or a spring catch to hold the mold closed. Either type (spring or clamp) works well, except that the mold usually will not stand upright while you are pouring. Some have legs to support them for casting, but even in some of these the bend of hooks clamped in place extends beyond the bottom of the mold (or the legs) making it impossible to keep it vertical. In cases like this either fashion a support for the mold or hold it in place with an asbestos glove or pliers while pouring.

In some cases hooks will not lie flat while being placed in the mold; this is because the surface area of the mold is not large enough and the overhanging part of the hook is heavier than the supported shank part. This is not a minor inconvenience; it means that the weight of the hook bend will raise the shank of the hook, making it virtually impossible to close the mold without disturbing the hook position. If you get a mold like this, return it and ask for an exchange, or a different style mold. Otherwise, each time the mold is used place a small block of wood against the bottom of the mold to support the bend of the hooks until it is closed. An alternative is to build a extension on the bottom of one side of the mold that will serve the same purpose.

Some bucktail molds come with the weight of the completed lure and the correct hook size marked on the mold; others do not. (This information is available in the catalogs and in stores from which molds are purchased.) If this information is not marked on the mold, keep a sheet with the mold number, hook size, and lure size, or scratch it into the side of the mold with an awl. (I use a small engraving tool to write this information on any of my molds that lack it.) Having these data handy saves time when it comes to choosing hooks for molds or molding bucktails of specific weight.

BUCKTAIL HOOKS

Special hooks are required to make lead heads for bucktails. These hooks come in a wide variety of sizes and styles, but all of them have a right angle bend in the shank near the eye of the hook. This bend both holds the hook in place in the head and places the eye of the hook on the top of the lure for proper lure action in the water. They come in both regular and heavy wire in sizes 12 to 9/0, the latter to accommodate stronger saltwater fish. O'Shaughnessy and Aberdeen styles of hooks are offered in jig-hook styles by both Eagle Claw and Mustad; Herter's offers a Model Perfect bend jig hook.

Hook finishes come in bronze, gold, tinned, and cadmium. Any of these platings will work with freshwater jigs. Saltwater anglers should choose non-rusting hooks in tinned, gold, and cadmium finishes. The cadmium finish will powder as it oxidizes, but will retain its strength and otherwise not corrode. Stainless steel jig hooks would be a welcome addition to the tackle maker's supplies for saltwater lead heads.

It is important to use the right size hook in each mold. Since the eye must fit into a small round depression in the mold half, and the shank of the hook into a slot at the tail of the mold cavity, this is easy to determine. With the eye in the round depression, the shank should fit straight and correctly in the slot made for it. If it's cocked at an angle, it means that the hook is too large or too small. In *neither* case can the mold be properly closed and a good casting made.

SOURCES OF LEAD

All service stations that change tires or mount new tires on cars have ample supplies of old lead in the tire weights that come off the wheels. Large stations often sell their old weights, but some smaller stations are glad to have them taken off their hands. Unfortunately, these weights have a steel bracket in them which must be skimmed off the top during melting. Another disadvantage is that the weights are dirty and greasy from long use on the road, and, they are really an alloy of lead, about 10 percent antimony. There is considerable slag and some fumes from the use of these, but the price is right, and they will do the job.

Other sources of lead and lead alloys are plumbing supply houses, junk yards, and scrap metal yards. Lead pipe and cable sheathing used in telephone lines is relatively pure lead—above 98 percent—but take care not to use any of the solder used in joining sections of sheathing or pipe; these are lead alloys.

It is better to keep pure lead from any less pure samples, though with experimentation, these alloys might prove acceptable for molding. Even if it has to be bought, lead is cheap enough as a lure material. Lead from junk metal sources currently sells for under 20 cents per pound.

HEAT SOURCES

The actual process of molding lead-head lures is a simple one, but one that must be carried out carefully and with forethought, both for safety and best results.

The first consideration is the place where the molding will be done. The kitchen stove is the obvious place for melting the lead and pouring the lures. It's a good place for several reasons: first, there are several burners, so that several pots of lead can be kept hot at once; this is important if a large quantity of lures is to be made or if each lure takes a lot of lead. Also, many kitchen stoves have exhaust fans above them. Since there can be some toxic fumes released in melting lead (even "pure" lead contains trace elements of toxic substances), an exhaust fan should be run throughout the operation. If no exhaust fan is available, open windows will help to reduce the slight danger from fumes.

Another advantage of using the kitchen stove area is that usually there is ample counter or table space for laying out molds, hooks, and the few tools required. Of utmost importance in using any kitchen area, if you want to be allowed in the house again, is to cover all working surfaces with a protective layer of ¼ inch or thicker plywood, masonite-over-asbestos, hot pads, or some similar sturdy, non-heat-conducting material. Many plastic laminates used on kitchen counter tops will burn. Better still, use the above materials covered with a sheet of aluminum or stainless steel. Scrap or spilled molten lead will not stick to these metal surfaces as it will to wood, so it will be easier to clean up when you've finished a molding session.

Lacking a suitable kitchen space in which to work, it is possible to use gasoline camping stoves, propane and butane stoves and torches, as well as some hot plates, again with due caution as to where and how they are used.

Electric lead-melting furnaces are generally used only in molding bullets for hand loaders, but they can be modified to work with bucktail molds. They work best on a production basis using precision single-cavity molds. The furnaces keep the lead at the right temperature and discharge the lead through a spout on the bottom, so that the lead fills the mold cavity under gravity pressure. This helps eliminate air pockets and defects caused by slow hand-molding. All the slag floats to the surface and does not enter the mold cavity. (I have never used one, since the prices of $25 to $35 make it economical only for a club or someone going into the business, but claims are that up to 350 jigs per hour can be made using one of these furnaces and a precision mold.)

The best area for molding bucktails is often the kitchen, with counter-space well protected by scrap-wood, masonite, or thick cardboard. Here, the author molds bucktails.

Some of these electric melting furnaces come with thermostatic controls to give a heat range of from 500° to 800° F., making it an ideal tool for the tackle tinkerer who might be using type metal (used in the printing industry), tin, or other alloys with melting temperatures different from that of lead.

There are also electric melting pots that sell for about $25 and hold up to 20 pounds of lead. You'll have to use a ladle to transfer the lead from the self-heating pot to the mold. And there is a long-handled electric melting pot by Palmers called a Hot Pot; it holds 4 pounds of lead and can be used to pour directly into a mold. One advantage of electric melting pots is that they permit molding in places other than the family kitchen; all that is required is a clear protected working space and an electric outlet.

Regardless of the heat source, be sure that you have a solid support for the lead melting pot. The best pots for melting lead are those made for plumbers. These are sold in several sizes by some of the companies listed in the Appendix, as well as at local hardware and plumbing stores. They hold from 6 to 10 pounds of lead. This may sound like a lot, until you start to fill up molds. In making 4-ounce bucktails, for example, in a four-cavity mold, one pound of lead is consumed in each pouring.

The melting pot is too big to pour from, so a small, long-handled ladle holding 2 to 4 pounds of lead is a must. There is even one special type of ladle with a partition across half the bowl. Holes in the bottom of the partition allow the molten lead to flow from one side to the other. In use, lead is picked up on one side of the ladle and poured from the other. Since the lead can only flow to the pouring side through the holes in the partition, all the slag (which floats to the top) is left behind. The result is clean lures with no impurities or defects.

If necessary, you can get by with a soup ladle and a discarded cooking pot, but special pots and ladles are much better, since they are constructed of thick-wall cast iron that holds the heat better. Melting pots and ladles vary in price from about $2.50 to $5.00 each.

No matter where, when, or how you decide on molding lead lures, safety is paramount. Mold *only* when other family members (particularly small children and pets) are not in the same area. Lead melts at 621° F. and can cause severe burns if spilled.

MOLDING TECHNIQUES

While the lead is melting, lay out the molds, tools, hooks, and other materials, and review a systematic method of molding. Plan to have everything within reach, and plan on making a lot of molded lead heads at once. I like to mold lures, but I do not like to prolong the process by molding only a few at a time on successive days. It's a waste of both time and natural gas or electricity every time the lead is remelted. Once the lead is melted, more lead can easily be added to keep the operation going. Thus it is simpler and more economical to mold 50 to 100 lead heads of a favorite lure at one time, even though such a supply may well last for several fishing seasons.

If there is any trick to molding lead heads for bucktails, it is in having the lead *hot* and the mold *warm*. When the lead first melts, it will be a bright, glistening silvery color, almost the sheen of highly polished sterling silver or a brand-new silver-plated spoon. As more lead is added the temperature will drop and the lead will turn "mushy," approaching the consistency of oatmeal or mashed potatoes. The lead must be heated beyond either of these points, to the point at which it will pour rapidly through the sprue hole of the mold. It must be hot enough to completely fill the mold cavity before cooling. The easiest way to judge this temperature is to heat the lead until it becomes a golden to purple color. Since this is a higher heat, it might also bring to the surface some additional impurities, giving the surface a slightly scummy appearance. This is to be expected; it does not matter unless the scum and slag are so excessive that they will interfere with the proper filling of the mold with pure lead. If they do seem excessive, skim them off with an old tablespoon, reserved just for that purpose.

The melting pot provides a ready "stock" of melted lead, the ladle an easy way to pour the lead into the mold. Still, many beginners have problems in using the ladle to dip lead from the pot. The problems usually result from using a cold ladle; a cold ladle cools the lead so rapidly that it begins to solidify before it can fill the mold cavity. A better, surer method: heat the lead-filled ladle on the stove, slipping it into the lead pot only to refill the ladle. Or, leave the ladle in the stock pot so that the ladle is thoroughly heated before pouring. Take care, however, that the long-handled ladle does not tip the pot over as lead is removed from the pot.

If the aluminum mold is not kept warm, it will dissipate the heat of the molten lead so rapidly that the lead cannot fill the cavity completely before becoming cooled and solid again.

Repeated casting with the same mold will in time heat it enough to make good castings, but when starting out, I find it best to heat the mold slightly over

Melting pot and ladle should be kept on the stove at all times. Note the supporting block of wood under the ladle handle to keep the ladle level.

a low flame on the stove, turning it over from time to time, to be sure that it is evenly warm. I generally like my molds to be just too hot for the touch, but experience will soon dictate whether or not the mold and lead are hot enough. Ill-formed lures mean that either the lead or the mold or both must be hotter. However, be careful not to overheat the mold. Excess heat can warp an aluminum mold.

There are several other ways that ill-formed bucktail bodies can occur. Sometimes the sprue hole is just not large enough for the size of the cavity to fill the lure body rapidly enough before cooling takes place. I recall one mold of mine that makes four bullet-shaped bucktails, all of the same size. No matter how hot I had the mold, or the lead, or which sprue hole I filled first, one cavity always produced a bad lure. I reamed out the sprue hole slightly, and since then it has worked fine. If you find this necessary, just be careful that reaming or drilling is confined to the sprue hole, and does not ruin the cavity.

Sometimes the mold and lead can both be hot enough, yet the bucktails will have ripples on them. This usually happens only in the larger cavity molds and can be corrected by drilling the sprue hole larger, as mentioned above, or by smoking the inside of the mold cavity with a candle flame. The smoked cavity prevents ripples.

While both lead and mold must be hot, they can also be too hot. The lures will be perfectly formed, but too hot a mold or lead increases the incidence of "flash" at the edge of the lure where the mold halves come together. It can happen to a slight degree with any of the standard molds. (It will not happen with a single cavity "professional" mold since the inside mold faces are machined smooth.) The less lead flash that occurs, the less work there is in removing it later.

MOLDING STEPS

The actual steps of molding are simple. First, place the special jig hooks in the mold, making sure that they are the right size for the mold and finished lure and that the eyes and shanks fit into the special depressions made for them.

After the hooks are properly positioned, close the mold carefully and hold or clamp it securely. Remove the ladle from the stove and pour the molten lead rapidly and smoothly through the sprue hole of each cavity until the lead fills the sprue hole, indicating that the cavity is filled.

Wait a few minutes for the lead to cool and then open the mold carefully. The lead heads are still hot, so lift them out of the mold with pliers, or with a hot pad glove, and lay them aside. Put more hooks in the mold and you are ready to cast again.

The excess lead that forms in the sprue hole of each lead-head casting can be cut away with wire cutters. This excess lead, sometimes called "sprue" for the entrance hole into the mold of the same name can be added to the lead stock pot.

If you don't want to keep the lead in the pot when you're finished molding, buy some ingot molds (which cost about $3 for a six-cavity, 7-ounce model). Pour the lead into them to form "pigs" before the lead cools. Actually, there is nothing wrong with leaving the lead in the pot until the next pouring session. You still might want the ingot molds, however, if you get lead in odd shapes and sizes and want to melt it down to usable bars. If you're using different alloys, work out a system of marking the pigs with a chisel or scratch awl.

One of the best ways of turning out a quantity of heads in short time is to use several molds and to work with a fishing buddy. Working together, it is possible to turn out far more lures in less time than either could individually.

Special jig hooks are placed in the open bucktail mold. Presmoked molds (smoked with a candle flame) will form the best bucktails. Note also that the correct hook size has been engraved on the mold to make hook choice easy.

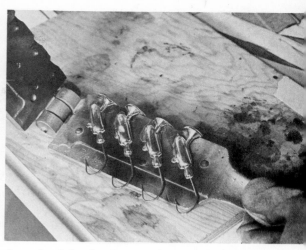

The molten lead should be poured rapidly into the sprue hole of each cavity of the mold. Fill the cavity all the way to the top of the sprue hole.

Completed bucktails being removed from the mold. Some flash along the edge of several bucktails can be noted but this is easily removed with a file.

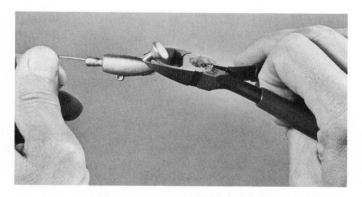

After the bucktail is removed from the mold, the sprue (excess lead at the sprue hole) can be removed with wire cutters.

After a molding session, excess lead can be poured into ingot molds for future use.

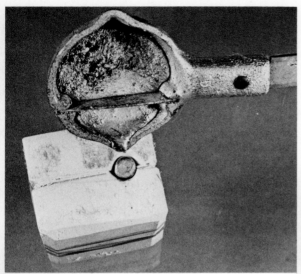

Two-piece homemade plaster molds can also be used. Directions for making these molds can be found in Chapter 13.

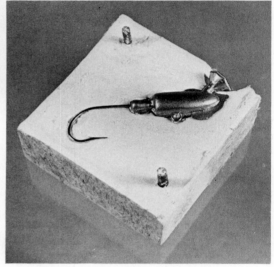

Molded bucktail ready to be removed from plaster mold.

One man can be responsible for placing the hooks in the molds and prewarming the molds to the proper temperature while the other takes charge of the actual lead melting and pouring process. With several molds—perhaps of different styles or size lures—it is easy to keep a rotation system going and turn out several hundred lead heads in only a few hours.

FINISHING MOLDED BUCKTAILS

Once all the heads have been molded, there is still work to do before the lure can be tied to the end of a line. Check the hook eyes carefully to be sure that no lead has filled them. If it has, use a small pair of side cutting wire cutters to remove it by cutting around the base of the eye and twisting, loosening the lead. Do not clamp hard with the wire cutters, or you may cut the hook eye off!

The flash on the body is easily removed with a coarse file. Regular files are designed to be used with steel and other hard metals, and while they will work, there are special files on the market designed for use with special metals. There

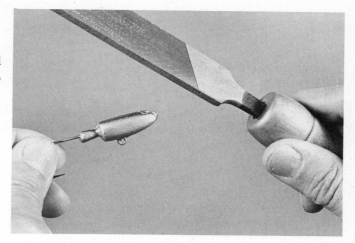

Completed bucktail heads should be trimmed and all flash removed, using files or wire cutters.

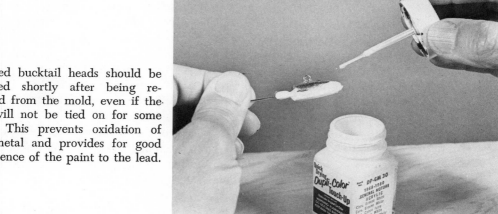

Molded bucktail heads should be painted shortly after being removed from the mold, even if the tail will not be tied on for some time. This prevents oxidation of the metal and provides for good adherence of the paint to the lead.

are lead files in flat and half round shapes, as well as brass and aluminum files for other metal-working. Prices are about $2.00 to $3.00 as compared to $0.75 to $1.75 for regular files.

If you are turning out a quantity of bucktails, and not tying them all into lures at once, paint all of them anyway *shortly after molding*. Any color of good paint will work well, although white is preferred; white is a good base for any finishing color to be added to the lure later. If the heads are not painted the lead will slowly oxidize. Neither paint nor lacquer adheres well to oxidized lead.

The choice of paint is a difficult one since the problem with any lead-head lure is that the paint chips off readily if the lure hits a rock. This is true even of commercially made bucktails. The pros and cons of various types of lacquers, enamels, and paints, and the methods of using them on bucktails as well as other lures, are covered thoroughly in Chapter 12.

After the first coat of paint to prevent oxidation, the lead head can be left indefinitely without finishing. I usually keep a stock supply of different styles and sizes of lead heads on hand, all painted a base coat of white, to tie up in my leisure or as needed.

WRAPPING TAILS ON LEAD HOOKS

To finish the bucktail, place the hook of the painted lead head in a vise to tie on the tail. A fly-tying vise works best for this step, but any other small vise or clamp can be used. Take thread and wrap it several times around the shank of the hook just behind the lead head or around the special shoulder at the rear of the head of some bucktails. Fly-tying or rod-wrapping thread is best, in size 2/0 for small bucktails, size A for medium ones and size E for large lures.

After wrapping the thread around the hook shank several times, wrap over the previous wraps, to hold the thread in place. Cut off the excess thread.

The tail material can be of bucktail, some of the new artificial fur, saddle hackles, crinkly nylon, polypropylene fibers (unraveled from polypropylene rope), marabou, or similar materials.

Once the proper amount and length of tail material is decided, there are two basic ways that it can be tied on. One way is to take a large bunch of hair, hold it over the hook shank or molded shoulder and tie it all in place at once. The best way to accomplish this neatly is to make several loose wraps of thread around the hair and hook shank. Pull them tight, spiraling the hair completely around the hook shank or shoulder to cover it completely.

When the bucktail is stiff, this method is difficult, especially for the beginner or tackle tinkerer without fly-tying experience. It can be made easier by soaking the butt end of the cut bucktail in hot water for a few minutes to soften it.

The second method is easier, but will take longer, since the hair is added in several sections at different positions around the hook shank, to cover the shank completely. Although it's more time-consuming, this method is usually easier for the beginner who has not yet mastered fly-tying techniques.

This method is also the one to use when tying on a tail with mixed colors as in a blue-and-white-tailed salt-water bucktail. Some bucktails have both fur and long saddle-hackle tails. These too must be tied in separately.

It is also possible to wind hackle between the lead head and the tail. To do this, wrap a large hackle feather in place by the center vane or shaft of the feather. Then the feather is wrapped around the tail and hook shank so that the feather fibers spring out from the body of the lure. The end of the hackle feather is wrapped down and cut off and the wrappings finished. This type of wrap, sometimes spiraled up along the tail, is most often seen in freshwater jigs and crappie-type lures.

Some materials are more difficult to work with than others. Nylon tail material has a tendency to pull out from under the thread wrappings. It's a good idea to soak the butt ends with a clear fingernail polish or fly-tyer's head cement while it is being wrapped on. This will help hold the nylon in place.

Polypropylene tail material can be made from a piece of rope. A jig or bucktail with this material on it proves to be a highly successful lure for some fish. Along the Gulf Coast these lures are advertised and sold as being excellent for ling, also called cobia.

Add polypropylene by tying a short piece of rope to the hook shank of the bucktail. Make sure that the polypropylene fibers completely encircle the hook shank. After the rope is tied in place, unravel the fibers carefully, using an awl,

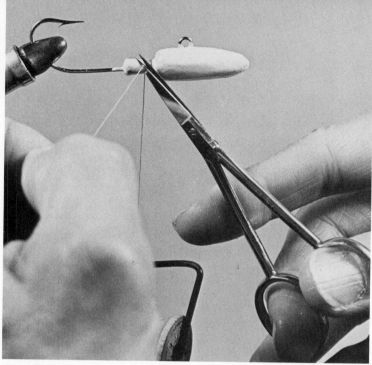

Prepainted bucktails are clamped in a vise and wrapped with fly-tying thread.

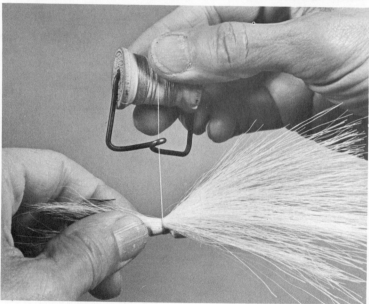

Once the thread is tied down, the tail material is tied in place.

After all the tail material is added, it should be wrapped several times with the thread to hold it securely before the excess tail material is trimmed.

bodkin, needle, nail, or other sharp tool. Do not try to unravel it too rapidly, but instead concentrate on freeing a few fibers at a time.

After tying down any of these tail materials, clip the excess from in front of the thread and wrap the thread securely over the tail. Finish it smoothly by covering all the butt ends of the tail material. Make several half hitches over the thread wrapping to tie the end of thread down. Pull these down securely, cinching each half hitch into the one previously made, clip the thread, and the bucktail is almost finished. It can be used as is (painted white) but the thread wrapping should be protected with a coat of fly-tying cement or clear fingernail polish. Another way to protect the thread windings from unwrapping is to cover with several layers of narrow vinyl adhesive tape. Painting bucktails, adding eyes, and finishing bucktails with special metallic and flocked finishes are completely covered in Chapter 12.

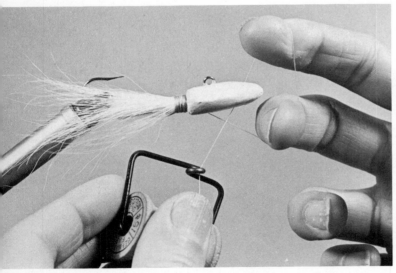

Once the excess tail material is trimmed, the wraps are finished and then the bucktail tied off with a series of 3 to 4 half-hitches as shown.

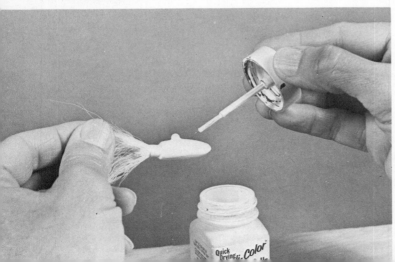

After the tail is wrapped, the bucktail can be given a base coat of color and then finished as outlined in Chapter 12. Note that the thread wrappings here have been painted to protect them from wear.

Finished bucktails. Top to bottom: natural fur tails, artificial fur tails, feather tails, nylon tails, marabou tails, and polypropylene tails.

JIGS AND BUCKTAIL KITS

Those who prefer not to make their own bucktail bodies can buy either the component parts or kits that include everything needed to make effective jigs and bucktails. Finnysports, Herter's, Cabela's, Netcraft, E. Hille, Midland, Reed, Ament, Lure-Craft, and other mail-order outfits all carry the unfinished lead heads, bucktails, tying thread, paints, and/or other needed materials. The Worth Company and Tack-L-Tyers both offer jig-making kits. The Worth kit (about $6.95) includes prepainted finished bodies, thread, and a small inexpensive fly-tying vise to clamp the jigs while finishing them. This kit makes 24 jigs in assorted sizes, colors, and shapes. Tack-L-Tyers has four similar jig-tying kits. Herb's Hairjig Kit, just on the market from Netcraft and selling for about $10, makes it possible to mold tail material into the jigs. The high-quality four-mold kit has a special electric gun that makes possible seating tail material in the molds, so that no tying or wrapping is necessary. After molding with lead, the jigs can be used as they are or the head can be painted.

Variations of bucktails. Left row: finished spinner baits; center row: lead head lures; right row: bucktail bodies rigged with plastic worm, split rubber tubing, and small molded squid.

←

An alternate method of cleaning flash from bucktails is shown by Dick Savage. An electric router is used under a plexiglass covered box to cut away the excess lead. The covered box prevents the lead from being scattered around the room.

Left, Herb's Hairjig mold closed, the hair in place and ready to be filled with lead. The two-part mold has holes at both ends, one to accommodate the tail, the other for pouring in the lead. Below, completed jigs out of Herb's Hairjig. *Photos courtesy The Netcraft Company.*

COST OF BUCKTAILS

The cost of any single lure is low. Taking a simple ½ ounce bullet-head bucktail as an example, the materials will come to something like this:

Hook, size 2/0	$1.85 per hundred	$0.0185 each
Lead—free from		
tire weights		
Thread	0.20 per 50 yards	0.0040 per yard
		(enough for one bucktail)
Bucktail	1.30 per tail	
	(enough for 100 lures)	0.013 per bunch
Paint, two coats (estimate only)		0.05 for several coatings
	TOTAL	$0.0855

That same bucktail lure that costs less than 9 cents would probably retail for 50 cents or more. Of course, the cost of molding must include the cost of the molds, ladle, pot, file, and wire cutters, assuming that none of these are currently in your home workshop. Then the figures would run something like this:

	MINIMUM	MAXIMUM
Mold	$3.00	$6.00
Pot	2.50	5.00
Ladle	2.00	4.00
File	1.00	2.00
Wire cutters	2.75	5.75
TOTAL	$11.25	$22.75

Sound too expensive? Cost-averaged over 100 bucktails, as above, the total would come to $20.75 to $31.25 (tool cost plus $8.50 material costs for the 100 lures). That brings the cost of those 100 bucktails up to 20 to 30 cents each, still half the cost of the store-bought models of the same style, even if another lure is never made and the tools never again used. But in continued use over a long period of time, the cost quickly drops. For a lure so simple to make, the economic benefits of a long-term arangement are obvious.

With a world-wide reputation as one of the best lures in both freshwater and saltwater, jigs and bucktails are not only easy to make but also easy to fish. Any angler should have a good selection of them in his tackle box.

4

SINKERS AND TIN SQUIDS

SINKER TYPES · SINKER SIZES · COSTS ·
MOLDING TECHNIQUES · TIN SQUIDS

BASIC TOOLS	HELPFUL TOOLS
Old cooking pot	Plumber's melting pot
Cheap gravy ladle or large	Plumber's ladle
serving spoon	Heavy pliers
Sinker or tin squid molds	
Hot pads, gloves, and safety goggles	

♘ SINKERS CAN BE MOLDED JUST AS EASILY AS BUCKTAIL BODIES, BY the methods described in the previous chapter. In one sense, they are more satisfying for the beginner, since once a sinker is popped from the mold and the excess lead (left from pouring through the sprue hole) removed, it's ready to use.

Sinker molds come in the same styles as those for bucktails, namely in pinned, clamped, and hinged-handled molds. However, there are some differences. Not all sinker molds are made of aluminum as are the jig and bucktail molds. The Reading Instrument Company has a complete line of sinker molds and several squid molds made from cast iron, with machined molding surfaces. Because the cast-iron molds rust when not in use, they suggest a way to make the molds rust-resistant. They recommend mixing equal parts of motor oil and kerosene, dipping the mold in the solution, and standing it on edge on newspapers for several days to drain before using.

SINKER TYPES

Many sinkers have molded-in eyes, but some, such as pyramid sinkers, bass (also called dipsy or bell sinkers), trolling sinkers, and cushion sinkers (sinkers shaped like round pillows) have brass or swivel eyes that must be placed in

47

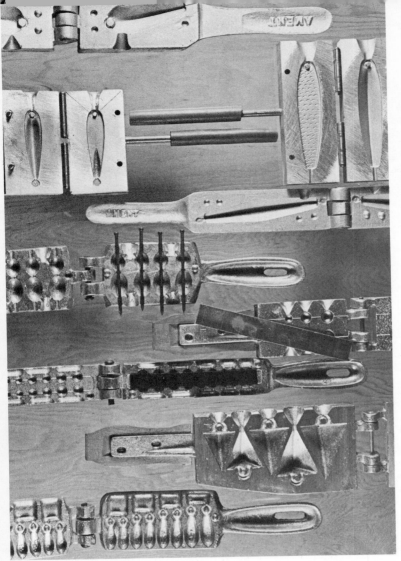

Typical sinker and tin squid molds. Top to bottom: 4 tin squid molds, egg sinker mold, 2 split shot molds, pyramid sinker mold, and bank sinker mold. Note the core pins in the egg sinker that form the holes in the sinker, and the plates that form the slot in the split-shot sinkers.

the mold before pouring. The eyes and proper swivels are available from the sinker supplier, tackle store, or mail-order outfit.

In addition, there are egg sinkers, which require the use of rods, sometimes called core rods, to form the hole in the sinker. Split-shot, ear-grip (or clamp-on) sinkers use a metal plate in the mold to form the slot into which the fishing line is placed and clamped in use. These plates and core rods are supplied with the sinker molds.

The cost of aluminum sinker molds is about the same as that of the bucktail molds—between $2 and $5, although cast-iron molds run generally higher, between $4 and $10. The eyes used in some of the sinkers are available in lots of 100 or by the pound, or by 5 pounds. Prices vary from $0.35 to $1.00 per 100, depending upon the style, or $2.00 to $2.50 per pound. The low variation in the price per pound is due to the fact that the difference in the eyes is mostly a matter of size. The larger-size eyes yield less per pound, even though the amount of brass used in making the eyes is the same for all sizes. (Eyes for sinkers and tin squids can also be formed on a homemade wire former—see Chapters 10 and 13.)

Swivel eyes for dipsy, trolling sinkers are generally standard brass swivels, available for $0.25 to $0.35 per dozen, $1.75 to $2.50 per gross, depending upon size. Sinker molds that will make any size weight are also available, most molds making from three to eight sinkers in one pouring.

SINKER SIZES

Some popular sizes of sinkers currently available include the following, though not all are from the same mold, or even from molds of the same company.

pyramid sinkers—1 to 8 ounces   snagless sinkers—1 to 7 ounces
bank sinkers—$\frac{3}{8}$ to 20 ounces   cushion sinkers—1 to $3\frac{1}{2}$ ounces
egg sinkers—$\frac{1}{2}$ to 8 ounces   split shot—BB to size 4
trolling sinkers—$\frac{1}{2}$ to 12 ounces   ear grip or clamp-on sinkers—$\frac{1}{16}$ to 2 ounces
bass or bell sinkers—$\frac{1}{8}$ to 3 ounces   worm slip-sinker molds—mostly $\frac{1}{4}$ ounce

(Molds with a greater size range may be forthcoming with the increased popularity of worm fishing for bass.)

Molds that require core pins include the egg and worm-slip sinkers. Those that use plates (to form a slot in the side of the sinker in which to place the line) include split-shot and ear clamp-on sinkers. Using molds with core pins or plates is no different from molding regular sinkers, except that the plates and pins must be removed after molding.

The plates can easily be pried from the completed sinker, but pins are usually a little more difficult to remove. They can usually be pulled out with pliers, or the core pin put in a vise and the sinker pulled away from it. Often it is easier to pull the pins before removing the sinkers from the mold. A light coating of soap on the core pin lubricates it slightly and makes the pin easier to remove. Just as in molding bucktails, there will be some flash on the sinker where the two mold halves come together, but usually it's minimal. Since the sinkers are not used to attract fish, the flash does not have to be removed unless its removal is desired for aesthetic purposes. The same applies to removing any other rough spots.

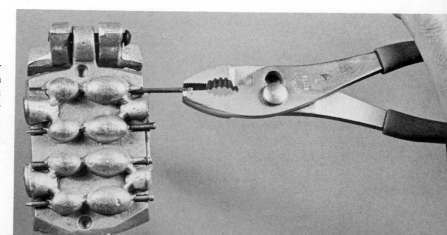

Core pins are best removed from sinkers with pliers while the sinker is still in the mold. Normally the mold is kept closed, but is shown here open for clarity.

COSTS

Assuming that lead can be obtained free from old lead pipe, cable sheathing, or tire weights, the cost of lead sinkers molded in the home is minimal. If you use old pots and soup ladles for tools and kitchen hot pads and old gloves, the only cost will be the sinker mold, which will vary from $2 to $10, depending upon whether the mold is aluminum or cast iron, and the size and style of the sinker and number of mold cavities.

Pyramid sinkers as they are removed from the mold after pouring. Pouring techniques are identical to those for bucktails.

Once the sprue is removed from a sinker, it is ready to be used. Wire cutters cut the sprue off.

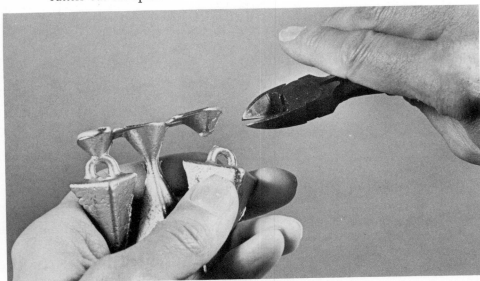

MOLDING TECHNIQUES

The molding technique is identical to that used for bucktails, in terms of working space, safety, choice of metals, heat factors, tools, and methods.

Just as the hooks are placed in bucktail molds, so the core-rods, eyes, swivels, and plates must be put in the molds before making egg, pyramid, split-shot, and clamp-on sinkers. While brass eyes are standard for pyramid, bass, and keel sinkers, it may be preferable to mold the sinker without them. Certainly it is quicker (since the eyes do not have to be placed in the mold for each pouring) and less expensive, although the cost of the brass eyes makes this a minor consideration.

There is one additional advantage, as well as one disadvantage. The advantage of the molded eye in fishing rocky or snaggy areas is that a hung sinker can frequently be broken off when snagged. A properly molded-in-brass eye will never break. If the eye of the sinker breaks, the loss is only an easily made sinker, whereas if the eyes are used, the line must be broken, resulting in a loss of lures, hooks, bobbers, or other terminal gear. Some molds are made with this "breakaway" feature in mind. The mold cavity is made slightly larger in the eyes, allowing the user either to use the brass eyes, or to mold a solid lead eye.

However, if the sinker is to be tied directly to the line and used continuously, there is a slight danger of the rough lead in the large molded eye wearing the line, causing it to part. Of course, this is not like the loss of a lure or fish, but when or if it happens, a new sinker must be tied on. One way to avoid this is to tie the line to a large snap and snap the sinker on.

With a $4 eight-cavity bank sinker mold, 25 pourings will make 200 sinkers for just 2 cents each, plus a little time. With sinkers selling in most stores for about 5 cents an ounce, the savings are obviously considerable.

TIN SQUIDS

Tin squids are used by surf anglers, and are highly regarded as one of the best lures in certain situations, either alone or rigged with pork rind or a skirt of some type. Tin squids are made by the same techniques used in molding sinkers and bucktail heads, except for one important difference: the metal used in molding tin squids is usually pure block tin.

Tin is generally preferred for squids, since surf anglers often bend these lures slightly to increase their action in the water. Lead and other alloys such as type metal (used by printers) cannot be bent by hand to shape, and these heavier metals also make the lures less maneuverable in the water.

The tin lure is lighter than a lead one of the same size, and the tin stays bright, where lead will not. Since these lures are used unpainted, the bright finish is important as a fish-attracting factor.

The difference in weight is about a 5 to 8 ratio; i.e., a tin lure of 2½ ounces would weigh 4 ounces if molded of lead. Tin squid molds, depending upon the size and type of squid, vary from as low as $4 for some of the aluminum single-cavity molds to as high as $16 for multiple-cavity cast-iron molds. Most of the molds available are single-cavity.

The necessary eyes and hooks are placed in tin squid molds, which have been smoked by a candle flame.

Pouring molten tin into the mold.

Once cooled, the squid can be removed from the mold and have any flash or sprue cut off.

One-piece molds for tin squids are not commercially available, but because these lures are generally flat on one side, homemade one-piece molds can be made and used, according to the directions in Chapter 13.

Using an open-face mold for tin squids is simple, in that there are no sprue holes or hinged halves. There is just an open cavity the shape of the lure. But it is important to use a small ladle to control the pouring of the tin so as not to overflow the mold cavity.

Position the mold near the melting tin, pour the mold rapidly, and allow to cool. Open-face molds can be made with a small slot at one end to hold the hook in place. Or the hook can be slipped into the molten tin and held in place briefly until the metal solidifies. Wear asbestos gloves or use pliers to hold the hook, since it will become hot as the metal cools.

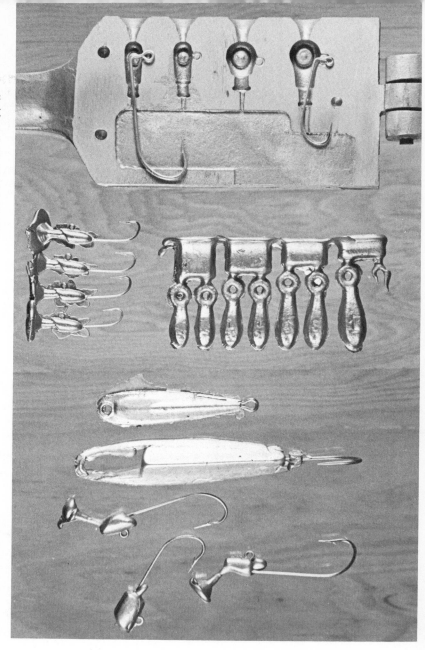

Defects in molded lures include hooks the wrong size for the mold (top), misplaced hooks that cause excessive flash (second row left), lead becoming too cool before completing molding (second row right), too cool a mold or not hot enough lead (third row and fourth row).

Typical home-molded sinkers and squids. Clockwise from twelve o'clock: egg sinker, split shot, worm slip sinker, tin squids, pyramid sinkers, bank sinkers, keeled trolling sinkers.

Some tin squids are not molded with the hook in place but instead have an eye molded at each end. As they come from the mold, they look like angular-shaped trolling sinkers. Add a split ring to one of the molded-in brass eyes, and a hook to the split ring at the same time. In use, the line is tied to the other eye and the hook swings free. The hook can be either a single or treble hook, left plain or dressed with fur, feathers, or attractor tubing.

Brass wire can be used for the eyes or the eyes can be molded in. Generally, since these are lures and presumably will have the pull of a fish on them, it is preferable to use a brass wire eye at each end of the lure so that there is no danger of the eye being pulled out and a fish lost. (Eyes can also be formed in a homemade wire former—see Chapters 10 and 13.)

Some fishermen prefer tin squids made of type metal, which is heavier than pure block tin, but does stay bright. Usually this is used in diamond jigs and squids that are jigged in deep water rather than cast from the surf, where it is sometimes necessary to bend them for best action. Type metal is hard and brittle and cannot be reshaped once the lure is molded.

While a large variety of sizes of sinkers are available, the most weight is generally used by the surf angler, the river catfish and carp fisherman, the saltwater troller, and other anglers after big fish or plumbing deep waters. Sinkers come in up to 28-ounce sizes, although average sizes would probably be 8 ounces for trolling, 4 ounces for surf pyramid sinkers, and 2 ounces for freshwater bank sinkers.

When you're molding sinkers or tin squids, be sure that enough lead or tin is at hand. Since most sinker molds have multiple cavities, up to 5 pounds of lead can be used per pouring in large bank or trolling sinker molds. A check of several mold companies shows that bank sinker molds use from 6 ounces to 2 pounds of lead; pyramid sinker molds from 6 to 20 ounces; trolling sinker molds from 4 ounces to 5½ pounds. Sinker molds take a lot of lead, a hot fire, a large pot, and a large ladle, if many sinkers are to be made at one pouring.

COSTS

As with sinkers, the cost of molding tin squids is minimal. Most take single hooks, costing about 2 cents each. If the tin or type metal can be obtained free, the only other cost is that of the mold. Assuming an average mold (costing approximately $6), molding 100 tin squids will cost about $8, including the cost of both mold and hooks. Each lure will cost only 8 cents, exclusive of the metal.

If you must purchase the metal, the price rises some, since the retail price of pure tin is currently about $1.50 per pound. But even then the cost of a typical 2-ounce squid will only be about 28 cents, far less than the average store cost. Of course, as with all molded lures, the more the mold is used and its cost amortized, the cheaper the cost of each individual lure.

The technique of molding sinkers and tin squids is easy. With the cost of lead sinkers constantly rising, molding your own not only makes sense, but saves cents as well. Starting with these easy-to-make tackle items is a natural for anyone who wants to cut the cost of angling, while adding to the wintertime pleasure of tackle craft.

5

SOFT PLASTIC LURES

BASIC TOOLS	HELPFUL TOOLS
Rubber or aluminum molds	Hot plate or special melting stove
Melting pot	
Stirring sticks	
Molding plastic	

Many Anglers Who Buy Soft Plastic Worms Are Not Aware that worms just this soft, just as good, and in a variety of sizes and colors can be made at home for but a few pennies each. And while worms may seem to be the most popular of the soft lures for bass, soft plastic crickets, minnows, crayfish, frogs, tadpoles, salamanders, and other lures are made just as easily.

MOLDING PROCESSES

There are two processes by which soft plastic lures can be made. One involves heating a metal open-face mold and adding a liquid plastic which cures to the proper consistency with heat. The second method involves heating liquid

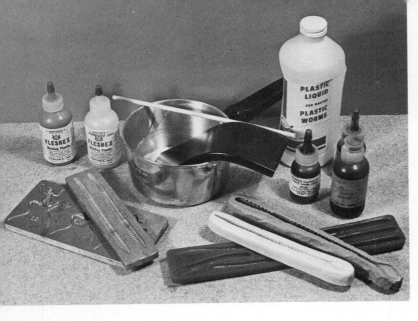

Tools and materials in molding soft plastic lures. Included are metal molds, rubber molds, three types of molding plastic, and melting pot.

→

Typical soft plastic lure molds. Top row: worm molds; second row: worm, crayfish molds; third row: frog and insect molds; fourth row: minnow, frog, insect, and crayfish molds; fifth, sixth, and seventh rows: worm molds. Top four rows are metal molds, bottom three are made of rubber.

plastic to 350° F., pouring it into a hard rubber, plastic, or similar mold, and allowing the lure to cool slightly before removing it from the mold.

> CAUTION: There is one important thing to remember in using all liquid molding plastics, as well as in handling the completed lures. The plastics will chemically attack most furniture finishes, as well as some tackle boxes and most paint and plastic finishes on lures. Be careful not to spill any plastic on anything but the scrap board used at the molding area. Do not allow completed lures to come in contact with anything except the inside of a plastic bag or worm-proof tackle box. This applies to commercially made soft plastic lures as well.

MOLDS

The molds vary, depending upon the molding process used. The metal molds are usually aluminum and come in single-cavity or multiple-cavity models. Most are multiple-cavity models and sell for about $1.50 to $2.50 each. Typical molds available include those for worms of all types from 6 inches to 9 inches, hellgrammites, crayfish, mayfly nymphs, grasshoppers, crickets, dragonfly nymphs, stone fly nymphs, grubs, large and small frogs, shrimp, mayflies, garden worms, minnows, and similar lures. Most are rectangular and open-face.

All Herter's molds are made in small aluminum squares, designed to be used either over an open flame or in their Mold Heater. Some molds, such as the Herter's mold for a minnow, have two cavities, one each for a right and left half of the lure. In practice, the two halves are molded together to form one single lure.

The rubber and plastic molds are not heated, but are used with the heated liquid plastic. However, they are said to be able to withstand heat to 600° F., well above the 350° temperature of the liquid plastic.

Because the molds are of rubber and because they are used with very soft plastic, most rubber open-face molds are made with a deeper more rounded cavity than is found in an aluminum mold. Thus a more rounded lure is pos-

sible with rubber molds than aluminum molds. These are certainly popular molds, and come in a tremendous variety of sizes and shapes.

Limit Manufacturing Company, and Ottawa Supply Company list 46 rubber molds, while Lure-Craft Company lists 205 molds. Maumelle, Carver Plastisols, M-F Manufacturing, and Super-Sport also carry a variety of molds. These include worms of all sizes (from 4 inches to 16 inches) with standard heads, knobby heads, spiraled heads, round tails, flat tails, split tails, smooth bodies, segmented bodies, and all types of fins. Due to the current popularity of bass fishing, worms make up the bulk of the molds, but there are also molds to make spring lizards, eels, split tails for spinner baits, plastic "pork chunks," grubs, crayfish, jig tails, mud-puppies, frogs, tadpoles, and some lures that defy description.

Many of these come in single-cavity molds, selling at about $1.50 to $6.50 each, depending upon the size and type of lure. Some of the Lure-Craft molds are multiple-cavity, making it possible to make up to twenty-four catalpa worms, six 9-inch bass worms, twelve small 4½-inch worms, and eighteen tadpoles. Multiple-cavity molds from Limit are usually three-cavity molds. They vary in price from $2.50 to $12.00, depending upon the type and size and number of cavities.

In addition to the open-face molds, two-piece molds are available for making round soft plastic lures. These will probably become more popular and readily available in the future, but at this writing, only Lure-Craft and Super-Sport list the two-piece molds. And all these are single-cavity only.

MOLDING PLASTICS

The plastic used for both types of molds is similar, and in some cases, identical. While the various manufacturing companies retain the formulation of the plastic, it is variously described as Plasnyl (by Finnysports), Fleshex (by Herter's), and liquid plastic by other suppliers. It comes in liquid form in pint to 5-gallon quantities, and in solid blocks sold by the pound.

Both types of plastic are reuseable, so any early "mistakes" in molding are not wasted but can be poured into the melting stock pot and used again.

The liquid plastic is milky white, of a slightly thick consistency, which turns clear upon being heated. The manufacturers claim that it never goes bad and can be reused over and over again. Heat serves as the curing agent; no catalyst is needed or added. At 350° F., it starts to turn clear, and becomes thicker and syrupy. A color additive must be used to obtain the shade of lure desired.

The block plastic is sold by the pound and comes in several colors, including transparent red, opaque red, blue, green, white, black, purple, and grape. Santee Lure and Tackle and Best Bet Lures both carry block plastic. It has the advantage of not having to be mixed with a coloring agent; a piece is cut off, placed in the melting pan, heated, and poured into the mold. But the fact that it comes in colored blocks is also a disadvantage, in that it is not possible to change the colors to get a lighter or darker shade than that of the plastic block.

Color must be added to the liquid plastic, if anything other than a clear lure is desired. The colors come in 2-ounce bottles, which most supply houses consider enough for one or two gallons of molding plastic. Use care in adding colors: it's easier to add more color than it is to double or triple the quantity of plastic molding compound to dilute the color and get a lighter shade.

The variety of colors available makes it possible to make any type of soft plastic lure in any color desired. One company lists the following as standard available colors for adding to their plastic: black, red, blue, avocado, amber, green, strawberry, raspberry, natural, lime, white, orange, violet, yellow, brown, purple, fluorescent green, fluorescent red, fluorescent yellow, fluorescent blue, fluorescent purple, fluorescent orange, fluorescent pink, phosphorescent blue, phosphorescent yellow, phosphorescent green, phosphorescent yellowish green, and pearl colors of sparkling white, yellow gold, worm bronze, and minnow silver. The phosphorescent colors glow in the dark (like electric wall-switch plates). They may be illegal to use for fishing lures in some states; check before ordering or making lures from this material. Fluorescent materials are extra bright, just like some plastic rainsuits, hunting jackets, and caps.

In addition, the colors can be mixed together. Usually white is mixed with a color to obtain a lighter shade, while most colors can be made in "pearl" shades by adding a drop or two of the standard color to the sparkling white pearl color. Do not overlook the fact that most colors can be made lighter just by adding less color than is called for to the basic plastic.

OTHER ADDITIVES

Various other additives may be mixed with the molding plastic. For example, while the molding plastic is ideal for molding most plastic lures for most fishermen, it is possible to make the plastic either harder or softer. Generally 2 ounces of hardener or softener to a pint of molding plastic is enough to change the consistency quite a bit. While most of the molding plastic has a slight buoyancy, plastic lures can be made higher-floating by the addition of a special floating agent. A few drops in a small pan of plastic forms bubbles in the plastic lure as it cures, increasing the flotation.

And as if the hardeners, softeners, and floating agents were not enough, there are also special flavoring agents that can be either mixed into the plastic, or added in the polyethylene bags in which most plastic worms are stored. Licorice, wild cherry, raspberry, cheddar cheese, anise, and fish flavors are common. More and more fishermen are becoming aware that the scent of people, gas, oil, and other "foreign" scents can sometimes repel fish. Presumably these flavors help disguise foreign fish-repelling odors.

There is also a plastic lubricant (in plain or fish scents) that can be added in small quantities to the polyethylene bags in which soft plastic lures should be stored. It makes the lures slick (they are dry and rubbery feeling when they come out of the molds) and helps to hide the foreign odors, and reportedly, increases chances of catching fish.

Prices for liquid plastic vary from $2 to $4 per pint, $10 to $20 per gallon. Solid plastic sells for about $2 per pound, equivalent to a pint. Color additives are a little more: typical current prices run about $0.50 per 2 ounces, $1.50 per

8 ounces, $3.00 per pint. Phosphorescent colors are even higher, averaging $1.50 to $2.00 per 2 ounces. Softeners, hardeners, and flotation additives are about $1 per half pint.

GENERAL MOLDING TECHNIQUES

The liquid (or solid) soft plastic lure-molding material can be heated in several ways. Since the plastic must be brought to 350° F. to cure properly, it's important to be able to control the heat. Overheating is just as bad as under-heating; while the material is not explosive, excess heat creates fumes and burns the material, destroying its color. And the fumes can be noxious. It is also flammable, so that heating over a gas flame is more hazardous than over an electric stove or hot plate; some companies sell two-burner hot plates just for molding. A suitable substitute for a burner can be made by building a support to hold an iron upside down, heating the plastic carefully by means of the controls on the iron; otherwise the kitchen stove is best for plastic molding.

If possible, use two burners for molding soft plastic lures, since it is best to keep a large supply of melted plastic on one burner in a large pot, adding it to a small pot for pouring into the mold cavity. Pouring the thick, syrupy melted plastic is an art in itself, since it has a tendency to run down the side of the pan (again the danger of fire over a gas or open flame). A small folded cloth or block of the soft molding plastic—made by melting a small amount of plastic in a small pan, allowing it to cool, and then removing it—will serve for wiping excess plastic from the pouring lip.

Another type of molding is also possible with the use of liquid plastic (such as that currently available from Herter's and Finnysports) poured into heated aluminum molds. The results are the same. The difference is that instead of pouring hot plastic into a cold mold, liquid plastic at room temperature is poured into the hot (about 350°) mold. Aluminum molds must be used for this type of molding.

There are several ways of heating the molds in this process, best described in the Finnysports catalog:

> To cure Plasnyl, that is, to change it from a liquid to a solid, you must have heat around 350° F. There are many ways you can go about providing the heat.
>
> The length of curing time needed varies as it takes longer for a thick tadpole to cure than for a thin mayfly. Usually 15 to 30 minutes if you bake them in an oven.
>
> We will give you several ways to cure the plastic as it depends what you are making as to which way is best. Your mold must be dry. If it's not the water will boil away and make bubbles and holes in your bait.
>
> OVEN CURING. You simply preheat the oven to 350° F. and then place your filled molds in the oven for 15 minutes or more, then take them out of the oven and allow mold to cool. You can dunk the mold in water to cool and strip out the bait or just let the mold cool for 5 minutes.
>
> GRIDDLE CURING. We like this way as you can add more Plasnyl to make

This special self-contained electric Herter's Mold Heater is used with special small open-faced molds that have separate lifting handles for easy mold removal.

the bait thicker or you can drop in a hook to let it be molded into the bait. This is a quicker way but you have to watch the molds all the time. You set a pancake griddle over electric or gas burners and keep the heat on low and place the molds on top of the griddle to cure. This way you can watch them, you know when to add more Plasnyl or coloring, when to drop in the hooks, and the exact time to remove the mold. If you spill any of the liquid you can scrape it off. Also, you can be preheating some molds on the back side of the griddle.

OPEN FLAME. You can also just place this over a low gas flame on a kitchen range and set the molds on the grates or on an electric range; just place the mold on the burner. But, if you spill anything it burns and it could be a mess to clean up. Protect the burner with even a cookie sheet or something.

CURING PLASNYL. It cures or starts to cure when the edges get darker. This is the time to add more plastic to make the bait thicker to get a nice fat worm, etc. You can't get a worm with markings on both sides as you are working with an open mold. A full round worm with markings on both sides is made on an injection molding machine, closed dies, etc. That has its drawbacks.*

Herter's has the same type of molding plastic. However, the rubber mold–heated plastic process formerly described is becoming more popular than the aluminum mold–cold pouring method that was first developed for making soft plastic lures.

Herter's furnishes all its smaller molds in a uniform square size for use in a special heater, much like the Mattel, Inc., Vac-U-Maker toy set designed for molding flexible plastic toys.

A special spring handle makes it possible to lift the mold out of the Herter's heater once the plastic is cured. New molds can be placed in the heater to warm as the first mold is cooling, to allow removal of the lures. Molding time for aluminum molds varies, from a few minutes up to 15 minutes for large molds with deeper cavities.

*Courtesy of Finnysports

USING RUBBER MOLDS*

First arrange all the necessary materials and tools. Two small aluminum pots for melting the plastic, hot pads for handling the pots, a shallow pan of water, molds, the plastic, and any additives complete the list. Use a gas stove, electric stove, or hot plate for heat, turned to low heat. If the heat is too low it is easy to increase gradually; on the other hand, if it is too high, it can scorch the plastic before the heat is reduced. Overheated plastic will also release toxic fumes. Work in a kitchen with an exhaust fan if possible, or leave the windows open until you are experienced enough to determine the correct heat.

Cover the kitchen counter with plywood, newspaper, or masonite to protect it against spilled plastic. Place the mold next to the stove. Fill the shallow pan with cold water in which to place lures for cooling. Place the two pots on the burners, adding the milky liquid plastic to each. Keep the smaller pot (or the pouring pot if they are the same size) just barely filled, since this will be the one used to pour plastic into the molds. Use the other pot for a "stock" solution to add melted plastic to the smaller pot.

Melt the plastic slowly, watching for the milky plastic to become thicker, and to turn clear and syrupy. Stir constantly; some bubbles may develop in the plastic as it is stirred, but these will come out as the plastic heats. Some of the additives (color, hardeners, softeners, scents, and so forth) mentioned previously are added before the plastic is melted; others can be added only after. Be sure to follow the supplier's instructions accordingly. In the case of the solid blocks of plastic, since no color is added, the plastic is used as supplied.

Once the plastic is melted and the additives mixed thoroughly, remove the small melting pot from the heat and pour the liquid plastic quickly into the mold cavities. Some manufacturers recommend pouring the head end first, others the tail end first. (I prefer the latter.) As the plastic cools (and it cools rather quickly), it becomes more difficult to get it into smaller parts of the mold cavity. This includes tails of worms, legs of frogs, and crayfish, insects, and the like. Pouring into these cavities when the plastic is hot helps to keep the detail of the mold without over-pouring so that excess plastic overflows the mold cavity.

In the case of molds with a lot of fine legs or similar details, the best procedure is to pour into the center of the mold rapidly. Generally, the plastic is still hot enough at this point to spread out evenly to the terminal parts of the mold.

Sometimes shaking the mold slightly or tapping it on the side helps to spread the plastic. Avoid going over the mold several times with the plastic; this tends to create uneven streaks and ripples in the finished lure.

---

* There are injection molding systems available for making plastic worms, such as the one offered by H & L Distributing Company, Inc., in Finger, Tennessee. But the price of these takes them out of the do-it-yourself realm.

The cheapest machine with one set of four cavity molds will produce up to 500 lures per hour and costs $8,000—perhaps an idea for a very large bass fishing club that might want to have its members kick in $10 to $30 each for the assurance of a continuous supply of worms.

The liquid plastic must be stirred constantly under low heat until it becomes puddinglike.

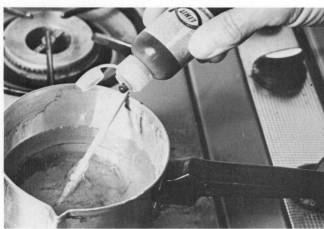

The liquid plastic, used as it comes, will yield clear lures, so color additives must be mixed in.

Once the color is added and the plastic becomes thin again, pour rapidly into the rubber molds.

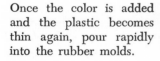

After several molds have been filled, wipe the lip of the pouring pot.

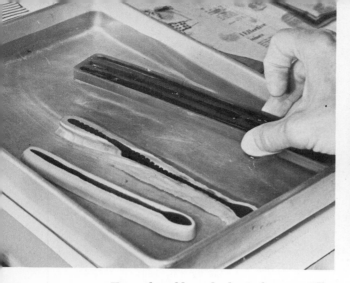

To cool molds and plastic lures rapidly, place in a shallow pan of water.

Molds then can be lifted from the water and the plastic lures carefully pulled out.

Since rubber molds are usually slightly undercut to give a rounded appearance to the finished lure, the mold can be "overfilled" slightly. This will round it without the plastic overflowing the sides of the mold. If the mold has several cavities, fill them all the same way.

Stop pouring at this point, wipe the lip of the small pot with a cloth or the plastic wiping block, and place it back on the stove. If most of the plastic has been used, add more from the stock solution kept at a low heat on the other burner. The small pot should never have more than enough for several pourings, since it might flow too rapidly and overfill the mold cavity. Once the mold is filled, allow it to cool or move it to a safe place while pouring another mold.

Often, faster curing is desirable, for speed of operations. To rapidly cool the mold and lure, place the mold in a shallow pan of water. Lift it carefully, taking care that the mold is kept horizontal. The plastic is still slightly liquid at this point, and lifting the mold at an angle will cause it to flow to one end, overflowing the mold.

After a few minutes, roll a finger or thumb over the lure at the edge of the mold to loosen it. Once an edge of the lure turns up, grasp the lure carefully and pull from the mold. If the lure (particularly in the case of a worm) stretches at this point, it is because it was not sufficiently cool when pulled from the mold. Folds and wrinkles can develop in the lure from the same causes. Any faulty lures can be thoroughly dried and then added to the stock pot of the plastic for reuse.

One disadvantage of curing rapidly in water is that the interior of the mold gets wet. It cannot be used wet, as the hot plastic will "spit" as it is poured into the mold the next time, creating a dangerous situation somewhat akin to grease spattering out of a frying pan. In addition, plastic cannot fill the mold wherever water droplets lodge. One solution to this problem is to remove the mold from the water after cooling and shake it forcefully. A quick wipe with soft absorbent toweling removes any remaining droplets.

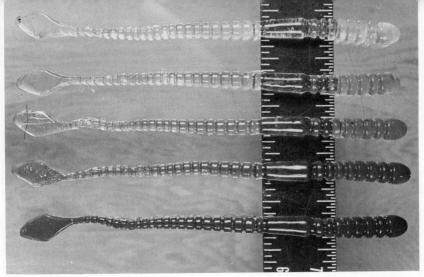

Variations in shades of color in plastic lures can be controlled by the amount of color additive mixed with the basic plastic.

For best results, use several molds at once on a rotation basis. This way new molds can be filled while others are cooling and drying. Also, if possible, use molds with cavities approximately the same size. The large cavity of a frog or crayfish mold takes much longer to cool properly than the mold of a thin worm or small imitation grub. Using molds the same size keeps the molding operation synchronized.

In addition to making solid-color lures, as just described, you can make lures with stripes, spots, or bars, or worms with different colored tails, or even red-spotted purple crayfish with fluorescent green claws!

The technique for multiple-color molding is the same as in single-color molding, only additional pots of the desired color plastic are needed.

STEPS IN MOLDING REPRESENTATIVE PLASTIC LURES

A few examples of this type of molding will show the principles involved.

Blue worm with a red tail. Keep two pots of red and blue on the stove. When both are of the proper syrupy consistency, pour blue plastic carefully into the head and center of the mold, pouring quickly to fill the mold completely except for the tail.

Putting this pot back on the burner, take the red pot, and rapidly pour the tail section of the worm. The two colors will meet in the middle or rear section of the worm (depending upon the amount of each color used), blending together so that there is no weak point in the lure. "Pork rind" chunks, eels, spinner-bait tails, and tadpoles can be similarly molded.

If the plastic from the first pouring flows too rapidly to the rear of the lure, this operation may have to be repeated in several steps, with the mold only partially filled each time.

Black worm with a single white longitudinal stripe. Use two pots of plastic, one black and one white, heating both to syrupy consistency. Take the white plastic pot and pour a thin stream of plastic rapidly from one end of the worm to the other. Allow to cool. Then fill the mold with the black plastic as in normal molding, removing the worm when cool.

Green frog with yellow legs and red eyes. Three colors of plastic are needed. To make the red eyes, dip a toothpick or nail into the red melted plastic, depositing the plastic evenly in the eye sockets of the mold. Repeat if necessary to fill out the eyes.

Now slowly fill the center cavity of the mold with the green plastic, taking care that the plastic does not flow into the legs of the mold. When the mold is filled, quickly pour the yellow plastic into the leg cavities of the mold.

As with the two-colored worm above, these steps may have to be repeated several times to build up the lure while keeping the leg and body colors separate. Minnows, salamanders, crickets, crayfish, tadpoles, mudpuppies, and similar lures can be molded the same way.

USING ALUMINUM MOLDS

Using aluminum molds differs little in basic principles from the procedure described above. The aluminum molds are heated in one of the several ways outlined earlier in the chapter, with the liquid plastic (at room temperature) poured into the heated mold to cure. Use plastic squeeze bottles for the liquid plastic. (Squeeze bottles are available from mail-order tackle companies if the plastic is not already packaged this way.)

> CAUTION: These bottles look like those used for dispensing mustard and catsup; do *not* use them for this or any similar purpose after the plastic is all used up. They *cannot* be cleaned sufficiently, and cannot be used safely for food products.

Once the aluminum mold is filled with plastic, watch for signs of curing—easily detected by the darkening around the edges. It can also be checked by touching the center of the lure with a toothpick or matchstick. If it is tacky and sticky, it is ready to be removed from the heat. If it is still liquid, it needs to cure longer.

Remove from the heat, place in a pan of cold water to cool, and remove after a few minutes as with the rubber molds above. One advantage in using aluminum molds is that any excess water droplets will be boiled out of the mold cavity when they are heated for the next lure.

Adding different colors to an aluminum mold is easier than adding them to the rubber molds, since two squeeze bottles can be used at the same time to fill up a mold. Dots can be added to a lure by dropping a small drop of liquid plastic all over the mold, then filling it with the base color when the dots are cured.

Eyes can be added in the same way. Alternate stripes can be added by

Cold plastic–hot mold method: aluminum molds are best heated by being placed on a cookie sheet on top of the stove.

The cold plastic is squeezed into the hot molds on the stove, or the molds can be filled prior to heating.

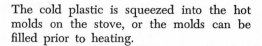

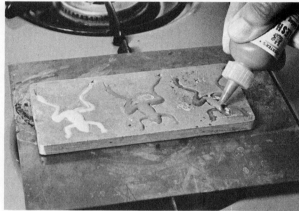

Using this method the plastic can be checked for proper curing by touching with a wood match or toothpick. When the plastic feels tacky, it is ready to be removed from the heat.

Samples of plastic lures being removed from aluminum molds.

running a length of plastic along the mold cavity, allowing it to cure, and repeating with a different color, as desired, until the mold is filled. Also, since the liquid plastic at room temperature is more fluid than the heated plastic, it is easier to use the cool plastic–hot mold technique for molding lures with many fine parts, long thin legs, and so forth. This is reflected in the molds available: there is a higher proportion of aluminum molds for insects, stone fly nymphs, dragon fly nymphs, crickets, and grasshoppers than of rubber molds.

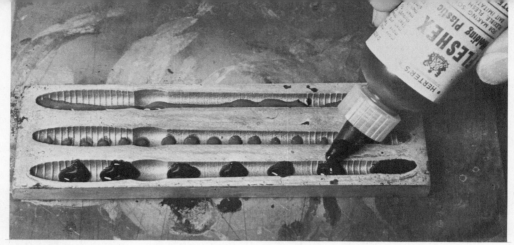

Striped, segmented, and dotted plastic lures are best made using the hot mold–cold plastic method. The dots or stripes can be added first and cured, the second color added later.

MOLDING ROUND LURES

Aluminum molds also come in two single-cavity lure molds, such as for making the two sides of a minnow. The proper technique is to mold one side, cool it and remove all the water, then place it on top of the other side, which has just been poured, so that the two sides will blend and cure together to make a rounded minnow. In practice, the technique is to mold two sides separately, cool and dry, then mold two more, placing the already molded sides on the opposite curing minnow halves. It saves time and the results are just the same as with the slower method.

TWO-PIECE AND ONE-PIECE PLASTER MOLDS

There is an easier way to mold round worms or lures that have two sides, by the use of a two-piece mold. Such molds are not readily available, although a few two-piece round molds are listed by Lure-Craft and Super-Sport for worms and minnows.

However, by using techniques similar to those for making plaster of Paris bucktail molds, it is possible to make two-piece molds using a commercial or other round worm or two-sided lure as a model. Complete details for making this kind of mold are described in Chapter 13.

Using such a mold is similar to the molding of bucktails, except that hot plastic is used instead of molten lead. The plastic is prepared in the same fashion as it is for one-piece molds, following the hot plastic–cold mold method, previously described. The two-piece plaster mold is clamped together with rubber bands; place the mold upright and pour the liquid plastic through the sprue hole in the top of the mold.

It is extremely important to have the liquid plastic properly prepared and with no lumps. A lump of cold plastic will fill up the sprue hole, preventing the passage of additional plastic, and result in an unusable, defective lure.

If there is one trick to this pouring, it is to pour the hot liquid plastic carefully down one side of the sprue hole. This allows the plastic to run all the way

Homemade one-piece plaster molds can also be used for plastic worms. Details on making this type of mold can be found in Chapter 13.

An open two-piece plaster mold, showing a completed plastic worm.

to the bottom of the mold cavity, while the air escapes through the sprue hole. If a lot of plastic is dumped into the sprue hole, it will clog the hole, preventing the escape of air and the downward flow of the hot plastic. All too often, the plastic will begin to cool and cure before the mold can be completely filled.

If, after you follow the above instructions carefully, the mold cavity still does not fill with plastic, enlarge the sprue hole. (This is also detailed in the directions for making the molds.) I like a sprue hole in two-piece molds of about the diameter of the head of the worm. It makes it easy to get perfect lures this way, and the excess plastic is easy to cut off and use over.

Unlike the one-piece rubber mold method in which the mold can be immersed in water for cooling, plaster molds must cure in air. Together with the two-piece mold that allows only slow transfer of heat and curing of the lures, this process is slower than molding with one-piece rubber molds. One solution is to make several two-piece molds of any chosen lure, so as to mold in a rotation system that allows each poured lure to cure completely before it is removed from the mold cavity. An alternative method is to use the two-piece plaster mold alternately with regular one-piece rubber molds.

Making one-piece plaster molds is completely described in Chapter 13. Their use is exactly the same as that of rubber molds, except that they cannot be placed in water for cooling and must be air-cooled and cured as with the two-piece plaster molds described above.

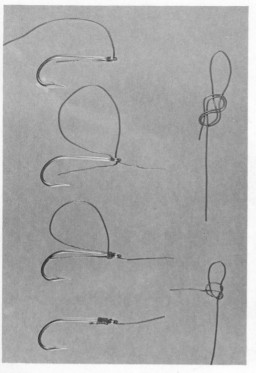

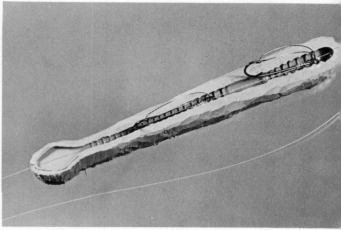

Details of snelling a hook and two types of loop knot for rigging hook harnesses to be molded into the plastic lure.

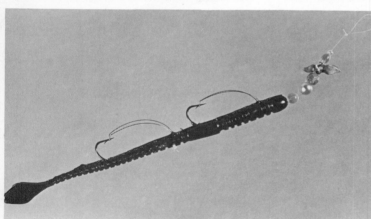

Snelled hooks on monofilament leader can be placed in slits at each end of the plastic mold.

A completed rigged plastic worm with beads and spinner blade at the head end. A loop knot was tied and excess monofilament trimmed from the knot and the tail of the lure.

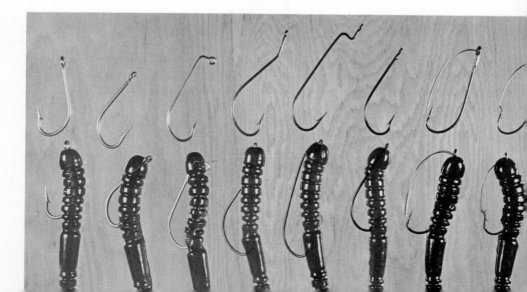

MOLDING IN HOOKS AND LEADERS

All of the lures described above are soft plastic without the addition of any hooks or snells. Most anglers prefer their lures this way, especially bass anglers, each of whom has his own favorite rigging method.

But any of these plastic lures can be molded with single hooks or hook harnesses (a monofilament leader with several hooks) molded into the lure. Lure-Craft supplies its molds either plain or, for a slight additional fee, with harness rings that allow the hooks and leaders to be molded easily in place in the lure. Even without the harness rings, it is possible to mold hooks and leaders into rubber molds by slitting each end of the mold to hold the leader in place while you're molding.

To mold leaders in place in a mold prepared this way, take an 18-inch piece of monofilament, 15- to 30-pound test (it should be stronger than the line used for fishing the lure), and snell a hook to the mono, leaving a long tail of mono that can be secured to the slit in the tail of the mold. One, two, or three hooks can be snelled to the mono. Then slip the two ends of the mono into the slits at either ends of the mold; pour the mold normally. The result is a worm, minnow, or other soft lure with molded-in leader and hooks.

To finish the lure, take the longer piece of mono (that at the head end of the worm), add beads and spinner or propellor blades as desired; finish by tying a loop knot. Use a figure-eight loop knot or perfection loop knot. Leave the mono extending from the tail of the worm so that the loop knot can be pulled tight. Then clip this end short, trim the knot, and the lure is ready to go fishing.

Many anglers prefer to rig their worms and other soft plastic lures on the water, using one of the many types of special worm-hooks now available. Some more popular riggings of soft plastic lures are illustrated in the accompanying photo.

COSTS

Once the mold is bought, the only cost is the molding plastic, since discarded pots and pans can be used for melting the plastic. Naturally, sizes of lures can vary greatly and will require widely differing quantities of plastic. Taking a standard lure—the plastic worm—I found that an ounce of plastic will make three full-bodied, 8-inch worms. Thus a pint will make about 45 to 50 worms of this size, depending upon waste and the fullness of each lure.

Methods of single-hook riggings on plastic worms. Left to right: standard method, weedless method, weedless method with jig hook, three weedless methods with bass hooks, two riggings with weedless hooks. In addition, each of the above can have the hook eye buried in the head of the plastic worm, with a toothpick (cut off) run through the eye to prevent the hook from sliding through the worm body. Worms can be fished as they are or rigged with slip sinkers.

Average costs based on these figures and on an estimated $2 per pint for plastic, would be about 4 cents per worm. The addition of colors, hardeners, softeners, flotation, and so forth, may raise this to about 7 cents per worm, but this is still far less than the retail price of good loose plastic worms. Rigging the worm with two molded-in hooks would raise the price to 11 cents, figuring the cost of hooks at about 2 cents each.

If you like the rigged plastic worms with molded hooks, leader, and spinner blade and beads, you can save even more. Assuming the cost with two molded-in hooks at 11 cents average and adding a few cents for beads and propellor blade, the cost might be raised to 15 cents. An average lure of this type bought in a tackle store would cost 55 to 75 cents.

The cost of getting into the plastic-lure-molding hobby is also minimal, and would be approximately as follows:

Quart of molding plastic	$ 4.00
Colors—red, black, blue	1.50
($0.50 each)	
Mold—single-cavity, 9″ worm	4.00
Mold—single-cavity, spring lizard 8″	4.00
TOTAL	$13.50

With two molds and three colors figured into the above listing, the cost per 100 lures still averages less than 14 cents each. The molds, of course, can be used for hundreds of lures, quickly amortizing the cost of over half of the above expense.

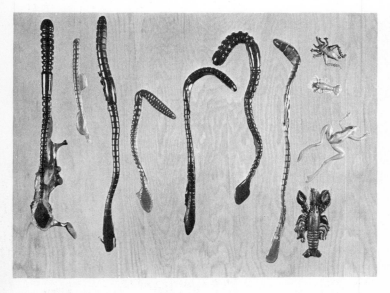

Defects in molding plastic worms. Left to right: three examples of overfilling a mold; four examples of removing lures before they are cured, causing the lures to become misshapen; and right, top to bottom: burned lure, overfilled lure, dirty lure, and overfilled crayfish lure. The worms were made in rubber molds, other lures in aluminum molds.

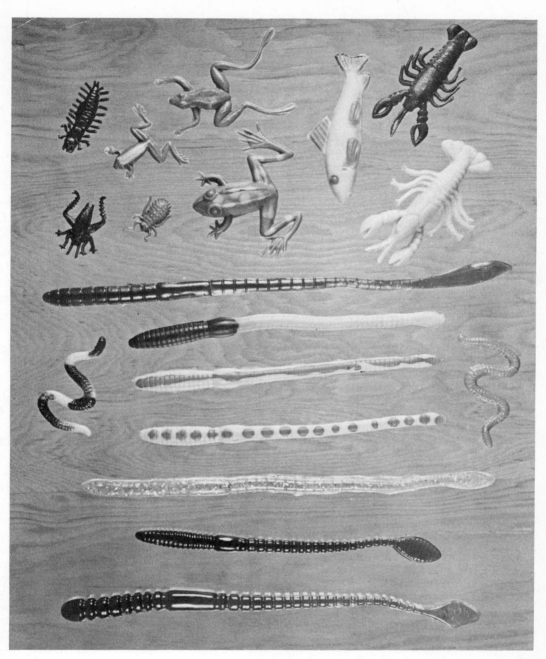

Examples of plastic lures. Top row: insects, frogs, crayfish, and minnows; bottom rows: examples of plastic worms. All are unrigged.

Excess plastic from overfilled molds can be removed from plastic lures with a revolving pizza cutter.

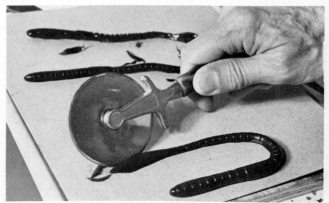

PLASTIC LURE KITS

Kits are also available for molding soft plastic lures. Santee Lure and Tackle Company has a kit that includes three blocks of solid molding plastic (black, purple, and blue), a pouring pan, and a four-cavity worm mold. Santee reasons that since the solid plastic blocks do not require color additives, they are easier for the beginner to use. The proper amount of molding plastic is cut off the block and melted in the pan, which makes it unnecessary to use bottles that can leak or spill.

Maumelle Plastics Company has a kit that includes one pint of the clear molding plastic, two bottles of color, a pan, stirring sticks, and a worm mold.

Lure-Craft has a "starter kit" selling for about $13 that includes three molds (one each: 8-inch worm, 6-inch worm, and beetle), one pint each of two plastic formulations, worm lubricant, two pouring pans, four colors, plastic worm bags, and stirring sticks.

Super-Sport has a Worm Maker Kit that includes an open-face mold for eight lures, plastic and colors, heating pans, slip sinkers for worms, and hooks; it sells for $14.95 list.

A kit by M-F Manufacturing includes a four-cavity mold, colors, and plastic, and sells for about $10.

The Carver Plastisols, Inc., kit includes a three-cavity mold, plastic, scents, and colors, and sells for about $6.95.

Toledo Manufacturing Company has an introductory kit consisting of a three-cavity mold, pan, plastic, colors, and scents for $8.95.

All seven companies as well as Limit Manufacturing Company, supply the individual components for making soft plastic lures.

Soft plastic lures have revolutionized fishing in the relatively short time that they have been around. Molding them is an easy, pleasurable, and inexpensive way to make sure that your tackle box stays full of favorite styles, colors, and sizes of these lures for all species of fish.

6

SPOONS

TOOLS · HARDWARE · SPOON CONSTRUCTION ·
MAKING SPOON BLADES · STEPS IN MAKING
SPOON BLADES · HAMMERING BLADES TO
SHAPE · HAMMERED AND CUT FINISHES ·
FIXED HOOK SPOONS · MISCELLANEOUS SPOONS
AND METAL LURES · TESTING · COST · SPOON KITS

BASIC TOOLS	HELPFUL TOOLS
For assembly:	Jeweler's saw
Small round-nose pliers	Anvil
Worth split-ring pliers	Plastic and rubber hammer
For cutting and hammering blades:	Metal chisel
Tin snips or aviation snips, or hack-	Nail set
saw files	Punch
Electric drill and bits	Soldering iron
Ball peen hammer	

No Special Talents Are Needed to Construct Spoons That Are almost identical to those found in every tackle store—all it takes is a pair of small round-nose pliers and the correct components.

With just this one tool, the spoon "blades," treble hooks, split rings, and swivels can be put together into workable lures in just a few minutes' time.

TOOLS

Serious spoon makers should also invest in a pair of the split-ring pliers manufactured by the Worth Company. They are inexpensive pliers with a small

Tools and materials needed for making spoons. Sheet metal, file, tin snips, aviation snips, awl, ball peen hammer, split ring pliers, and punches. These tools are not needed for assembling blades and hooks.

overlapping "tooth" at the end of one jaw that makes it easy to open split rings without deforming them. These pliers also have a notch farther back on the jaws for crimping leader sleeves in making wire leaders, while the pointed tip can also be used to open split shot.

Of course, for those with original ideas, or those hardcore do-it-yourselfers, spoons can be built from raw materials. In this case metal snips, aviation compound cutting snips, jeweler's saw, several small files, anvil, ball peen hammer, and soldering iron are all either useful or necessary, depending upon the lure and the process.

Metal snips are used for cutting out light metal spoon blades, while the compound cutting aviation snips are used for cutting out heavier metals. For extremely heavy metals, a small jeweler's saw will be needed. Various ball peen hammers, anvils, and blocks of wood are used for forming curves and hammered finishes in the lures, discussed later in this chapter.

Similarly, punches, nail sets, and small chisels can also be used to finish spoons. An electric drill will be necessary to drill holes for hook and line attachment; small drill bits, $\frac{1}{16}$ to $\frac{1}{8}$ inch, are the best sizes. A soldering iron will help in fastening hooks to small spinner blades to make ice fishing lures for crappie, panfish, and trout.

HARDWARE

The basic parts of any spoon are the hook, spoon blade, and split rings. Many home craftsmen, and even some commercial spoon manufacturers, make up spoons only of the hook and blade, with a split ring joining the two parts. The spoon is tied to the line or leader at the hole at the other end. It is much better, however, to add another split ring to the "line end" hole. Without this, the hole in the spoon will often cut through the line while you are casting or playing a fish. The main part—the spoon blades—comes in a variety of sizes and shapes from tiny 1-inch blades to huge blades 4 inches long designed for muskies, northern pike, and saltwater fishing.

As with spinner blades, they are available in a variety of finishes, including nickel, brass, and gold, and are even painted, as with the popular red and white striped pike spoon.

The cost of spoon blades varies with the thickness and finish. Small blades can cost as little as 10 cents each; large heavy gold-plated blades can cost 30 cents or more each. The cost of spinner blades varies from about 2 cents to 10 cents each in dozen lots, as previously noted in Chapter 2.

Any spoon fisherman who wants greater variety, particularly for smaller spoons, can easily take a spinner blade, drill a hole in the base end, and rig the blade as a lightweight spoon.

With spinner blades there is greater variety, varying from narrow willow-leaf blades to wide bear-paw blades, all in nickle, silver, gold, brass, and copper, as well as hammered, corrugated, stamped, and painted finishes. These same blades in small sizes, soldered to a single hook and painted or left bright, are ideal for ice fishing.

Split rings are necessary in all phases of spoon-making, and cost approximately one cent each in quantity. For spoons that have a tendency to twist line or revolve, I like to go one additional step and add a swivel to the front split ring, tying the line to the swivel. When trolling, sometimes this is not even enough to prevent twist. Then, in-line trolling rudders and sinkers between the line and the leader are the answer.

Naturally, if there is a tendency toward twisting, the best swivels should be used, to save on line troubles and replacement. One of the best is the ball-bearing swivel such as that made by Sampo and the Kelar swivels by Gladding. Solid ring swivels, split ring and lock snaps, split rings and safety snaps, solid ring and coastlock snaps, and solid ring pompanette snaps are also manufactured in ball-bearing styles.

Bead Chain Tackle Company also makes freely turning swivels, along with single-snap swivels, double-snap swivels, and lock-type snap swivels. Swivels like Sampo, Kelar, or Bead Chain can add 15 cents or more to the cost of the lure. In cases like this, rather than go to the expense of adding ball-bearing swivels to each lure, keep a supply on hand, tying them to the line or leader as needed.

Hooks used in spoons include single hooks, double hooks, and treble hooks. All three types are used for spoons with free-swinging hooks. Single hooks are used most often when the hook is firmly attached to the spoon. For the free-swinging type of spoon, the treble hook is the most popular. However, in some saltwater spoons and western freshwater models, the single hook is preferred.

All three types of hooks come in a full range of sizes. Treble hooks range from size 18 up to 5/0, in regular shank, short shank, and extra-strong shanks. Bronze, cadmium, nickel, gold, and stainless steel finishes are all available.

Double hooks are formed out of one piece of wire so that the hook can be added to any lure by spreading apart the shanks to slip it on a screw eye or split ring. They range in size from 14 through 5/0, and come in both 90° and 120° spreads. Siwash single hooks are often preferred in free-swing spoons because of their strength. They come nickel-plated or in stainless steel. Sizes range from 10 to 8/0, and all have an open eye for easy lure attachment. The hook eye can be slipped over any screw eye or split ring and then closed with pliers.

Actually, all three types of hooks can be added to spoons without the use of split rings. Siwash salmon hooks always have an open eye, and all double hooks have an open ring formed by the double hook shanks. Mustad also makes two types of treble hooks with open eyes. One type has an open ring. A second type has an open ring and a split shank, similar to that of double hooks. Saltwater anglers should always use stainless steel hooks. If stainless steel is not available, gold-plated or cadmium-plated hooks are an acceptable substitute. Consider hooks with extra-strong shanks for big fish and/or fast waters. Hook prices will range from 3 cents each for small bronze trebles up to 8 cents each for large stainless steel trebles.

SPOON CONSTRUCTION

Construction of a spoon from readily available parts is quite easy: choose the spoon blade that you want for your lure, then choose a hook to match it. The split ring connecting the hook and the blade should not be overly large, but must be strong enough not to pull apart during the strike or subsequent playing of the fish. It should also be large enough to provide clearance between the spoon eye and the hook eye without binding.

With round-nose pliers, or the Worth split-ring pliers, take the split ring, open it, and place it in the hole in the spoon to hold it open. Using the Worth split-ring pliers, insert the sharp-pointed tip of one jaw into the groove of the split ring, close to where the two ends of the ring meet, squeeze lightly, and the ring will open; Using regular needle-nose or round-nose pliers, pull one end of the split ring out and slip one jaw of the pliers into the gap to hold the ring open. (An alternative, although not recommended, method is to open the split ring with the point of a knife, slipping it onto the spoon eye.)

Place the eye of the hook over the spoon blade hole so that the split ring goes through both openings at once. The advantage is that, in turning the split ring through the two eyes at the same time, the lure is completed in one operation. If you go only through the eye of the spoon blade, you must repeat the whole operation again to place the hook on the split ring—a waste of time and also one more operation that will tend to spread the split ring. A split ring on the other eye (where the line is tied on) completes the lure; add a swivel at this point if desired.

Many spoons are shaped so that the two ends can be reversed, to effectively make two spoons with completely different actions in the water. Fish-It Co. markets a do-it-yourself spoon kit that not only has different-colored tapes for quick finishing of the lure, but also provides spoon blanks with several holes at each end, so that both the line and the hook position can be changed at will. To make it easy to change the hooks, double hooks are provided so that the hook can be quickly added to or taken off the lure, without the use of split rings. Anybody could do the same with commercial spoons or spoon blanks, using an electric drill and small $\frac{1}{16}$-inch bit to drill the several holes at each end of the spoon blade.

MAKING SPOON BLADES

Making spoon blanks from sheet metal is a more complex operation. You can be as original as you want, using any variety of materials in a wide variety of shapes, thicknesses, metals, sizes of spoon blades, and finishes. Sheet metals

Manufactured spoon blades can be rigged with hooks using split rings as shown.

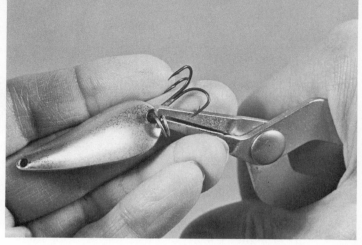

Split rings or swivels should be added to all spoons.

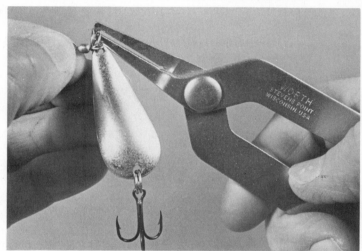

that have been used in spoon-blade making include copper, brass, steel, stainless steel, and aluminum, as well as nickel, gold, and silver-plated metals. Other metals can be used but are generally too costly or difficult to obtain to be useful.

Obtaining various sheet metals for spoon-making is not difficult. Aluminum sheet and ⅛-inch-thick bar stock are available from hardware stores. Copper tubing, such as used in home plumbing and available from plumbing and hardware stores, can be cut open and flattened to make copper spoons. Many hobby shops carry small squares of various sheet metals; and a trip to a junk yard will often turn up other sheet metals that can be used in spoon-making.

Obviously, the same size and shape of lure made of each of these metals will have different cutting and finishing qualities, weight, and action in the water. But, some generalities about spoon blanks are possible.

Thin sheet metals (nontempered, up to 20 gauge) can be cut with regular tin snips. Often, these metals are too thin for making spoon blanks, but they are ideal for spinner blades, which can also be made by the process described here.

For thicker metal that cannot be cut with tin snips, there are two other tool choices. One is aviation snips (compound leverage cutters), which can exert greater pressure than tin snips. The disadvantage of these is that three snips are required for complete metal-working: one type of snip cuts left-hand circles, one cuts right-hand circles, and one cuts straight. If the spoon and spinner blanks are of simple shapes, it might be possible to get by with one set of snips, say those cutting to the left (easiest to use for most right-handed persons). If your spoon-making plans are more complex and require more elaborate cutting, be prepared to lay out $15 or more for a set of three cutters. There are, however, several cheaper compound leverage cutters that can be used to cut left and right as well as straight, and these sell for less than $5 a pair.

Even the compound-cutting aviation snips have their limits when it comes to cutting thicker metals such as might be desired for some lake, western stream, and saltwater spoons. Perhaps the easiest cutting tool to use is the fine-bladed hacksaw or small metal saw. One disadvantage of the hacksaw is that it will only cut straight. A heavy file must be used for rounding off corners. Small metal or jeweler's saws have narrower blades (¼ inch on a metal saw compared with ½ inch on a hacksaw) and cut curves better.

Hobbyists who have electric jigsaws with metal cutting blades will find these a distinct advantage as they cut quickly and are easy to use. But they're expensive and purchasing one should be considered only by the tackle hobbyists interested in lure-making as a long-time occupation.

STEPS IN MAKING SPOON BLADES

The first step in making any spoon or spinner blade is to determine the shape and size of the blade. To do this, draw several spoon outlines on paper until you're satisfied with one, then copy this shape on a heavy cardboard or metal template.

Most spoons are bilaterally symmetrical; that is, they have the same curve on both sides of the spoon. Since our eyes, in making freehand drawings, are less than perfect, it's better to draw only one side of the spoon shape on a sheet of paper, cut out that side, fold it down the center, and trace the other side. This paper pattern can then be traced onto a heavier material for permanent use. Assuming that the blank is one that you will want to continue using, this template can become one of a permanent stock of guides, templates, and stencils. Other templates will be used in making wood plugs and cork rod handles, as well as stencils for painting.

Using a sharp-pointed awl, trace the pattern from the template onto the piece of sheet metal. Trace it next to an edge or a corner of the sheet metal, so that there will be the least possible waste of metal when you cut out the blade.

Cut out the spoon blade using your tin snips, aviation snips, a hacksaw, or

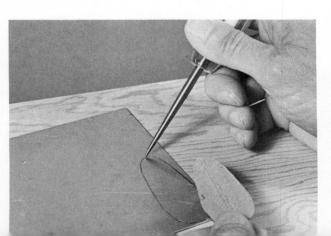

Cutting out spoon blades requires a cardboard or paper template, the design traced with an awl on the selected sheet metal.

After the spoon blade has been cut out, it should be hammered flat before the next step.

Any rough edges on the spoon blade can be smoothed with files or an old grindstone.

a jeweler's saw. The first two are best held by hand, holding both the sheet metal and tools. Clamp the metal securely in a vise when using a saw. Machinist vises have scored jaws, so that some protective material must be used between the vise jaw and the metal to prevent scarring the finish. Thin scraps of wood, small pieces of sheet metal (which can be folded around the vise jaws to hold them in place), and plastic sheeting can all be used. Be sure to clamp the metal close to where it is to be cut, otherwise the saw will "chatter" as the metal bends with each stroke.

After rough cutting, smooth the spoon blade with a large quick-cutting file. Use successively finer files to smooth the edges, ending with emery cloth or an old cheap sharpening stone, if you find it easier to work on. (Use only an *old* sharpening stone as noted, since, in time, smoothing the edges of the spoons will groove the stone and ruin it for sharpening knives.) Once the spoon blank is shaped, it must be drilled at each end, hammered into the proper curvature, and finished, if desired, with a hammered, scaled, lined, or painted finish.

It's best to drill both holes first, while the blade is still flat; the drill will have less of a tendency to "walk-off," slip, or (if the metal is thin) to deform the blank from the pressure of drilling. A hand drill can be used for soft metals (aluminum, brass, copper), but an electric drill is preferable. In fact, it is a necessity when cutting the tougher metals, such as stainless steel. Quarter-inch electric drills are far cheaper today than ever before; a serviceable model can be bought for less than $10, and sometimes even cheaper at discount or mail-order store sales.

The flat spoon blade should be drilled at each end. Make a slight depression in the blade first with an awl or prick punch before drilling to keep the drill from slipping on the metal.

Drill a small, ⅟₁₆ to ⅛ inch, hole using fast-cutting hardened drills designed for metal. Cheaper drills designed for wood only will dull rapidy, and the hardened metal-cutting drills can be used for wood and plastic as well as metal.

Hole size will be relative to the size of the spoons and hook used, but it is always better to make holes too large than too small. Any hole in a spoon that does prove too small should be redrilled or reamed to the proper size.

HAMMERING BLADE TO SHAPE

Take care to drill both holes exactly on the center line of the spoon, unless of course, some erratic wobbling action is desired; experimenting with off-center drilling may give interesting results. Once it is cut, polished, and drilled, hammer the blade into the desired curve, and add any hammered finishing marks. Actually, either of these operations can be completed first, and there are advantages and disadvantages to each method.

Hammering the curve into the lure first makes it more difficult to add any finishing hammered marks to the convex side of the lure later. It is easy to hammer a finish on the *concave* side of the lure, since it can be done while hammering the spoon blade to shape.

To add hammered finishes to the convex side of the bent spoon requires a special anvil which will be discussed later. Also, it is difficult to hold the blade in place on the anvil while positioning the chisel or hammer; adding hammered finishes to the blade on a flat surface will take the curve out of the spoon.

Hammering the finish first tends to put a curve in the blade, with the finish on the concave side; thus, if you want the finish on the convex side, the finished blade must be hammered flat again and then bent to the desired curve.

After it has been drilled, hammer the spoon into shape. Either way a hammered finish is easily done with a ball peen hammer on a small anvil.

If you want a smooth finish, or if some other type of finish will be added later on, use a rubber or plastic-head hammer, working the spoon on a hard flat or shaped wood block. Hammer it evenly, all over the part of the spoon to be curved. The hammering will gradually produce a concavity on the hammered side, so the anvil or block side will be convex. With practice, you will be able

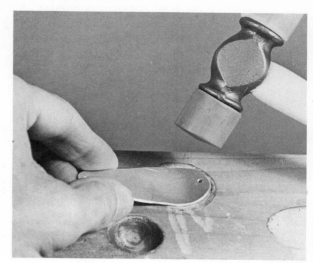

The drill-finished spoon blank is then hammered into the proper curvatures on an anvil or as shown by hammering with a rubber nylon-faced hammer in small depressions carved in a block of wood.

to hammer spoons into almost any degree or type of curvature, including a reverse or S-shaped curve.

If you want deep curves in the blade, carve a round depression in a hard wood block into which the spoon blank is hammered to fit. This method can also be used to duplicate curvatures in successive spoons of the same design.

HAMMERED AND CUT FINISHES

One easy way to decorate a spoon is to give it a hammered finish, either while forming the curve in the spoon, or later, after the spoon is shaped. If the hammering is to be on the concave surface, it is easy to place the spoon on the wood block and hammer until the desired effect is achieved.

If you want the hammered finish on the convex side of the spoon, there's an additional problem. Hammering the spoon on the wood block would destroy the curve, since there is no support under the spoon. This problem is easily overcome by making a wooden "anvil": drill holes of the proper size in a base and insert short, 2- to 3-inch, lengths of various-size wood dowels that have been rounded on the exposed end. Egg-shaped darners (used to darn or sew socks and other small pieces of clothing), placed on a short dowel, also work well as wood anvils for finishing spoons.

Place the spoon concave side down on the appropriate rounded dowel or anvil, and hammer the finish with the ball peen hammer. A short block of 2 x 4 lumber drilled with ½-inch to 1½-inch holes for the dowels is ideal. Do *not* glue the dowels in place, since it is best to remove those rounded dowels not in use for better clearance in handling and turning the spoon. It does, however, take some juggling to hold the spoon blade in place, while holding the chisel or nail set, and the hammer.

An alternate method, previously described, is to hammer the finish in the cut-out spoon blade, later forming the blade into the proper curves. A rubber or plastic-faced hammer must be used to add any curves, so as not to scar the finish already on the spoon.

Hammered finishes are easy to create. For example, a "punched" appearance is easy to put on any spoon or spinner, by hammering the blade with a center punch, creating small depressions.

A hammered finish can be given to a spoon by hammering with the round end of a ball peen hammer on an anvil.

Different types of hammered finishes can be made with different-size ball peen hammers and by hammering on different materials such as wood or steel blocks.

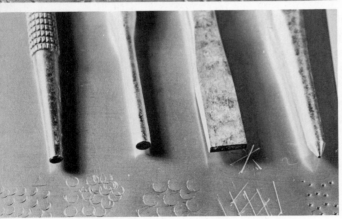

Different finishes on spoons can be made with nail sets, punches, chisels, and prick punches. Left to right: crescents and circles hammered with a nail set, crescents hammered with a punch, cuts hammered with a chisel, dots hammered with a prick punch.

A finish of small circles is easy to make by hammering the blade successively with a large nail set. Made to punch finishing nails beneath the surface of wood, a nail set has a small cuplike depression in its face. It can also be used to make scale finishes on spoons. Just hammer the nail set off-center, so that only one side of the nail set makes an impression on the metal. The result is a series of small, half-round marks that from a distance look like scales of a fish. Similar half-round marks can be made with special stamps cut from hardened nails. (See Chapter 13 for directions for making these.) Various straight lines and designs on a spoon can be made with a cold chisel. Just as with the nail set or center punch, hammer the cold chisel into the spoon, creating either parallel lines or random patterns.

Spoons and spinner blades can also be painted, though most fishermen prefer metallic-finished blades and spoons. There are times when fish will change their preferences in lures, as a few years ago in the Chesapeake Bay when the spring runs of big striped bass suddenly showed a marked preference for yellow and white painted spoons instead of the standard nickel-plated spoons that had proved effective in the past. Red and white striped spoons are practically a standard item in tackle boxes of northern-bound anglers, where big pike go after this lure like kids after a candy bar. Painting of spoons, as well as other finishes of tape, glitter, and flocked materials, is covered in Chapter 12.

FIXED HOOK SPOONS

You can make spoons in which the single hook is attached to the concave surface of the blade, instead of swinging free from a split ring. There are no commercially made blanks designed for this, although they can be modified in the same way that start-from-scratch blades are fashioned. In either case, once the blade is finished, redrill the lower (hook end) hole in the blank to a larger size through which the hook point can be inserted.

Bend the lip of metal at the edge of the hole toward the concave surface. This provides clearance for the hook shank when it extends out from the blade. Insert the hook point through this hole and position the hook eye on the center of the spoon blank; mark the center of the hook eye on the blank. Drill the spoon blade at this point. Bend it to shape, and add any hammered finish desired. Using pop rivets, split rivets, or a very small, short nut and bolt, fasten the hook eye to the blank. The result is not unlike many commercially made spoons, such as the Huntington Drone, Tony Accetta Pet Spoon, and others.

An alternate method is to solder the hook to the spoon blade. However, except when used on small ice-fishing spoons for relatively small fish, this method is not recommended, since the soldered connection could weaken with wear and result in the loss of a good fish.

MISCELLANEOUS SPOONS AND METAL LURES

In addition to standard types of free-swinging and fixed-hook spoons, there are other metal lures that fall loosely into the spoon category that can be just as easily made. For example, small-diameter copper tubing and galvanized conduit can be cut in 2- to 6-inch lengths, hammered flat, drilled at each end, and fitted with hardware.

A variation of this type of tube lure can be made by hammering the tube only partially flat, or hammering only one end flat, leaving the other end with a round or eliptical cross-section. The partially open tubing can be filled with lead for additional weight, if desired. As with the spoons, these lures can be hammered into curves, painted, and otherwise finished.

The same tubing can be left round and cut on a sharp diagonal to create another type of lure. Square, rectangular, or round bar stock can be cut on the diagonal to make a heavy slab-side lure. But unless you use a metal-cutting power saw, the time it takes to cut through bar stock is not usually worth the effort.

TESTING

Before making any blade in quantity, or even before finishing a blade, test it in open water to be sure that it has the action you desire.

COST

The cost of making spoons is slight, since the components of blades, split rings, hooks, and swivels are all readily available. Using an average, 2½-inch, standard red and white pike spoon as an example, prices would average about as follows:

	BULK COST	INDIVIDUAL COST
Spoon blades	$0.60 per 3	$0.20
Split rings	.15 per 12	.03 (2 used in lure)
Swivel	.25 per 12	.02
Bronzed treble hook	.60 per 12	.05
TOTAL		$0.30

This represents a saving of at least half over similar lures available in tackle stores. Since the hooks, split rings, swivels, and spoon blades are all available in lots of a dozen or less, the investment cost can be as low as $3.50 for the basic materials for a dozen lures.

SPOON KITS

As with the construction of most other lures, there are even kits available for those who would rather get everything in one box. Aspen Lures (who also make spinner kits) have a kit that includes two dozen 16-gauge solid brass blades, along with the proper hooks, split rings, and stencils for painting. Current retail price: $5. A can of spray paint is all that is needed to finish the lures, or they can be left as is. Herter's and Netcraft also carry complete spoon-making kits.

The parts, including spoon blades in painted, plain, or hammered brass are also available. Herter's and Finnysports, Netcraft, Reed, Hille, and others all carry the components with a variety of blade sizes, finishes, and styles.

Ever since an angler dropped a teaspoon in the water while fishing a lake, only to see a large fish strike at it, spoons have occupied an important spot in both freshwater and saltwater tackle boxes; by making your own, it is possible to get exactly what you want at a fraction of the cost of similar commercial lures.

Examples of finished spoons. Left to right: two spoons made from hammered copper tubing, spoons made from sheet metal and teaspoon, assembled spoons (the bottom two lures have several holes for different hook and line attachment and are provided by the manufacturer this way), assembled shiny spoons, painted assembled spoons (two rows), and various tape and glitter finishes on spoons (last row).

7

WOOD AND PLASTIC PLUGS

*TOOLS · PLUG HARDWARE · PLASTIC PLUG
BODIES · WOOD PLUG BODIES · WOOD STOCK
USED IN MAKING PLUG BODIES · CARVING
WOOD PLUGS · USE OF POWER TOOLS IN
PLUG-MAKING · SEALING AND PAINTING ·
ADDING PLUG HARDWARE · THROUGH-WIRE
CONSTRUCTION · COSTS · PLUG-MAKING KITS*

BASIC TOOLS	HELPFUL TOOLS	
A. Assembling of Plugs	Carving Plugs	Sandpaper, assorted grades
Small screwdriver	Electric drill	Glue
Pliers	Wood rasp	Countersink
B. Carving Plugs	Long-shank or	Contour gauge
Pocketknife	aircraft drills	Calipers
Sandpaper	Electric drill routers	Awl
Countersink	Knife	Saw
	File set	

⟋ WHEN I WAS A BOY, MOST BASS FISHING PLUGS SOLD FOR ABOUT 85 cents. That was pretty steep for a lad with a paper route as his only source of income. While I am making more money now, with the price of plugs at $1.65 on up to $3.00 for saltwater models, I am not so sure that I am any better off.

One answer to this economic squeeze (which gets worse everytime a big bass runs off with a lure or a line breaks on a snagged lure) is to make your own. The advantages of savings, custom finishes, specially designed plug shapes, and similar features are offset only by the time it takes to make them.

At one time, all commercially manufactured plugs were made of wood; now almost all of them are plastic. Homemade plugs can be made of either material,

Tools and materials needed for carving wood plugs. Blocks of wood, pocket knife, wood rasp, screwdrivers, and several grades of sandpaper.

using preformed wood or plastic bodies available from tackle supply catalogs, or wood blocks, carved to suit a particular need.

TOOLS

The tools required for making plugs vary, depending upon the method of construction. For building plugs from plastic blanks and hardware—nothing more than an assembly process really—all that is needed is a small screwdriver to add hook hangers and the wiggle plate. At the other extreme, a start-from-scratch plug builder could equip himself with a lathe to turn out lures quickly; but such an expenditure would be exceptional.

A pocket whittling knife, a wood rasp, and several grades of sandpaper are quite adequate for carving any plug from basswood or cedar. Any pocketknife can be used, but best are those with small, relatively straight blades, special whittlers' folding knives or wood-handled, small-bladed knives made exclusively for carving . Many such knives are available in hobby shops. I use an old and well-worn whittling knife.

For through-wire plug construction, a method by which all hook hangers and eyes are fastened securely to a wire running through the plug, an electric drill is useful. A wood saw is handy for cutting wood blocks to size. If you want to use cup or disc washers under the screw eyes on wood plugs, a regular electric drill countersink bit will be helpful in making the small depression into which the cup washer must fit.

A contour gauge and calipers will be useful in transferring dimensions and tracing the plug shape from a commercial model to a block of wood.

PLUG HARDWARE

Plastic plugs are the easiest to work with since the plug construction is essentially one of assembly, although gluing and painting are sometimes required

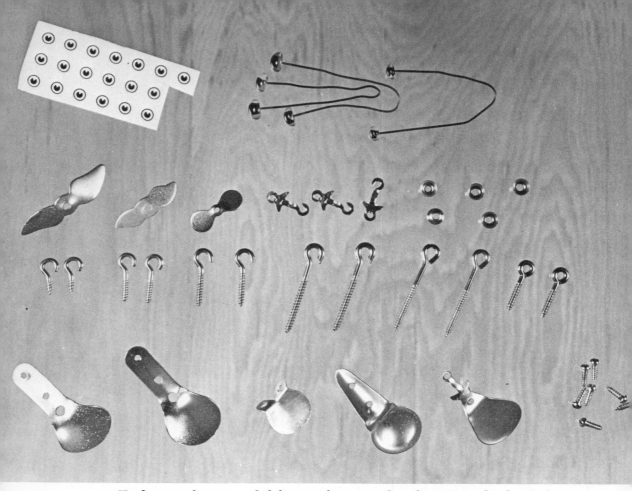

Hardware and parts needed for completing wooden plugs. Top: decal and glass eyes; second row: propellers, hook hangers, disc washers, and screw eyes; bottom row, scoops and bibs and screws for hook hangers.

as well. Some plastic plugs come in ready-to-make kits, which include plug blanks, hooks, holders, wiggle lips, paints, eyes, and any other needed parts for making a dozen or more lures. Plug hardware itself is not complicated and consists mostly of the screw eyes or hook hangers, treble hooks, and wiggle plates and propellors (for some surface plugs).

Screw eyes come in nickle-plated brass or stainless steel; the latter are more expensive. While the initial cost is greater, the stainless steel eyes are well worth it for plugs used in salt or brackish water. These screw eyes must not be confused with those available at local hardware stores; these are designed and made for plug construction. The wire used in them is smaller in diameter, and the eyes formed are smaller, too.

Both closed and open eyes are available; the former are for the line end of the plug. The open eyes allow hooks to be added to the screw eye. The eye is then closed with pliers and screwed into the plug. Stem lengths from ¼ inch to 1¼ inch are sold; the ¼-inch stem length for short plugs and ½-inch stem length for long plugs are optimum. Since they are used in almost every plug, they should be purchased in lots of 100; the cost per 100, depending upon size, length, and whether the eye is open or closed, will range from $0.50 to $1.50.

Sometimes screw eyes are used with cup or disc (plug) washers, although this is not absolutely necessary. Cup washers look like small regular washers bent into a bowl-like shape; disc washers are similar but look like miniature derby hats. Both are set into a countersunk depression in a plug before the screw eye is added. They supposedly give the plug a more "finished" appearance, but, more important, they limit the swing of the plug to prevent hook parts from scratching the plug finish. Disc washers are used in the belly of a plug; cup washers at the tail. Both are made from nickel-plated brass and sell for 25 to 75 cents per 100, depending on the size.

Hook hangers are small pieces of nickel-plated brass bent in the shape of a gardener's trowel. They are screwed in place with tiny round wood screws through holes in each end. The main advantage of hook hangers over screw eyes is that the screw eye, without washers, allows the hook to swing in a 360-degree circle, possibly tangling with other hooks or the line (as the center hook may also). Hook hangers restrict the movement of the hook in a forward (relative to the plug) direction, and thus prevent or lessen tangling.

Hangers come in several sizes, and cost less than one cent each in lots of 100. The screws needed for the hangers (two are needed for each hanger) are about $1.00 to $1.25 per 100. The screws come in several sizes, from $\frac{8}{32}$ to $\frac{14}{32}$ lengths, and are also used to hold wiggle lips and other hardware in place on plugs.

Wiggle plates for deep-diving, medium, and even shallow-running plugs sometimes include a hook hanger, for the front hook, and usually have a notched hole for adding a connecting link or split ring for line attachment. A dozen styles and sizes are available to be attached with two small screws, as are the hook hangers. Prices are about 4 cents to 10 cents each, in dozen lots.

Wiggle plates do not usually come with the connecting links, which must be ordered separately. *Never* tie the line directly to the slot punched into the wiggle lip: the edges of this slot are sharp and will cut the line, either in normal fishing wear, or worse, from the strike and fight of a fish.

The connectors can be a split ring, a figure-eight attachment, or a connector link, all of which come in a variety of sizes. Figure 8 attachments are about half a cent each in lots of 100; split rings about one cent each in packages of a dozen (cheaper in larger quantities), while connecting links are about one and a half cents each in dozen lots.

Treble hooks are a matter of personal preference. Some anglers like straight points while others prefer the Eagle Claw design, and some like larger or smaller hooks on a plug than others would choose. Personally I like bronzed No. 374 Eagle Claw treble hooks for freshwater plugs and Eagle Claw No. 77SS stainless steel treble hooks for saltwater plugs. Nickle- and bronze-plated treble hooks are about 5 cents each in the sizes used in plugs, while stainless steel trebles run 7 to 9 cents each in small packages.

Eyes (simulating the eyes of minnows) are usually molded into the plastic plugs, but must be added to wood plugs unless they are painted on. Several types of eyes are available including yellow and black decal eyes and glass eyes set on pins which are inserted into the completed plug body. The first style is

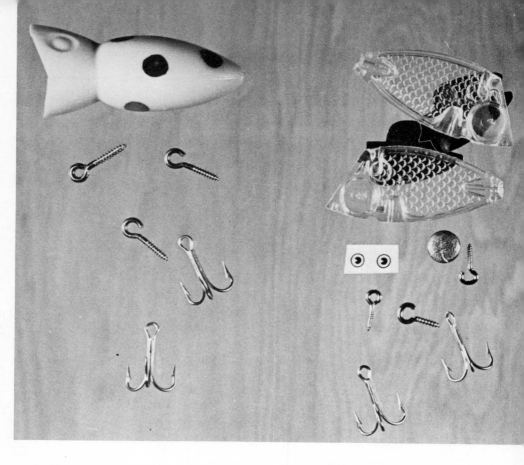

cheaper, about 10 cents per sheet of 50 eyes. Each decal is cut out, soaked in water, and transferred to the plug just as a window decal is applied. Glass eyes sell for about 10 cents a pair; they are set on long steel pins and have black pupils. The advantage of the glass eyes is that the underside of the eye can be painted any color desired to contrast with the plug, before the pins are clipped to approximately ½ inch in length, inserted, and glued in place.

"Map Tacs," in a variety of colors and several sizes, are available from stationery stores and can also be used for plug eyes. Map tacs have spherical heads and are used to pinpoint items on maps and graphs. Since they are spherical, the plug must be countersunk at the spot where the eye is to go so that the map tac can be recessed slightly.

Wiggle eyes—little lightweight plastic bubbles with a flat back and a dark little bead in the center that rolls around with the plug movement—can be glued in place. They sell for 1½ to 3 cents each, depending upon their size, which ranges from 5 to 12 millimeters diameter.

PLASTIC PLUG BODIES

Most of the molded plastic bodies are tenite, a tough plastic resistant to chipping, scratching, and breaking. It is the same material used in most commercially made plugs.

Plug bodies come two ways, as completed plugs and in halves ready to be cemented together. The completed plug blanks are the easier to work with, and come in a variety of styles, including banana-shaped plugs, minnow imitations,

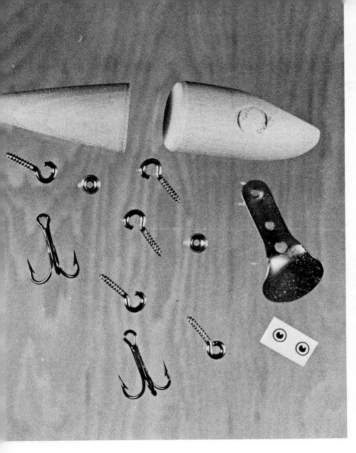

Plugs can be made by several different methods. Left: assembled plastic plug which requires only addition of hooks. Center: two-part plastic plug with metallic inserts. This must be glued together before hooks and screw eyes can be added. Right, preformed wood body which must be painted and then assembled with bib, screw eyes, hooks, and decal eyes.

deep-diving plugs, mid-depth running plugs, and a variety of surface poppers, plunkers, and injured minnow lures.

Herter's carries perhaps the most complete line of plug bodies, with 30 different styles of tenite plugs, some in up to four different sizes. Finnysports, Netcraft, and Hille also carry plug bodies.

Costs of plastic plug blanks vary according to size, with most plugs running between 6 and 30 cents each in freshwater sizes; 30 to 50 cents each for saltwater plugs. The average price for a single plug is about 15 cents. Prices are lower when the plugs are purchased in quantity; plugs are available in lots of 6, 12, 25, 100, and 1000. Only a small commercial company would be interested in the last, but clubs and groups of fishermen might want to consider lots of 25 or 100 for a single size and style of plug. Prices in lots of 100 are about half those listed above. Most of the plugs are hollow except for underwater and deep-diving plugs, which are usually molded of a solid plastic.

Two-part plastic plug bodies must be glued together with a special glue or plastic solvent, which in effect "welds" the plastic halves together by softening the plastic at the point of contact, evaporating later to leave a solid permanent bond.

In some cases plugs can be bought cheaper in the two halves than in the molded plug blanks, but this is not always the case. There is an advantage in buying plug blanks in two parts, however, for certain types of lures. For example, some lures have clear plastic sides so that inserts of silver or gold foil can be sandwiched between the halves to shine through and give a lifelike appearance. (Some of these lures have a scalelike pattern embossed in the sides.)

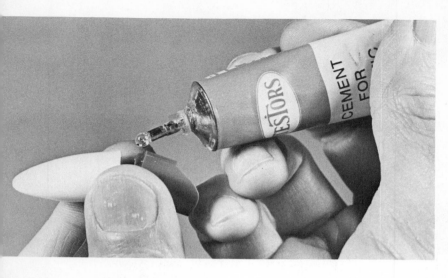

Two-piece plastic plugs should be glued together with special plastic cements.

This is true of many of the vibrator lures and some minnow imitations. Of course, other inserts can also be added to lures like this. Those with clear sides can be painted on the inside (which prevents any chipping of paint) and finished with different color "glitter"—small bright metallic flakes. Weights can be glued in to make the lure sink, add casting weight, and, if left loose, to give it a fish-attracting rattle. Be sure in adding weight to a plug that does not normally call for it that the extra weight does not adversely affect the lure's action.

In both types of bodies, holes for the front screw eye and the back and center treble hooks are molded into the lure. If small screw eyes, available from tackle stores and mail-order supply houses, are used, these holes are deep enough to hold any normal size fish.

One supply company advertises that their lures have caught fish weighing from 9 to 20 pounds with no danger of the hooks or front screw eye pulling out. For larger fish, or for plugs fished in saltwater, you should consider through-wire construction in wood plugs, described later in this chapter.

WOOD PLUG BODIES

Wood plugs are available to the tackle builder in a variety of shapes and sizes. Usually, they are round in cross section, and are mass produced on assembly line lathes in the same way that table legs are produced.

White cedar is the wood most often used for these plug blanks. Typical lures include a basic medium-running bass lure, medium-running pike lure, injured minnow surface lure, mouse imitation, and poppers and similar basic shapes. Usually they are nicely sanded and finished when received, although they do need some finishing touches, particularly at the two ends where they were held in the lathe.

WOOD STOCK USED IN MAKING PLUG BODIES

Homemade plugs can be cut from small blocks of wood, obtained from lumberyards, hardware stores, hobby shops, tackle stores, and fishing tackle supply houses. Cedar and basswood are the woods most often offered and used for fishing lures.

Cedar is the traditional plug wood. White cedar, while much more scarce than it once was, is still available in the small sizes required by lure carvers. Some companies offer small blocks, 1 inch by 1 inch by 4 or 5 inches, for carving plugs; others have it only in 4- to 8-inch boards of 1-inch, 2-inch and 3-inch thicknesses, which must be ripped (sawed) to size.

Cedar is a lightweight wood, gives good action as a lure, and is soft and easy to carve for the home craftsman. Basswood is slightly harder and lighter colored, and does not split as easily as cedar. Both are easy to work with, basswood being more readily available.

Other woods are also available for plugs; pine strips ¾ by ¾ inch, 1 by 1 inch, and 1½ by 1½ inch are available from hardware and lumber stores, and are easy to work. Balsawood is a very light soft wood, easy to carve and readily available at hobby shops. Because it is so soft, it is too fragile for standard plugs, although it is used in minnow imitations similar to the very popular Finnish Rapala lure (and some of its imitations). In using this wood, even for this type of lure, you must cover the lure completely with many coats of lacquer to give it a "surface" toughness and protection against chipping, denting, and puncturing.

Screw eyes do not hold well in balsa wood, and so the lure must have through-wire construction. This is a method of hooking the front eye and both hooks to a single strand of wire for strength. As in saltwater plugs (where a big fish can shatter a lure), the wire will still hold the hooks, so that the fish is not lost even though the plug is ruined. Balsa is also quite porous and can soak up water if punctured by a fish, ruining its action.

Wood dowels might seem to be likely material for the plug maker, since they are already round and are available in a wide variety of thicknesses. But such is not the case; dowels are made of very hard wood and are difficult to carve. I do know some plug makers who use dowels, but they use rotary rasps in electric drills for carving the proper taper and the popping face in the end of the plug. Wood dowels are also heavier in the water than cedar or basswood and have a heavier or more sluggish action—something to consider in making any lure.

Wood lathes are ideal for carving plugs of cedar or basswood, although a lathe is not available to most hobbyists or home craftsmen. To spend the $100 or so necessary for a good wood lathe and set of lathe carving tools just to carve plugs is obviously false economy.

CARVING WOOD PLUGS

Anyone can carve plugs from wood blocks using nothing more than a pocketknife or a wood-carving knife. Essential to the use of any of these tools is a sharp blade; a good sharpening stone or two is just as necessary as the knife. Knife-sharpening instructions come with most good knives and with the better sharpening stone sets.

Before beginning, first decide the style and design of the plug to be carved from each stock piece of wood. Random carving, with hopes of producing

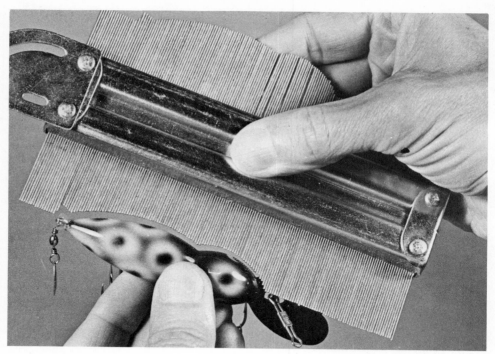

A contour gauge makes it easy to copy exactly the shape of another plug and duplicate the pattern on a template.

Template patterns for plugs are traced on the wood block, making sure that the pattern is lined up with the center axis of the plug.

something, usually produces only a pile of wood chips. *Before touching the knife to the wood,* draw several designs or trace a design from a favorite commercially made plug.

Original design plugs must be drawn freehand; designs of standard commercial plugs can be identically traced by means of a contour guide. These tools, made principally for exactly duplicating the contour of molding strips and decorative woodwork, can be purchased for about $1 and are especially useful for tracing patterns of plugs, rod handles, spoons, and similar fishing tackle. Consisting of a series of short wires mounted in a clamp, the contour guide is pushed against any object to determine its exact outline. In using the contour guide make sure it is pushed all the way to the center axis of the plug, so as to measure the plug's full thickness. After using a contour gauge, draw the outline on a paper, turning the contour gauge over to trace both sides. Check the plug with a pair of calipers at several points to be compared with the final drawing.

Plugs can be drawn freehand also. The best way to do this is to draw a center line for the plug, and then draw the pattern desired lightly on one side, until the proper shape is determined. Then fold the paper along the center line and trace the same pattern on the other side of the paper, so that the plug pattern will be symmetrical.

Now cut out the outline of the plug, and trace the pattern on the block of wood, using the center lines drawn on each of the four surfaces of the block. If the plug is to be symmetrical, trace the pattern on all four sides of the block, to aid the carving. If the pattern is not symmetrical, separate patterns must be made for top and bottom and sides, and the appropriate tracing made on the respective sides of the block.

If a number of plugs of the same design are to be carved, make a heavy-duty template or pattern by tracing the paper design on sturdy cardboard, sheet metal, or sheet plastic, cutting out the pattern with metal snips or stout shears. Keep the pattern on file with other templates and design patterns.

Once the pattern is traced on the wood, start carving, cutting away a little at a time, being careful to cut only away from you. Do not cut toward you, or cut in any way in which a slip could result in a cut or accident.

As the wood is cut away, it may be necessary to redraw the pattern several times and to look at the plug from both ends to be sure that it will be symmetrical, or true to the shape desired, when you're finished.

When the plug is completely roughed out, start rounding it with a wood rasp to the finished shape. Remember that final finishing with sandpaper will also take off some wood, so don't rasp the plug down to the final dimensions. I prefer to leave the plug about $1/16$ inch larger than final dimensions when it is rasped to shape, and then remove any remaining wood with sandpaper. (If the $1/16$ inch figure sounds like too much wood to leave on, remember—it's only $1/32$ inch per side.)

Start sanding with grade 1 paper, progressing to finer grades until using grade 6/0 to 8/0. For a final smooth finish, take a tip from cabinet workers: save some of the fine sawdust, sprinkle it on the plug, and polish the plug with the back (paper) side of the finest grade sandpaper. At this stage the shaping of the plug is complete.

98

Carving the block of wood with a pocketknife.

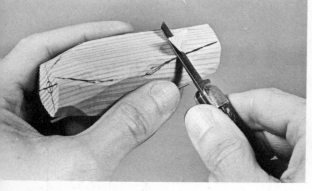

After the plug is roughed out with the pocketknife, it can be rounded with a wood rasp.

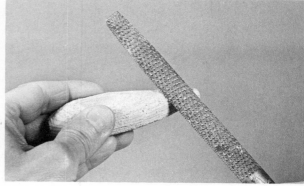

Final sanding of the wood plug is necessary for a smooth finish of the painted lure.

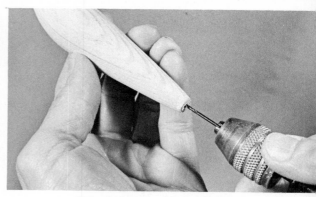

Pilot holes should be drilled wherever screw eyes or hook hangers are to be added.

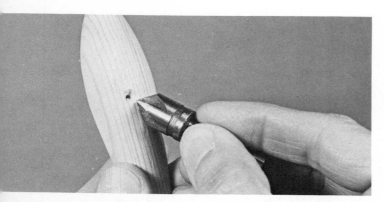

Plugs should be countersunk where cup washers are to be used under the screw eye.

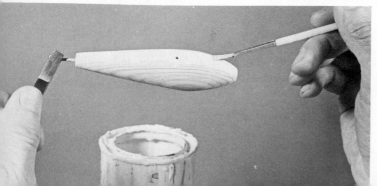

Finished plugs should be given a base coat of white paint or wood sealer.

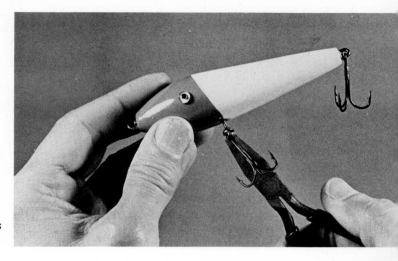

After the plug is painted, the hooks and other hardware are added.

One point to keep in mind in carving any original design lure is that the simple lures are always best. The most successful commercial plugs usually have a simple design or shape even though they may have a wobbling, vibrating, or erratic action in the water.

USE OF POWER TOOLS IN PLUG-MAKING

Plugs can be sawed to shape with a jigsaw, following the drawn outline. Some jigsaws also have belt sanders or sanding discs built into them, which makes it even easy to further shape the plug, using coarse sandpaper. Rotary rasps and stones on an electric drill are also useful, especially for forming the cupped heads of popping plugs. But, final finishing of any plug should be done by hand; power tools just take off too much wood too quickly at this critical state. An exception to this would be a small belt sander in which fine, 5/0 to 7/0, paper can be used.

SEALING AND PAINTING

Once shaping of the plug blank is finished, it should be sealed with a clear lacquer, or base paint, before any further work is done. Use several coats, sanding lightly between each coat for better bonding of the sealer. This waterproofs the plug and prevents the final coats of paint from being absorbed into the plug, resulting in a splotchy or uneven coat. After the plug is sealed, it can be laid away for final finishing.

At this point the plug can be painted, or finished in some other way. A variety of finishes are available, including paints and lacquers, scale finishes, masked patterns, glitter or metallic dust finishes, glue-on finishing sheets, and so forth. Since finishing methods for plugs, spoons, jigs, and other lures are similar, Chapter 12 has been devoted to finishing.

After the plug is completely painted or otherwise finished, it is completed by the addition of the necessary hardware: hooks, hook hangers, screw eyes, and lips.

ADDING PLUG HARDWARE

There is no particular order in which the hardware must be added to the lure. I prefer to start at the front end and add the closed screw eye to which the line or leader is tied. Use a closed screw eye, preferably one as long as possible to give added "bite" into the wood to keep the screw eye from pulling out. Some of those supplied in kits and even some found in commercially made plugs seem too short for my taste. I like a long screw eye because it is generally screwed in *parallel with* the grain of wood, rather than across the grain (as in the center treble hook of the plug, where it holds better for a given length of screw thread).

Actually, I may be slightly over-cautious about this subject. As a test, I once screwed a ¼-inch-long screw eye into the end grain of a one-inch-thick block of basswood used for making plugs and pulled it against an industrial grade tension tester, accurate to ± 0.5 percent. It did not pull out, and the screw eye finally deformed at 24 pounds pull. This is far more tension than would normally be exerted on the plug while landing a fish.

One the other hand, I have heard too many tales of screw eyes coming out of both commercial and homemade plugs to be complacent. Plugs are not just thrown in the water to occasionally retrieve a fish. They get hooked on snags and stumps and knocked about in tackle boxes, and lines are snapped off plugs to change lures, all of which can weaken the hold of a short screw eye.

Using a long screw eye also creates problems; I have occasionally had the "eye" part of the screw eye twist off while I was still turning the thread into the wood. This will happen in basswood or cedar with screw eyes approaching one inch in length or in very hard woods (wood dowels, etc.) in shorter lengths. If using very long screw eyes, pre-drill with a small diameter drill bit to avoid this problem. Also, a bit of soap on the threads of any screw eye makes it easier to turn in and less likely to twist off.

Cup washers, through which the screw eyes are fastened into the plug, are not necessary, but they do add a professional touch. Deeper cut washers, called disc washers, serve the same purpose as the hook hangers, preventing the hook points from scratching the finish of the plug and also from tangling together. Without them, the hook eye and screw eye can sometimes become twisted together, preventing the hook from hanging naturally. Regular cup washers are normally used in the head and tail of the plug.

The spot where the cup washer is to be placed must be carved for insertion of the cup or disc washer. Since the disc washers are deeper and cylindrical, it is best to drill slightly into the plug, but only enough to seat the disc washer. Cup washers can be placed into a small depression made with an electric drill countersink bit.

Plastic plugs have a preformed socket in the plug for the screw eye and will accommodate only the length for which the socket is designed. A longer screw eye will twist off, crack the plastic, or make a hole in a hollow plug that will in time pick up water.

Sometimes screw eyes are not used at all, and the line attachment is made

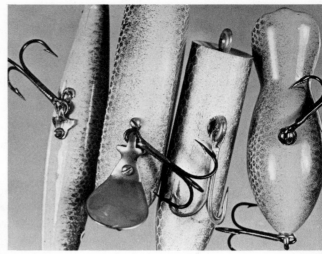

Methods of hook attachment. Left to right: hook hanger, hook hanger on bib, screw eye, and screw eye with cup washer.

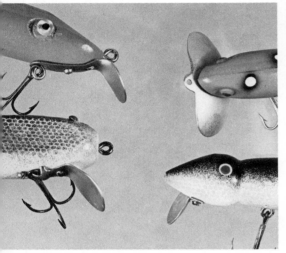

Different types of metal bibs and plates attached to the head of wood lures.

through a connector ring, split ring, or connector link or swivel attached to the wiggle plate on deep-running and diving plugs. These wiggle plates are attached by small round-head wood screws made for plug construction, either supplied with the wiggle plate or available separately.

Some wiggle plates also have a hook hanger built in for placing the center treble hook. To attach it, line up the wiggle plate on the plug, mark with an awl the spots for the screw hole (plastic plugs will have the holes formed in the plug), and screw in the small round-head screws to hold it in place.

Add the tail screw eye and treble hook just as the front eye is added. Use an open screw eye to add the treble hook; place the hook on the open screw eye, close with pliers, and turn it into the plug. The tail treble hook can also be fastened with a hook hanger and the small round-head screws.

Surface plugs often have propellers for added flash and noise. On some plugs they are at the tail, on others, at both ends. Add these to the shaft of the screw eye before turning it in the plug. Use small cup washers to provide bearing surface fore and aft of the propeller. Also take care not to draw the screw eye up tight, preventing the prop from turning.

If you're making plugs with propellers both fore and aft, it may be wise to take one of the propellers and turn the pitch of the blades so that it turns in the opposite direction from the other prop. Do it carefully so as not to twist

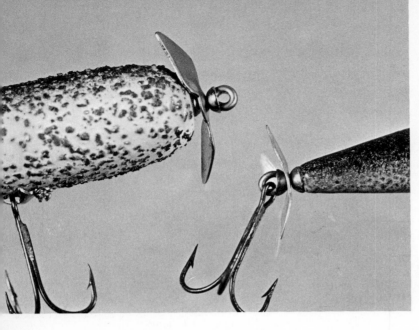

Propellers may be attached to the front, rear, or both ends of a surface lure. Cup washers should be used on both sides of the propeller as shown, with enough play in the screw eye shaft to allow the propeller to revolve.

the prop. With both props turning in the same direction, the plug may have a tendency to revolve as it is retrieved, which will twist line and also could cause a missed fish, if a strike comes when the plug is turned belly up. Many twin-prop commerical plugs have this same disadvantage; however, the props on commercial plugs can be changed in the same way. This is particularly a problem on small lightweight spinning surface plugs, but I have seen it happen with large saltwater lures as well.

THROUGH-WIRE CONSTRUCTION

Through-wire construction of plugs is also possible with both homemade and preshaped wood bodies. Through-wire construction is the process of rigging the eye to which the line is tied, and all hooks, to a single strong wire running through the longitudinal axis of the plug. It is generally not possible with plastic bodies, since forming a slot or hole for the wire and sealing the plug again is either impossible or not worth the effort.

Through-wire construction absolutely excludes the possibility of losing a fish because of a pulled screw eye, or because a plug is shattered by the strike of an exceptionally strong fish. It is used in almost all commercially made salt-water plugs for just these reasons.

There are two ways to rig a wood plug with through-wire construction. The first involves drilling a hole through the long axis of the plug, the second by sawing a slot in the belly of the plug, inserting the wire, and sealing the plug with glue.

The first method is most adaptable with small (or at least short) plugs. Most $\frac{1}{16}$- or $\frac{1}{8}$-inch drills are not long enough to drill all the way through long plugs, and the longer a plug is, the easier it is to drill off center and end up with an eccentric hole through the plug, ruining it for all practical purposes. Even with short plugs there is the problem of drilling, since most $\frac{1}{16}$- or $\frac{1}{8}$-inch drills are no more than 1 or 2 inches long—hardly long enough for any but an ultra-light spinning plug, where this construction is unnecessary.

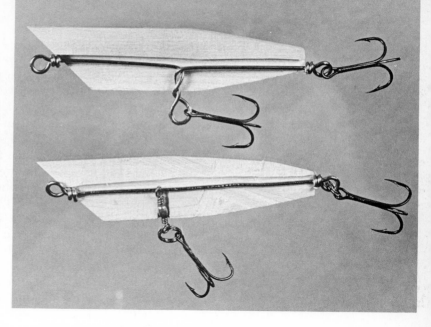

Cut-away view of two methods of through-wire construction. Top: a slot is cut in the belly of the lure, and a preformed wire hook attachment dropped into place and glued. Bottom: two holes are drilled in the plug. One hole runs through the axis of the plug while the second hole holds the belly hook. (Construction details in text.)

To drill longer holes, use 6-inch-long aircraft drill bits (12-inch lengths are also available, although these are hardly necessary for the job.) They're not easily available, but some large hardware stores and specialty tool mail-order houses do carry them—$\frac{1}{16}$, $\frac{3}{32}$, and $\frac{1}{8}$ inch are the best sizes. (One company that carries aircraft drill bits is the Brookstone Company; see Appendix.)

Drill the plug from either end, preferably with the electric drill in a small press (small drill presses that hold electric drills are available from hardware and mail-order stores in $15 to $25 price ranges). Use a bench vise or some support to hold the plug absolutely vertical, on line with the drill bit.

A vertical support can be easily constructed from nothing more than three pieces of wood screwed together to make a "corner." Providing that it has been made carefully and that the corner and the drill bit are parallel, the bit will drill the plug exactly through the center.

An easier way to drill plugs is to cut out blocks of the wood to the proper size, drill the center holes, and then carve the plug around the holes already drilled. This way even if the block is drilled slightly off center, the plug can be carved accordingly, so that the end result is an on-center hole. Once the hole is drilled, it is easy to wrap an eye on one end of a length of brass wire, run it through the plug, and start another eye, adding a hook before twisting the eye closed.

If a center hook is to be added to the plug, drill a second hole in from the belly of the plug to intersect the center axis hole. Insert a swivel into this hole, running the wire through the plug and the swivel eye at the same time. After completing the plug, add a hook to the exposed swivel eye with a split ring. Obviously, the plug should be painted before through-wire rigging is added.

Hook styles, sizes, and placement are important in large saltwater plugs with through-wire construction. For example, while treble hooks are practically standard on most lures, single hooks are sometimes better. In plugging for large fish or those with a mouth full of teeth, prying out a single hook with a pair of pliers is far easier than working loose three hook points.

By the same token, hook size in relation to the plug size can often mean the difference between landed fish and lost strikes. Many Florida anglers turn their own cedar or white pine surface chugger plugs on a lathe. And they frequently use single hooks with a gap larger than the greatest diameter of the plug body. The reason is that in striking a large saltwater fish with a smaller hook the plug can be pulled away from the fish. By using a hook gap larger than the diameter of the plug, the hook is sure to sink in the fish.

It is also possible to form the wires as described above, dropping them into a slot sawed in the plug after it is carved out. Place the carved plug belly up in a vise or clamp, using wood blocks or vise jaw protectors to prevent scarring the plug. Saw the plug lengthwise, stopping when the center line is reached. This way the completed wire rigging, with eyes preformed and with hooks attached, can be dropped in place. Naturally, the position of the center hook must be predetermined. It is not necessary to use a swivel for this type of construction, since the wire can be twisted to include the center hook as well. It may be necessary to enlarge the slot by drilling at the point where the center hook hanger wire is placed. Drop the wire in place and glue the slot shut with several applications of epoxy or household waterproof glue.

In this type of construction, it is best to paint the lure first, touching up the glued slot in the belly of the plug once the lure is finally completed. Painting and adding eyes and other finishes of plugs are fully described in Chapter 12.

The wire used in through-wire construction can be of almost any type as long as it is heavy enough to hold the fish, and noncorrosive. This is especially important in fishing saltwater, where the through-wire construction is almost mandatory for bigger fish. Brass or copper wire in size .060 is good, with brass wire this size used on many commercially made saltwater plugs. South Florida anglers who make their own plugs are using stainless steel No. 15 leader wire with equally good results.

Obviously, as in any fishing tackle construction, it is far better to work out an assembly-line production as much as possible, assuming that several plugs of the same design and size are desired. Thus, a dozen plugs should all go through each of the above operations together, rather than one at a time. The exception to this rule is designing the first plug of every new lot, or in trying an untested design. Even in duplicating "exactly" a commercial plug, the balance of the plug, the weight of hardware, and other factors will be different enough to affect the action. Check at least one example of each plug design in the bathtub or on a pond before gearing up for production.

COST

The cost of homemade plugs will be only pennies each. As mentioned earlier, the cost of the hardware and plug bodies is small, assuming the purchase of reasonable amounts of necessary supplies.

⟶

Examples of finished plastic and wood plugs. Left two rows are plastic plugs, right two rows are wood plugs. Far-right row of plugs were all carved by hand. Other wood plugs came preformed in kits.

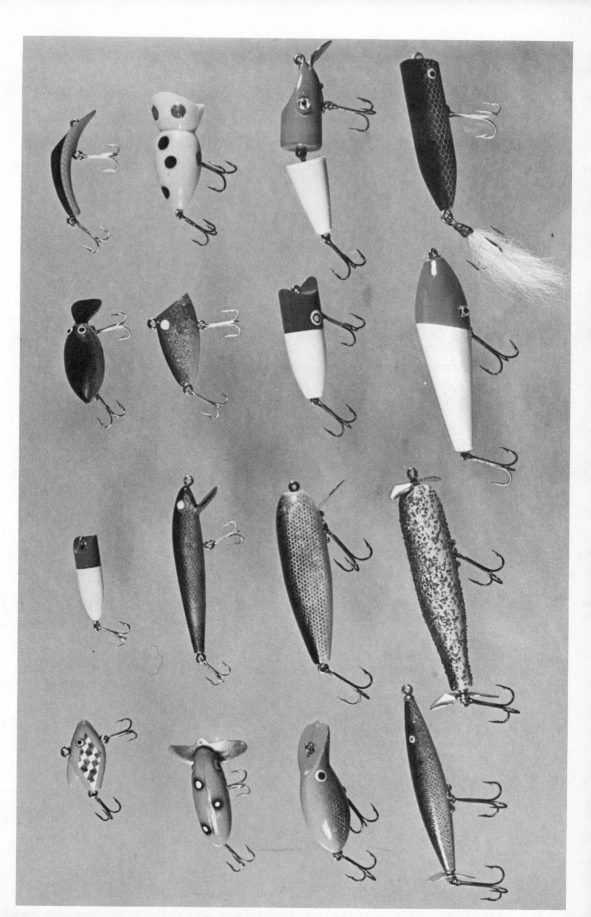

Given a typical banana-shaped red and white plastic bass plug, the cost would look approximately like this, based on current (1973) prices:

Plastic plug bodies	$0.71/6	or	$0.1183 each
Closed screw eyes	.54/100	or	.0054 each
Open screw eyes	.60/100	or	.0120 (2 used)
Lacquer—red	.59/2 oz.		.01 each
Lacquer—white	.59/2 oz.		.01 each
Decal eyes	.15/50		.0060 pair
Hooks—#6 treble	1.30/36		.0722 (2 used)
TOTAL			$ .2339

The completed plastic plug costs just a little under 24 cents, with relatively little time involved, on the production basis previously described. Most plugs would average about this same cost, with the only variables being the variety of plug bodies used, the size and number of hooks in each lure, and the variety of colors used in finishing. Hand-carved wood plugs will be even cheaper. Only rarely will a plug run more than 20 to 22 cents each—cheap enough for plugs that are custom-made and frequently just as good as or better than those commercially available.

PLUG-MAKING KITS

As with spinners and spoons, kits are available containing complete plug bodies and hardware for anywhere from six to a dozen lures. Netcraft has several such kits, one consisting of finished plastic plug bodies that have only to be assembled. Other kits include wood plug bodies that must be finished and kits of two-piece plastic plugs that must be glued together before finishing and assembling. Typical kits include one each of several popular shapes of lures; some kits contain three to four colors of paint for finishing.

Kits range in price from about $2 for a wood plug kit to $5 for a kit of a dozen finished plastic bodies. In addition, Herter's has an arrangement whereby any of their thirty styles of plug bodies can be ordered with hardware for a slight additional fee, usually less than 20 cents each. By this method, any number of specific shapes and sizes of lures can be ordered, without the sometimes wasteful process of getting a kit that may contain some lure shapes and sizes that are virtually useless for the waters you'll be fishing.

The one disadvantage of any home-finished lure is that unless the plug bodies are already prefinished, the paints used are seldom as durable as those on commercial plugs. But with a total lure cost of about a tenth to a sixth the cost of a store-bought lure, an occasional refinishing is a small price to pay for the basic economy and ease of making plugs.

8

FLY, BAIT CASTING, SPINNING, AND SALTWATER RODS

*TOOLS · ROD BLANKS · FERRULES · GUIDES
AND TIP TOPS · REEL SEATS · REEL SEAT
BUSHINGS · CORK RINGS AND CORK GRIPS ·
HANDLES · BUTT CAPS · WINDING CHECKS AND
ROD HOSELS · MISCELLANEOUS MATERIALS · SPINE OF
A ROD · FILING GUIDE FEET · WRAPPING GUIDES · TYPES
OF GUIDE WRAPPINGS · OTHER WRAPS AND
DECORATIVE WINDINGS · VARNISHING GUIDES
AND DECORATIVE WINDINGS · SEATING METAL
FERRULES · MAKING GLASS-TO-GLASS FERRULES
GLUING CORK HANDLES · STEPS IN BUILDING
SPINNING RODS · VARIATIONS OF SPINNING
ROD CONSTRUCTION · STEPS IN BUILDING
CASTING RODS · VARIATIONS OF CASTING
RODS · STEPS IN BUILDING FLY RODS ·
VARIATIONS OF FLY RODS · STEPS IN BUILDING
BOAT, TROLLING, AND BIG GAME RODS ·
COSTS · ROD KITS*

BASIC TOOLS	HELPFUL TOOLS
Old book (for guide winding)	Wood rasp
File	Rod winder
Sandpaper	
Razor blade	

ᗡ YES, RODS ARE EASY TO BUILD, AND REQUIRE VIRTUALLY NO TOOLS, except sandpaper and a coarse file. For those planning to make a number of rods

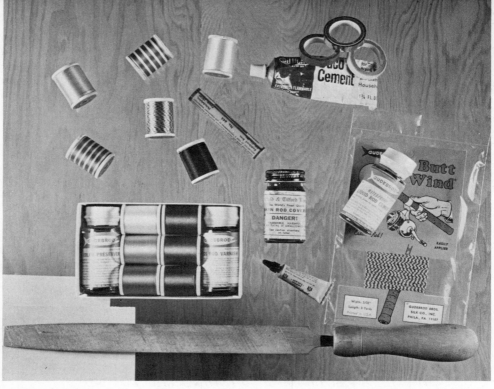

Materials required for building rods. Thread, color preservative, rod varnish, ferrule cement, file, and sandpaper.

there are special rod winders available, but rod guides can be wrapped without them.

Actually, building rods today is really just the assembling of the various components—the rod blanks, ferrules, guides, handles, and so forth. At one time some home craftsmen built split-bamboo rods, a craft requiring skill, patience, and experience. It also required an investment in special V blocks for splitting cane, and wrapping machines for pressure-gluing the six strips together into the rod blanks. This equipment is not now generally available.

Rods can still be built of bamboo, and some companies carry split-bamboo rod blanks that can be assembled into complete rods as are glass rod blanks. Phillipson, Dunton, Orvis, Leonard, and Thomas and Thomas all supply bamboo rod blanks.

The basic components of any rod are all the same. They include the rod blank, handle, reel seat, guides, keeper ring, ferrules, and thread windings.

TOOLS

Few tools are needed for rod building. Commercial rod winders are available, but even these are not necessary. Guides can be wrapped by hand, running the thread through a book to achieve the proper tension. If you use this method, use an old book or discarded telephone directory, since the thread will scar the pages. Additional tension can be gained by adding more books or weight on top of the book through which the thread runs.

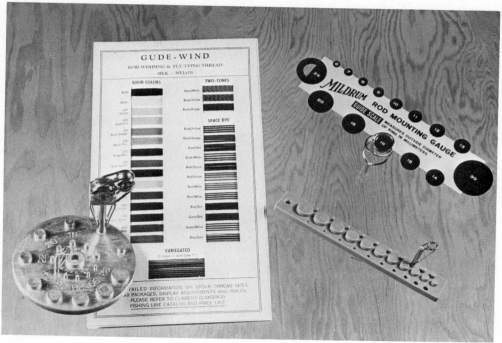

Tackle stores often have guides and charts to help in rod building. Left, a Gudebrod thread chart and Allan tip-top gauge. Right, Mildrum guide gauge and tip-top gauge.

While the rod can be wrapped freehand, it is far easier to use some sort of stand to support the rod blank. One can be made by nailing an upright—3 to 4 inches high—to each end of a 1- to 2-inch board. (Make sure that the uprights are high enough so that the guides will clear the baseboard when the blank is rotated.) Cut a V into the top of each end of the uprights.

Commercial rod winders such as those offered by Herter's consist of a small bracket that clamps to a table top, surmounted with an adjustable spring-loaded shaft to hold a spool of thread. A thumb screw adjusts the tension on the thread; arms extend out in front of the bracket to hold the rod blank. However, the support bracket mentioned is far easier to use than the arms that come with these commercial rod winders.

For making a number of rods, you may want to consider using a rod winder together with easily made frictionless support brackets. I use support brackets made from a set of four 2-inch hostess tray casters (or rollers). Two adjoining casters mounted upside down, with a tiny gap between them, will roll with a rod blank making the winding task very easy. Since two brackets are needed to support the rod blank, a total of four casters are required. Electric winders are also a possibility; construction details of both of these are included in Chapter 13.

In addition to a rod winder of some sort, a file and sandpaper will be needed to finish the rod grip. A coarse file or wood rasp can be used for rough-shaping the grip, but sandpaper is needed to finish it. Use a razor blade to cut the excess thread, once a guide is wrapped in place.

ROD BLANKS

The most important part of any rod is the blank onto which all the assembled component parts are built. Most rod blanks available today are made of hollow glass, although some solid glass rod blanks are available. Hollow glass blanks are lighter and have better casting action; solid glass rods are quite satisfactory for boat rods, trolling tackle, and ice-fishing rods.

In quite another class are the split-bamboo rod blanks. Some fishermen, particularly fly fishermen, still prefer the slower action of the split-bamboo rod to the faster action of the glass rod. Also, with fly fishing and especially trout and salmon fishing, sports loaded with tradition, there is no small amount of nostalgia in the choice of split-bamboo fly rods.

"Fast" and "Slow"—two commonly used terms in rods and rod building—do not really explain the action of the rod. "Fast" action is also called "tip action." A rod with this type of action will have a stiff butt in relation to a very flexible tip. The idea of this type of action is that relatively small baits and lures can be thrown with the tip of the rod while enough backbone is maintained in the rod butt to land big fish. Once popular, it is today primarily favored by West Coast fishermen, who must meet the small bait–big fish combination if they are to have any sport.

"Slow action," sometimes called "parabolic action," is an action in which the rod has a more progressive, even bend from tip to butt. Some slow rods— fly rods and light spinning rods especially—have an action in which the bend of the rod can be felt all the way down into the rod handle. There are other rod actions between these two extremes.

Hollow glass revolutionized rod building in the post-World War II days and over the years has proved superior to all other rod-building materials such as steel, beryllium copper, laminated wood (sometimes used in heavy boat and trolling rods), and similar materials now only rarely found in rods.

Glass rod blanks are exactly that—glass just like that found in any windowpane. The difference is that the glass is melted and drawn into fine threads and these threads woven into a cloth, not unlike fiberglass curtains available for the home. The glass cloth is then cut into a roughly triangular shape, almost as cloth is cut from a pattern for a pair of pants. Wrapped on a steel mandrel and baked with resins, the result is a solid cylinder of glass, the rod blank. After baking, the steel mandrel is pulled from the hollow rod, and the blank is trimmed to size, ready to be finished.

The resins in a glass rod are just glue, binding the layers of glass together. The real strength and action of the rod is in the glass fibers. Different manufacturers have different methods of building glass rod blanks, and different ideas about the thickness of the glass fibers in the blank, the wall thickness of the rod, and even the action.

The action of a rod is controlled by the amount of glass in the blank, as well as the way the glass is cut before being wrapped on the steel mandrel prior to baking. The amount of glass will determine how stiff or light the rod is; the curve cut in the hypotenuse of the glass "cloth" triangle will determine the action. A convex curve will make a stiff rod with a light tip action—the so-called fast tip action—because of the thick wall of the lower rod section. A concave curve cut into the glass cloth will result in a light rod with stiffer action far down in the butt section. A straight cut of the glass cloth will result in an even, parabolic action rod, that bends uniformly from tip to butt.

Glass rods come in all colors, from black to white, with various shades of brown and tan the most popular colors. Some of the extremes of color are spray-painted over a basic brown blank. Rod blanks come in all styles and sizes, ranging from 5-foot ultra-light blanks to 14-foot surf-rod blanks. They come one-piece, two-piece, multiple-sectioned, and both ferruled and unferruled.

Rod companies vary greatly in the number of rod blanks that they make available for amateur rod-building. Some offer only a few blanks in a few styles and sizes; Fenwick currently stocks 72 rod blanks. Their complete selection includes fly-rod, ultra-light spinning, freshwater-spinning, saltwater-spinning, steelhead, casting, spin casting, live-bait saltwater, jigging surf, boat, and regulation IGFA trolling blanks. Most of these are available either ferruled or unferruled.

Rod blanks are generally purchased ferruled. Saltwater, fly-rod, and spinning-rod blanks come both center and off-center ferruled. Center-ferruled rods have the ferrules placed in the exact middle of the rod. Off-center ferruled rods are ferruled in two unequal lengths. The tip section is always the longer, the idea being that the off-center ferrule will give better action than the center ferrule.

One disadvantage of off-center ferruled blanks is that the unequal rod sections require a longer rod case than do center-ferruled rods. I have found little practical fishing difference between the two types of rods, and I usually build center-ferruled rods, since they are easier to carry.

Sometimes off-center ferruled rods are called butt-ferruled. This term is *not* to be confused with the special ferrule that goes on the butt of a one-piece casting rod for attachment of the blank to the casting-rod handle.

Blank prices vary widely, depending upon the brand, length, and style of rod. It can be as little as a few dollars for a short, ultra-light spinning blank, to almost $50 for a fine quality, 130-pound class regulation IGFA blank.

FERRULES

Ferrules vary widely depending upon the type of rod on which they are used. For standard two-piece rods, such as spinning rods, fly rods, two-piece casting rods, and saltwater rods, the ferrules consist of two parts, a male section and a female section into which the male fits. And the old adage of "you get what you pay for" is nowhere more important than in choosing rod ferrules. Cheap ferrules are false economy; they tend to become loose, so that the tip section may slide off the rod, or the two rod sections may rattle during casting.

One type of ferrule that has gained wide acceptance with both the home rod builder and the tackle manufacturer is the Featherweight "Armor Plate Sizmatic" ferrule. This ferrule utilizes a rubber O ring in the tip and a tapered shoulder at the base of the male ferrule. The result is that the fit of the male into the female section is tight with the O ring and shoulder providing a solid joint. O rings can be replaced if they ever become worn. Prices are about

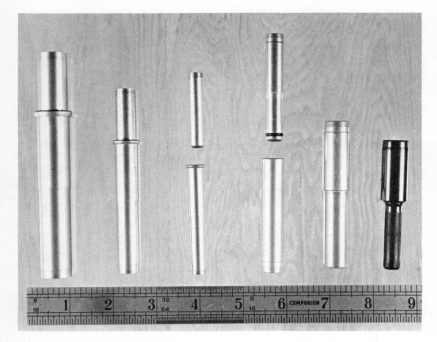

Types of ferrules. The two right-hand ferrules are for casting rods and are often called butt ferrules.

Courtesy of Featherweight Products

EXPLANATION OF "DIMENSIONAL DROP" IN FEATHERWEIGHT FERRULES

Example: Size 17/64"

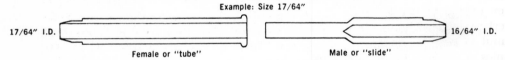

17/64" I.D.   16/64" I.D.

Female or "tube"   Male or "slide"

All Featherweight ferrules have varying "dimensional drops" between the size of the female (or "tube") and the male (or "slide"). In every case, the inside diameter of the male half of the ferrule is **smaller** than the female half. In the example above, while the size of the ferrule is 17/64" only the female half has this inside diameter; the male half carries a full 1/64" "dimensional drop" and is 16/64" inside diameter. Thus, the "dimensional drop" is an important sizing factor of all Featherweight ferrules according to the attached dimensional drop chart.

TYPE OF FERRULE	SIZES	DIMENSIONAL DROP
"Armor Plate Sizmatic"	11/64" thru 16/64"	approx. .010"
	17/64" thru 43/64"	full 1/64"
"Brass Chrome"	30/64" thru 40/64"	full 3/64"

$1.25 to $3.75, depending on size. Sizes range from 11/64 to 48/64 inches.

German nickel-silver ferrules are widely used, the male section smoothly mated to the female to provide a firm fit without any looseness.

Casting-rod ferrules fit the butt of the rod, and come in standard shank diameters to fit the collets (like a drill chuck) of casting and spin-casting rod handles. These ferrules are available in a variety of inside diameters to fit a number of different-size rod butts. Sometimes measured in decimals, but more commonly in 64ths, ferrules are available in sizes from 20/64 to 4/64ths. Prices are $ .75 to $1.25.

Fenwick also has available a Vee ferrule/casting handle combination for casting and spin-casting rods. This ferrule, which fits only Fenwick handles designed for it, has a tapered shank with a self-aligning feature so that the guides cannot twist out of line with the handle. They come in inside ferrule sizes from 24/64 to 41/64ths. These ferrules sell for less than $1 each; the casting handle designed for use with them selling for around $5.

Boat and trolling rods use different ferrules, since the female section of the ferrule is incorporated into the reel seat of the rod, the male ferrule positioned at the butt end of the rod section and below the foregrip. Depending upon the quality of the ferrule-reel seat, the male section may or may not have a slot on the end to key into the ridge in the bottom of the female section, again to assure guide and handle alignment.

Prices vary greatly, depending upon the size, usually 13/16, 7/8, or 1 inch inside diameter ferrules. Prices are around $2 to $3 for a boat rod ferrule-reel seat, but can go as high as $25 each for the heavy-duty, solid-brass chrome-plated double-locking ferrule-seat used on big game rods. Of course, the price includes not only the ferrule but also the reel seat. Most of the better types have ferrules with a knurled ring that screws onto the reel seat–female ferrule portion to assure that the tip section will not come out or get out of alignment while a large fish is being played.

One of the most popular ideas in ferrules to come along since Izaak Walton used a rod is the glass-to-glass ferrule developed by the Fenwick/Sevenstrand Tackle Manufacturing Company, makers of Fenwick rods. This idea has been copied in various ways—glass to glass, metal to glass, glass male plugs, overlapping female glass ferrules to fit over the glass butt section. Today most manufacturers offer at least some rods with this type of ferrule, and some companies, such as Phillipson, Fenwick, Fuji, Orvis, and others, sell glass-to-glass ferruled rod blanks for the rod builder.

GUIDES AND TIP TOPS

Sometimes called "eyes" by the novice fisherman, guides force the line to run the length of the rod from the reel, allow for ease in casting, and even help distribute the strain on the rod when you are playing a big fish. They can be broken down into a number of basic styles according to the rod on which they are to be used.

Snake Guides: There are the small guides used in fly rods and are presumably so named because of their twisted appearance when viewed from the top. They come in about ten different sizes suitable for the smallest stream rod to the heftiest saltwater fly rod. They come in bronze, black, gold, nickel-plated, chrome, and stainless steel, the last a must for fly rods used in salt-and brackish water.

The cost of these guides is minimal, about 2 to 4 cents each, depending upon size, with matched assortments of 12 to 15 guides, ranging from about 50 cents to $1.50. Fly-rod tip tops are small rings fitted to a tube, in sizes from 4½/64ths to 9/64ths. Prices are about 25 cents each.

Casting Guides. Used for both casting rods and spin-casting rods, casting guides consist of small round rings, mounted in a bracket that terminates in a "foot" at each end. The foot is wrapped to the rod blank. The mountings vary, depending upon the manufacturer. Common mountings for the rings include stamped frames, and round wire frames in both V and U styles.

Sizes range from about 7 to 18 millimeters in diameter. Most guides are measured by the outside diameter, but some manufacturers and styles measure the inside opening diameter. When you're buying guides, *check* to be sure which way the guides are measured, since the difference between an outside and inside measurement can be several millimeters. (A guide millimeter sizing chart is located in the Appendix.)

Usually larger guides are used on spin-casting rods than on casting rods. On all rods, the sizes for the guides are graduated, with the smallest near the tip top, the largest near the handle.

Materials commonly used are stainless steel, chromed stainless steel, gold plate, Carboloy (tungsten carbide), gold-plated Carboloy rings, agate rings, and now a ceramic ring made of aluminum oxide, one of the space-age materials.

Guide costs range widely, depending upon the size of the guide, the quality of construction, and the material used in the ring. Single casting guides sell for as little as 25 cents to as much as $2.00 each. The more expensive guides include those of Carboloy, aluminum oxide, and agate rings. Guide sets of four to five guides are also available at prices of $1.50 to $5.00.

Spin-casting guides are, in some cases, exactly the same as casting rod guides, and in all cases similar. The rings are larger and placed higher in the frame, something like a compromise between a spinning and a casting guide in height. Prices and materials are the same as for casting guides.

Tip tops come in the same ring materials as the guides and are mounted, by wire supports, on metal tubes to fit the diameter of the tip of the rod blank.

Standard sizes for tip tops for casting and spin-casting rods vary from 5/64ths up. Since the same type of tip top is used on trolling and boat rods, sizes will run to 16/64ths. They cost from 50 cents to $1.50, depending on size and quality.

Spinning Guides. Essentially like lightweight casting-rod guides, these are different from the former in two important ways. First, they have much larger rings to accommodate the large loops of line coming off the spinning reel when you are making a cast. Second, they are placed on a higher frame than in casting guides, to prevent line slap as the loops of line fly off the spinning reel.

In size, the rings used in the guides range from a small ring of perhaps 6 millimeters in diameter used near the tip top, to a large ring of 24 to 27 millimeters used as the first guide on a freshwater spinning rod. Saltwater spinning rods have larger rings, ranging up to 50 millimeters for the butt guide.

The ring frame can be V or U shaped, made of either stamped metal or, in better quality guides, round wire. Materials for the rings are the same as those for casting rod guides, i.e., Carboloy, gold-plated Carboloy, stainless steel, chrome agate, aluminum oxide.

There is an additional consideration in the choice of guides for spinning

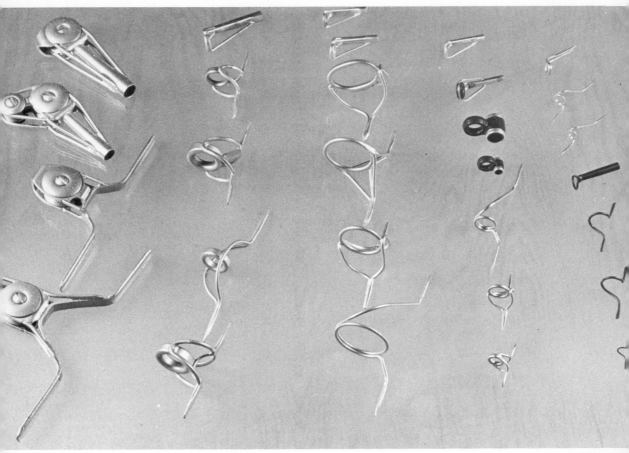

Examples of some guides and tip tops. Left to right: big game roller guides, trolling rod guides, spinning guides, casting guides, and fly rod snake guides.

rods. Guide weight affects rod action, and no finished rod will have exactly the same action as the unfinished rod blank. For this reason, it is unwise to add the heavier Carboloy or agate guides to an ultra-light spinning rod. These rods are light, and the addition of any excess weight only makes the action sluggish, slow, and "heavy."

In addition, while the Carboloy and agate guides are ideal in preventing grooving, the small fish caught and the light lines and lures used with ultra-light tackle make such considerations unnecessary. Good choices for ultra-light rods are the lightweight Aetna guides by Gudebrod, or similar guides by Allen and other companies.

Carboloy or aluminum oxide guides (distributed by Lew Childre and Sanders) are excellent for heavier tackle where line-grooved guides from throwing big plugs and fighting heavier fish are a distinct possibility.

Agate guides, extremely hard and also excellent in preventing line grooving, do have the disadvantage of being extremely brittle. A slight knock can crack them and the crack can cut the line.

While the use of large guides is standard in the industry and among most anglers building their own spinning rods, there is some question as to whether the larger ring is really necessary in spinning tackle. The basic idea, of course, is that the large guides serve to "gather" the loops of cast line, so that by the time the line leaves the rod tip, it is traveling in a straight path.

But that reasoning may be more theoretical than actual. Several years ago, I fished with Ralph Delph and Art Blacker of Miami, both excellent anglers (Ralph had three world records at the time). Among the arsenal of tackle we used, both anglers had special spinning rods that incorporated a first butt guide of a tiny Carboloy ring mounted in simple supports. The other guides were standard spinning guides, though not overly large. Their explanation was that the rods were used for fishing when especially long casts were needed. I commented on the small first guide, expecting that it would cut distance. But they told me that the small guide "clears" all the loops from the line as it comes off the reel, allowing the line to run friction-free and without line slap through the rest of the guides, thus giving longer distance than regular spinning guides. Far be it from me to argue with the holder of three world records in the specialized sport of light-tackle saltwater fishing.

Similarly, several years ago, Heddon sold spinning rods mounted with small-ring, high-frame guides. Talking with their representatives, I learned that according to their tests, the smaller rings made no difference in casting distance. The high frame was necessary to prevent line slap against the rod, but try as they might, they could not convince the fishing public of this and so discontinued the rods from the market several years later.

The average fisherman is still conditioned to using rods with large spinning guides, although someone with an inquisitive mind may learn some interesting things by experimenting with several rods, taping different-size guides in place to compare casting distance.

Spinning tip tops are generally the same as those used for casting rod, although a little lighter in weight, and often have a smaller ring through which the line flows. Cost for the guides and tip top is about the same as for casting rod guides.

Other Spinning and Casting Rod Guides and Tip Tops. Some types of guides used for spinning, spin casting, and casting rods do not fit into the category of guides already discussed. These include guides with different mounting methods, single foot guides, and split tip tops (to fit any size rod).

One of the most unusual guide ideas to come along in recent years is the Fuji Speed guides and tops, made in Japan and distributed in this country by Lew Childre and Sanders, Inc. These guides, made for both casting and spinning rods, do not have the two feet by which most guides are wrapped to the rod. Called slip-on guides, they consist of an aluminum oxide ring in a hard, durable polyacetyl plastic frame. This frame is incorporated into a wide band of the same plastic, designed to slip over the rod blank.

They come in several styles: a mini-guide with a small ring for fly rods, a low frame guide for casting and spin-casting rods, and a high frame guide for spinning rods. Claims for the new types of guides are that the aluminum oxide ring is harder and "faster" (less friction) than wire or tungsten carbide and that the plastic frame is lighter-weight than the standard metal frames. Finally, the wide plastic band that holds the guide to the rod blank requires no winding;

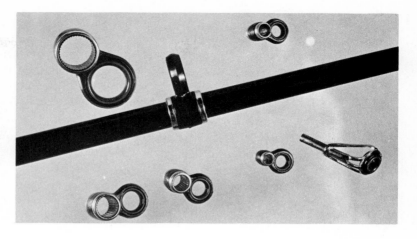

Examples of Lew's Speed Guides of aluminum oxide rings and a plastic frame that is slipped on the rod blank without any thread wrapping. Note the ridges in the ring that slips on the rod, which prevent any twisting of the guide.

inner ridges in the band hold the guide without twisting. The spinning and casting guides range from $^{13}/_{32}$ to $^{60}/_{32}$ inch, the fly rod mini-guides range in sizes down to $^{8}/_{32}$ inch. They also manufacture standard guides incorporating the aluminum oxide rings.

Tip tops with the aluminum oxide rings are also available in the hard plastic tube. However, most tip tops come in the standard metal tubes and must be cemented in place with ferrule cement as with regular tip tops. Lew Childre and Sanders manufacture rods with these types of guides, as well as selling the component parts for rod builders. One problem with these guides is that they must be bought in the exact size diameter of the rod blank where the guide is to be placed. This means that it's impossible to order a rod and guides, since you won't know the taper of the rod and the exact blank dimension at the spot where the guide should be placed.

To rectify this, Lew Childre and Sanders are placing "Lew's Speed Merchants" in local tackle stores. The Speed Merchant is a dealer's display that includes blanks, guides, ferrules, and casting and spinning rod handles, making it possible to build a rod in minutes by a simple method of measuring the rod blank at the point where a guide is desired, picking the correct guide, and slipping it onto the rod blank, progressing in this manner until the rod is built. But that is getting ahead of our story on guides.

Other types of guides include the Aetna guides and tops, manufactured by Gudebrod. These guides look almost like an enlarged snake guide, with an additional loop of wire to form a complete ring for the line to run through. They can be bought individually or in a number of different sets, for fly rod, spinning rod, casting rod, spin casting, and heavy duty fishing. It is important to get the right type of guide set if these guides are chosen, since the wire diameters vary from a light 0.025 model for fly rod guides, to a heavy 0.093 for heavy saltwater fishing. Prices of individual guides range from about $0.50 to $1.00 per guide and from $3.25 to $8.60 per set, depending upon the number and size of guides in each set.

The advantage of Aetna guides is the extreme flexibility of the single-wire construction, which means that little rod action is lost. Disadvantages are that these guides, in the lightweight styles, are easily bent. With their simple construction, they weigh only about one-half as much as regular guides, which combined with their flexibility makes them especially good for light spinning and casting rods. This does not mean that they are unsuitable for heavy fishing. Many Florida anglers I know, true experts in light-tackle saltwater fishing, use heavy-wire Aetna guides on their casting and jigging rods.

Unlike other guides (measured in millimeters), Aetna guides are measured in fractions of inches, ranging from $\frac{5}{32}$ to 1¾ inch. (A size chart for these guides is located in the Appendix). Allan Manufacturing Co. has a similar guide called the Spiralite, of chrome-plated stainless steel, in 8 to 50 millimeter ring sizes, similar in price to that of the Aetna.

Flexon guides are also made of single-wire construction, but the two ends of the wire are folded back together, forming one foot, by which the guide is wrapped. They are made of chromed stainless steel in sizes from $\frac{3}{16}$ inch to 1½ inches and have the singular advantage of requiring only half the wrapping of an ordinary guide.

A similar type of guide that need be wrapped only once is the Uniguide, in which the two feet are parallel and on opposite sides of the rod blank, and require only a single wrap.

Ceramic guides are also becoming popular for fishing and utilize a ceramic ring placed in a metal frame. These are similar in appearance to the aluminum oxide rings used in some of the Lew Childre and Sanders Fuji guides, and boast a tough hard ring that can't be grooved (even with a file) and one that is less breakable (from pressure or knocks) than Carboloy or agate, according to the manufacturers.

Many rod companies are just starting to use these guides on their rods and they are also becoming available to the home rod builder.

In addition, some new styles of guides that look quite interesting may soon be available. Gene Bullard of Gene Bullard Custom Rods is at this writing considering importing some Sintox ceramic guides of English design that are different in appearance from our American guides. But he also insists that the English manufacturer, Sapphrite Laurels Ltd., will make guides of American design if desired. So just what ultimately appears on the American market along this line remains to be seen.

Boat Rod Guides. Boat guides are similar to those for casting rods, except that they are beefed up, heavier in both ring and frame, and generally larger. The rings are Carboloy or stainless steel, and the frames are heavy wire or stamped out on some of the less expensive guides. Some are mounted on a longer frame, called a Belmar frame, but most are in a simple U mount frame, with a brazed or forged foot. While there are extremes, average ring sizes range from 6 to 18 millimeters.

Prices are higher than those for casting guides and range, depending upon size and quality from about 75 cents to $2 each. Sets of trolling and boat guides are available. The tip tops are also similar to, but sturdier than those for casting rods. Sizes range from $\frac{5}{64}$ to $\frac{32}{64}$ inch inside tube diameter.

Big Game Rod Guides. As might be expected, these are extra-strong guides, designed to withstand the rigors of fighting big fish with heavy tackle. Many are similar to standard casting and boat guides, with the addition of a reinforcing

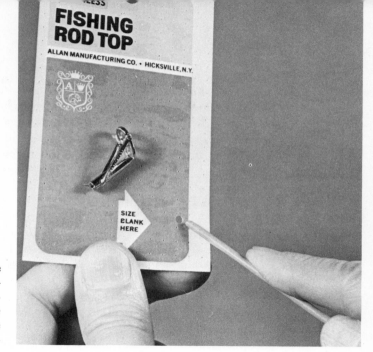

FISHING
ROD TOP
ALLAN MANUFACTURING CO. • HICKSVILLE, N.Y.

SIZE
BLANK
HERE

Some fishing hardware manufacturers, such as Allan Manufacturing Company, provide holes in the tip top cards for sizing the blank.

brace running from the feet to the lower part of the guide ring. There are also guides with bridge or Belmar frames.

Big game guides also come with Belmar frames, ending in feet that straddle the rod blank. The four feet (two at each end of the guide straddling the rod blank) give greater support to the guide and resist any tendency of the guide to deflect to the side when pumping a big fish. The rings in these guides are stainless steel or Carboloy. (Mildrum, which makes a number of these big game guides, refers to its Carboloy guides in Mildarbide. Actually, both materials are the same tungsten carbide materials, Carboloy being a trademark of General Electric).

Most true big game rods, however, use roller guides, large guides which incorporate a roller over which the line runs, reducing friction and wear. Allan Manufacturing Company and Mildrum Manufacturing Company make roller guides and matched roller sets for use on big game rods.

Essentially, these guides are large (weight is no problem on a big game rod) with two long, wide feet for attachment to the rod blank, surmounted by a frame holding the roller over which the line runs. Since they are used primarily in saltwater they all have corrosion-proof or resistant construction of plastic, stainless steel, phosphor bronze or Oilite bearings and chrome plating. They come in both straddle mount and top rod mounting types.

The first (butt) guide usually has two rollers, and the line runs between them. This is because the line coming off many big game reels is not in a direct line with the plane of the first guide; without the top roller, the line would scrape against a frame support. Roller tip tops are also available and some have a swivel top action that allows the roller to rotate in any direction, regardless of the position of the line. All roller guides come in several sizes to accommodate a variety of rod classes with tip tops in $7/64$ to $32/64$ inch. Prices are as low as $1.50 each for less expensive and cheaply built models, to $5.00 each for better guides. Roller tops are $2.00 to $3.00 each.

Hook Keepers. Keeper rings or hook keepers are small, guidelike devices wrapped onto the rod just above the winding check, to hold a hook or lure when the tackle is not being used. They are used on many types of rods, including spinning, casting, spin casting, fly and light tackle saltwater spinning rods. They come in chrome and gold, and cost from 10 to 20 cents each.

REEL SEATS

Reel seats hold the reel in place on the rod. Their construction varies widely, from the light skeletal reel seats on an ultra-light fly rod to the thick heavily chromed double-locking reel seats for big-game rods.

Fly Rod Reel Seats. These vary, but basically are small, lightweight reel seats capped at one end, designed to fit on the end of the fly rod. Inside diameters are ½ inch, ⅝ inch, ¾ inch, and ⅞ inch. They come with either single or double knurled rings to hold the movable hood in place over the reel foot. Most are of aluminum, with several anodized colors and color combinations available. Skeletal reel seats are also available in which a light butt hood (to hold the reel foot) is riveted or pinned in place on a walnut or cork insert. A second hood and threaded lock nut fits at the other end of the seat. These are more expensive than the $1 or $2 regular fly rod reel seats, and are generally only used on expensive rods or light rods where weight is a critical factor.

Spinning Rod Reel Seats. Similar to fly rod reel seats, these are open at both ends so they can be slipped on the rod while the handle is being built. Inside diameters range from ⅝ inch to ¾ inch freshwater and $1\frac{3}{16}$ to 1 inch saltwater. Since no spinning rod blank is this thick, a wood or fiber bushing or small cork rings are placed between the blank and the reel seat. In several color combinations, spinning reel seats come in single and double locking models and also several types of sliding reel seats that can be positioned anywhere on the handle, before the reel is locked in place. Prices vary from $1.00 to $3.50 each.

Boat Rod, Trolling Rod, and Big Game Reel Seats. These are large, usually double-locking reel seats, with a built-in ferrule. Ferrule sizes are standard and range from 0.625 to 1 inch. Some have locking collet nuts on the outer part of the female ferrule to fit the threads on the base of the male ferrule so that the rod cannot come apart, once joined. They are designed for saltwater use, are usually more heavily chrome plated, and range from $3 to $8 each. Big game reel seats for heavy offshore tackle are similar, but can cost up to $25 each for a 1⅛ inch diameter, 8-inch-long, heavily chromed brass reel seat.

Miscellaneous Reel Seats. Popping rods, used along the Gulf and southern coasts, are heavy-duty casting rods in which the reel seat is not offset as with freshwater tackle, but built over the rod blank, as are spinning rods. Popping rod reel seats are like spinning rod reel seats, except that they have a trigger on the rear part of the seat, much like that used on an offset casting handle. They are designed to hold conventional, revolving spool reels.

Examples of reel seats. Top row, left to right: reel seats for popping rods, surf rods, trolling, and big game rods. Bottom row, left to right: reel seats for spinning rods, sliding spinning rod reel seat, spinning rod reel bands, and fly rod reel seats. To the far right is a fly rod reel seat that takes a fitted extension butt.

Surf-rod reel seats are very similar to those used for spinning tackle except that they are heavy-duty, heavily chromed, and large diameter, both to fit on the larger rods and also to accommodate the big reels used in surf casting.

Spinning-rod reel rings are not really reel seats, but are still reel attachments. Two snugly fitting rings on the cork handle keep the reel in place by slipping the rings over the foot of the reel. Many spin-fishing anglers like them because they are more comfortable to hold, and because the reel can be placed anywhere along the cork handle; a disadvantage is that the reel will have a greater tendency to slip than when placed in a regular reel seat.

REEL-SEAT BUSHINGS

A bushing must be used under any reel seat on fly rods, spinning rods, popping rods, and similar rods where the reel seat is mounted directly on the rod blank. The bushing fills the space between the rod blank and the inner walls of the reel seats. They come in a variety of inside and outside diameters to fit different rod blank and reel seat combinations.

Fiber bushings listed in one current catalog range in size from 0.620 to 1.175 outside diameter and 0.390 to 1.000 inside diameter. The outside diameter is matched to the inside diameter of the reel seat, the inside diameter to the approximate diameter of the rod at the point where the reel seat is to be placed.

Bushings are made out of several materials, including cork, fiber, and wood. In addition, small cork rings are available as bushing material—usually used on fly rods. And of course, standard cork rings can be glued in place and filed down to fit under any reel seat. Prices range from 20 to 75 cents each for bushings, depending upon size and material.

CORK RINGS AND CORK GRIPS

Cork rings are used almost universally to make fishing rod handles. Exceptions are the wood, soft plastic, fiberglass, and aluminum handles used on boat and big game rods, and the separate rod handle-reel seat assemblings for casting and spin-casting rods; these latter frequently have cork ring grips but are sold as finished handles.

There are two different types of cork rings. Specie cork, cork in which the natural cork pits run parallel to the handle (the same direction as the center drilled hole in the cork) is the best. Mustard cork rings are cheaper, and are cut so that the holes run at right angles to the handle or ring hole.

The disadvantage of the mustard cork rings is that, in turning down or rounding a handle, often a large hole or pit is uncovered; the only recourse is to fill the hole with a combination of cork dust and glue. Many lower priced rods have mustard cork ring handles; higher priced rods almost always have specie cork handles.

Cork rings come in several different diameters and a number of different size predrilled holes, but all are ½ inch in actual thickness.

Sizes include 1⅛-, 1½-, and 2-inch outside diameters. The large 2-inch rings (these have a 1-inch diameter hole) are used solely for large saltwater rod handles and foregrips.

Inside diameters of the 1⅛-inch and 1½-inch rings range from 0.345 to 0.750; prices vary depending upon size. Cork rings are sold in lots of 14 (enough for a 7-inch fly rod handle), 24 (enough for a 12-inch spinning rod handle), or in bags of 100.

If you're only building one rod, buy just enough cork rings for that one rod; make sure the inside diameter of the rings fits the rod butt. Otherwise, buy 100 at a time, those with the smallest inside diameter hole; that way, the cork will fit the smallest rod, and can be reamed out to fit larger rods as needed. If the hole is too large for the blank, it is almost impossible to use enough filler or glue and/or thread to fit the handle properly in place, but slight differences in the rod and cork ring diameter can be adjusted, as I'll explain later.

Prices for specie cork are $0.75 to $1.50 per 14, $1.50 to $2.50 per 24, $5.00 to $9.00 per 100. The large (2-inch) rings are about $15.00 per 100.

In addition to the cork rings used in building up fishing rod handles, preformed cork grips are available. Featherweight Products offers a complete line of grips in casting, fly, spinning, and saltwater sizes and shapes to fit any rod. Both fore and butt grips are available for spinning tackle. They are predrilled, some with tapered holes, and are glued on to the rod blank as one unit. Prices range from about $1.50 to $4.50.

Featherweight also makes grip components in a soft but firm Hypalon plastic. Four grip lengths are available in sizes from 4½ to 11¾ inches. All are ⅝-inch inside diameter, but, because they are elastic, will fit blanks to 1-inch diameter. Prices range from about $2 to less than $5, depending upon length.

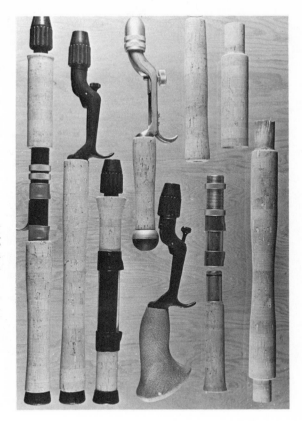

Examples of casting rod handles. Left to right: popping rod, long-handled steelhead handle, general purpose spinning, conventional casting, and pistol grip casting. To the right are preformed cork grips and a fly rod-extension butt reel seat.

HANDLES

Assembled handles are an obvious necessity but the ways in which they are incorporated into the rod vary with the type of tackle.

Casting and Spin-Casting Handles. Usually referred to as an offset handle, these incorporate the reel seat, as well as the chuck into which the rod blank butt ferrule is fitted.

The basic part of the handle-reel seat is metal, with cork rings or composition cork glued onto the metal rod at the rear of the reel seat. A butt cap or rubber button at the end of the handle protects the cork handle end from damage.

Cork has proved to be the most comfortable and lightest material to use in making handles for most fishing rods. Only recently has it been threatened by some of the newer plastics.

Casting-rod handles come in different lengths, with those of 5½, 9, and 12 inches (the latter used mostly for West Coast salmon fishing) standard. They also come with, or without, cork foregrips placed between the reel seat and the ferrule chuck.

The chuck at the fore end of the casting rod handle is similar to that used in a drill. A collar is turned to tighten the chuck jaws on the male butt ferrule of the casting rod; most collets fit ferrules of from $^{18}/_{64}$ to $^{28}/_{64}$ inch. Because of the possibility of twisting of the rod blank in the handle chuck,

Fenwick introduced a Vee ferrule casting handle incorporating a tapered, keyed butt ferrule that fits into a special handle chuck. The advantages are that it is self-aligning, does not rattle, and is positive locking. They are available for about $5, with ferrules in eight sizes from 0.380 to 0.640 inches costing about $1 each.

Some handles, such as some Champion casting handles by Featherweight, have adjustable handle positioning, or at least adjustable trigger positions. Prices range from $3 for a simple nonadjustable handle up to $6 for an adjustable handle; all handles are complete as furnished and have only to be fitted to the rod butt ferrule to be made ready for fishing.

Recently some of the new plastics have replaced the cork grip on some casting handles. The so-called "pistol," "Bass," or "comfort" handles, now used widely by bass anglers, are made of both hard plastic and several types of soft plastic.

Boat Rod Handles. These are long handles which incorporate a ferrule as part of the reel seat. Boat handles are used on conventional (revolving-spool tackle) rods used in party-boat fishing, small-boat bottom fishing, pier fishing, and some heavy inland fishing. Usually made of wood, they average 16 to 20 inches long. A rubber or metal button at the base of the wood handle protects against splits and is more comfortable when you are fighting a fish and the rod is pressed into a rod belt.

The wood handle varies in shape, but is usually made of tapered hickory, over which a reel seat is glued at the fore end. The upper part of the reel seat is hollow, to accommodate the male part of the rod ferrule, to which is also attached a foregrip of wood or cork.

Standard ferrule sizes on the boat rods include inside diameters of 0.624 to 0.875 and fit male ferrules of the same dimensions.

The hooded reel seat holds the reel foot in place and often has two locking knurled rings. Some reel seats have the ferrules "keyed." A bar or ridge at the bottom of the female ferrule lines up with a slot on the male ferrule to prevent twisting of the rod, and to provide perfect alignment of the reel with the guides. Many also have a knurled locking ring at the outside upper end of the reel-seat ferrule, which engages threads at the base of the male ferrule attached to the rod blank. Prices for boat rod handles and 30-inch-long surf-rod handles vary from $5 to $12.

Trolling Big Game Handles. Trolling and big-game rod handles are very similar to boat handles. They are usually heavier, and have stronger components, including a double slotted ball or tapered gimbal butt cap designed to fit into a socket and bar on a fighting chair. Many big game rods are today equipped with aluminum handles, or fiberglass handles such as those available from Fenwick. Prices are high, about $40 to $80 for the handle with standard fittings; they come in several sizes to match IGFA class rods.

BUTT CAPS

Butt caps are fitted onto all rods. They are designed to protect the rod butt, or in the case of trolling rods that are fitted with a gimbal rod holder, for playing a fish. No rod butts are used on fly rods, but only because the reel seat at the butt of the rod serves the same purpose.

Polyethylene butt caps, in a variety of colors and several sizes, look very much like the plastic caps for chair legs, but are designed to fit on the cork rings at the butt of a rod. About ½ inch high and with an inside diameter of $15\frac{5}{16}$ inch, they sell for 10 to 20 cents each. If they are not available, good substitutes that come in sizes from ½ to 1 inch are the plastic chair leg tips sold in hardware stores.

Many other types and styles of rubber butt caps are sold, ranging from $11\frac{1}{16}$ to $15\frac{5}{16}$ inch inside diameter and from ½ to 1½ inches in length. Prices are nominal, about 25 cents each.

Butt caps like these serve well on spinning rods, surf rods, casting rod handles, popping rods, and all other rods with a wood or cork butt. Some anglers do not like the weight or size of the plastic and rubber butt caps on ultra-light spinning rods. In place of these, small lightweight metal butt plates are available, to be fastened with glue and a screw.

Gimbals are specialized butt caps for saltwater rods. They are used only on big-game tackle where the fish is fought from a chair or from a gimbal rod belt. Gimbals—sometimes called "knocks"—are longer rod butts with a slot or sometimes two slots forming an X cut into the bottom. The slot fits onto a bar at the bottom of a socket in the rod belt or fighting chair. Their purpose is to keep the rod from twisting with the strain of fighting the fish. They come in chrome-plated brass and nylon; prices range from $1 to $4 each.

WINDING CHECKS AND ROD HOSELS

Winding checks and rod hosels are used at the forward end of rod grips, for a finished appearance between the grip and the rod blank. Winding checks are slightly dished round discs, with a hole in the center. Winding checks with a ¾-inch outside diameter are available with center holes ranging from $18\frac{8}{64}$ to $39\frac{9}{64}$ inch to fit rod blanks in these sizes. Winding checks with an outside diameter of 0.922 are available with inner-hole diameters of $40\frac{0}{64}$ to $49\frac{9}{64}$ inch. Black, gold, and brown are available; prices are about 20 cents each.

Rod hosels are usually made of plastic and serve the same purpose as a winding check. They come in different shapes, however, and are usually used on larger saltwater trolling and boat surf rods, and other similar rods. They come in a variety of colors and sell for about 25 cents each. Inside-hole diameters range from 0.484 to 0.783. Similar to the rod hosels are deep-draw winding checks that can be used on both wood and cork handles. They come in inside diameters of 0.410 to 0.687 and cost about 20 cents each.

MISCELLANEOUS MATERIALS

Thread is needed both for wrapping the guides in place and for the trim windings that go at the tip tops, ferrules, and in front of the handle. Both silk and nylon rod-winding threads are available; the nylon is more popular.

The advantage of silk is that it does not stretch, and so will not come loose even in time. Its disadvantages are that it can rot and break down quicker than nylon thread. The stretch factor of nylon today is less than it once was, and some stretch can even be an advantage, if even tension is maintained when the guides are wrapped; in fact, tension *must* be maintained to get a good wrap. Nylon thread comes in several sizes, ranging from a thin 2/0 through A, D, E, EE, and FF, the heaviest. (Lighter threads, 3/0 through 8/0, are available, but these are used only for fly-tying.)

Recommended Thread Size for Rods.

2/0 • light and medium fly rods, ultra-light spinning rods
 A • heavy fly rods, casting and spin-casting rods, light- and medium-action spinning rods
 D • freshwater spinning rods, heavy casting rods
 E • heavy freshwater and light to medium saltwater rods
EE • surf rods, boat rods, trolling rods, and light-tackle big-game rods
FF • heaviest big-game rods

All the sizes given above come in a variety of solid colors. Gudebrod, a major manufacturer of fly-tying and rod-winding threads, supplies them in black, white, purple, goldenrod, emerald, beige, azure blue, medium brown, dark scarlet, chartreuse, gray, burnt orange, king's blue, yellow, and maroon.

In addition, Gudebrod has a "space dye" thread, with two contrasting colors in size E only. The predominant color (the first named) extends approximately 28 inches, alternating with 16 inches of the second color. Colors include black/green, green/red, black/yellow, red/white, blue/gold, green/white, black/red, blue/white, black/orange, red/yellow, black/white, and blue/red. Two-tone colors in black/yellow, black/white, and black/orange are also available in sizes A and E. The very short lengths of the alternating colors give a mottled effect. A variegated, five-color thread is available for a rainbow effect; it has 7-inch lengths of each color.

Standard nylon or silk thread requires color preservative to be added before the protective rod varnish. Failure to add two coats of color preservative before the varnish will result in the light-color threads becoming practically transparent (or completely transparent in the case of white) and will turn all other threads very dark. As an option, Gudebrod sells all their size A thread in an "N.C.P." (No Color Preservative) nylon, which requires no color preservative. Varnish can be applied directly over these windings. The thread comes in 1-, 4-, and 8-ounce spools only and must be marked N.C.P. Prices are the same as for regular thread. Prices vary from $0.25 to $0.35 per 50-yard spool, depending upon colors and size. One-ounce spools, the largest a home tackle-builder will ever need, retail from about $1.75 to $2.75, depending on the thread type.

Gudebrod also has rod-wrapping kits with either size A or size E thread. Each kit includes six 50-yard spools of thread, one bottle each of color preservative and varnish, and an instruction booklet. The size A kit is under $3; the size E kit under $4.

Color preservative, as previously mentioned, is necessary to preserve the color of the thread windings. It is available from a number of sources, is usually sold in one-ounce bottles, and sells for less than $1 per bottle. Rod varnish, also in one-ounce bottles, sells for about the same price.

In addition to the standard color preservative–rod varnish finish on rod guides, there are at this writing just appearing some new finishing materials for rod wrappings. Epoxy finish material has just become available from Feather-weight and Gene Bullard Custom Rods. The advantages cited for these new rod wrap finishes include a harder tougher finish, single or at the most two-coat finishing, and application with brush or finger without leaving air bubbles, brush strokes, or finger prints.

Ferrule cement is used not only for seating ferrules, but also for cementing the tip tops to the rod. It comes in stick form and must be melted over a flame. The advantage of ferrule cement is that the ferrule or tip top can always be heated and removed if replacement is necessary, which is not possible using waterproof or epoxy cements. Sticks of ferrule cement sell for about 50 cents each. Various other glues are necessary to cement the component parts of trolling rod handles, add cork rings to the blank when building up a rod grip, and glue winding checks, rod hosels, and butt caps in place. I prefer waterproof cements such as Duco, Seal-All, Ambroid, and Pliobond. They come in small tubes, and are inexpensive and readily available at hardware stores, hobby shops, and even drugstores.

SPINE OF A ROD

Glass rod blanks do not have exactly the same wall thickness throughout their circumference, because of the way the rods are built. They are made from glass cloth, wrapped around a steel mandrel, the size and shape of the cloth determining the stiffness and type of action. Because of this method of construction, all glass rods are stiffer in one plane than in any other. It is true that this line of stiffness, or "spine" of the rod, is markedly reduced compared to that of the early days of glass rod construction, but it is still an unavoidable quality of glass rod construction.

It is extremely important to determine the spine of the rod blank *before* beginning rod construction. It is in this plane (either on the same side or the opposite side of the stiffness or spine) that the guides must be placed. This is particularly important in a rod used for casting, since if the guides are not in line with the spine, the rod will cast "off" to one side. It is also important in a trolling or big game rod that the rod does not bend to one side while pumping a fish, and that the strongest side of the rod will be used in fighting the fish.

To find the spine of a rod, place the butt end on the floor and lean the tip section against a table. Roll the rod along the floor and table, bending it as you do so. As you roll the rod, you will feel a marked difference in its resistance at one point; this is the heaviest section of the rod, its spine. Mark this side of the rod and be sure to place the guides either on the *same side* as the spine *or directly* opposite it. On big game rods, or rods used primarily for trolling instead of casting, the guides should aways be placed on the side of the spine or stiffest resistance. Determining the spine *must* be done before the rod is wrapped or handles and reel seats placed on it.

FILING GUIDE FEET

Before guides are wrapped onto a rod, the guide feet must be filed. Guide feet, as manufactured, do not end in a smooth knife edge, but have a blunt edge. If they're used this way, the thread will not cover the edge of the foot and will create an unsightly gap in which the end of the metal guide foot shows through. This blunt edge also makes the guide harder to wrap, since it is difficult to begin the wrap over the guide foot, even though previous wraps are already on the rod blank.

In order to prevent this, each guide foot must be filed down to a knife edge. File each guide foot with a smooth clean file until it tapers to a knife edge. Thus size of the file will vary depending upon the size of the guide. A jeweler's file may be all that's needed for a fly-rod snake guide, while a coarser workshop file may be necessary to dress a big game guide.

WRAPPING GUIDES

The technique of wrapping guides or decorative windings on a rod is the same, whether it is on a big-game 130-pound-test International Game Fish Association class rod, or an ultra-light 6½ foot fly rod. Of course, the size of thread would vary (see the section dealing with construction of each type rod), but the basic technique is identical.

First, take out all the guides to be used (previously filed as outlined above) and arrange them according to size. Surf rods, casting rods, and short spinning rods have only a few guides; others, such as fly rods, have many. Before starting, tape the guides in place at what seems to be the best position for the type of rod you're building. (Masking tape is best, but friction or cellophane tape will do.) This placement will vary with the rod action; check with the guide-positioning charts in the Appendix to help in lining up guides for most rods. After taping the guides in place, run a line through the guides and flex the rod lightly (do not pull the guides loose), to be sure that the strain will be distributed evenly when you are casting and fighting a fish.

If necessary, reposition the guides, and remember that while too many guides can be placed on a rod, too few guides frequently cause more trouble. Too few guides will cause the line to slap against the rod blank during the casting and the strain to be unevenly distributed on the blank while you are fighting a fish. In the severe stress of fighting a fish with conventional tackle, too few guides will cause the line to rub against the side of the rod blank.

Once the guides are properly positioned, place the thread in the rod winder, or run it through the pages of an old book, catalog, or phone directory to create tension. Do not use a good book, since the thread will score and mar the pages. Tension can be increased by adding more books on top of the book through which the thread runs.

Regardless of the method used to wind the rod, it is important that the winding be identical on both sides of a guide. The wrapping length for each guide will vary depending upon the number and size of the guides on the rod. To ensure an equal wrap, measure from the center of the guide perhaps ¾ to 1

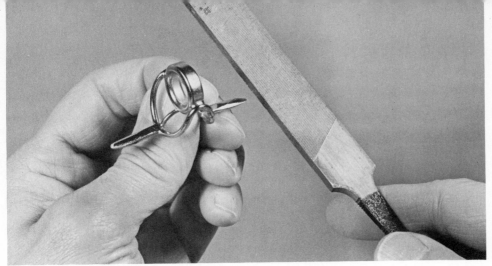

Steps in wrapping a guide: Guide feet should be filed down before wrapping.

Guide must be taped in place and tape wrapped around the rod to mark the position for the end of the wrappings.

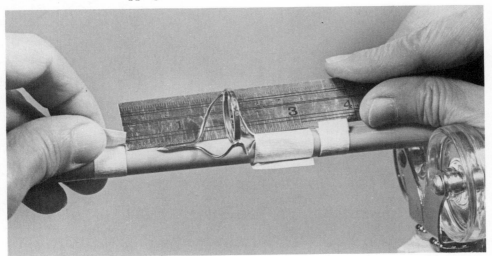

inch beyond the end of the guide foot. Mark this spot with a piece of masking tape or with a washable ink felt-tip marker. Start the winding on the rod blank, making sure that the thread being wrapped down is on top of the rod where it can be seen. Do not start the wrapping on the guide foot, because the thread will slip off at the end of the foot, leaving gaps in the winding.

Wrap the winding thread around the rod blank several times in a loose spiral, with the spiral pointed toward the guide foot. Then begin wrapping the thread around the rod blank, over the first spiral wrap; make sure that the beginning of this wrap is at the point marked by the tape or ink mark.

After marking several wraps, you may find it necessary to push the wraps together or to adjust them slightly so that they are not crooked, or at an angle. Wrap several more times, and after five to ten turns cut the excess from the end of the thread.

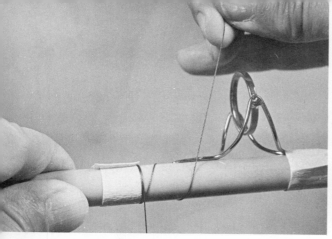

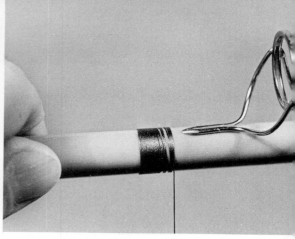

Begin the guide wrap by wrapping the thread loosely around the rod, wrapping over the loose wraps to hold the thread down.

Be careful not to make the mistake of leaving gaps between the thread windings as shown here.

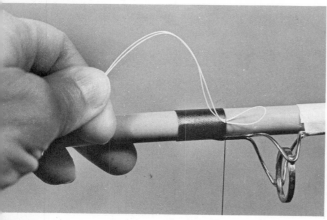

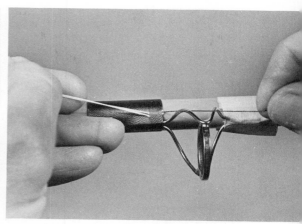

Six to seven turns from the end of the wrap, wrap over a loop of cord as shown. This allows the end of the thread to be pulled under the windings once completed.

The end of the thread is trimmed with a razor blade close to the windings.

The end of the thread is cut, slipped through the cord loop, and the cord loop pulled through.

An alternate method of finishing a winding is to cut the thread after it is slipped through the loop. The end of the thread must be shorter than the distance under the wraps of the loop.

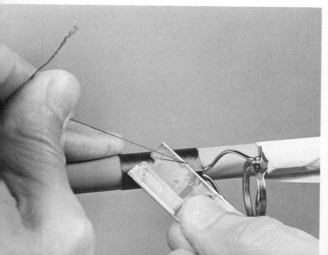

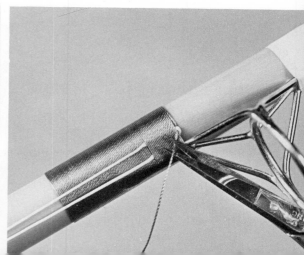

Continue the windings, going over the guide foot. When five to six windings away from the end of the wrap, take a loop of heavier thread, monofilament, or braided fishing line, and lay it alongside the guide foot, with the loop pointing toward what will be the end of the wrap.

Continue winding over this loop until the end of the wrap is reached as the guide foot separates into the two upright portions of the frame. Hold the thread so that the winding will not come undone; cut the winding thread (leaving plenty of excess), stick the end through the loop of thread or line, and pull the loop tight. The loop, and the end of the winding thread, will be pulled out through the winding, and the excess thread can be trimmed with a razor blade.

Sometimes this method will leave a slight gap in the wrapping as the thread end and loop are pulled through. Push the windings together with a thumbnail to close the gap. But there is a way, not generally known, to finish wraps that makes it unnecessary to trim the end and risk cutting the windings.

At the point where the loop is wrapped over the winding, cut the thread, again leaving excess, and stick the end through the loop. But instead of pulling the loop through quickly, pull it snug against the end of the windings to lock the thread in place.

Now cut the end of the thread so that the length of the cut end extending from the loop is shorter than the distance it will be pulled under the wrapping. Pull the loop through, and the end of the winding will be hidden under the wrap; no thread will protrude.

Each guide in turn is wrapped by the same procedure; make sure, of course, that each successive guide is in line with all the others previously wrapped. Decorative windings at the winding check, rod tip, and ferrules are wrapped using the same method.

TYPES OF GUIDE WRAPPING

There are a number of ways in which a rod can be wrapped. The one I have outlined is a simple single wrap, often used on fly rods, light spinning, and casting rods. There are other, more complex methods, as well as some that have specific advantages for certain tackle.

Double Wrapping. A rod can be double-wrapped, using the technique described above, except that when the guide frame is reached, the thread is wrapped back over previous windings to double-wrap the guide in place. This is usually only done part way back on the top of the other winding, since the thread might slip if it's wrapped down over the end of the guide foot. (Sometimes this can be done, since the first wrapping makes a slip at this point less likely.) The wrapping is finished exactly as the single wrapping above, using a loop of line to lock the thread end under the wrap.

Underwrapping. Rods can be under-wrapped; this is nothing more than wrapping on the rod blank at the point where the guide will be placed. Under-wrapping is usually completed in one wrapping, so that it will show under the

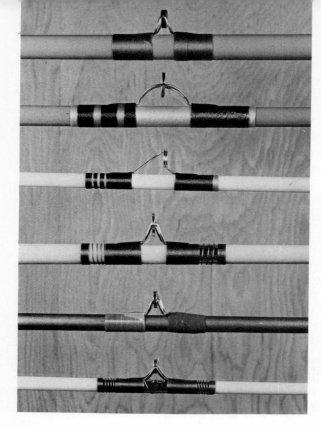

Examples of rod wrappings top to bottom, left to right: single wrap, double wrap, space dye over underwrap, two-tone thread over underwrap, space wrapping, single wrap with trim winding at end, spiral wrap, spiral wrap over mylar, monofilament wrap, tape wrap, and all-in-one guide wrap made by jumping thread from one side of the guide to the other.

center of the guide. It can also be completed in two separate sections, or it can be spiraled in the middle for decorative effect. The under-wrapping is almost always made a contrasting color to the guide wrapping, again for decorative effect.

Its main purpose is not decorative, however; the purpose of under-wrapping is to provide a cushion for the guide foot, so that it will be less likely to be forced into the rod blank, possibly cutting, crushing, or otherwise damaging it. This is not a problem with light freshwater tackle, and underwrapping is used mostly in heavy rods and saltwater tackle.

Spiral Wrapping. The rod guide wrapping can be spirally wrapped at the ends to give a decorative effect with the rod blank showing through. The technique is the same as for a single wrapped rod, except that, after starting the winding, deliberate but even gaps are left between the windings for several turns before the winding is closed prior to wrapping up on the guide foot.

Spiral Wrapping with Mylar Tape. This is nothing more than the above spiral wrap, with Mylar or other tape placed under the spiraled portion—again only for decoration. Measure the rod windings and measure for proper tape placement; wrap the tape on the rod blank and then wrap as above, allowing the Mylar to show through the spirals. Ironically, this flashy type of rod winding is seen mostly on cheaper commercially manufactured rods and is usually not found on expensive models.

On a good split-bamboo rod, it would be looked on about as favorably as salmon-fishing the Miramichi with a party boat cod-fishing rod.

Space Winding. A guide can be wrapped into place leaving several large gaps in the winding to allow the rod blank to show through for decorative effect. Of course, one thread will show on the rod as it runs from one winding to the next; usually, half of the thread wrap will show on the rod as the winding gap is made, and usually this is positioned opposite the guide so as to be as inconspicuous as possible.

Monofilament Fishing Line. The same stuff that goes on your reel can be used for thread in winding guides for a different look. With most colorless mono, the winding will virtually disappear once varnished. The advantages are that the mono is tough and fray-resistant. Do not use extremely stretchable nylon, however, as it does not permit enough tension to hold the guides in place. The same transparent look, if desired, can be duplicated with white thread, varnishing the winding without adding color preservative first. The thread becomes as clear as water.

Two-Tone Wrap. Using the same methods as for the single wrap, you can decorate windings by wrapping with a different color thread on the end of each guide wrapping. Of a contrasting color, these additional windings are not functional (since they are only wrapped on the rod, not the guide) but merely dress up the end of the wrap.

The same effect can be gained by using an under-wrap, allowing it to extend ⅛ to ¾ inch beyond the end of the over-wrap. Rod-winding thread comes in fifteen colors, making any color combination possible. Generally, two-tone rod-winding threads are used only on the top windings, not on the underwrap.

Tape. It is also possible to use tape to wrap guides in place, although this is usually recommended only as an emergency procedure for fishermen caught out in the boondocks with a damaged guide or fraying windings. Plastic tape comes in narrow, ¼-inch widths in a variety of colors. Stretching the plastic tape while wrapping helps hold the guide in place. While it is effective, it is not as attractive or permanent as the thread windings.

Stainless Steel Wire. Stainless steel wire wraps on commercially built rods gained some popularity several years ago, and were truthfully advertised as being permanent wrappings that never needed any maintenance. The only problem was that regular guides were used on the rods, rather than Carboloy, aluminum oxide, agate, or similar permanent nongrooving guides. The result was that even though the windings were permanent, the guides were not, and wore out before the wire. The major difficulty with wrapping with stainless steel wire is that it is springy and difficult to handle. Also, since it has no elasticity as thread does, too much pressure can crush or damage the rod, while too little will leave the guide wrapped loosely in place.

Personally, I do not care for it, and know few rod builders who do. If you do decide to use it, proceed carefully, and use permanent Carboloy, agate, or aluminum oxide guides that will not groove and do not have to be replaced unless broken. If possible, practice first on an old rod blank.

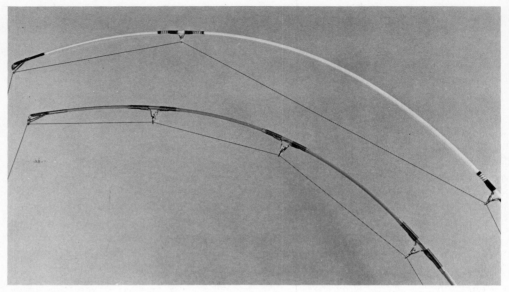

Proper alignment and placement of guides on a rod are extremely important for effective fishing. Top: a rod with improperly spaced guides; bottom: properly spaced guides.

Two-Tone Color Thread. All of the windings mentioned above can be done not only in the fifteen solid colors of winding thread available, but also in two-color "space dye" threads. The width of each color wrap on a rod blank depends upon the thickness of the blank.

Gudebrod also has two-tone colors, with short lengths of each color to give a striped effect. Variegated colors include 7 inches each of five colors to give a rainbow-hued rod wrapping. If "space dye" or two or variegated colors are used, they should be used in a simple wrap to avoid rod windings that are too complex or gaudy. The wrappings should complement the appointments of the rod to give an overall pleasing effect, not overpower the rod to the point where it looks like a carnival advertisement.

OTHER WRAPS AND DECORATIVE WINDINGS*

Decorative wrappings, done exactly as outlined previously for the single wrapping of guides, can be added to several other parts of the rod. Wrappings are added to the rod blank at the rod tip for decoration since only the rod blank is wrapped. The decorative winding is finished at the edge of the tip top, already cemented into place, and not wrapped up over the metal tube of the tip top. Similar decorative wraps go at both the male and female ferrules at the winding check or rod hosel just above the handle.

In addition, a decorative wrap can be added to the rod blank, 4 to 10 inches above the winding at the rod hosel or winding check. Usually this is done to give an attractive "framing" to any rod specifications, name and address, line

---

* Decorative windings are sometimes called "trim" windings, but because the word "trim" is a verb, adjective, and noun, its usage can cause confusion. As a result, it has not been used in this section.

weight (for fly rods), or similar data inked on the rod butt to add to the usefulness of the rod. (Any specifications like this are best added with a fine pen
and India ink, after the varnish is gently scraped or sanded from the rod blank.
Once it's dry, cover it with several coats of varnish.)

Diamond butt-winding the rod just above the handle has become increasing
popular in recent years. First associated with custom-built rods or expensive
rods from small factories, the butt wind is being seen today on more and more
commercially built rods and many rods made by do-it-yourselfers.

Essentially a spiral winding of different-color threads, the butt wind is a
diamond wrap placed just above the rod-winding check or hosel. One easy
way to add it is to use the Butt Wind manufactured by Gudebrod. Available
in six color combinations, it is a flat braided tape that gives a finished look in
one wrapping operation.

Tape the end of the Butt Wind to the rod, just above the winding check.
Wrap the Butt Wind spirally up the rod as many turns as desired, maintaining
tension. Reverse the direction of the wrap so that the now intersecting winding
crosses the rod on the top or bottom, i.e., directly in line with or opposite the
guides.

Continue wrapping the Butt Wind back toward the handle. Be sure that
the windings cross each other in a straight line; upon completing the wrapping,
tape the end of the Butt Wind in place and cut any excess.

Wrapping the butt wind material in place with tape.

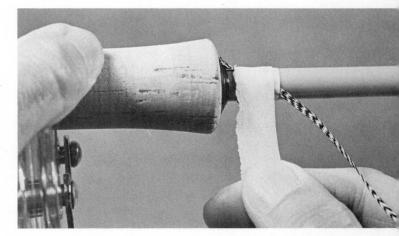

Steps in butt winding: spiraling the butt wind thread up
and back on the rod.

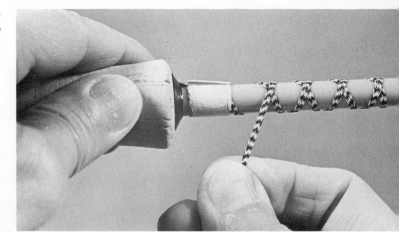

Now start the regular decorative winding of the rod blank that would normally be found in front of the winding check. Begin forward of the tape holding the Butt Wind in place; once the end of this trim winding is secure, remove the tape holding the Butt Wind. The decorative winding will now hold the Butt Wind in place. Finish the winding as outlined previously.

A second method, the traditional way of adding butt winding, utilizes the same method, only instead of the wide flat Butt Wind being wrapped all at once, it is wrapped one thread at a time. Usually the central thread is wound first, the other threads wrapped one at a time, each individually taped in place at the winding check with masking or friction tape. Depending upon the size of the rod, thread size, and decoration desired, seven to eleven individual wraps of thread are required.

Other decorative windings at the butt and elsewhere are also possible employing some of the winding methods mentioned previously. Double wraps,

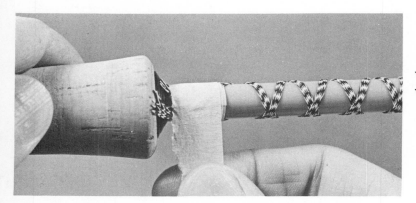

Wrapping the end of the butt wind down with tape.

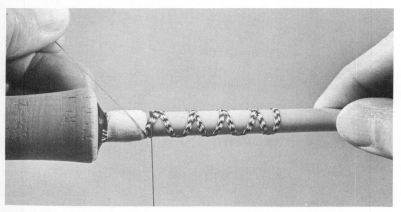

Beginning a regular rod wind over the butt wind and above the tape.

Once the rod winding is secure, the tape may be removed.

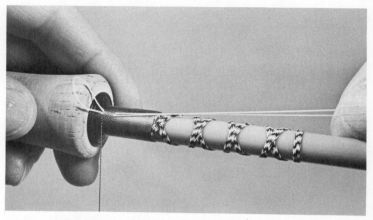

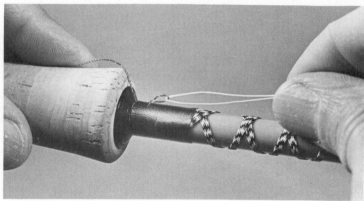

The rod winding is finished with a loop of cord the same as is done for wrapping a guide.

two-tone wraps, spiral wraps, spiral wraps over Mylar tape are all possible in endless variations, in decorative as well as guide windings.

VARNISHING GUIDE AND DECORATIVE WINDINGS

Once all the guides and decorative windings are in place, they must be covered with varnish to protect them from wear, the effects of sun and water, and fraying. Color preservative must be added first to prevent the thread colors from changing. Added directly to thread, varnish will turn dark threads almost black and turn light yellow and white almost transparent. (Protecting with color preservative can be avoided if Gudebrod "N.C.P." thread is used, and varnish can then be added directly without changing the thread color.)

The trick is to add enough color preservative or varnish to get enough on the wrappings to protect and color, without adding so much liquid that the varnish runs or dries in droplets. A half-dozen thin coats are better protection than two or three thick coats, so it is better to be skimpy whenever adding protective varnish.

Begin by adding the color preservative. It's thinner and has a tendency to

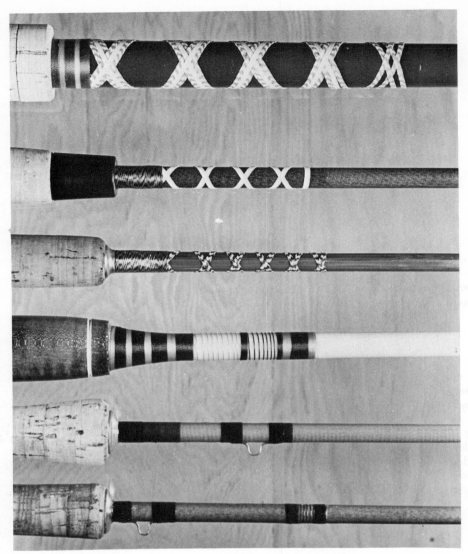

Examples of various types of butt and trim windings and decorations.

run, but it also is soaked up rapidly by the dry thread windings. There are several ways to add the color preservative. One way is to use a small brush, supporting the rod on the rod-wrapping supports, rotating the rod to cover all the wraps.

I usually use this method for the two to three coats of color preservative necessary to protect the wraps from changing color. Since the thread soaks up the preservative, there is little chance of getting bubbles in the finish. It is extremely important to allow each coat to dry (usually overnight) before adding the next coat.

After three coats of color preservative have been added and are dry, add the varnish. Three coats of varnish are sometimes enough, although more coats will not hurt; on the contrary, they will protect better, give a more glossy finish, and look more professional.

I prefer to add varnish with my finger. If you use a brush, there is always a chance that the strokes of the brush will leave a bubble. There is also a chance (especially when using cheap brushes) that one or more hairs will come out of the brush and become embedded in the finish. If you use a finger, just lightly touched in the varnish, there is no danger of this happening. Each coat of varnish should be allowed to dry before the next is added.

Whether you use color preservative or varnish, it is important to coat only the winding, being careful not to get any color preservative or varnish on the rod blank or guide. It won't hurt the blank or guide, but it won't look professional either. I make one exception to this rule: I think that it's important to get varnish well worked in around the foot of the guide at the top, where the windings wrap up over the guide foot. Windings do not last forever, and the better the job done here initially, the easier it is to touch them up each year with another coat or two of varnish. If an adequate job is not done in the beginning, the windings will quickly become frayed and broken, and require a complete rewrapping each year or even sooner.

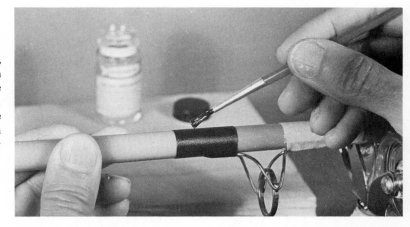

After windings are finished, they should be singed with an alcohol flame to remove any fuzz from the thread. Color preservative can be added to the wrappings with a brush or the end of your finger.

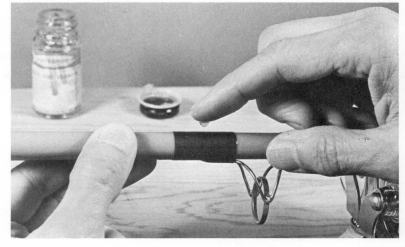

After two coats of color preservative, several coats of rod varnish should be added with the tip of your finger.

Sometimes in refinishing a rod, or in varnishing a bamboo blank before guides are added, it's necessary to coat the entire rod blank with several coats of varnish. An easy way to do this is to soak a nylon stocking in a little varnish and wipe it quickly up and down the rod blank. This method gives the entire rod a smooth even coat, something impossible to do with a finger or brush. For all varnishing operations, use a good quality rod varnish.

SEATING METAL FERRULES

While many rod blanks come with metal ferrules already fitted, some do not. Unless you're making glass-to-glass ferrules (which will be discussed later) metal ferrules are a must for multiple-section rods. In some cases, mail-order houses will match the ferrules of your choice to the rod; otherwise, it's best to match ferrules to the rod blank at a local sporting-goods store to be sure of a proper fit. If this is impossible, use the ferrule size chart in the Appendix.

Ideally, the male and female ferrules should fit securely on the rod sections. The female part goes on the butt section; the male on the tip section of a two-piece rod; additional ferrules are arranged the same way on multiple-section rods.

If the ferrules are a little tight on the rod, it is possible to sand the glass rod lightly (or to sand the corners on a bamboo rod) to fit the rod to the ferrule. Do *not* do this unless the ferrule will partially fit on the rod; it is usually necessary only on the butt section of the rod because of the rod taper; if there is any question, try the next larger ferrule set.

The male ferrule should be seated all the way over the butt of the tip section; check it by fitting the ferrule on the rod, marking the rod at this point, removing the ferrule, and checking the depth of seating against the outside of the rod.

Some female ferrules have a "stop" dividing the ferrule in half. This prevents the ferrule from being slipped too far onto the butt section of the rod and also keeps water, dust, and dirt out of the hollow rod section. If there is no stop, a hollow rod may be sealed with a small rubber or cork stopper, cutting the stopper flush with the end of the rod blank. This must be done before the ferrule is installed.

There is still the problem of fitting the female ferrule to the rod while avoiding seating it too deep or too shallow. One solution is to fit the female ferrule onto the male ferrule, then fit the female ferrule onto the rod section until the rod hits the end of the male ferrule. Raise the female ferrule approximately ⅛ inch and mark the rod; separate the parts and prepare to seat the ferrules. The ⅛-inch gap will assure that the male ferrule will not "bottom" before being seated firmly.

To seat the female ferrule, take a stick of ferrule cement, melt the end of it with a match, and smear the cement liberally on the part of the rod to be covered by the ferrule. Often, as this is done, the ferrule cement will start to cool and harden so that an even distribution of the ferrule cement is not possible. The solution is to remelt the ferrule cement stick, spreading the cement until the rod end is completely covered.

Seating ferrules: A loose ferrule can be tightened on the rod by adding several threads between the rod and the ferrule.

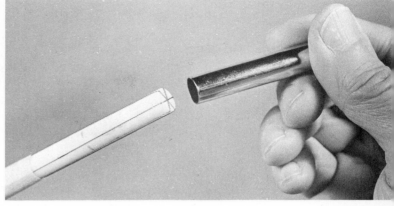

Once the ferrule cement is added to the rod, the ferrule can be slipped on.

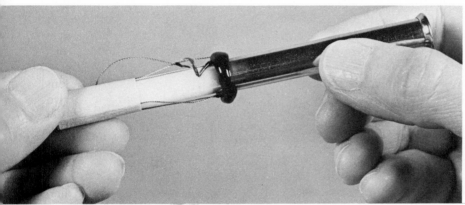

Now remelt the ferrule cement on the rod end, carefully turning and twirling the rod to prevent hot spots; glass rods will burn and can be damaged by excessive heat. The goal is to remelt all the cement, all the way around the rod. As soon as the cement is liquid, quickly push the female ferrule onto the rod end, all the way to the measured mark. If the cement has flowed over the measured mark on the rod, as often happens, check the seating of the ferrule with a measured stick (the length of the seated male ferrule plus ⅛ inch) by measuring the inside depth of the female ferrule from the ferrule opening to the rod section. This must be done immediately, before the ferrule cement solidifies; if the cement does solidify before the ferrule is properly positioned, heat the ferrule, revolving it to remelt all the cement. Once liquid, quickly adjust the ferrule to its proper position. The same method is used to remove a ferrule that must be replaced.

The male ferrule is easier to seat, since the only requirement is that the rod section fit all the way to the end of the ferrule. The same method of placing the ferrule cement, melting the cement, and placing the ferrule is employed.

An alternative method, and one preferred by some rod builders, is heating the ferrules, instead of the cement. This way the ferrule is filled with the liquid cement by touching the heated ferrule to the cement stick. The male or female ferrule can be partially filled with the heated liquid cement and the ferrule then carefully seated at the end of the rod.

Proponents of this method argue that the heated ferrule will retain heat

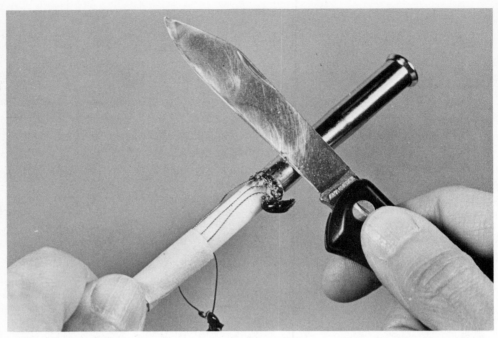

Allow excess ferrule cement to cool thoroughly and then crack it off with a blunt object. Threads are cut, and then a decorative wrap placed over the ferrule.

longer than the cement smeared on the rod, allowing greater time for seating the ferrule properly and assuring complete contact between the rod and the metal ferrule. Naturally, the heated ferrule cannot be held by hand and must be held on the end of a dowel (that fits the female ferrule), or in the case of the male ferrule, with pliers, the jaws wrapped with rags or masking tape, to prevent scarring the ferrule finish. Do not try to remove any excess cement right away; it will still be soft and will only smear over the rest of the rod. Wait until it is completely hardened and at room temperature (or lower, if possible), then strike it with a blunt edge such as the back of a knife, and the cement will chip off cleanly. This same technique is used to mount the tip top on a rod.

In case the ferrules are slightly large for the rod, some corrections will be necessary. A ferrule with any amount of play will become a loose ferrule at a later date. To avoid this, place several lengths of winding thread over the end of the rod section so that the strands lie parallel around the perimeter of the rod end. Two, three, or four lengths of thread can be used to provide four, six, or eight threads around the perimeter.

These threads fill the space between the rod and the ferrule and provide for a tight fit. Test first to be sure that the threads do give a tight fit. Hold the threads in place with masking, adhesive, friction, or cellophane tape and place the ferrule on as previously described. If the addition of thread does not give a tight fit, the ferrules are too loose for that rod, and a size smaller should be substituted.

Once the ferrules are seated, put the rod sections together, and sight down the rod blank. Ideally, the rod should be completely straight, allowing of course for the gravity pull on the end of the rod. Sometimes, however, this is not the case; there may be a "dog leg" in the rod at the ferrule. Often this can be cured by loosening the ferrules slightly, twisting the rod, and resighting until the rod

Ferrule cement is heated and smeared on the end of the rod to seat the tip top.

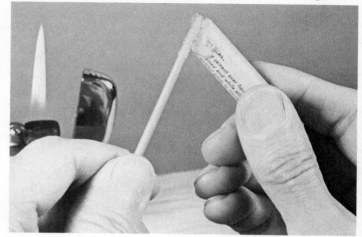

The tip top is then slid into place on the rod.

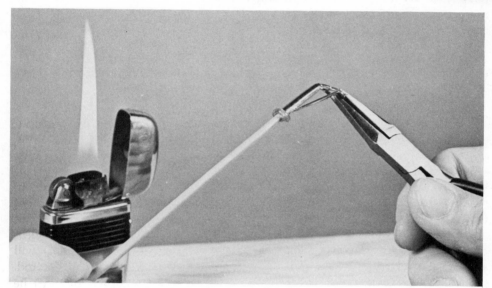

is properly lined up. Put a tiny scratch mark or a tiny dent made with a prick punch at the point on both the male and female ferrules to align the rod sections. That way, as the rod is worked on, it can be assembled and broken down as desired, still keeping the proper alignment for guide placement and subsequent fishing. Later on, these tiny marks can be replaced with small dots of paint, touched to the ferrules with the head of a pin.

In cases where the rod cannot be properly lined up even when the ferrules are completely rotated, it will be necessary to remove one or both ferrules and reseat them. This is rarely necessary and when required usually indicates some serious mistake in seating the ferrules to begin with or an attempt to use ferrules that are too large for the rod.

MAKING GLASS-TO-GLASS FERRULES

Though this is not yet widely known, it is possible for the home craftsman to make his own glass-to-glass ferrules. There are two methods of making glass-to-glass ferrules, and credit for both, at least as far as my having learned about them, must go to Poul Jorgensen, expert fly-tyer and tackle-builder of Towson, Maryland. Poul has been making his own rods for years, and for several of those years with glass-to-glass ferrules. Using the methods outlined below, he has tested and fished them extensively, without trouble.

One method involves inserting a plug cut from a rod blank into the butt section of the rod to form the male portion of the ferrule. The result is somewhat like the ferrules in the commercially available Scientific Anglers and Berkley rods. The second method involves sliding a short section of a hollow rod blank over the tip section so that it overlaps, making a ferrule not unlike the original Fenwick rod (although Fenwick rods incorporate the overlapping female portion of the tip section as an integral part of the blank, rather than a separate added piece, as in home-built rods). Note that *both* types of ferrules are made *before* rod handles, reel seats, or guides are added to the rod. Once a butt cap was added to the rod, it would be impossible to drop the male portion of the ferrule through the blank. It would be equally impossible to add a female ferrule over the tip if the guides were on.

A separate blank will be needed for the ferrule parts for building both types of ferrules on glass rods. The additional blank is cut up for ferrules and can be used for ferrules on up to a dozen different rods of various sizes, making the cost of each glass-to-glass ferrule less than the cost of a set of metal ferrules. Glass fly and spinning rod blanks are available at a number of tackle stores for less than $10, which brings the cost of the ferrule to less than $1 each. Obviously, for the angler only building one or two rods, the cost would be much higher and hardly worth it. Glass-to-glass ferrules are equally impractical for the rod builder making numerous rods all of the same size, since the diameters of the ferrules would all have to be the same size, impossible when using tapered rods.

Poul Jorgensen builds many rods at a time, and when he starts out on a rod-building binge, he buys an extra blank just for the ferrules. He also finds that he can sometimes use pieces trimmed from either the butt end or the tip end of a one-piece blank, since all rod blanks are trimmed to gain a lighter or heavier action for a given length. Poul usually buys one-piece blanks so that the trimming is possible, and so that the rod center can be center ferruled or off-center ferruled, as he chooses.

Of the two types of ferrules, that with the plug extending up from the butt section is the easiest to construct. First, cut the rod to length, trimming the butt or tip of the one-piece blank as needed. Then cut the rod where the ferrule is desired, usually in the center. Actually, to end up with the two rod sections of equal lengths, it is necessary to cut the butt section shorter by one-half the length of the plug that forms the male ferrule. Otherwise, while the original rod sections will be the same length, the male ferrule inserted in the butt section of the rod will add 2 inches in length to that section. Cutting the rod 1 inch off-center toward the butt section "justifies" for the added ferrule.

Glass-to-glass ferrules: The first step is to cut a spare rod blank into sections for the ferrules.

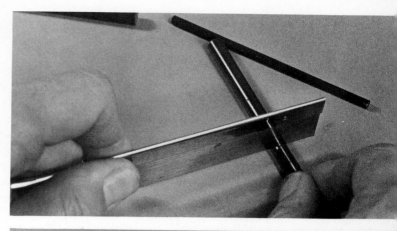

To make a butt ferrule, choose a section of glass rod blank that will fit snugly into the top of the rod butt section.

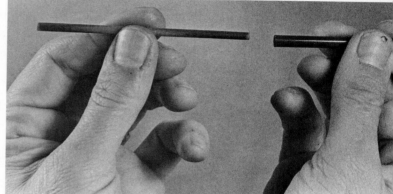

Smear glue on the lower part of the ferrule plug and slide into place.

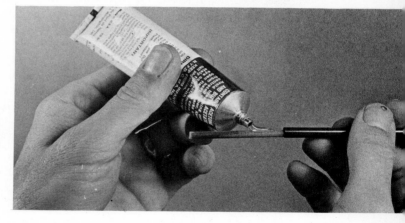

(For instance, mark the rod in the center, and make a cut with a fine-blade saw 1 inch lower on the rod from that mark. This will result in a 2-inch difference in the rod section lengths—the 2 inches taken up by the glass ferrule to be inserted into the butt section.)

Next, drop the glass rod to be used for the ferrule into the butt section, pull it snug, and cut it off 2 inches beyond the point where it extends from the butt section. Remove the rod from the butt section and cut the glass ferrule to a length of approximately 4 inches. This will leave 2 inches to be glued inside the rod and 2 inches extending from the butt section; the extended 2 inches fits into the tip section for joining the rod.

Using a small stick, pipe cleaner, or small cheap paintbrush, smear a good epoxy glue on the butt portion of the ferrule; drop the glass ferrule into place, pull tight, carefully clean any excess glue (though there should be none) from the exposed ferrule, and allow to cure overnight (if the ferrule does not drop all the way through the rod, shove it in place with another rod blank); the result is a permanently bonded ferrule. You may find that the tip section does not fit tightly onto the male glass ferrule before butting against the butt section of the glass rod. If this happens, cut a ⅛-inch section from the female ferrule part of the tip section. This will allow the two parts of the ferrule to come tight before the two ends of the rod meet. It also helps to add a little beeswax to the male ferrule. This helps to tighten a ferrule, while household paraffin helps to loosen ferrules—something to keep in mind in care and maintenance of rods with glass-to-glass fittings.

Building the second type of ferrule, that of an overlapping female section, is no more complicated, but does take more careful measurements. First, cut the one-piece rod blank into two parts. As in the first type of ferrule, measure to the center (if it is to be a center-ferruled rod), but here, cut the rod 1 inch *above* this mark on the tip, so that the tip section will be 2 inches shorter than the butt section. When the overlapping 2-inch section of the glass ferrule is added to the tip, the lengths of the two rod sections will be equal.

Now it is necessary to cut a section of ferrule that will fit tightly onto the lower part of the tip section, yet overlap by 2 inches to fit onto the butt section of the rod. Sometimes, with semitranslucent rod blanks, the rod blank to be used for the ferrule can be dropped over the tip section and measurements taken, holding the telescoping rods to a light to mark off that portion to cut for the ferrule. On many rods, however, this technique is impossible, since the rods are opaque.

In these cases the only possible method, as Poul explains, is to measure the diameter of the ferrule end of the tip section. Make a note of this measurement and then measure the wall thickness of the rod at this point. Double the wall thickness measurement and add it to the rod tip section diameter; set a pair of calipers to this total figure, and then locate and mark this diameter on the glass blank to be used for the ferrule. Cut it 3 inches to each side of this mark.

The reasoning behind this procedure is that the outside diameter of the tip section will equal the inside diameter of the glass ferrule. And since most rods of similar diameter have similar wall thicknesses, adding the wall thickness of the cut rod at this point will be approximately the same as the wall thickness of the ferrule section. Cutting 3 inches to either side of the measured mark gives some leeway in adjusting the ferrule if the measurement is slightly off.

Fit the 6-inch ferrule section onto the rod tip, measure and trim any excess so that the ferrule will be 4 inches in length. Leave 2 inches for the ferrule proper.

Smear epoxy glue on the ferrule end of the tip section, drop the ferrule in place, pull tight, and wipe the inner surface (use a pipe cleaner wrapped with a rag) of any traces of glue; allow to dry for twenty-four hours. As with the first type of ferrule, you may find that the butt and tip section of the rod meet before the ferrule is sufficiently tight on the butt section, and the solution is

Once the ferrule plug is pulled tight and cured over night, the ferrule is complete and ready to use.

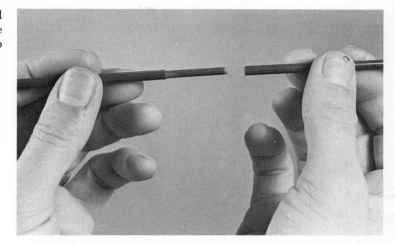

Making a female ferrule on the tip section of the rod is more difficult. The ferrule section must be measured by adding the outside diameter of the lower part of the tip section of the rod, together with the wall thickness of the glass blank.

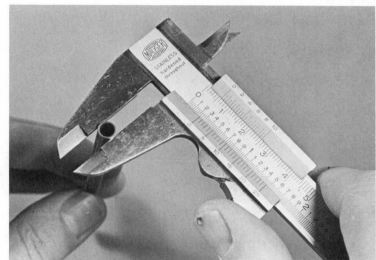

Glass-to-glass ferrules: the glass ferrule is slipped over the rod.

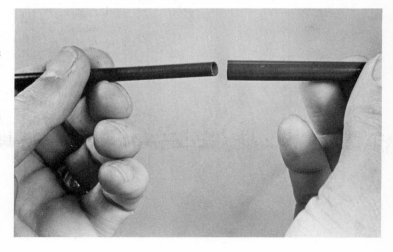

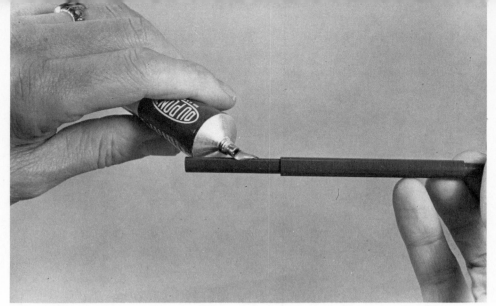

Glass-to-glass ferrules: glue is smeared on the lower part of the tip section and the glass ferrule pulled snugly into place.

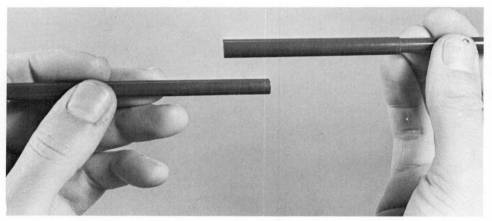

A cured and finished female glass ferrule that will fit snugly on the butt section of the rod.

Finished ferrules can be disguised by positioning a guide over them as shown here.

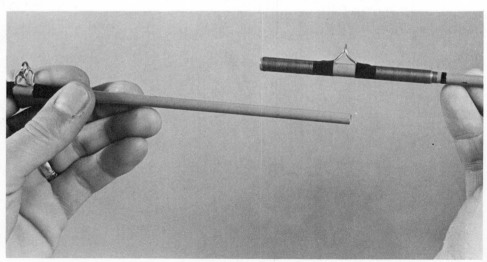

the same as for the first type of ferrule. Cut ⅛ inch from the butt section to leave a gap, and/or use a little beeswax to tighten the ferrule.

Both types of ferrules should be wrapped with thread windings when finished to complement or match those on the rest of the rod and guides. In addition, the thread winding gives strength to the joint.

GLUING CORK HANDLES

Cork handles on rods are built up, ring-by-ring, adding the ½-inch-thick cork rings to the rod blank. This is one of the first steps in building any rod, and it must be done before guides are added to the butt section. Because of the rod taper, the cork rings are slipped over the ferrule end of the butt section.

Essentially, the process is one of reaming out the hole in the cork ring to the diameter of the rod blank. This will vary, depending upon whether the ring will fit at the lower or upper part of the handle; so it's best to buy cork rings with the smallest diameter holes and ream them out as needed for the rod or rods.

Cork rings have a tendency to crack if they aren't reamed out enough, although the fit should be a tight one. One way both to get a tight fit *and* prevent any possibility of cracking, is to soak the rings in hot water until they are soft. Dry them (they will still remain soft) and, before gluing them to the handle, take each ring and ream it out to the proper size. Since the hole size will be slightly different in each ring, be sure to keep them in order once they are removed from the rod for gluing.

Do not use epoxy cement for gluing the cork rings. Epoxy glue makes too solid a joint to permit the cork rings to be removed for repairs. An all-purpose waterproof cement—such as Duco, Seal-All, Ambroid, or Pliobond—is better. All of these glues hold well, yet are easy to work with if repairs must be made.

Cork rings are glued individually onto the rod blanks.

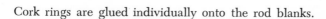

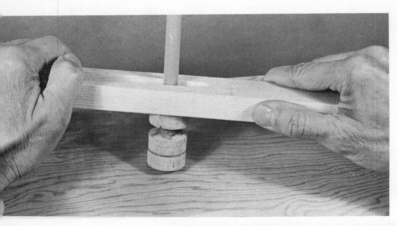

A special tool like this can be used to firmly seat each cork ring.

Tool made from strip of lumber to push cork rings closely together when rod handle is being glued. Note different-size slots for different-diameter rods.

Working with one cork ring at a time, smear a light, even coating of glue on the rod butt and quickly slip the cork ring onto the rod blank. Rotate it slightly when it is in position at the end of the blank to assure even distribution of glue. Now smear a light coating of glue on the upper face of the cork ring and the rod blank just above it. Slide the next cork ring into place, rotating it to spread the glue for a good contact between the rod blank and the cork ring and the touching surfaces of both cork rings.

To aid in seating the cork rings, a "seating tool" can be used. This is nothing more than a 1-by-2-by-10-inch strip of wood with a slot cut into the center from the side or end. The slot must be larger than the diameter of the rod. In use, the tool is positioned behind cork rings as each is placed on the rod, to push each ring down firmly against the other rings.

In case one or more of the cork rings is reamed out too large, it will be necessary to wrap the rod blank at this point with thread or cord to build up the rod diameter for a firm fit. This is best done after all the corks are reamed, before any gluing is started. Use cord of sufficient thickness to fill up the gap between the cork ring and the rod blank.

Continue adding the cork rings one at a time. It will soon be obvious that

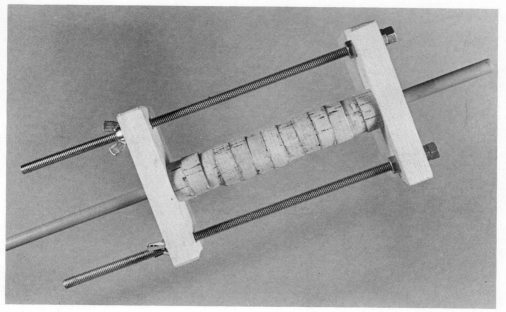

Once all the cork rings are in place, a special cork ring gluing clamp can be used while the glue dries.

the cork rings will not line up exactly; this is no cause for concern since they will be sanded down to finish the handle anyway. For the same reasons, any excess glue spilling onto the outer surface of the cork rings will be removed as the handle is reduced and shaped. Once all the rings are added for the handle, allow them to dry for twenty-four hours.

To assure that the cork rings are firmly seated against each other, a gluing clamp or vise can be used while the glue in the handle is drying. This clamp is nothing more than a specialized vise to clamp the cork rings while the glue is drying. This clamp is easily made from strips of wood, threaded rod, nuts, and wing nuts; directions are found in Chapter 13.

After the glue is dry, begin finishing the rod handles by removing any of the unwanted cork. This is best done in two stages: first, remove the top layer of the cork with a wood rasp or coarse file; then, sand down with successively finer grades of sandpaper to finish the grip. (One alternative not generally available to rod builders is to place the rod handle in a lathe, and turn to size and shape with coarse sandpaper, finishing with fine sandpaper.)

A good job can be done with the rasp and sandpaper, rotating the rod handle carefully to keep the grip round and centered on the rod blank. Before beginning to remove any cork, draw a handle design or carefully check the measurements on the handle of a favorite rod to make a template and adhere closely to it in finishing the grip. One of the most common mistakes made by beginners is to remove too much cork initially with the wood rasp or file. Cork is a soft, very porous material and it crumbles easily. Leave at least ⅛ inch excess cork on all sides of the rod handle. Then switch to coarse sandpaper,

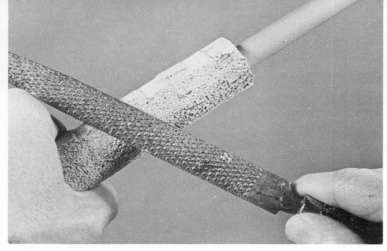

Once the glue is dry, the handle can be shaped with a wood rasp.

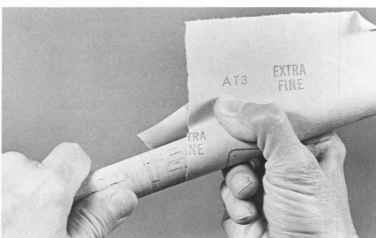

The handle is finished by sanding with successively finer grades of sandpaper.

working gradually finer grades of paper until the rod handle is finished. Once it is finished, it may be necessary to fill some pits in the cork with a mixture of cork dust and glue; save a little cork dust just for this possibility. If this is required, mix the glue and cork dust together, add to the pit or hole, allow to dry, and finish with sandpaper.

Obviously, it's only rarely that a cork handle is completed and finished in one step. With fly rods, the reel seat is added first to the rod blank. Since the rod blank is always smaller than the reel seat, some sort of bushing is necessary between the blank and the seat, which can be made from cork rings sanded down to fit.

Similarly, cork rings can be used as the bushing under the reel seat of a fly rod, spinning rod, popping rod, or surf rod. In the case of reel bands used on a spinning rod in place of the reel seat, the final two cork rings of the handles are left off until the glue dries. Then the handle is sanded to size and finished. The reel bands are slipped on and the final two cork rings glued in place and finished. Details of construction of specific rods are discussed later in step-by-step rod-building directions.

STEPS IN BUILDING BASIC TYPES OF RODS: SPINNING RODS

The parts needed for an average 6½-foot spinning rod with a fixed reel seat include the following: a 6½-foot two-piece rod blank, a set of ferrules (unless the rod comes ferruled), a set (usually five) of spinning guides, a spinning tip top to fit the rod, a hook holder (keeper rings), 24 cork rings (½-inch thick each) or assembled cork fore-and-aft grip along with a reel seat bushing, a spinning reel seat, a winding check to fit the rod blank in front of the grip, a butt cap for the butt of the grip, one spool of size A thread (or several spools if several colors are to be used in the decorative and guide windings), a stick of ferrule cement, and one bottle each of color preservative and rod varnish.

Begin by determining the "spine" of the rod, as previously described, and marking for guide placement. Seat the ferrules as previously outlined, unless, of course, the rod blank comes with ferrules intact. Next glue the cork rings on the butt section of the blank, following previous instructions.

Ten to fifteen cork rings are used in a rear grip since these vary in length between 5 and 7½ inches. If a bushing is used between the rod blank and the reel seat, add it next, using the same gluing methods as outlined previously for gluing the cork rings. If a bushing is not being used, add another eight, nine, or ten cork rings depending upon the reel seat length. (Reel seats come in 4-inch, 4½-inch, and 5-inch lengths for light spinning tackle).

Stop at this point and allow the glue to dry overnight. When the glue has cured, file and sand the aft cork grip to shape as previously outlined. (If the reel seat is added before filing the handle to shape, there is a danger of scarring the metal reel seat with a file, a rasp, or even sandpaper. Also, if a bushing is not used, it is necessary to allow the glue to dry so that the cork bushing rings can be sanded to fit the reel seat.)

At this point, spread glue on the bushing, slide the reel seat in place and twist it to assure good glue contact; align the reel seat hoods with the spine of the rod. Now add the rest of the rings to end up with a total handle length of 12 inches. (However, the handle length can be made shorter or longer as desired.) Allow to cure overnight.

Parts needed for a typical spinning rod: rod blank, reel seat, cork rings, rod butt cap, winding check, guides, and tip top.

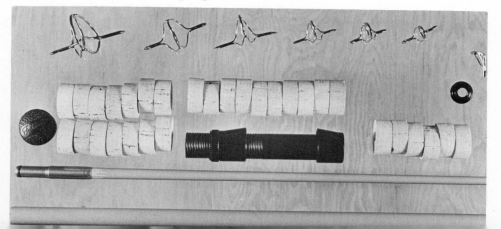

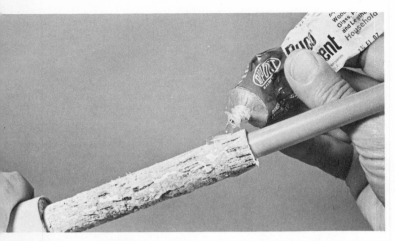

Cork rings can be used as a bushing under the reel seat. This is added as the handle is built, then filed down to fit the reel seat. It can be left rough for added tooth in gluing.

The reel seat is slipped over the bushing once it is saturated with glue.

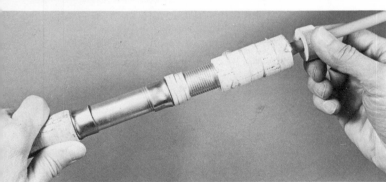

Additional cork rings are then added to the rod blank to shape the fore grip.

A view of a finished spinning rod handle with fixed reel seat.

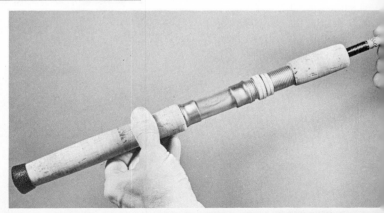

File and finish the fore grip on the handle. To keep from scarring the reel seat while doing this, cover the reel seat with an old rag secured with masking or friction tape. Glue the butt cap to the butt of the grip and glue the winding check in place in front of the grip.

Assuming that the rod has been previously checked and aligned as noted in the suggestions on seating ferrules, the rod should be perfectly straight.

Cement the tip top on the rod with ferrule cement (in line with the rod spine) using the same method previously described for seating ferrules. The use of the ferrule cement allows the tip top to be replaced easily if it becomes bent, broken, or grooved. Make sure that the tip top is lined up with the reel seat when the rod is assembled.

File the guide feet. Using measurements from the guide spacing chart in the Appendix, a similar good commercial rod, or the rod kit instructions, tape the guides in place. Some trial and error is necessary here to adjust the guides properly before starting to wrap them with thread. Run a line through the guides and flex the rod lightly (so as not to pull loose the taped guides) to check the guide placement.

Remove the tape from one of the guide feet and start winding, using the directions and one of the wraps previously described. Wrap each guide this way, checking the guide alignment frequently; add a keeper ring if desired. Finish with decorative windings at the winding check, both ferrules, and the tip top. Cover with color preservative and varnish as previously described and the rod is ready to use.

VARIATIONS OF SPINNING ROD CONSTRUCTION

Variation No. 1

Many spinning-tackle anglers prefer a cork grip with two light metal bands to hold the reel foot, instead of a fixed reel seat. The advantages are that the handle is more comfortable than the fixed reel seat that becomes cold in chilly weather, and the reel can be positioned anywhere on the handle. The disadvantages of the sliding ring arrangement are that the rings must be tightened several times a day to keep the reel from coming loose, and the reel has a tendency to rotate slightly on the handle.

To make this type of handle, glue all except two of the cork rings of the handle into place initially. For a 12-inch grip, this means that 22 rings are glued on at once. Then file the handle and sand it down (after curing), leaving a swelling at the butt end so that the metal reel bands will not slip off. Sand the handle so that the reel bands will fit on *snugly;* otherwise the reel will be loose on the handle.

When the handle is completely sanded and finished, slip the reel bands on the handle, glue two more cork rings in place, and allow to dry. Finish the two remaining cork rings. Leave these swollen too (as with the butt end) so that the reel bands will not come off the front; the same procedure is used in adding a sliding reel seat to a cork-handled spinning rod.

Variation No. 2

In the Santee-Cooper bass lakes of South Carolina the anglers use casting tackle almost exclusively for fishing among the stumps and flooded forests for largemouth. But several times during the year, they switch to spinning tackle to throw light spinners under the cypress trees. Almost to a man, they use short one-piece wood-handled spinning rods. They build their rods with very large guides to cope with the heavy 15- to 17-pound test spinning line needed to horse the bass out of the rough cover.

Most Santee-Cooper bass anglers build their own rods on a short ten-inch wood handle. Old broomsticks have been used for handles, although more elaborate handles are sometimes turned on lathes. To make a rod like this is simpler and quicker than making the cork-handled rod described above. First measure the diameter of the butt end of the rod blank; drill a 4-inch deep hole of this diameter into one end of the wood handle. Smear epoxy glue on the rod butt and in the hole and seat the butt section into the handle. Add a winding check if desired and wrap the guides in place.

No reel seat is needed on these rods; instead the reel foot is taped semi-permanently to the wood handle. For more comfort in fishing, some anglers, such as Joe Avin of Summerton, South Carolina, recess the handle so that the foot of the reel is flush with the outer diameter of the rod handle when taped in place. The rest of the rod is finished as above.

A variation of a spinning rod handle is this wood-laminated handle with the reel taped in place, used in Santee Cooper Lakes, South Carolina.

Another variation of a spinning rod handle is this cord-wrapped grip.

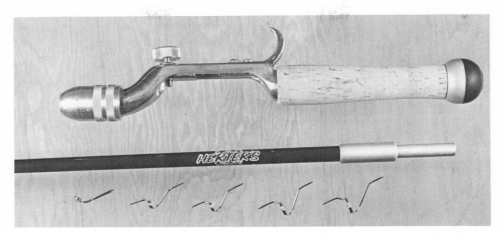

Parts for a typical casting rod: handle, blank, guides, and tip top.

STEPS IN BUILDING CASTING RODS

The components for building a standard 6-foot casting rod include the following: 5-foot 3-inch one-piece rod blank, offset casting rod handle, casting rod butt ferrule (unless the rod blank comes ferruled), a set (usually five) of casting guides, a casting tip top to fit the rod, a hook holder (keeper ring), one spool of size A thread, a stick of ferrule cement, and one bottle each of color preservative and rod varnish.

Casting rods are about the easiest and quickest rods to assemble, since the entire rod grip, reel seat, and chuck to hold the rod blank come completely assembled. If the rod is not ferruled, attach the butt ferrule, using the instructions for seating ferrules. Determine the spine of the rod and cement the tip top in place and in line with the spine. As previously detailed, use the ferrule cement for attaching the tip top.

File the guide feet and tape the guides in place in line with the tip top, using the guide spacing chart in the Appendix. Run a line through the guides, flex the rod slightly, check guide placement, and readjust if necessary; wrap the guides, checking frequently to be sure that they are in perfect alignment. Wrap a keeper ring next to the butt ferrule and finish with trim windings at the butt ferrule and at the tip top. Cover with color preservative and rod varnish as discussed previously, check the ferrule into the handle, and the rod is ready to use.

VARIATIONS OF CASTING RODS

Some anglers prefer a straight handle built on the rod blank to one of the many types of commercially available offset handles. This type of handle is frequently used on southern and Gulf coast popping rods for casting big plugs to big fish. A special type of reel seat with an index finger "trigger" is required, but otherwise the instructions for building this type of handle are the same as for building a standard spinning rod handle. See these instructions for details on adding and finishing the cork grips and adding the reel seat.

STEPS IN BUILDING FLY RODS

The parts needed for building a standard 8-foot fly rod include the following: a two-piece 8-foot fly-rod blank, a set of ferrules (unless the rod blank comes ferruled), a set of snake guides, a fly-rod tip top to fit the rod, a hook holder (keeper ring), 14 cork rings, a reel seat, a reel seat bushing (or another 7 to 9 cork rings, depending upon the length of the reel seat), a winding check, one spool of size 2/0 or A thread, a stick of ferrule cement, and one bottle each of color preservative and rod varnish.

Begin by seating the ferrules, as previously described, unless the rod blank comes with ferrules attached. Using waterproof cement, glue the reel seat bushing to the lower end of the rod butt section, cover the bushing with glue,

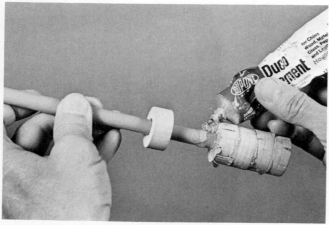

Cork rings added to the rod blank can serve as a bushing under the fly rod reel seat.

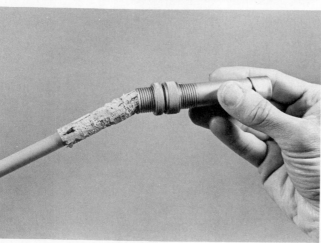

Add the fly rod reel seat.

The handle is then rasped and sanded to shape. Note that the reel seat has been taped to prevent any scratching.

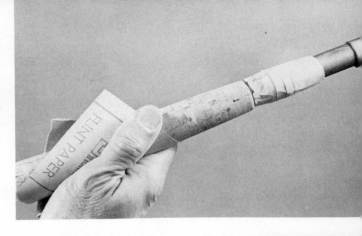

Finished fly rod handle.

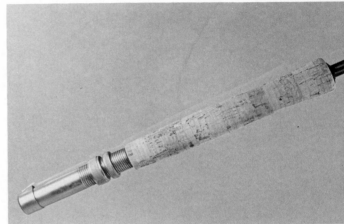

and place the reel seat over it. In case the reel seat has two open ends (the lower opening for the placement of an extension butt or rubber button), make sure that the fixed hood on the seat is at the butt end of the rod. If a bushing is not used or not available to fit the rod blank and reel seat, glue cork rings on the blank and allow to dry. File the cork rings down to size and glue the reel seat in place. (In place of bushings and cork rings, several wraps of masking tape can be used to fill the gap between the rod blank and the reel seat. Glue the reel seat to the built-up tape.)

Next glue on the 14 cork rings for the grip, and allow to dry overnight. Tape a rag over the reel seat to protect it and file and sand the handle to size and shape. (An alternative method is to add the reel seat bushing and cork rings first, sand the grip to shape, and then glue the reel seat in place). Glue the winding check to the front of the cork grip.

Assuming that the rod has been previously checked and aligned as noted in the suggestions for seating the ferrules, the rod should be perfectly straight. Cement the tip top on the rod using ferrule cement as previously described. Using the guide spacing chart in the Appendix, tape the guides in place, after first filing the guide feet. Run a line through the guides and flex the rod slightly (so as not to pull loose the guides) to check for proper guide placement; wrap each of the guides, checking alignment after each winding. Wrap the keeper ring above the cork grip, finish with trim windings at the winding check, at both ferrules and at the tip top. Cover with several thin coats of color preservative and varnish as previously described.

Examples of three types of extension butts: a short plastic extension butt, long bicycle grip extension butt, and cork ring extension butt also built on a dowel.

VARIATIONS OF FLY RODS

Most fly rods are standardized, but some variations are commonly made in the length and shape of the cork grip. Western anglers often prefer a longer straighter grip than those fishing eastern streams. In addition, some bass bug, salmon, and saltwater anglers like to use very light fly rod Aetna foulproof guides in place of the standard snake guides. These add weight to a rod and should be used only on very large rods. The argument for Aetna guides, although never confirmed, is that they will add casting distance by creating less line slap and guide friction than snake guides. Some other variations that can be included on any rod include:

Extension Butts: These are used only on very large saltwater and salmon fly rods to provide additional leverage while playing large fish. The extension butt is a removable 2- to 6-inch extension that is slipped into an open end reel seat of a fly rod while playing a fish; they are removed when casting.

Extension butts can be added in several ways. Featherweight Products makes a combination reel seat–extension butt. The extension butt uses an O ring fitting similar to that found on Featherweight ferrules, and fits the inside of the reel seat. The only difference in adding this reel seat to the rod blank and bushing is that the 1½-inch space must be left at the butt end of the reel seat to accommodate the extension butt.

Extension butts can also be built and added to any standard open-end reel seat. Many fly rod reel seats have a metal hood at the end, although some of the newer ones have two open ends, with a rubber button filling the butt end. Of course, lightweight spinning reel seats can also be used. They can be used with an extension butt, by using only half of the reel seat bushing and cementing only the forward part of the reel seat. Leave a space of about 1 to 1½ inches at the rear.

An extension butt to fit any of these types of fly rod reel seats can also be made from a large wood dowel or broom handle. The extension portion itself can be built up of reamed-out cork rings, glued in place as on a rod handle. After gluing on enough cork rings for a 2- to 6-inch extension butt, allow to

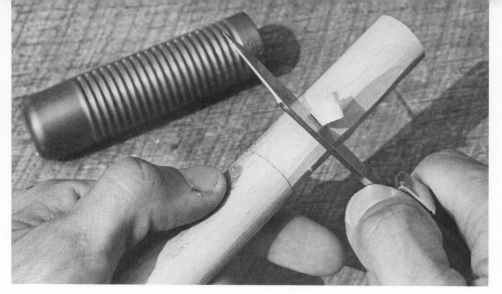

The dowel is whittled to fit in the end of the fly rod reel seat.

dry, and sand to shape. Glue on a butt cap and cut the remaining wood dowel to a length of 1½ inches. Carefully whittle and sand it to fit snugly into the reel seat. The result is an extension butt just as good as those commercially available.

For a simpler and just as efficient extension butt, a bicycle grip can be cut to the desired length and glued on the wood dowel.

NOTE: Anyone making extension butts to use in fly rod tournaments should carefully check the rules first. Some tournaments restrict the length of extension butts to only 2 or 3 inches.

It is also possible to make an extension butt similar to the built-in extension found on Pflueger saltwater fly rods. This built-in extension butt consists of a butt cap fitted to the end of a small rod that fits into the reel seat. When the rod is pulled out to its full extension, a spring-loaded catch locks the extension butt open. The spring lock is pushed in to slide the extension butt back into the reel seat.

Poul Jorgensen adapted this method to some of his own home-built saltwater fly rods, using the locking mechanism from a discarded umbrella for the extension butt. The small vane that extends from the center shaft of the umbrella to hold the umbrella ribs up and the umbrella open serves as the lock. The extension butt is made by utilizing this section of the umbrella, fitting the outer sleeve of the center shaft into the reel seat and adding a butt cap to the end of the rod. Poul makes his extension butts with a friction fit of the outer sleeve of the umbrella slide to fit into the reel seat. This way the entire extension butt arrangement can be removed if desired.

Skeletal Reel Seat: Skeletal reel seats are used on very lightweight fly rods, or on expensive fly rods for both appearance and weight. Skeletal reel seats come in different styles. The simplest is nothing more than two small metal bands over a cork seat. The two bands are slipped over the feet of the fly reel to hold it in place exactly as spinning reel bands on a cork-handled spinning rod hold spinning reels.

A removable collapsible extension butt built on an umbrella shaft by Poul Jorgensen.

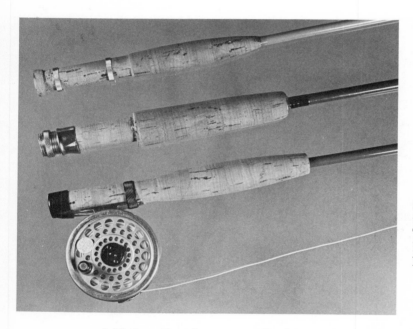

Several examples of skeletal reel seats on fly rod. Top: two bands; center: locking hood; bottom: hood and sliding band.

Add 6 or 7 cork rings to the butt end of the rod blank (enough for the reel seat). Add the rest of the cork rings for the handle, file and sand to shape and size. The cork grip will be the same as on any regular fly rod, but the cork rings forming the skeletal reel seat must be sanded to a ⅝- or ¾-inch diameter, depending upon the size ring used to hold the reel in place. Spinning rod rings (standard 1-inch inside diameter) are too large.

Unfortunately, most tackle suppliers do not carry small enough rings for skeletal reel seats, but I have successfully used large-sized "friendship rings," sold as jewelry in most stores. Add the rings, then glue one additional cork ring to the butt end, sanding it down to "button" shape to keep the rings from coming off.

A second way to make a skeletal reel seat is to use the metal butt cap, walnut dowel, and sliding ring supplied by Leonard Rod Company. The pre-drilled walnut dowel is glued to the rod blank, then one side is filed and sanded flat to hold the reel foot. Any varnish, polish, or finishing is best put on the dowel at this point, before the sliding ring and butt cap are added. Once it is polished, add the sliding ring, and glue and pin the butt cap in place.

A regular reel seat can also be cut apart to make a skeletal reel seat; by cutting out the middle section of a fly rod reel seat with a fine jeweler's saw, the hood, threads, and knurled rings can be used with cork, walnut, or other fine wood as a center spacer.

To make this type of reel seat, add the wood or cork rings to the rod blank. Cut the hood end and threads from a standard fly rod reel seat, filing any rough edges on the parts to be used. File and sand the cork rings or wood to a diameter equal to the outer diameter of the cut-apart reel seat. Then measure the length of the hood against the end of the wood or cork spacer, mark this length on the spacer, and sand it lightly to fit the inside hood. This keeps the cork or wood spacers flush with the base of the reel seat hood. Glue the hood in place. Measure the length of the feet of any reels to be used on the rod, and allow enough room to fit the foot into the hood and under the locking knurled rings. Mark where the threads are to be placed on the wood or cork spacer and sand this section down slightly to receive the threaded section. Slide the threads over the rod blank onto the spacer and glue in place; then the rest of the handle and rod can be completed as previously described.

The same arrangement can be used with the threads and hood reversed, with the hood hidden under the rear of the cork grip. An open end hood must be used or the metal plate sawed from the end of the standard hooded reel seat to do it. The parts are placed on in reverse order from that given above, and the rear cork ring of the grip enlarged to fit over and hide the metal hood.

STEPS IN BUILDING BOAT, TROLLING, AND BIG-GAME RODS

All of these are similar in their construction, varying in the size of fittings and style of guides and butts. Fighting rods, meant to be used in fishing chairs, have slotted gimbal butts where regular boat rods have metal, plastic, or rubber butt caps.

The parts needed for an average 7-foot boat rod will include the following: one piece 5½-foot boat rod blank, a set (four or five) of trolling guides, a trolling tip top to fit the rod, a wood rear handle, a wood fore handle, a combination reel seat and ferrule to fit the handle parts, a rubber butt cap, a winding check or rod hosel, one spool of size E thread, waterproof cement, a stick of ferrule cement, and one bottle each of color preservative and rod varnish.

Because trolling and boat rods consist of a handle assembly and the rod tip, the two parts can be worked on independently. I prefer to assemble the rod, slip the rod hosel on the blank, and tape the guides in place. (Use the guide placement charts in the Appendix). Test for action and reposition the guides if necessary. Then wrap the guides, checking for alignment. On big game rods, it is best to underwrap—see rod wrapping directions for details. Cement the tip top in place with ferrule cement.

The wood foregrip glued to the butt end of the rod blank before the

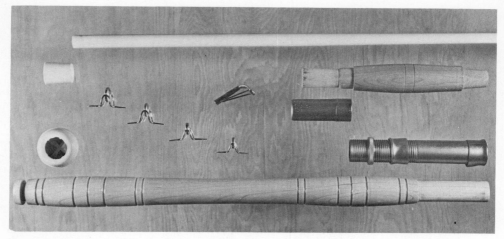

Parts needed for building a boat rod: blank, rod hosel, fore and rear grips, reel seat-ferrule, butt cap, guides, and tip top.

guides are wrapped will make the guide wrapping process more difficult. The extra weight on the end of the rod makes it difficult to wrap the guides unless a support is arranged to hold the butt end in line with the rest of the rod. Glue the rod blank into the wood foregrip, glue the rod hosel over the end of the foregrip. Check the fit of the wood foregrip into the male ferrule. If the fit is snug, glue in place. If the fit is too tight, sand down to a snug fit. If there is too much play between the ferrule and the wood grip, wrap the wood grip spirally with thread or cord until a tight fit is achieved. Soak the cord-wrapped foregrip with glue and fit into the ferrule.

Use the same procedure to glue the reel seat-ferrule over the end of the rear wood handle. Add the butt cap; rubber butt caps usually slip onto wood handles, plastic ones usually glue on, and metal butt caps are glued and pinned. Wrap decorative windings at the tip top and ahead of the rod hosel, add several coats of color preservative and rod varnish, and the rod is complete.

Rod blank being glued to wood fore grip.

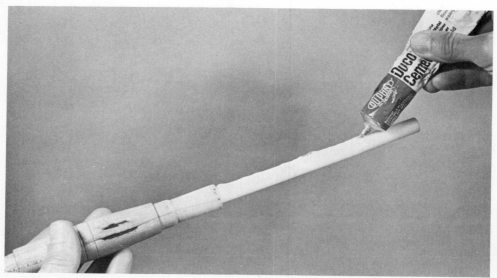

Rod hosel of boat rod being glued in place on wood fore grip.

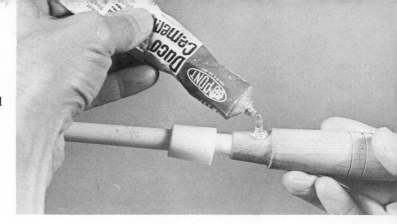

Gluing the male metal ferrule in place on the wood fore grip of a boat rod.

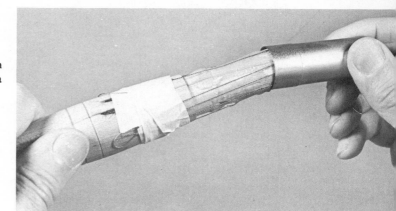

Gluing the reel seat–female ferrule onto the rear wood grip of a boat rod.

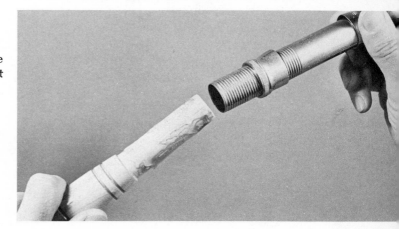

Finished handle of a boat rod.

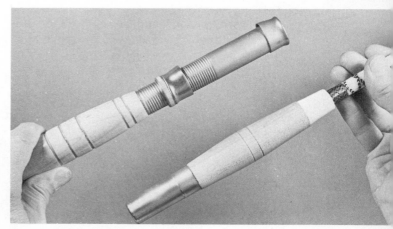

Different types of butt caps are used on saltwater rods, depending upon their usage. Top: butt cap for rod belt; center: slotted gimbal for gimbal rod belt; bottom: standard rubber butt cap on surf rod for surf rod belt.

VARIATIONS OF BOAT, TROLLING, AND BIG-GAME RODS

Since boat rod combination reel seat-ferrules come in standard sizes, much of the procedure outlined above is unnecessary. In buying an already assembled handle, all that is required is the guide wrapping, gluing the rod blank, wood grip, and male ferrule together, and fitting to the rear handle assembly.

Fighting rods are built the same way, only a slotted gimbal is used instead of the butt cap. The slotted butt cap must be aligned properly so that the reel seat and guides are on top of the rod when the butt is in a gimbal socket.

Also, better trolling rods are built with a locking slotted reel seat-ferrule to prevent any turning of the rod tip while fighting a fish. If this type of reel seat-ferrule is used, take care to align the slot on the male ferrule with the guides so that the reel seat and guides are in the same plane.

COSTS

Because of the tremendous variety of rods and component parts, the cost of making each type of rod will be different. However, the 6½-foot spinning rod mentioned first in the step-by-step instructions would work out as follows:

6½-foot Fenwick ferruled spinning rod blank	$11.25
Set of 5 Carboloy spinning guides	3.82
Carboloy tip top	.70
Hook holder	.10
24 cork rings	1.43
Reel seat	.99
Winding check	.20
Butt cap	.25
Thread, one 50-yard spool	.20
Ferrule cement—$0.50 per stick	.05 per rod
One-ounce bottle color preservative—$0.75	.25 per rod
One-ounce bottle rod varnish—$0.75	.25 per rod
TOTAL	$19.49

While the total of $19.49 is not necessarily inexpensive, it is a low figure for a custom-built rod made of the best materials known; a rod of this type in a tackle store would cost approximately $50. If further savings were desired they could be realized by using a cheaper rod blank, chrome guides, and tip top instead of Carboloy, as well as cheaper cork rings. By using these expensive fittings, a good spinning rod can be made for about $10.

ROD KITS

If you prefer not to buy the separate components from tackle stores and mail-order houses, you can use one of the numerous kits that supply everything needed to make a rod. Kits are available for making fly rods, spinning rods, casting rods, spin casting rods, saltwater spinning rods, surf rods, trolling rods, and boat rods.

Herter's carries kits for all of the above, with prices ranging from $10 to $23, depending upon the style of rod. Hille, Reed Tackle, and Anglers Pro Shop also have fly, spinning, and casting rod kits, while Netcraft has these as well as trolling rod kits. Fireside Angler and Sewell N. Dunton & Son carry fly rod kits, while Phillipson and Orvis have both fly and spinning rod kits available.

9
TACKLE BOXES

TOOLS · MATERIALS · TACKLE BOX DESIGN ·
TACKLE BOX CONSTRUCTION · COSTS

BASIC TOOLS		HELPFUL TOOLS
Cross-cut saw	Wood rasp	Bench saw, sabre saw, or jig saw
Screwdriver	Sandpaper	Electric drill
Hacksaw	Hand drill	
Files	Drill bits	

GIVEN THE DIVERSITY OF TACKLE BOXES ON THE MARKET TODAY, making one may seem to be an exercise in futility. Commercially available boxes include tiny boxes for a few dollars each and giant boxes that, when filled with lures, are almost too big for even a strong man to lift. Special boxes are available for spinning, worm fishing, saltwater fishing, fly fishing, reservoir bass fishing, and coho salmon fishing; and some boxes are fitted for night fishing with lights that turn on when the lid lifts.

Still, there is a place for the homemade box. For boat anglers, for example, there is a definite advantage to building a box to fit under a seat, between boat ribs, or in a tight spot under a forward deck, or, to implement new ideas, that incorporates a flat wood top that can also be used as a bait-cutting board, for example.

The shore-bound angler can build a box with rod holders on the top to carry several rods from one spot to the next. The big game angler might want a large open box in which to carry several large big game reels, rigging tools, wire, and the heavy hooks used in offshore fishing. Slide-out trays might be an important part of a special box designed to fit under the seat of a canoe or small boat.

Example of homemade wood tackle box showing lift-out tray with removable partitions for the compartments.

TOOLS

The tools needed for making tackle boxes will depend on the materials used and the construction methods. A wood handsaw is basic for any box made of wood, marine plywood, or masonite. Cross-cut saws that have finer and closer teeth are better than rip saws; they will give a smoother sawed edge. Some combination saws are also available. The average saw cost will vary between $2 and $10. If you have an electric sabre saw, jigsaw, or circular saw, it will be helpful, although not really worth acquiring just to build tackle boxes.

Each type of power saw has it advantages and disadvantages. The circular saw (or table saw) will cut far straighter than will a sabre saw or jigsaw; both jigsaws and sabre saws will cut curves, something which is impossible with the circular saw. The sabre saw is generally better for cutting curves for large pieces of work, since the arm on an electric jigsaw will restrict the size of the work that can be cut.

Hand coping saws, selling for less than $2, also cut curves, although they are limited in working on large pieces because most have a 6½-inch throat.

A hacksaw (about $3 to $4) will be necessary for cutting any channel aluminum, aluminum or brass piano hinge, or other metals.

Assorted screwdrivers will be necessary, since a tackle box should be screwed, not nailed together. An electric drill will come in handy for drilling pilot holes for screws; regular drill bits can be used, although special pilot bits are available.

Wood rasps, files, and assorted grades of sandpaper will be needed to finish up the box.

MATERIALS

Marine plywood gets the nod for most homemade tackle boxes. As the name indicates, marine plywood is made for boats, and is therefore eminently suited for tackle boxes. If possible, purchase plywood in AA grade, which indicates that both outside surfaces of the veneer are flawless—no knotholes or splits. Marine plywood comes in sizes from ¼ inch to 1 inch, ½ inch is a good thickness for tackle boxes.

Thin shelving pine and similar woods are also suitable for tackle boxes, the only disadvantage being that they are thicker than necessary and usually make up into heavy boxes. Weight is not a factor when the box is a permanent or semipermanent boat box, but should be a consideration if the tackle box is to be carried much.

Aluminum sheeting is an ideal exterior material for a tackle box, but it must be backed with a heavier wood, fiberboard, or masonite base. The Reynolds do-it-yourself sheeting, in plain or embossed sheets, comes in an 0.020 thickness—too thin to be used without such backing—at about four dollars per 36-by-36-inch sheet.

Masonite or similar hardboard is also suitable for tackle boxes, provided that it is treated to withstand moisture. Some Masonite is tempered or hardened on both surfaces to withstand water, which makes it ideal for use in combination with the thin sheet aluminum.

One easy way to make a basic frame for a tackle box is to utilize Reynolds do-it-yourself aluminum corner posts. Available in 8-foot lengths only, these slotted corner channels come in three sizes to allow the use of ¼-inch, ½-inch, or ¾-inch materials. They make the measuring of any angles or the complicated butting of joints unnecessary; the materials are slid into the channels, then screwed or glued into place. Corners of boxes are easily formed by cutting the corner posts on a mitred angle. Prices range from $3 to $5 per 8-foot length, depending upon size.

Hinges are needed for any tackle box lid, the best being aluminum brass-plated or polypropylene piano hinges. The aluminum or polypropylene hinges are preferred, since they will not chip or rust as will the brass-plated ones. Prices are about $3.50 per 6-foot length of aluminum or polypropylene with brass hinges about $1.40 per foot in short lengths.

Many other fittings such as brass corner reinforcements; brass, aluminum, and stainless steel nonrusting screws; and handles are all available at better hardware stores.

TACKLE BOX DESIGN

Before making a tackle box, it is important to design the interior layout. Whether the box is to have pull-out trays or lift-out trays or be arranged to hold commercially molded plastic lure boxes will determine its ultimate size. shape, and even construction.

The best and simplest design is a large box with a hinged lid, something like a small foot-locker. Lift-out trays, only slightly smaller than the inside box dimensions and of a height determined by the lures or tackle, can be fitted into the box.

The tackle box can be filled with trays, or a compartment can be left in the bottom for reels, sinkers, pork rind bottles, bait knives, and similar large gear. The easiest way to adjust the height of this bottom compartment is to glue strips of wood in the box to prevent the lure trays from dropping down into the box. Two horizontal strips of wood across the ends or the long side of the inside of the box will work, as will four upright strips of wood glued in each corner.

Trays can be made by the construction methods used in making the main box. Lighter wood for the sides and bottom is suggested; ¼-inch plywood is most practical. (Be careful, however, in cutting plywood, since it will splinter unless a finetooth saw is used.)

The dimensions of the trays should be just smaller than the inside of the tackle box in width and depth, with a height suitable for the lures stored in them. Usually this height will be about 1 inch for freshwater boxes and 1½ to 1¾ inches for saltwater boxes. The deeper trays in saltwater boxes are needed to accommodate the larger saltwater lures.

The inside of the tray can be partitioned with light plywood (¼-inch), Masonite, or similar thin material. These partitions can be permanently glued into place; grooves can be cut into the sides and end of the tray to allow the partitions to be removed or arranged for the tackle carried. Grooving of these sides must be done before the tray is assembled. It is best done with a dado on a circular saw but can be done with care with a regular hand saw.

For long life the trays should be glued together with a waterproof glue, with light brass wood screws in each joint.

The individual trays (usually two or three) are placed on top of each other in the main box with enough clearance left to close the box. Some method must be devised to lift the trays out of the main tackle box. The easiest way is to drill small finger-size holes in the center of each tray, so that the tray can be removed with two fingers. Another method is to staple or otherwise fasten small rope handles at each end. Light ⅛-inch nylon parachute cord or similar nylon cord will work well.

It is also possible to fasten two small screw eyes on the inside of each end of the tray, and put a small C-shaped handle of coat hanger wire through the two screw eyes. The handle must be shorter than the depth of the tray so that the handle will drop into the tray when another tray is stored on top. With the handle loose, it can be lifted up enough (usually about 1 inch) to provide a good grip for lifting the trays out of the box.

Some anglers prefer to have several holes in a central divider of each tray, to lift the tray with two fingers of one hand. This makes it easier to get the trays out, provided that they are lifted straight up. But if heavy lures are on one side of the tray and light lures on the other, the tray may cant, and catch on the insides of the box.

Swing-out trays such as are found on commercial tackle boxes are difficult to make, since special side supports are needed to lift the trays clear as the lid of the tackle box is raised.

It is possible to make a tackle box with slide-out trays, such as can be

Detail close-up of partitions in wood tray.

Detail (circled) of wood support to hold tackle box tray.

found on commercial boxes like those by Kennedy and the 747 and 727 by Plano. The main box is made the same as any other tackle box, except that the front is left open. Then light Masonite plywood shelf supports are placed horizontally in the box to hold the individual trays. An alternate method is to place angle aluminum on the inside of the main box to support the edges of the individual trays.

Naturally, the trays must be held in place so that they do not slide out when the box is closed. One method of accomplishing this is to place a strip of metal along the rear edge of each tray and glue a magnetic strip of metal along the inside of the main tackle box. Then when the tray is slid shut, the magnet will hold it in place. Usually this is adequate for temporary tray closure while fishing, but not adequate for carrying the tackle box. A lightweight bottom- or top-hinged front that fastens in place, or a metal rod that drops vertically through both the front of the tackle box and holes in the front of each try, are two ways to provide secure closure.

If a top- or bottom-hinged front is used, this front can also be useful in other ways. It can be used as a bait-cutting board, or, if some clearance is left between the front and the trays, springs for snelled hook attachments can be fastened to the inside lid.

This type of box can also be combined with a top compartment or several lift-out trays, depending upon the size of the box and trays.

TACKLE BOX CONSTRUCTION

Construction of wood tackle boxes involves basic carpentry. Cabinetmak- ing techniques—dovetailed or mitred joints—are even better, if you have the tools and experience for this type of work. Tackle boxes, because of the hard use to which they are put, should never be nailed together. All joints should be glued with a good glue and screwed together as well.

The various epoxy glues and also casein and other glues designed ex- pressedly for wood are best. In choosing the glue, make sure that it is water- proof; tackle boxes sit on wet shorelines, and in the bottoms of leaky boats, and anything other than a waterproof glue is an invitation to disaster.

Before cutting out all the pieces, draw pians for the box and carefully determine the dimensions for each part of the box and trays. The old car- penters' adage of "measure twice and saw once" is nowhere more important than in cutting out parts for a tackle box and the trays that must fit it. If pos- sible, use the type of cross-cut wood saw with the greatest number of teeth per inch. It gives a smoother cut to the finished box, and less finishing will be required.

If the box is to be made of plywood, try several ways of laying out the various parts. Often one layout of parts will make maximum use of the 4 by 8 sheets of plywood, whereas other layouts of the parts will waste wood. Once all the parts are cut out, sand all the cut edges, but keep the cut edges square with the flat surfaces of the wood. Once all the parts are completely cut out and finished, the box can be assembled.

Often it is best to clamp or lightly nail (with small thin brads) the box together, so that pilot holes for the screws can be drilled first. A pilot hole should be drilled that is smaller than the diameter of the shaft of the screw. Special pilot hole drills are available that will drill and countersink (for flat- head screws) at the same time.

After the pilot holes are drilled, spread glue evenly on contact edges of the box and screw them in place; do it one side and piece at a time. Once the main box is complete, assemble each tray, following the above directions. The screws used in the lighter wood of a tray should be smaller and shorter. If possible, use stainless steel or brass screws throughout, since they will be more rust-resistant than steel screws.

Homemade battery box used for running electric motors. Note special pins (circled) that allow removal of the handle so that batteries may be changed.

Once the box is completed, it must be painted. Epoxy paint forms a tough, hard, long-lasting surface. These paints come in two cans (just as epoxy glues come in two tubes); equal parts of the two cans (or the entire contents of both) are mixed together and used immediately. Several good coats of varnish is an alternative. Once the box is completed, hinges, brass corners, latches, handles, and other hardware are added.

COSTS

The cost of a homemade box will depend greatly upon the box size and the thickness of plywood, and the amount of sheet aluminum, corner bracing, and miscellaneous hardware used. Top-quality ½-inch marine AA grade plywood currently sells for about $1.00 per square foot in 4-by-8-foot sheets; ¼-inch plywood sells for about $0.75 per square foot.

Assuming a very large tackle box of 12 by 12 by 24 inches (the average large commercial box is about 9 by 12 by 18 inches), the box will require 10 square feet of ½-inch plywood, costing $10. Additional handles, hinges, brass corners, screws, and miscellaneous hardware will come to $3 to $4. Two inside trays using ¼-inch plywood for the tray bottom will cost about $4 for all materials.

Thus, the total cost for the completed "jumbo" size box will be about $18, less than a smaller commercial box. But the real advantage is that the box can be custom-designed as to size, tray arrangement, lure-compartment size, and other features, to complement the tackle of the individual angler.

10

WIRE LEADERS, TERMINAL RIGS, AND MISCELLANEOUS LURES

*TOOLS AND MATERIALS · USING LEADER SLEEVES ·
BASIC SINGLE-STRAND WIRE CONSTRUCTION ·
TERMINAL TACKLE AND LURE RIGGINGS · WEED
GUARDS, SPINNER SHAFTS, LEADERS, BOTTOM
RIGS, LAKE TROLLING RIGS, RIGGING TROLLING
SKIRTS, SURGICAL EELS, SNUBBERS, HOOK LEARS,
BOTTOM SPREADERS · COSTS AND KITS*

BASIC TOOLS	HELPFUL TOOLS
Pliers	Round-nose pliers
	Wire former
	Leader sleeve pliers
	Wire cutters

∿ EVEN THOUGH RODS AND MANY LURES HAVE BEEN CONSIDERED THE proper domain for the tackle craftsman for years, wire leaders and some lure riggings have often been ignored.

Actually, wire leaders and terminal rigs of all types are among the easiest of tackle items to make, requiring only the simplest tools and no expensive materials. There are special wire formers on the market that can run several dollars or more, but they're not needed except by the angler whose hobby might turn into a part-time business, or who fishes extensively and must replace a lot of equipment.

Wire leaders, terminal rigs, and rigged lures can encompass a wide range of tackle ideas. Simple wire leaders, bottom fishing spreaders, surf-fishing bottom rigs (made out of wire as well as the more popular nylon), surgical eel lures, spinner shafts for making spinners, hook lears, drop-sinker trolling rigs, spinner-bait rigs, weedless hooks, rigged vinyl lures, and a host of other items all fall into this broad category.

TOOLS AND MATERIALS

The tools required will vary widely depending upon the tackle to be made. Round-nose pliers, needle-nose pliers, or wire formers will be needed to make hook lears, wire spreaders, spinner shafts, drop-sinker trolling rigs, and similar items. If side cutters come on the pliers, as they do with many long-nose models, wire cutters will not be necessary. Prices for pliers vary from $2 to $5 or $6, depending upon quality, type, and size.

Do not overlook the Bernard Sportmate pliers, which have compound-action parallel-jaw pliers, cutters, and a small drilled hole in one jaw that makes it easy to form right-angle bends in any light wire.

Leader crimping pliers are special tools for crimping the small leader sleeves that make wire leader construction so easy today. They come in several styles. Berkley sells its pliers separately as well as in kits that include wire and sleeves. Fenwick/Sevenstrand has two crimping pliers with wire cutters included on the deluxe model. Both crimp all sizes of Sevenstrand leader sleeves, as well as those of most other manufacturers. Prices of crimping pliers vary from about $2 to $6.

The new crimping sleeves are for use with twisted-wire leader material, but can also be used in a wide variety of connections, including crimping nylon. They come in over a dozen different sizes to fit all wire from 9- to 400-pound test. Sleeves retail in lots of 25, 100, and 1,000, priced about $0.50 to $2.00 per 25, depending upon size.

The wire used in leaders, bottom surf rigs, and some rigged lures comes either plain or nylon-covered twisted, in both bright and bronze finishes. There are also special big-game trolling wires such as the Sevenstrand Duratest and single-strand stainless steel wire. Coiled leader wire is sold in several ways, usually in 25- or 30-foot coils, but also in 300- and 1,000-foot spools and the quarter-pound and 1-pound coils for heavy users.

Wire sizes are generally listed in pound test, for the twisted wires, and vary from 8- to 250-pound test, diameters from 0.008 to 0.039. Nylon-covered wire is obviously thicker, ranging from 0.012 (for the same 8-pound test listed above) to 0.075 (for 250-pound test).

Single-strand leader wire is either tinned "music" wire or stainless steel. The music wire is stiffer than the stainless steel and generally preferred for making tackle such as spinner shafts. The stainless steel is more often used in long wire leaders for offshore trolling for big game fish. Neither of these single-strand wires is designed to be used with the above-mentioned leader sleeves, but instead must have a wrapped eye.

Prices depend upon the size and type of wire, ranging from $0.50 to $1.50 per 25-foot coil. Spinner shafts must be made from prestraightened wire, since it is impossible to get the curve out of coiled wire. Spinner shafts are made of single-strand, tinned music wire. In sizes from 0.024 to 0.035 it sells for about

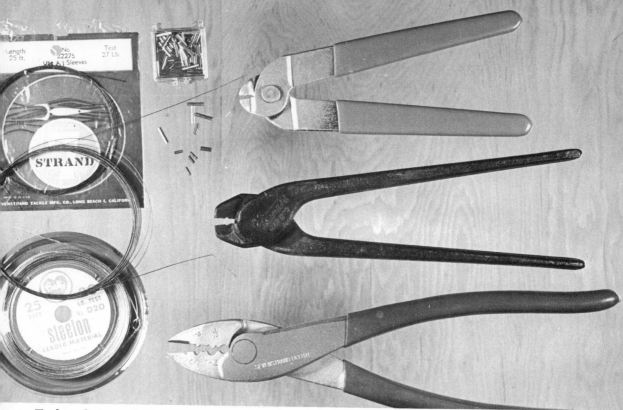

Tools and materials used in making wire leaders. Left: twisted leader wire; top center: leader sleeves; right: three styles of leader crimping pliers.

Hooks, pliers, sinkers, wire, and swivels carried by the average saltwater fisherman for rigging wire leaders.

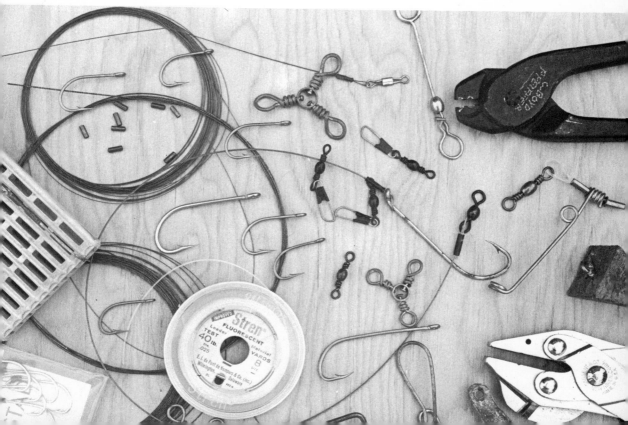

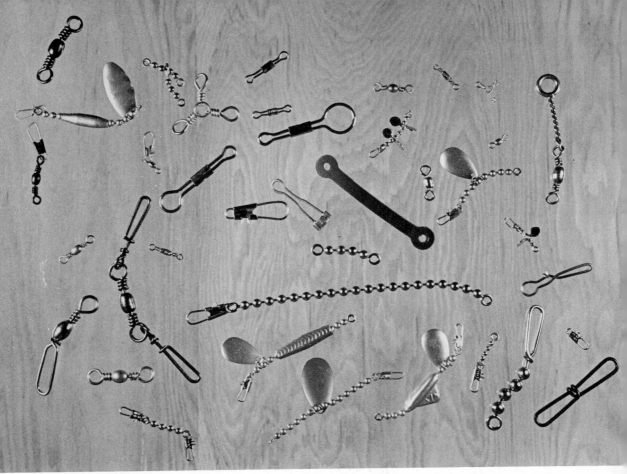

Various types of swivels, connecting links, and snaps available to the tackle tinkerer.

$1.00 for a dozen 18-inch lengths. It also comes in prestraightened coils, with most but not all of the curve removed. Available in sizes 0.009 to 0.045, it sells for about $0.40 to $1.00 per 25-foot coil, but also comes in quarter-, half-, and 1-pound coils.

Brass wire is a handy wire to use for surf-fishing rigs, flounder spreaders, hook lears, drop-sinker trolling rigs, sinker eyes, and similar miscellaneous terminal tackle. It can be purchased in sizes 0.029 diameter and larger. Commercially made bottom spreaders that I have "miked" measure 0.065. One company sells spring brass wire for about $2 per quarter-pound coil, in sizes from 0.029 to 0.045. Lacking brass wire, electricians' solid copper wire will serve just as well, and comes in different gauges. The 14 gauge measures about 0.065, just right for bottom rigs, and is easy to work with pliers or wire formers. It is more expensive than brass, but at about 4 cents per foot in 100-foot coils, it is still reasonable.

The many types of wire sizes, finishes, coatings, and materials may sound confusing, but only indicate that a wide variety of wire supplies is available to give the tackle tinkerer a choice. Obviously, certain sizes and types of wire are a must for certain procedures. For example, for making weedless lures,

0.009 or 0.012 single-strand stainless steel is recommended. For making the straight shafts used in construction of spinning lures, 0.024 single-strand (straightened lengths only for best results!) is used. Naturally, heavier or lighter wire can be used in these and other applications, if personal experience or conditions warrant it.

USING LEADER SLEEVES

To construct a basic leader, slip the proper size leader sleeve up over the wire, then double the end of the wire back into the sleeve to make a wire loop. Fastened with crimping pliers, it makes a permanent connection that will not pull out, and can be used to make a wide variety of wire devices; two wires can be joined together the same way.

For an even stronger connection when making a loop, slip the tag end of the wire back into the sleeve (a slightly larger sleeve might be necessary in some cases); then crimp. This also prevents any short, sharp ends of wire from sticking out of the end of the sleeve. In addition, the Fenwick/Sevenstrand catalog lists a method whereby the leader material is threaded through the leader sleeve and hook eye, making a double overhand knot (like a surgeon's knot) going through the hook eye a second time, and running the end of the wire back through the sleeve; draw the loop up and crimp twice to complete the loop. Fenwick recommends this improved loop especially for use with their Sevalon and Duratest wire material. They also recommend the use of two sleeves spaced one inch apart on the 90- to 400-pound test leader material.

Using these leader sleeves, it is a simple matter to attach hooks directly to leaders, to make leaders with snaps at one end and swivels at the other, and to construct one- and two-hook surf bottom rigs and similar items.

BASIC SINGLE-STRAND WIRE CONSTRUCTION

The basic methods used to make wire terminal rigging and fishing tackle are the same, no matter what types, sizes, or finishes of single-strand wire are

Technique of crimping a leader sleeve to make a loop in wire leaders.

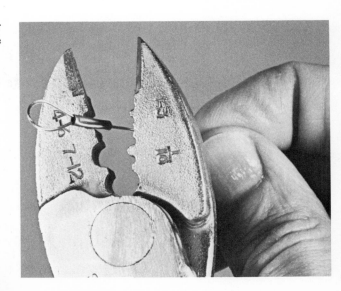

used. Naturally, the size and type do make for some slight differences, but these can easily be dealt with as one gets more experienced in wire-handling and forming.

Probably the most basic technique is in forming an eye in wire, which can be done with any of the types of wire mentioned in this chapter except the flexible twisted wire. Round-nose pliers and wire cutters are all you'll need, although needle-nose pliers, Bernard Sportmate pliers, and various wire formers can also be used.

Assuming that the bare minimum of equipment is to be used—the round-nose pliers—select a piece of wire that is long enough for the job; allow an additional 1½ or 2 inches for the formation of the eye. Bear in mind that if another eye is to be formed on the other end of the wire, another 1½ to 2 inches must be allowed also for that eye. While it is true that the eye will not take this much extra wire for the eye and wrap alone, the extra wire is needed for leverage in wrapping the eye.

Grip the wire 1½ to 2 inches from one end with the round-nose pliers and bend the other end (usually the longer end) of the wire at a slight angle to the main shaft. Now grasp the short (1½ to 2-inch) end and wrap it smoothly and evenly around one jaw of the round-nose pliers. Do this in stages, since the other jaw of the pliers will prevent your making a complete even circle without shifting the grip. Stop when the short length of the wire is crossed over and at right angles to the main shaft. Still holding the eye in the pliers, begin wrapping the short end around the main shaft, taking care that the wrap is tight, with the coils close together.

Make at least several wraps for strength and then finish by cutting the excess wire close to the main shaft with close-cutting wire cutters. A pair of Bernard Sportmate pliers does this nicely. (Note that one side of the wire cutters on the pliers will cut closer than the other side; use the close-cutting side.)

It is also possible to break the wire off smoothly by bending the excess wire at right angles to the direction of the wrap (in other words, bend back and forth parallel to the main shaft). The wire should break after several bends, provided that a sharp bend is made in the beginning and the excess wire is bent rapidly. The advantage of this method is that the wire will break much closer to the main shaft than it can be cut. It takes some experience to do this accurately since a common error is to fail to get the bend close to the main shaft.

The leverage needed for making the wrap and also for breaking off the wire is the reason that the extra length of wire must be used.

Wire can be saved and eyes made allowing only enough wire for the wrap, if a wire former is used. Wire formers come with complete instructions and make the wrap by holding the wire end in a small groove or special clamp while turning the eye by means of a handle.

TERMINAL TACKLE AND LURE RIGGINGS

Though there is an endless variety of rigs and tackle that can be made with wire, often with regional differences, there are certain basics of construction applicable to all.

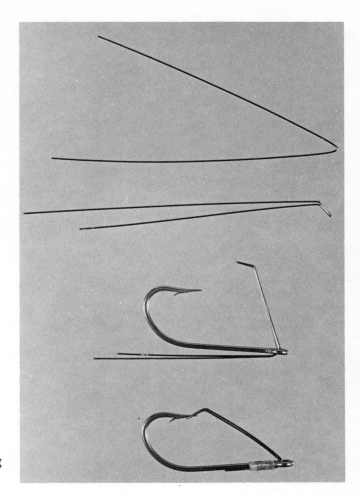

Top to bottom, steps in making
weedless hook arrangements.

Weed Guards. Weed guards to protect the point of a hook are easy to make.
Size 0.009 to 0.012 spring wire should be used for most fish and fishing conditions. Cut a piece of wire about 1 inch longer than twice the length from the
eye of the hook to the barb of the hook; double the wire in the center and
bend the two wires slightly about ⅛ inch from the doubled end. This will be the
loop that fits at the hook points. Hold the bent part at the hook point between
the point and the barb, measuring to the eye of the hook. Bend again at this
point so that the two ends of the wire can be slipped through the hook eye and
fastened to the shank of the hook.

Obviously, the length of wire needed for each size and style of hook will
differ slightly, so if any number of weedless wires are to be made, keep a
record of the length of wire needed for each size hook.

Fastening the weed guard in place can be accomplished by several means.
First, the two ends of the weed guard can be wrapped to the hook shank with
size A or E thread. The technique is just that of tying a fly on a hook, or wrapping a guide onto a rod. (See Chapter 8 for this technique.) However, instead
of tying off the wrap by pulling the end of thread under the last wraps, finish
it with a series of half hitches (a commonly used fly-tying technique). The weed
guard can also be wrapped on with wire or soldered in place.

And, there are alternate methods of construction. For example, cut the light
wire to length (as outlined above) and fold it in half. Make a sharp bend in

the two wires ½ inch from the previous bend, slip the folded end through the eye of the hook, and fasten this end in place at the eye of the hook as outlined above. Then spread the two ends above the hook point and cut the wire to length, slightly beyond the point of the hook.

Spinner Shafts. Spinner shafts come in several different styles—with a wrapped eye, a spring closed eye, and a self-lock snap type of eye. All three types can easily be made in the home workshop from straightened piano wire. There is a fourth type that incorporates "half" of a barrel swivel to prevent twisting, but this type is impossible to make at the home workbench, although a barrel swivel can be added during construction to the eye of any of the first three types.

The use of each of the three types of spinner shafts is fully discussed in Chapter 2, on spinner making. A check with the photos found there will show the steps necessary in making each of the three types of shaft eyes.

Leaders. Leaders are perhaps the easiest of all wire tackle to make. All that is required is the proper length and test of leader wire, a snap, and a swivel. Or, a snap swivel can be fastened to one end, the other end left as a loop of wire.

The best wire to use is twisted stainless steel, either in the bright finish or the coffee camouflage color. Test to suit the fishing conditions. Nylon-covered wire can be used, if desired.

Using this wire, the crimping sleeves make any fastening of snaps and swivels easy, quick, and sure and give professional results with no experience or even talent required.

Bottom Rigs. Using the same basic techniques, bottom rigs can be made to hold a sinker and snelled hooks. These are usually about 18 inches long and can be made simply by adding two loops to the middle part of the rig by means of the leader sleeves. If any twisting is anticipated, the rig can be made in sections, using a brass barrel crossline swivel or a three-way swivel at each point where a snelled hook is to be added. The wire leader is attached to two of the swivel eyes, the loop of the snelled hook run through the third extra eye placed on the side of the swivel. In all cases in rigs of this type, a large snap at the bottom for sinker attachment is a must, since many sinkers (particularly bank sinkers) have large molded-in lead eyes that will not fit on small snaps. Special sinker snaps such as ice tong snaps or Duo-Lock snaps are available.

Lake Trolling Rigs. Using long flexible braided wire, it is easy to make lake trolling rigs, sometimes called cowbells because of the series of large spinner blades used as a fish attractor ahead of the lure or fly. Typically used in western lake trolling for salmon and trout, lake trolling rigs vary from 2 to 6 feet in length. They have a rudder near the front of the rig, to keep it from twisting, followed by three to seven blades ending in a split ring or snap for easy lure hook-up. The metal spoon blades and rudders are available from mail-order and tackle supply stores.

To make one of these rigs, take a 6-inch length of braided wire, form a loop in one end with a leader sleeve, slipping a split ring or swivel over the

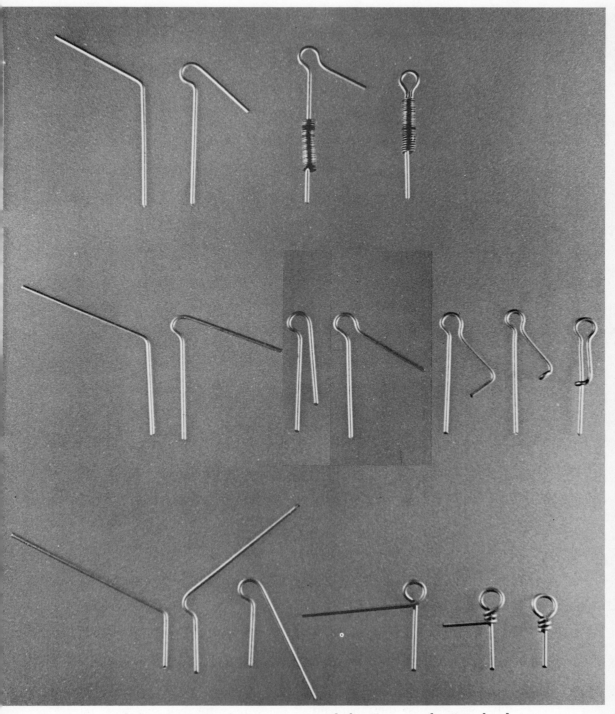

Steps in making three types of eyes on spinner shafts. Top: a coil-spring closed eye; center: a self-locked snap eye; bottom: a wrapped eye.

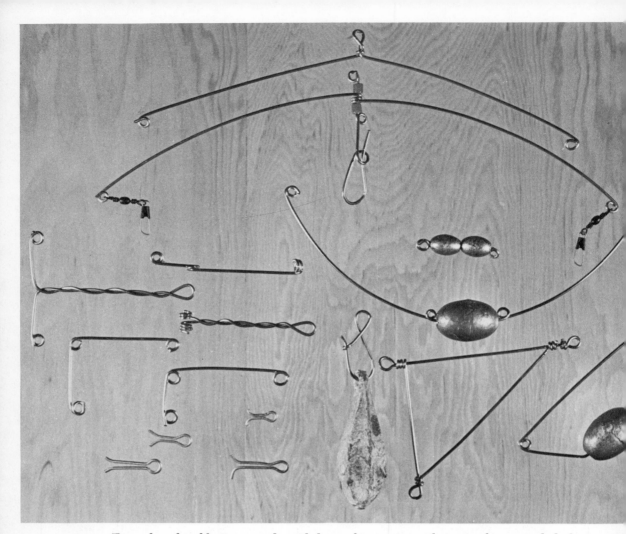

Examples of tackle items made with heavy brass wire with a wire former include bottom spreaders, hook lears, trolling sinkers, and bucktail-tin squid-sinker eyes.

end of the wire before running the end of the wire back into the leader sleeve for crimping. Form a similar loop in the other end of the wire, slipping the wire of the loop through the hole in the forward end of the metal rudder before crimping.

Now cut braided wire the desired length of the trolling rig and form another loop through the eye at the other end of the rudder. Slip the largest spinner blade on a suitable clevis and slip the clevis onto the wire; follow with a small bead or "unie" and a larger red plastic bead. Run these up the wire, follow with a leader sleeve, and crimp the sleeve at the point on the wire where the first blade is to be positioned. Continue the same way with all the other blades, positioning each several inches to a foot apart. Usually the last blade is positioned at the loop, making separate leader sleeve here unnecessary. Form the loop on the other end of the wire, slipping a split ring, swivel, or snap here for lure attachment.

Lake trolls like this can be made any length, using any type of large spinner blades, with or without the rudder that precedes them. Generally, large willow-leaf or special lake-troll fluted spinner blades are used. Heavy nylon can be used in place of the wire leader if desired, crimping the loops and positioning the spinners as above.

Rigging Trolling Skirts. Trolling lures such as vinyl skirts, squids, and soft plastic bait fish imitations can be bought rigged or unrigged. Generally, the cost of a rigged lure is several times that of one unrigged. They can be rigged quickly, and at little cost. The only materials needed are mono leader, wire leader or light chain, the hook, plastic beads (available at dime stores), and an egg sinker.

Vinyl trolling skirts are offered by Fenwick, Weber, and several smaller companies. To rig them onto your lure, run a wire or mono leader through the head of the lure, slip on a plastic bead, an egg sinker, and additional beads. Use enough beads so that when the egg sinker is seated against the head of the vinyl skirt, the hook will be hidden by the skirt. Using a leader sleeve, make a loop in the terminal end of the leader, slipping the hook eye on the loop before crimping.

There is an alternate method: slip the wire leader through the skirt, add a plastic bead, and the proper size egg sinker, and crimp the leader loop to a split ring, rigging another very short leader from the split ring to the hook eye to adjust for the hook position in the skirt. A brass or noncorrosive chain can be used in place of the leader connection between the split ring and hook (No. 1/0 brass safety chain tests about 35-pounds, No. 16 single brass jack chain about 10-pounds). Wire or chain at the terminal end of the lure is essential when fishing for toothy fish such as bluefish, barracuda, and king mackerel.

Surgical Eels. Surgical tubing eels have gained popularity over the past several years, especially for East Coast striped bass fishing, and eels are good for bluefish and other saltwater species as well. Basically nothing more than a length of curved rubber or plastic tubing over a hook and short leader, attached to a barrel swivel, the "surge" lures can be bought ready-rigged but are extremely simple to make.

The tubing comes in a variety of sizes and colors, including clear and red fluorescent. It is available at the better-stocked tackle stores and mail-order houses as well as surgical supply houses. Hooks should be strong saltwater single hooks. Either wire or heavy mono is used for the leader.

Determine the length you desire (eels will vary between 6 and 18 inches in length); fasten the leader material to the hook with a leader sleeve. The size of the barrel swivel will be determined by the inside diameter of the tubing, since the tubing should fit snugly around the center barrel of the swivel. Cut one end of the tubing on a sharp angle so that this short "tail" will extend beyond the bend of the hook.

Lay the tubing alongside the prepared hook and leader, placing the forward part of the slanted cut at the bend of the hook; cut to length. Measure and cut the wire leader, allowing enough wire to form the eye at the end. Run the leader through the tubing, and grasp the leader with pliers and roll the tubing back on the leader wire and up onto the bend of the hook. This is to allow room for forming the eye in the leader for attaching the barrel swivel. While

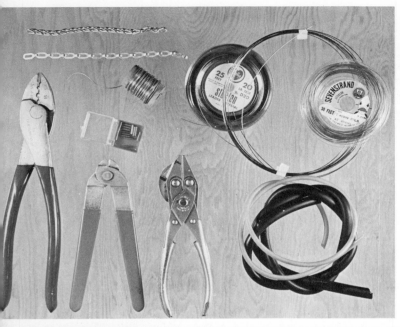

Tools and materials needed for making surgical tube eels and for rigging vinyl skirt lures include leader crimping pliers, Sportmate pliers, leader wire, chain, and surgical hose.

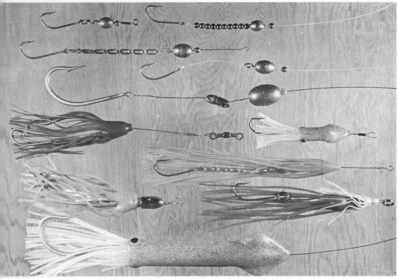

Vinyl trolling lures and rigging methods. Top: several methods of rigging vinyl skirts with an egg sinker for weight; bottom, finished rigged lures. Included are vinyl skirts and two sizes of vinyl trolling squids.

Herter's wire former makes it possible to work with several sizes of wire and to do a number of operations, such as rigging surgical eels.

holding the tubing back, run a leader crimping sleeve onto the wire and crimp it. Slide the tubing off the bend of the hook and back in place on the wire, slipping the forward end of the tubing over the barrel swivel.

It is also possible to premeasure the tubing against the wire leader complete with hook and barrel swivel. Slip the swivel eye over a long doubled wire (straightened coat hanger wire will do) and thread the surgical eel over the double wire, pulling it down onto the leader and hook. Once the swivel is clear at the end of the tubing, remove the double wire.

Since the tubing will form tightly around the barrel swivel, be especially careful not to slip and run the hook into your hand. A little warm soap, teflon spray, or similar lubricant rubbed on the barrel swivel, or soaking the tubing briefly in a very soapy solution, helps greatly. The lubricant or soap can then be washed off.

Properly done, the hook will be facing the inside curve of the tubing. (All tubing will have a curve, since it comes in coils. In fact, the curve of the tubing gives it the erratic fish-attracting movement in the water.)

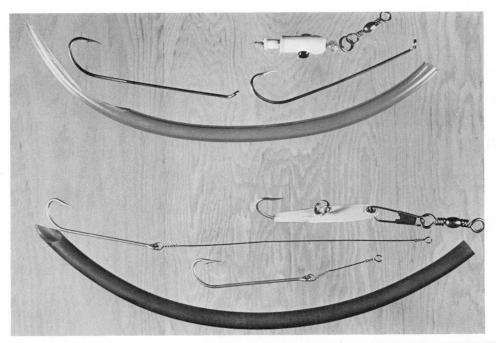

Two ways of rigging surgical tube lures, used for trolling for saltwater game fish. Top, a two-hook method, hooking the long shank hooks together. Bottom, rigging two hooks by means of different lengths of leader wire.

By forcing the eye of the lower hook through the slit in the center of the hole, it is possible to insert the second hook.

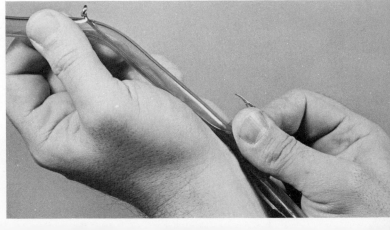

To rig the eel on a bucktail head, use tubing longer than the wire, push the tubing down on the hook to expose the leader, which has previously had an eye formed in it. Then slip the bucktail hook into the tubing, going through the small loop (eye) in the wire at the same time, and bringing the hook point out through the side of the tubing so that the tubing will extend up to the rear of the jig head.

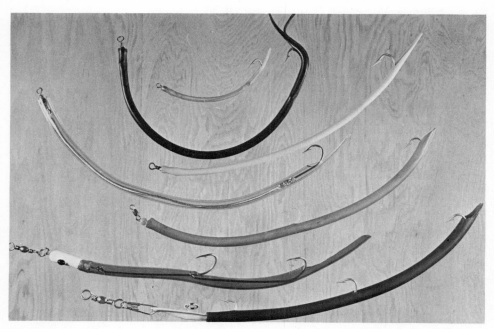

Examples of finished rigged surgical tube lure. Note that the fourth surgical hose from the top has been made of clear plastic tubing with a braided mylar insert for flash.

Materials for rubber snubbers include rubber surgical tubing, Dacron fishing line, snaps and/or swivels, and brass wire. Bottom, completed rubber snubber.

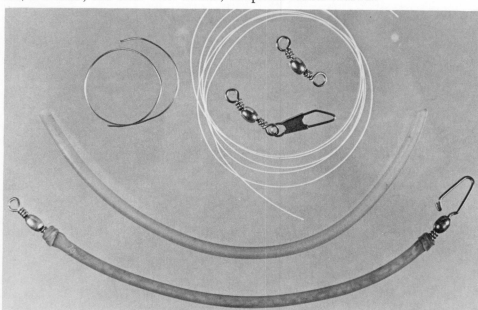

Of course, you don't have to use wire for surgical eels. Heavy mono is also used, tying the mono to the swivel and tying or snelling it to the hook.

In addition to colored tubing, clear plastic vinyl tubing can be used with inserts of mylar tubing. The easiest way to accomplish this is to use a mylar piping, available in fly-tying and tackle supply houses as well as millinery stores. Remove the inner cord from the piping, slip the piping over the leader wire, and finish the lure as above. It may be desirable to tie the nylon piping at the barrel swivel to keep it from slipping.

Snubbers.   Used when trolling for trout and salmon with long lake trolls, snubbers are nothing more than surgical latex tubing, secured with braided line running through the center with a swivel or snap swivel on each end. In use they are placed between the long lake trolling rig and the short leader and lure, to take up some of the shock when a strong fish hits.

To make a snubber, first gather the parts—two swivels (or two snap swivels or one of each), a 6-inch length of light surgical tubing, 15 to 20 inches of heavy—50- to 100-pound test—braided fishing line, and some light copper or brass wire. Any size surgical tubing can be used, with thicker tubing requiring a stronger pull (strike) to reach full stretch.

First, tie the braided line to one eye of the swivel or snap swivel using a clinch, improved clinch, or similar knot. Using a long upholstery needle or fine doubled wire, run the end of the braided line through the 6-inch length of the tubing. Pull the tubing up close to the eye of the swivel, slip it over the swivel eye; wrap and twist light copper or brass wire around the tubing to hold it in place. Now pull the tubing out to full stretch, allowing the braided line to run freely in the center of the tube while doing so; pinch the end of the tubing to hold the line, relax the stretch on the rubber tubing, and the braided line will fold up on itself in the tubing.

Tie the end of the line to the eye of the second swivel. If some slack occurs while pulling the knot tight, adjust for this before tying the knot by pulling some of the braided line out of the tubing; cut any excess line. Pull the rubber tubing out to full stretch and slip it over the swivel eye. Release and then secure the tubing around the eye with copper wire. Fold the ends (about ¼ inch) of the rubber tubing over the wire wrappings, and the snubber is ready for use.

Hook Lears.   To keep the snelled hooks well out from the bottom rig to prevent tangling, hook lears (stiff extensions of leader wire to hold hooks out from the main fishing line) can be made from heavier brass wire and attached to a bottom rig at two points for hook attachment.

Hook lears can be used in wire riggings, as above, or tied into mono terminal rigs. Construction should be of brass or copper wire of sufficient thickness to hold hooks straight out from the rest of the rigging to prevent tangles.

Form a right angle in the wire by bending an eye at the right angle bend, then bend an eye at each end of the wire. Make sure that one end of the wire is longer than the other. The short end should be about 2 inches long, the long end about 4 inches. The terminal rigging is attached at the eye on the short end of the wire and again at the center eye, the snelled hook looped through the eye on the longer shaft. Other types of hook lears can be created from

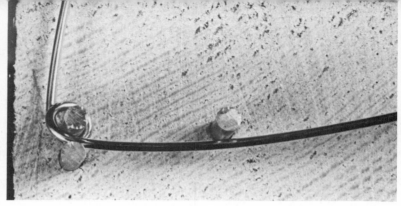

Completed eye formed in brass wire.

Completed hook lear. This is used in a bottom rig for saltwater fishing.

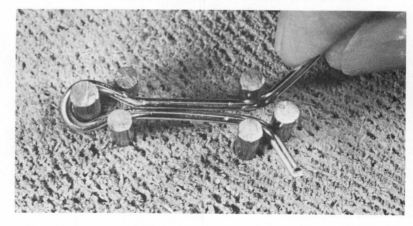

Sinker or tin squid eye made on homemade wire former.

Homemade Gulf Coast hootie, used for king mackerel trolling. This is made by fraying out short strands of rope.

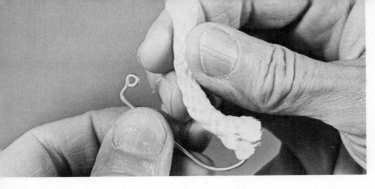

A "rope tail" lure made from a hunk of nylon rope. Here, short length of rope is threaded on hook.

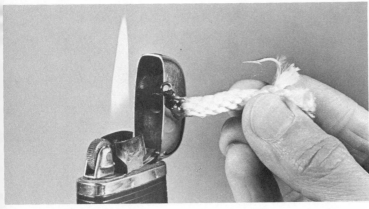

Heating head end of lure with flame to melt nylon around hook.

Fraying out nylon rope strands to complete lure. A kit for this lure is available from Lure Kits, Joppa, Maryland.

lighter wire, twisting the wires together to get additional stiffness. (See photos for additional examples.) Check Chapter 13 for a description of a homemade wire former that makes it easy to duplicate many hook lears.

Bottom Spreaders. Bottom spreaders and three-way trolling rigs for hanging a drop sinker between the line and leader are similarly made, as illustrated.

COSTS AND KITS

There are no kits for making any of the items mentioned in this chapter—perhaps because they are so simple to make with only a few tools and materials.

Cost will vary widely with the item but will average anywhere from one-fifth to one-third of the retail cost of a similar commercially made item. While the savings can be substantial, the real value in making wire leaders, rigging lures, and similar terminal tackle items is that each can be custom made for your area and your fishing style, something money can't buy.

11

OTHER FISHING TACKLE

*NETS • NET FRAMES • PLUG RETRIEVER • GAFFS •
ROD HOLDER, SAND SPIKES, ROD RACKS, AND ROD
CASES • WADING STAFFS • FISHING FLOATS •
CHUM POTS • BAIT BOXES • ICE-FISHING RODS •
FISHING MARKERS • LEADER STRAIGHTENER*

BASIC TOOLS		HELPFUL TOOLS
Nets	*Gaffs*	*Nets*
Shuttle	Wood gouge	Net wheel
Mesh gauge	Drill	*Net Frames*
Net Frames	*Rod Holders*	Electric drill
Hacksaw	Hacksaw	Wood gouge
Wood saw	Electric drill	
Bending jig	Wood rasp	
Plug Retriever	*Wading Staff*	
Hacksaw	Wood rasp	
Lead pouring ladle	Hacksaw	
Electric drill		
Masking tape		
Screwdriver		

∾ IN ADDITION TO THE STANDARD PLUGS, PLASTIC WORMS, SINKERS, RODS, bucktails, and spinners that are most often thought of in making tackle, there are also a number of other items that can be easily constructed.

Ice-fishing tip-ups and equipment for the northern states, plug retrievers, sand spikes, wading staffs, and similar items are all easily made at home. Let's look at a few of these items along with some simple instructions on how they can be inexpensively added to your stock of equipment.

NETS

As inexpensive as both original landing nets and replacement bags are, it might seem foolish even to consider making one—but there are several advantages to doing just that. First, the net can be made to any size or dimension desired. Then, it can be made of any thickness of cord, with any size mesh, and of either cotton or nylon. Once the basic net knot is learned, it's easy to turn out a large-boat landing net in one evening.

Several tools are required: shuttles to hold the netting cord, and mesh gauges to keep the net openings uniform. These are inexpensive, costing about 25 cents each. Sets of 8 to 10 shuttles or mesh gauges are available. This is the best way to buy them, since it is necessary to decrease the mesh size in working toward the bottom of the net. A set of shuttles sells for slightly over $2, a set of gauges for slightly over $1.

Either nylon or cotton cord can be used for nets; nylon is more expensive but also longer-lasting and stronger for any given size. Bonded nylon, made especially for netting, is the best, since the bonding process gives the nylon a "tackiness" that helps to "lock" the knots securely and prevent slipping. Regular nylon can be used, but it's more difficult to work with and more likely to slip.

Nylon comes in several sizes, varying from a size 3 with 8300 feet per pound of cord, to size 48, with only 360 feet per pound. Generally sizes 3, 5, 7, and 9 are used for landing nets. A large 36-inch-deep landing net made from size 7 nylon requires about 4 ounces of cord.

The cord must be transferred from the spool to the proper size shuttle, which is determined by the mesh size of the net. Most nets have a large mesh near the net wheel and progress to smaller mesh near the bottom of the net. The plastic shuttles are flexible; the illustrations show how to load the shuttle easily and quickly. Essentially, the nylon is tucked around the tongue of the shuttle, then wound around the foot and back around the tongue again, the steps repeated until the shuttle is filled.

In practice, I find it easiest to hold the shuttle by one edge in my left hand, alternately pushing the tongue out from the main body of the shuttle to slip the cord over it. Once the shuttle is loaded, you can begin in one of several ways. One way is to make a straight square net (like a short commercial gill net), joining the two sides with the netting knots once the net is finished. But by using a "net wheel," it is possible to make one continuous net, working toward the bottom without any seams. The net wheel, available from Netcraft, a major supplier of net-making tools and materials, is a wire wheel, with 40 clips around the circumference to hold the beginning loops of cord.

In using the net wheel, leave several feet of cord at one end and then clip the cord to the first loop. Measure each loop of cord before slipping it onto the wheel rim, making sure that all loops are equal and of the proper size for the mesh gauge chosen for the net.

At this point, it's well to realize that net meshes are measured in two different ways—stretched and square. Square measurement is the size of each square of mesh, from one side of the square opening to the other (from one

Materials and tools needed for net-making. Left: mesh gauges; right: shuttles; bottom: nylon net twine.

Method of locking the nylon net twine in place on the shuttle.

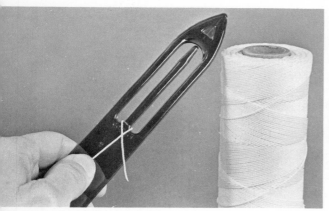

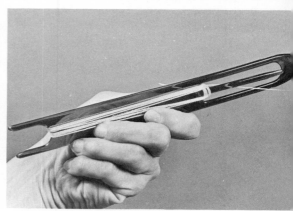

Shuttle is wrapped alternately from side to side with the net twine, wrapping the cord around the tongue of the shuttle each time.

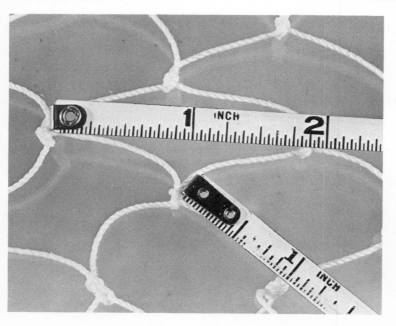

Two methods of measuring net mesh size. Top: stretched mesh, measuring the net meshes stretched into a slit. Bottom: square measurement, measuring the side of the square mesh opening from one knot to the next.

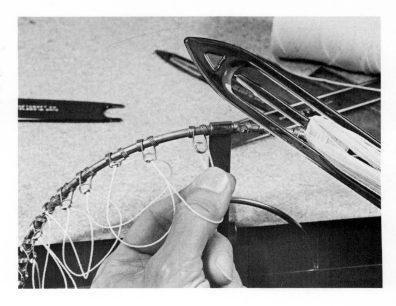

Clipping the nylon net twine into the clips on a net wheel. Nylon loops must all be the same size.

knot to the next knot). A net mesh measuring 1 inch from one knot to the next would be 1-inch square mesh. The same mesh would be a 2-inch stretched mesh, since this measurement is taken with mesh stretched, measuring the length of the slit of mesh formed.

The mesh gauge you use determines the square mesh measurement. Thus, a 1-inch-thick mesh gauge would form 1-inch-square mesh netting, or 2-inch stretched netting.

Once the nylon is clipped around the net wheel (and not all the clips have to be used—in case smaller nets are being made) tie the running end and the short end together. (A "short" end of several feet is necessary to knot the net together each time a row of mesh is completed.)

The construction of a net from this point on is nothing more than repeating the basic net knot, formed in each hanging loop of the net cord. This knot is best described as basically a sheet bend, but the accompanying photos show it in close-up and tying views.

After filling the net wheel, tie the two ends with a net knot. Hold the mesh gauge against the knot just tied, and bring the shuttle with the cord around the gauge and up behind and through the next loop. For a right-handed worker this next loop will be the one to the right of the knot. Pull tight, still holding the mesh gauge against the knot and the bottom of the adjoining loop. I find it easier to pull the shuttle (in my right hand) across my left hand at this point, holding the cord securely with my left thumb (see photos). Flip the loose cord up above the net. Take the shuttle, right to left behind the two cords forming the upper loop, and bring it through the loose loop just thrown up by the shuttle hand. Pull the shuttle tight, down, and at an angle, securing the knot. If the knot is going to slip, it will be at this point: the just-formed knot may slip below and off the loop. Correct this when it happens since the slipped knot will make for uneven meshes.

Repeat this procedure with the adjoining loops all the way around the net until you reach the loose end of cord once again. Tie the shuttle end with the short end, using the same knot, and continue as before. If you follow these instructions (learning how should take only a few minutes' practice), the net will proceed rapidly with even, strong meshes.

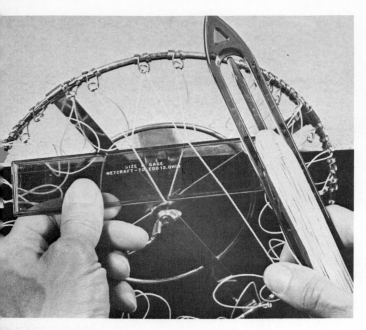

Beginning the first row of meshes by bringing the nylon twine around the mesh gauge and through the first loop

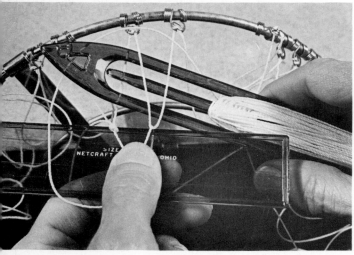

Holding the mesh gauge in place and running the shuttle behind the loop to form a sheet bend, the knot used in making nets.

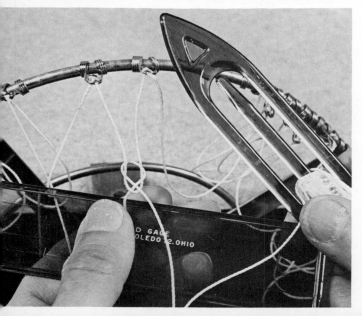

Netting knot just before it is pulled tight.

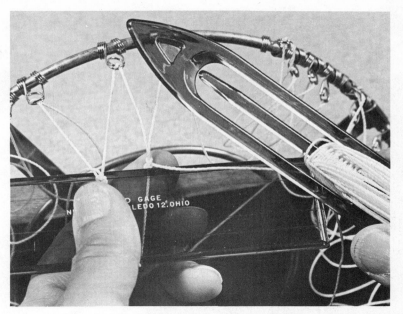

Netting knot pulled tight, ready to make the next mesh through the adjoining loop.

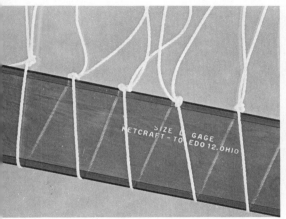

Series of mesh loops on a mesh gauge. This is how they would look as the net is being made.

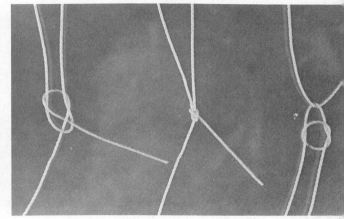

Details of netting knots. Left: open view of proper net knot; center: net knot pulled tight; right: net knot that has slipped and must be corrected.

As the net progresses, you will want to decrease the number of loops, to form a tapered shape. To do this, run the shuttle through two loops at several points around the net. For example, when using the net wheel with 40 clips, you could decrease the number of loops to 36 by picking up two loops at four equidistant points (every 9th loop) around the net; the next decrease could drop it another four by picking up two loops every 8th loop.

Similarly, the size of the net can be decreased by changing to smaller mesh gauges as the net progresses. This is easiest to do when one shuttle runs out of cord, since the smaller mesh gauge requires a smaller shuttle to run it through the mesh loops. It's also possible to widen a net by adding an additional loop over one already tied in. This means that two net knots are tied over one loop so that two loops are hanging from the same point.

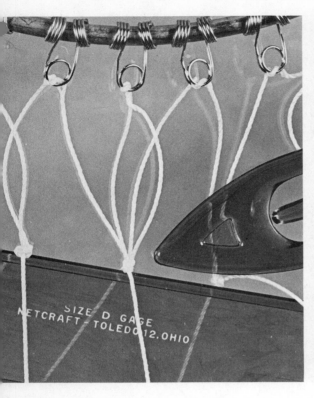
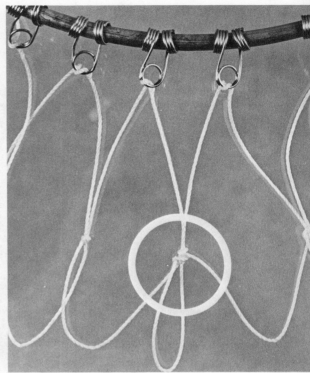

There are several ways to finish the net; one way is to decrease the net loops down to 10 to 15 loops, then finish it off with a small 1-inch-diameter curtain ring. Either half-hitch the cord around the ring and each loop until the net is finished, or make one more row of loops, looping them around the ring instead of the mesh gauge. The first method is usually the easier.

If a narrow net is not desirable, continue to make rows of mesh loops until the proper depth is reached, then lay the net out flat, alternately making the netting knot from one loop on one side to a loop on the other. This results in a net with a squared, rather than rounded, bottom.

This same technique is used for closing the seam on a net when a net wheel is not used. Using this method, a chain of mesh is first tied, using the mesh gauge, then the chain is transferred to a rod. After this, the rows of meshes are formed as above, except that instead of being worked in one direction, they must be worked alternately left to right and right to left.

NET FRAMES

Woven nets can be used in several different ways. First, they can be used for replacement of rotted nets in standard landing net frames. Alternately, they can be placed in discarded tennis, squash, and badminton racket frames. Almost every house has in it somewhere an old racket or two that may be easily converted into a landing net.

Method of decreasing the size of a net by running the shuttle through two loops at once. Shuttle points to knot made with two loops.

Method of increasing size of net by adding loop to perimeter of net. Several loops like this would be added to each row.

←

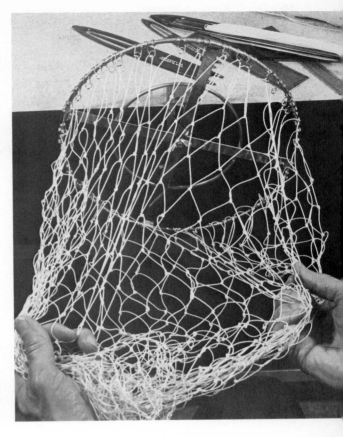

Net near completion. Note net wheel that makes it possible to make seamless nets.

Frame sizes of the three rackets are 10¾ by 8 inches for tennis, 9¼ by 7¼ inches for badminton, and 7⅝ by 6¾ inches for squash, all inside diameter. Of the three, the badminton racket is most useful since the tennis frame is a bit heavy, the squash frame opening a bit on the small side.

First remove the catgut from the frame, then cut the handle to length if desired. This will be necessary for the badminton and squash rackets being converted to streamside landing nets. It will not be necessary in making a boat net of a tennis racket, where the longer handle is desired.

A cork fishing rod grip (preformed or built up as described in Chapter 8), rubber fishing rod grip, or plastic bicycle grip can be used as a new handle over the racket shaft.

Once finished, the new landing net is attached to the frame by threading and lacing the net through the holes in the frame rim, or by looping the net to the frame with lacing cord spiraled around the net frame.

It's also possible to construct the rim and handle of your net. Heavy steel or aluminum wire, combined with a wood handle, can be used for the net rim. Or the entire frame of the net may be made with aluminum tubing.

The net frame must be bent in a circle, a job best accomplished with tube benders or with a wood jig made to bend tubing or steel wire to different radii. Steel or aluminum frames should be ¼-inch or ⅜-inch diameter rod; the length can be determined by multiplying 3½ times the chosen rim diameter. (The circumference of a circle is 3.1416 times the diameter—the additional wire is used for lugs to bind the net to the wood or aluminum handle.)

Bend the wire net frame on a jig made of a plywood disc fastened to a wood base, securing the straight end of the wire with wood strips and C-clamps. Use a plywood disc with a 6-inch radius, since most nets will not be smaller than 12 inches in diameter. Larger net rims can be formed by pulling lightly on the wire, repositioning it several times to form an even circle, or by using a larger bending jig. Once the frame is bent in a full circle, bend the two ends at right angles to and away from the frame rim, making each straight piece 3 to 4 inches long.

At each end of these pieces, bend short lugs inward, to fasten into the wood frame, to keep the net from canting sideways when landing a big fish. To make these final bends, it might be necessary to clamp the wire ends in a vise, hammering over the short lug. It's also possible to use a longer length of wire, bending over the lugs and then cutting them to length—an easier but more wasteful method.

Finish the net by making the wooden handle and attaching the frame to it; 1-inch-diameter wood dowels 24 to 48 inches long make good handles. To fit the frame to the handle, cut two grooves (parallel to handle length) in the terminal (net end) 4 inches of the handle, each groove the diameter of the steel rod used in the frame. Cut an additional hole or depression (it can be drilled) at the end of the groove, 4 inches from the net end of the handle. The lugs will slip into this slot; check the frame for fit.

Once the frame is fitted into the grooves, the net can be finished by clamping the rim in place on the handle, and wrapping it securely with light brass or stainless steel wire using the same method as in wrapping a rod (see Chapter 8).

Because the wire is stiff and harder to work than rod-wrapping thread, it may be necessary to finish the wrapping with a long staple or by wrapping the wire around a small nail or wood screw rather than pulling the wire underneath other wrappings as with thread.

The net can be added before the frame is put on the handle, or wrapped on the rim with a separate cord after the handle and frame are completed. I recommend the latter method, since any replacement nets will have to be put on in the same manner, unless the net and frame are taken apart.

Following the same directions to fasten the lugs of the frame onto a short 6-inch dowel of wood, you can place the frame on an aluminum handle, force-fitting the wood dowel into the aluminum tubing. (One-inch Reynolds do-it-yourself aluminum tubing makes a good handle.) The dowel should be the same diameter as the *inside* diameter of the tubing. If a dowel the correct size is not available, a larger dowel can be shaved to fit. Once the dowel is fitted in the tubing, pin the dowel in place with two long rivets or four small oval-head wood or sheet-metal screws.

With the same 6-inch diameter plywood disc-bending jig mentioned above (directions for making this jig are in Chapter 13), net frames can also be made of aluminum tubing. The Reynolds Metals Company for some years has been marketing do-it-yourself aluminum materials, including tubing, strap, rods, bars, channel, and sheets. The Reynolds aluminum tubing comes in either 6-foot or 8-foot lengths, in ¾-inch, 1-inch, and 1¼-inch diameters. Unfortunately, the ¾-inch diameter is too large for the rim of a frame, as it creates too much resistance in sweeping it through the water to lift a fish. But except for ½-inch aluminum tubing, found at some specialty shops of large aluminum fabricators, ¾-inch is the smallest generally available.

As with the wire, the framing length should be chosen by multiplying the diameter of the net by 3½ to determine the length of rim material required. The aluminum tubing can be bent in a circle; bend the tubing just a little each time on the bending jig. Bending jigs of several sizes will be required for bending tubing. Tubing bent at too sharp an angle or curve will deform and crack—examples can be readily found in old and abused aluminum lawn furniture.

The smallest bending radii recommended for the three diameters of Reynolds aluminum tubing are as follows:

¾-inch tubing	6 inches radius
1-inch tubing	11½ inches radius
1¼-inch tubing	13 inches radius

These maximum bends can be cut in half by tamping the portion of the tube to be bent with damp sand.

Once the tubing is bent in a circle, remove it from the jig, sand tamp both ends with damp sand, and place in a smaller 3-inch radius jig. (The sand used should be damp—not dry so that it falls apart when cupped in the hand, not so wet that water can be squeezed from it.) Plug the end and then bend the end of the tube in the jig, making the bend opposite the curve of the frame. Repeat with the other end. The two ends of the frame will now be parallel, so that they can be slipped in the aluminum handle.

Flatten the inside edges of the frame ends until they slip inside of the 1-inch aluminum tubing handle. Once the ends of the frame are securely in the handle, drill two ⅛-inch holes, each hole going through the handle and one of the frame ends. Add self-tapping sheet-metal screws to the handle to hold the frame in place, and the net is finished. The screws make it possible to remove the frame rim to add the net or replacement bags.

Cut the handle to the length desired. Nine-inch handles are standard for nets carried on the stream; 24-inch to 48-inch handles are standard for boats, depending upon the fish, waters, and conditions. The handle can be finished with a Reynolds aluminum spring snap cap in the end, or, as I prefer, finished with a crutch tip, chair tip, or bicycle grip of the proper size. In addition to the smooth aluminum tubing, 1-inch tubing is also available in oval-embossed, hexagonal-embossed, and rib-embossed patterns. The patterns make a more attractive net handle and also provide a better grip. There are also a number of other ideas and net-making tips in the $1 booklet "Popular Netcraft," by H. T. Ludgate, published by Netcraft, Toledo, Ohio.

PLUG RETRIEVER

With 4 feet of chain, a short length of tubing, a little lead, some heavy line, part of a broom handle, and a cheap reel, you can make a plug retriever

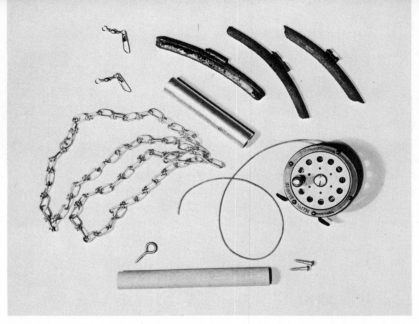

Parts needed for making plug retriever include lead, aluminum tubing, chain, snaps, fly reel, dowel, screw eye, screws, and heavy twine.

equal to the best on the market. It will have all the necessary ingredients of a good plug retriever: weight, plenty of chains to catch plug hooks if the plug will not knock off, and the strength to pull up a plug with a tree branch, as a last resort.

Its construction is simple: take ¾-inch or 1-inch aluminum tubing or conduit and cut it to a 4-inch length. Next drill four holes at equal distances around the sides near what will be the base or lower part of the plug retriever. The easy way to do this is to drill two holes straight through one end of the tube and then two more holes at right angles to the others and just above them. Using No. 3 Inco Coil chain, a ⅜-inch hole is just about the right size to allow the chain to pass through the holes. Then drill two small holes in a line along one side just large enough to allow for the passage of the swivel of a large snap-swivel.

Next, take the chain (No. 3 Inco Coil chain—a double-loop weldless wire chain) and cut it into three equal 12- to 14-inch lengths. Run one length of chain through the tube, leaving one link exposed at the upper end, then run the two lengths through the drilled holes, allowing an equal length of chain to hang from each side of the tube. Getting the last length of chain into position may be a little difficult but, by twisting the chain, it can be worked through. Place the snap swivels in the smaller holes with the snap exposed and the plane of the snap at right angles to the axis of the tube.

At this point, wrap the plug retriever with tape to hold the chain and snap swivels in position and also to prevent any leakage when the lead is poured into the top of the tube. Paper tape, such as masking tape, works better than plastic or rubber tape, which has a tendency to burn when the lead is poured. Wrap it as securely as possible all around the openings of the tubing except the end of the tubing at the top of the plug retriever. The bottom of the tube, the four holes for the chain, and the two holes for the snap swivels must all be securely wrapped. Place the plug retriever into a bucket or can of sand, leaving only the top opening exposed. The sand will prevent leakage of the

Drilling in the aluminum tube to accommodate the chain.

Slipping the chains and snap swivels into place in the drilled holes.

Wrapping the hole openings with tape.

Pouring the plug retriever full of lead. Note that the plug retriever is placed in a can of sand and that the top link of chain is held in place with a nail.

lead, will absorb the heat of the lead, and will safely hold the tube upright while you're pouring. If the top link of chain slides down inside the tube, hold it in place with a nail placed through the link and across the top of the tube.

If you have a ladle for pouring the lead, so much the better. If you do not, an old discarded pot or even a coffee can will do. Lead can be bought at a junkyard; in fact, discarded tire weights from a gas station will be enough for the few ounces you will need. While melting the lead, keep the kitchen fan on or leave a window open; lead fumes can be dangerous. In pouring the lead make sure that it is hot—this is one secret of getting a good plug retriever. A purplish cast on the surface of the melted lead indicates that it is hot enough. (See Chapter 3 for details of lead-melting procedures.)

Pour the lead rapidly into the tube, until it is filled. Make sure that the top link of chain is centered in the lead. It can be positioned in the liquid lead with a pair of pliers if necessary. Allow the lead time to cool and then remove the retriever from the sand and unwrap the tape. If all has gone well,

Screwing the inexpensive fly reel to the wood dowel.

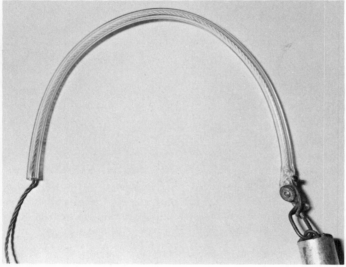

An 18-inch length of plastic vinyl tubing at the terminal end of the cord prevents fraying of the cord on rocks while retrieving lures.

Completed plug retriever.

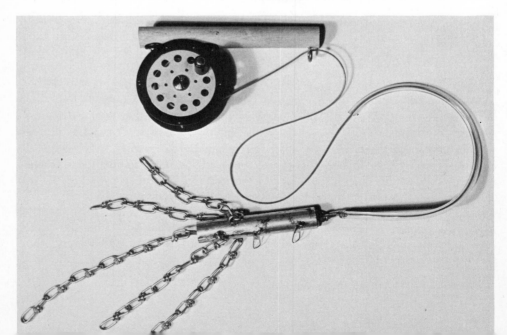

the tube will be completely filled with lead and no lead will have leaked through the wrapped openings. If a little lead has leaked through, remove it with a fine triangular file.

To make it easy to use the plug retriever, I mounted a cheap fly reel onto a 6-inch length of dowel and placed a screw eye in the end of the dowel for the retrieving line to run through. The best way to mount a reel on a dowel (or length of broom handle) is to drill holes in the two sides of the reel foot and screw the reel to the dowel. The dowel will then give you a short "handle" to hold, and the reel will store the heavy line needed to pull up your plugs.

Duke Nohe, a Maryland bass guide, arrived at the same plug-retriever idea independently, but he used a discarded casting reel to hold the line. Fifty to seventy-five feet of heavy line should be plenty to retrieve most plugs and will not overload the reel. One-hundred-and-seventy-pound test Nylon cord, available in spools from most hardware stores, is especially well suited for this task.

Since the plug retriever will be used around rough, rocky ledges, stumps and other underwater obstructions, the end of the heavy retrieving line can become frayed. To prevent this, get some thin vinyl plastic tubing and place a short, 18-inch, length of it over the end of the line; the type of tubing used to aerate aquarium tanks works well and is readily available. If you have trouble getting the line through the plastic tubing, run a doubled thin wire through the plastic tube, place the line through the loop of the wire, and pull the wire and line back through the tubing. Tie the line securely to the top link of chain in the plug retriever and slip the plastic tubing down over the line. Rivet or tie the plastic tubing to the upper chain link to hold it in place.

Using the plug retriever is simplicity itself. Once you are hung up on the bottom, secure the snaps of the plug retriever onto your fishing line and let the retriever descend to the plug. In most cases this will be sufficient to knock the lure free. In other cases it will be necessary to bounce the retriever up and down a few times to free the plug. If the plug remains snagged, continue to bounce the retriever, and it will catch a treble hook on one of the several chains. Wrap the line several times around the dowel and pull on the dowel, to prevent line cuts to your hands. Usually, you can pull the plug to the surface although you may bend or break one of the hooks. Once, while using this retriever, I pulled a plug up but left one of the treble hooks in a log. This was a minor loss since a new treble hook costs only 3 cents; a new plug would have cost $1.75.

GAFFS

It is possible to buy steel rod and wood handles and make a gaff from scratch, but I can't recommend it. Proper construction of a gaff hook requires equipment for bending ¼-inch steel rod and for tempering it—processes generally not possible for the home craftsman.

The best way to make gaffs is to buy the ready-made gaff hooks and se-

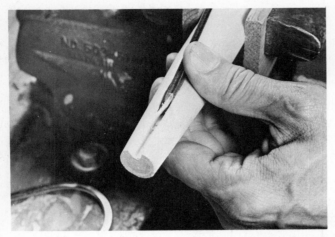

Grooving a wood handle for placement of a gaff tang.

Placing the gaff tang in place in the grooved handle.

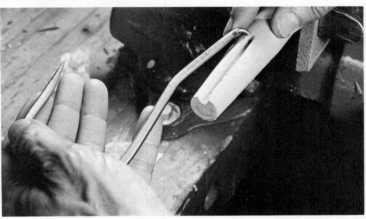

cure them to a wood or aluminum handle. Gaff hooks are made in both ⅝-inch and ¼-inch stock, are properly tempered, and have a built-in tang for attaching to the handle. Sizes from 1½-inch to 2½-inch gap are available from tackle and mail-order stores.

To make a wood-handled gaff, groove the gaff end of the handle and notch it to receive the tang and offset end, then wrap the gaff hook onto the handle with stainless steel wire. Aluminum wire, brass wire, and nylon cord might weaken or loosen in time and are not recommended. Wood gaff handles are generally tapered at the end, so that wrapping should begin at the gaff end.

The same technique is used here as in wrapping guides on a rod, except that the end of the stainless steel wrap may have to be stapled into place (using heavy staples—not those used for paper) rather than pulled under the previous wraps. A small round-head wood screw can be used; wrap the end of the wire around the shaft of the screw before it is tightened. If you do attempt to pull the end under previous wraps, do it carefully, clamping the gaff securely in a vise and pulling the loop with pliers.

Gaffs can also be made with aluminum handles, using 1-inch smooth or embossed aluminum tubing; these make a much better-looking gaff and are just as easy to make.

Take a short, 6-inch piece of dowel, one with a ⅞-inch diameter (or the proper size to fit snugly into the aluminum tubing). Groove and notch it to

Beginning the wrap of the gaff hook with wire.

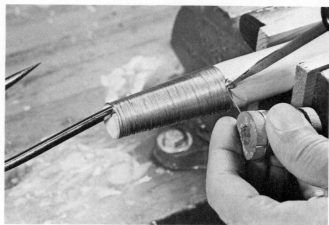

Completed wrapping of gaff hook, with end of wire wrapped around screw.

receive the gaff tang and offset end as described above for the wood-handled gaffs. Make sure that the groove in the dowel is deep enough so that the gaff tang is flush with the outer circumference of the dowel.

Fit the tang into place on the dowel and start the dowel into the end of the aluminum tubing. It should fit snugly, but not be so tight that it will risk splitting or deforming the metal wall of the tube.

Now hold the aluminum handle vertical on the floor (with something under it to prevent scarring the floor) and gently hammer the dowel and gaff hook into the tubing until the dowel is flush with the end of the handle. Once it's hammered home, drill the tubing and wood dowel through at two points, both holes at right angles to the plane of the gaff hook. Secure the gaff with a 1¼ inch aluminum rivet, a sheet metal screw, or a round-head ½-inch wood screw.

Another easy way to make a gaff is to get a large (7/0 to 10/0) needle-eye saltwater hook, file the barb off, and if necessary, bend the hook gap to shape. (Needle-eye hooks are used in big game saltwater fishing, and some of the hooks have the point bent in toward the shank, for increased strength. They are hardened and must be heated to be bent.)

Drill a hole in the wood handle large enough to insert the hook shank snuggly. Carefully measure the depth of the hole, then drive the hook shank home into the hole. Measure and drill another small hole through the side of the handle so that the drill will run through the needle-eye in the hook.

Seat the hook so that the hole is drilled across the grain, to prevent any possibility of splitting the wood. Insert a small bolt or pin to prevent the hook from pulling out, and the gaff is finished.

For an additional ounce of prevention, wrap the drilled section of the gaff to prevent any splitting or shearing of the wood if a fish lunges or twists on the gaff when being landed. The same procedure can be used to insert the hook in a wood plug, seating the plug in an aluminum handle and securing with four wood screws, sheet metal screws, or rivets. Slip a 1-inch-diameter bicycle grip on the end of the gaff handle, and it is ready to use.

If desired, a gaff point protector can easily be made from a piece of rubber or plastic tubing and a short length of friction tape. Pick flexible tubing that will fit snugly onto the gaff hook. Slip it over the gaff point for about 1 inch and then pierce the side of the tubing with the gaff point.

Continue to run the 1-inch length of tubing over the gaff hook, until it is against the end of the handle. Turn the tubing so that the loose end is opposite the gaff point, to keep the protector out of the way while gaffing fish, and secure the tubing in place with plastic tape. Now pull the tubing around one

Fitting the end of a needle-eye fish hook into a predrilled wooden plug.

Drilling the wood plug through the needle eye to receive a pin to hold the gaff hook in place.

Hammering the pin through the wood plug and needle eye of the hook.

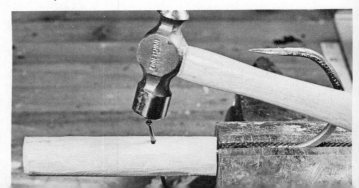

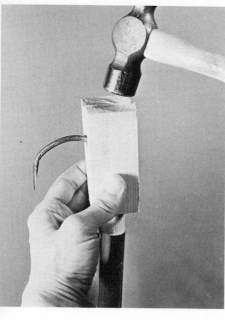

The plug is secured in the aluminum tube by means of wood or sheet metal screws.

Hammering the round wooden plug into the end of an aluminum tube.

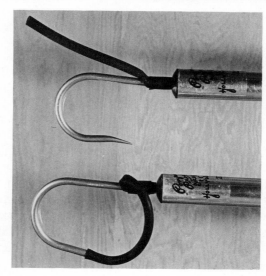

Gaff point protectors of rubber tubing. Top, out of the way and ready for gaffing; bottom, point protector in place on gaff.

side of the shaft and measure the tubing so that when cut, it can be slipped over the gaff point. Cut the tubing, and slip the protector in place. The protector will prevent accidents and damage from the gaff point, but when you're ready to gaff a fish, it can be quickly slipped off. It cannot get lost, as a loose point protector could, and it's out of the way.

ROD HOLDERS, SAND SPIKES, ROD RACKS, AND ROD CASES

ABS, RS, PVC, and CPVC plastic pipe can be used for a number of fishing tackle items not limited to the four items mentioned above. CPVC is an abbreviation for chlorinated polyvinyl chloride pipe, PVC stands for a similar polyvinyl chloride pipe, RS for rubber styrene plastic, ABS for acrylonitrile butadiene styrene. They are all rigid, will not rust, rot, or corrode; they are lightweight, easy to cut and work with hand tools, and readily available at hardware and plumbing supply houses.

Sizes for plastic pipes range from ½ inch to 4 inches, but not all pipes come in all sizes. Most useful for the do-it-yourself angler is the ABS, which comes in 1½-, 2-, and 3-inch diameters; the RS in 4-inch diameter, useful in making a large sturdy rod case for traveling; and the PVC in the larger 1¼- and 1½-inch sizes, for rod holders and rod cases. Commercial PVC comes in larger sizes.

All four plastic pipes are inexpensive, from $0.75 for a 10-foot length of ½-inch PVC pipe, to $2.50 for 1½-inch ABS, $3.50 for 2-inch ABS, and $7.00 for 3-inch ABS, also sold in 10-foot lengths. Ten feet of 4-inch RS pipe runs about $3.50.

Use the 1½-inch or 2-inch ABS pipe or 1½ PVC pipe for rod holders in boats. The 1½-inch size is best except where boat rods with large butts or butt caps require the larger pipe. Cut a 1-foot length with a hacksaw or a fine blade wood saw, and smooth any rough edges with a wood rasp or round rattail file.

If you desire, the pipe can be flared at the upper end where the rod is inserted to prevent the edge of the pipe from scratching or scarring the rod handle, although this is very unlikely. Heat it over a stove, taking care to keep the pipe away from the open flame. When the ·pipe is hot to the touch, press it firmly onto the neck of a soda bottle to flare the pipe rim. While it's highly unlikely that the bottle will break during this procedure, take care to hold the pipe well away from the end being flared, and to wrap your hand in a towel to protect it. The pipe will not flare enough with one heating, so repeat this process until it is flared sufficiently.

To make a vertical boat-rod holder, drill through the lower (unflared) end of the pipe, and insert a bolt, long rivet, or similar pin to prevent the end of a rod from dropping below the holder. Because of the variety of boat materials and boat construction, no exact mounting method can be described. Usual methods involve using pipe strap or short lengths of aluminum strap or U bolts·around the outside of the rod holder at two points. Drilling two holes through the sides of the rod holder, enlarging the hole on one side to fit a screwdriver, and screwing the holder to the boat also works.

If you're going to use spinning tackle, cut and file a notch in the upper part of the holder for the foot of the reel, to prevent it from swinging around in a bouncing boat. It will not interfere with carrying conventional or trolling rods in the same holder.

Surf anglers always like to have rods at the ready, but the 8- to 12-foot length of some surf sticks makes it hard to carry them in a beach buggy while roaming the dunes in search of fish or birds working over bait.

Rod holders fixed to the front bumper of the beach buggy hold the rods vertically and ready for instant use. ABS plastic pipe, 1½- or 2-inch, cut to length, flared and drilled as described above, and attached to the bumper or to a removable board, serves as an excellent surf-rod holder. Up to ten rod holders can be rigged together, leaving several inches between each holder so that the rods or reels do not rub together while traveling the beaches.

Method of flaring heated plastic pipe on soft drink bottle for making rod holders, sand spikes, and similar tackle.

Slot cut in top of rod holder prevents spinning outfits from swinging around. The slot holds the reel post.

One problem of using any type of beach buggy rod holder is that terminal bottom rigs can get tangled. Ken Lauer, surf-fishing guide for the Outer Banks of North Carolina at Cape Hatteras, solved this problem with a modification in his front bumper rod holders. Actually, he gives his wife, who is also a good guide and angler, credit for the idea of adding a short, 3-inch, length of plastic pipe next to the base of each rod holder. When the pyramid sinker is slipped into this pipe, the terminal tackle is stabilized and cannot swing around and get tangled with other lines.

Sand spikes can be made using the same techniques. Using 1½-inch ABS or PVC pipe, measure the desired length for the sand spike. Generally, 2 feet is a serviceable length, although commercial ones range from 20 inches to 36 inches. Five 24-inch sand spikes can be made from one 10-foot length of pipe at a cost of only a little more than 50 cents per spike. Actually, the 2-foot length is only an approximate figure, since if the pipe is cut at a 30-degree angle to make a sharp end to stick in the sand or bank, the spikes will come out about 3 inches longer than if the cut were made at a right angle.

Do not cut the tube into five equal squared-off lengths, but make each cut at an angle to form the slant of the lower face of the spike. This way, with five cuts (three slanted and two right-angle cuts) all five sand spikes can be cut out of one piece of 10-foot pipe.

Another view of rod holder clamped to front bumper of beach buggy.

Method of keeping terminal tackle from swinging around in beach buggy rod holders. Small piece of plastic pipe holds sinkers.

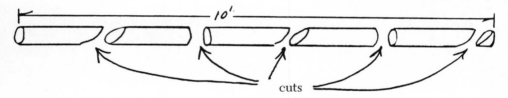

cuts

Measure off 21 inches, take a hacksaw and cut the pipe at a sharp 30-degree angle. Cutting the pipe at this angle will yield a sand spike about 27 inches long. If you want a spike of a specified length, measure that length of pipe and cut back toward the upper end of the sand spike; if the cutting angle is a little off, it will not affect the total length of the spike.

Now flare the upper end of the pipe (the squared end into which the rod will be placed), using the heat and soda bottle method mentioned for rod holders. To complete the sand spike, drill straight through the pipe 12 inches from the upper end (higher or lower if you desire the rod holder portion deep or shallow) using a ¼-inch drill. Insert a ¼-inch bolt (preferably of stainless steel or brass to prevent saltwater corrosion) through the hole and lock in place with a lock washer or by dropping epoxy or waterproof glue on the threads before tightening the nut. When the glue dries, the sand spike is finished, ready for use. The cost is only a few minutes' time and less than 60 cents for all materials including the bolt.

Even though sand spikes similar to this are available commercially, some surf anglers don't like them, claiming that they do not seat deeply enough in the sand and can be pulled out with the strike of a strong fish. Proper drag setting on the reel will usually prevent this, but Dr. Thad Wester of Lumberton, North Carolina, has come up with a modification of this basic sand spike for his fishing trips to Hatteras.

Dr. Wester takes a 20-inch length of 2-inch ABS tubing and fastens it to 36 inches of 1-inch angled (Reynolds do-it-yourself) aluminum, available at hardware stores. He cuts the aluminum at a sharp angle at the lower end to sink it deeply into the sand. Overlapping the aluminum and the ABS pipe by about 10 inches, he runs a bolt through the pipe and the aluminum at the lower end of the pipe, both to prevent the rod from dropping through when placed in the sand spike and to secure the two parts. The upper end he clamps with a stainless steel hose clamp. The result is a simple sand spike that can be driven deep into the sand, made from materials that will not corrode or rust with saltwater use.

The same ABS, PVC, or large-diameter 4-inch RS can be used for rod cases. The 1½-inch diameter pipe works well for individual rod cases, the larger 4-inch pipe for several rods, to conserve packing space on fishing trips. Caps are available for most pipes, along with special solvents permanently attaching the cap to the pipe. With the cap cemented in place on one end, lay the rod alongside the case and measure. Cut the pipe, allowing an additional 1 to 1½ inches of clearance at the end of the rod.

Since these pipes are not threaded, it takes some ingenuity to figure out how to add a removable cap. One way is to rivet the cap to a leather strap, and rivet one side of the strap to the top of the rod case, riveting a short strap and buckle to the other side. The cap can be closed with the strap and buckle, a method not unlike that used on many leather rod cases of years past.

An alternative is to buy a threaded adapter, cement it to the top of the rod case, and use a threaded end cap. Steve Hines of the National Rifle Association uses a case like this for his trout rod on western trips.

Typical sand spike made of plastic pipe.

Another type of sand spike made with aluminum angle and plastic pipe.

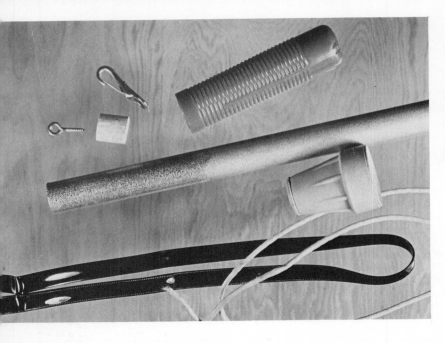

Parts needed for wading staff include aluminum tubing, crutch tip, plastic strap, nylon cord, bicycle grip, snap, wood plug, and screw eye.

Rod cases can also be made from Reynolds aluminum do-it-yourself tubing, available in 1¼-inch diameter and 6- or 8-foot lengths. By choosing the right length to make maximum usage of the aluminum, you can get two or three rod cases from each piece. Special aluminum end caps are available. The main disadvantage of the aluminum tubing is that the largest diameter tubing—1¼ inch—is only large enough for fly rods or light, one-piece spinning rods.

WADING STAFFS

Handy items for any river angler, wading staffs are easily made with the same do-it-yourself Reynolds aluminum mentioned above. One-inch tubing is best; the length is dependent on your individual preference and height. I find 55 inches a good length. Parts needed for the wading staff include 1-inch aluminum tubing, a heavy-duty rubber crutch tip, a bicycle grip, 30 inches of plastic strap, short wood plugs or dowels to fit the aluminum tubing, a screw eye, a 4-foot length of light rope, and a dog leash snap.

Cut the aluminum tubing to length, using a hacksaw. If there is any doubt about the proper length, cut it long—it can always be shortened later. Add the crutch tip to one end. (The best type of crutch tip, with a metal plate molded in place to prevent the metal tubing from cutting through, is available from some medical supply houses and better professional drugstores.) Cut a 4-inch length of wood dowel to fit snugly into the other end of the tubing and plane one side to allow room to wedge the plastic strap into place. Take 2½ feet of strap and place it along the flat side of the dowel as the dowel is tapped into place in the tubing. A 3-inch insertion of both ends will leave enough strap for an adequate loop extending out from the handle.

Tap the wood dowel home and add the 1-inch diameter bicycle grip. Since the grip will have to fit over both the aluminum tubing and the plastic strap, soak it first in hot water to soften it for an easier fit. Glycerine and special aerosol spray lubricants also help to slide the grip into place. With the grip in place, the strap will extend out from one side of the handle. Add

Seating the plastic strap in the top of the wading staff with the wood plug.

Slipping the bicycle grip in place for a handle.

Screw eye on top of completed wading staff is used to tie or snap the wading staff to fishing vest or clothing.

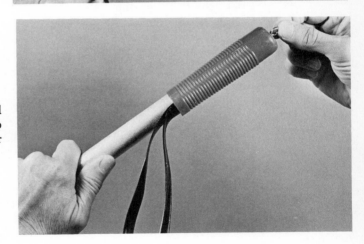

a screw eye to the top of the staff, through the hole in the plastic bicycle grip and into the wood plug.

Attach one end of the 4-foot cord (⅛-inch parachute cord, available at surplus stores, works well) to the screw eye or to the plastic handle, if you desire. Tie the other end to the dog leash snap. The cord prevents the wading staff from floating away while you're fishing, and the snap makes it easy to secure to clothing or a fishing vest.

While it does not really fit into the do-it-yourself category, a modified ski pole also works as well as a wading staff. Irv Swope of Frederick, Maryland, uses one and credits Jess Harden and Bill Hampt of Baltimore, Maryland, with the idea. Swope likes the ski pole better than the staff, citing that the sharp point gives a better hold on the stream bottom and the thin tubing of the pole creates minimal water resistance; also, ski poles are readily available.

Swope notes that used ski poles can be bought from many ski shops at a nominal price. Simply remove the webbing at the bottom. They come with a molded plastic handle and are available in many lengths. Instead of using a length of cord, Swope attaches the handle of the ski pole to a heavy-duty key-chain retriever which he can clip to any part of his clothing or fishing vest.

FLOATS

Fishing floats, or bobbers, can come in more styles than women's clothes, and all types of them are easy to make.

One of the easiest styles consists of nothing more than a bottle cork cut half way through along its length, into which the fishing line is slipped. It can be painted a bright color.

Going one step further, that same bottle cork can be drilled with a ⅛-inch hole and fitted with a short, ⅛-inch, dowel. The line runs through the hole in the cork and the short dowel is plugged into the hole when the cork is the proper length above the bait.

A bottle cork can also be fitted with a longer dowel glued into the hole, with a loop of 20-pound monofilament or heavy wire wrapped to the lower end. A bobber like this can be added to or removed from the line at will by running the line through the wire (or mono loop) to form a clinch knot.

The hole can be drilled or punched with an awl, the wire or mono loop wrapped with thread as a rod guide is wrapped in place. (See Chapter 8 for details on wrapping.) Similarly, round cork balls can be obtained in several sizes from any tackle store and used to build floats like those described above.

In addition to the round cork balls, slender tapered floats can be made by drilling a small, ⅛-inch, hole parallel with the grain of a block of balsawood. Then the float can be tapered to shape, using the hole as a center line, and finishing with sandpaper. Run the dowel through the hole, glue, add the loop, and the float's finished.

Porcupine quills are often used for delicate floats, and they can be bought from some tackle dealers and most fly-tying outlets. A loop of mono or wire wrapped to the lower end, and a small twist of spring wire or a small rubber band about the center of the float completes a quill float. The line is run through the loop in a clinch knot, and then clipped into place in the center of the float with the spring wire. If a rubber band fastener is used, the line must be run under the rubber band and through the loop at the bottom.

In all cases, bright or light colors are best for painting floats. White, or a combination of red and white or red and yellow, shows up well against water. Fluorescent colors painted over a white base coat have maximum brightness.

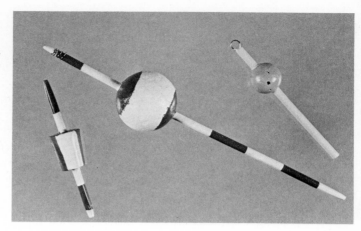

Examples of homemade cork-bodied floats.

CHUM POTS

These useful pieces of tackle have their place in freshwater fishing for carp and catfish, as well as in much saltwater fishing. Flounder, bluefish, striped bass, white perch, and other species can be attracted to a chum line. Sometimes chum is broadcast behind an anchored boat, but a chum pot is preferrable for many species. An easy way to make such a chum pot is to obtain a wide-mouth plastic jar. Mayonnaise and mustard are packaged for restaurants in these large jars, perfect for this purpose.

Take the jar, wash it thoroughly, and drill or punch a hole in the cap. Punch holes the size of the preferred chum bits in the sides of the plastic jar, using a drill, awl, reamer, red hot nail, or hot soldering iron. Weight the chum pot with several ounces of lead bars or sinkers screwed to the bottom.

A chum pot such as this can be made from a large plastic food jar, drilling holes in the sides to allow the chum to seep through. Weights in the bottom will sink the pot and a long line allows it to be tied to a boat or pier.

Knot a rope handle through two of the holes in the upper sides of the jar, with one end of the rope knotted through a hole in the lid to prevent loss. A rope tied to the handle when the chum pot is used can be untied and stored inside the pot.

In use, the chum pot is filled with the chum and lowered over the side by the rope; the weights in the pot sink it to the proper level, and the holes allow the chum to dissipate in the current or tide. Jiggling the chum pot rope helps to spread the chum.

BAIT BOXES

Bait boxes are still preferred by some boat fishermen for keeping minnows. The advantage of a floating bait box is that it can be easily constructed to any size and will keep the minnows in the water in which they are to be fished. There is no need to use battery-operated oxygen pumps, or to change the water at regular intervals, as is required with minnow buckets.

Basically, a floating bait box is like a small boat, except that the bottom is made of hardware cloth (a close mesh-wire screening) to allow the free flow of water.

General dimensions of a bait box are about 10 inches wide, 18 inches long, and 6 inches deep, although they can vary. Scrap wood can be used for the sides, ends, and top. However, if you use plywood, it should be marine type plywood, so that the plies do not separate with the constant contact of the water. The hardware cloth bottom is nailed or stapled in place.

Provision must be made for a lid in the top, through which to add or remove minnows. Usually this is made the full width of the top, centrally placed, with a simple toggle for closing. Any type of hinging arrangement can be used; perhaps the best is a stainless or brass piano hinge, or one of the newer polypropylene plastic piano hinges. All these materials are non-corrosive.

It is best to screw the box together with brass screws to prevent rusting. Fasten a large screw eye to one end of the bait box to tie the bait box to the boat. When varnished or painted, the box is ready to use.

ICE-FISHING RODS

Ice fishing for crappie, sunfish, pike, bass, and other fish calls for short sturdy rods. The sport is an old one, and is getting increasingly popular in all areas where ice gets thick enough in winter to support an angler's weight.

Ice-fishing rods are made in two basic styles, i.e., those used with spin-casting or other standard fishing reels and those in which the line is wrapped onto some device mounted on the handle. Since the variety of individual specifications for rods is limited only by the imaginations of the thousands of ice anglers, there are no standards in building this basic piece of equipment. But some general ideas will serve to illustrate the type of rods that can be easily made.

Most ice-fishing rods are short, both to give the lure or bait a sharp jigging action in the water, and to put the angler closer to the hole through which the quarry must be dragged. One way to modify regular tackle for ice fishing is to place a standard 3-foot tip section from a 6-foot spinning rod into a casting-rod handle, and use the resultant rod mounted with a spin-casting reel. Naturally, to fish a spin-casting reel, the rod guides will have to be mounted on top of the rod rather than underneath as in fishing open-face spinning reels.

A broken tip section of any type of light rod—spinning, fly, or casting—can be stripped, rewrapped with casting guides, and mounted on a spin-cast handle.

Components, including solid glass short-rod blanks especially for ice fishing, are available, enabling you to make any type of ice-fishing rod. The short blanks can be fitted with guides, according to the directions in Chapter 8, or guides can just be wrapped with tape for a simple, quickly built rod. The blank can be glued into a handle, also available from tackle stores and mail-order houses. Usually, ice-fishing handles are not designed to be used with reels, but will take a clamp-on device that will hold the line.

A 24-inch length of ½-inch dowel can be glued into the end of a 1-foot length of old broom handle or 1-inch dowel, to make an ice-fishing rod. These rods won't have the same action as those with a hollow or solid glass blank, but will give a jig, ice-fishing spoon, or dart a good action, the reasons being that the wooden "rod" will not bend while working the jig as will glass rods. Regular guides or just simple screw eyes at the middle and end of the rod can serve as line guides. A spin-casting reel can be taped to the middle of the wood handle or a simple clamp-on device used to wrap the excess line in place.

One simple, quick way to make an ice-fishing rod is to take a 1-foot length of scrap board 1 by 2 inches, and drill two ¼-inch holes in the side and another hole in one end. The hole in the end will be the same size as the glass rod blank or wood dowel to be glued in place. Two 2-inch lengths of ¼-inch dowel glued into the two holes in the sides of the "handle" serve as posts around which to wrap the line. It helps if the two holes are drilled at a slight angle, to slant the two posts away from each other slightly, and keep the line from slipping off.

Ice-fishing rods. Top, rod made from wood block and dowel, with safety pin guides taped on. Second row, casting rod handle fitted with short glass blank. Third row, ice-fishing rod with clamp-on line holder. Bottom, rod blank glued in wood dowel, reel taped to handle.

Ice fishing tip-ups. Left tip-up is inserted vertically next to hole drilled in ice. Right tip-up is laid across the center of hole drilled in ice. Line is draped across coat hanger hook. When fish hits, the hook is pulled down and the tip-up flies up, flying the red flag and signaling the angler.

FISHING MARKERS

Markers have a number of uses in both freshwater and saltwater fishing. Essentially a float with a line and sinker or weight attached, they serve to mark channels, fishing reefs, stream bottom in manmade lakes, drop-offs, points, and other fishing spots—most first located with a depth-finder.

Carried on a boat, they make it easy to mark a fishing spot temporarily, since they can be thrown out immediately and will unwind to mark the chosen spot. Once the fishing is over, they are picked up, rewound, and saved for the next trip.

Freshwater markers can be smaller and lighter than those used in saltwater since the area covered is usually smaller and the chop on the waters usually less. The buoy or marker for saltwater fishing must be larger, for both buoyancy and easy visibility.

To make a freshwater marker, cut a 1x4x5-inch board or similar sized plank into an H pattern. The center of the H is used to wind the cord, while the "wings" of the H keep marker from further unwinding once the sinker hits the bottom.

Any dimensions of the H, or for that matter any size of board, will do, depending upon individual preference. However, if the H is made too big or the center core cut too narrow, it will take a heavier sinker to unwind the board rapidly.

Once the board is cut out, paint it white, fluorescent orange (over a white base coat), or a similar bright color that will contrast with the water.

Tie and wrap light nylon cord on the center of the H, wrapping on enough cord to hit the bottom in the deepest hole of any fishing waters. For fresh-water fishing, this is usually 25 feet in ponds and shallow rivers, 50 feet in deeper ponds, rivers, and shallow lakes, and 100 feet in the deepest lakes. A

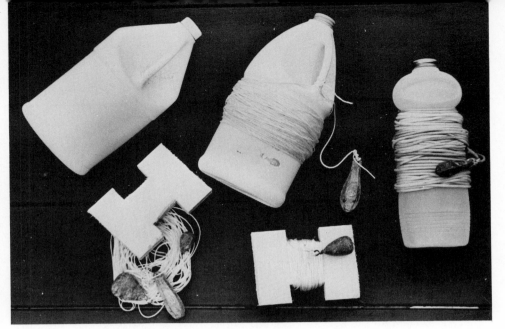

Fishing markers can be made from scraps of wood or plastic household product bottles. Wood is cut into an H shape as shown. Cord ending with sinker is wrapped around bottle or board marker to serve as temporary buoy in marking good fishing spots.

sinker of several ounces tied to the end completes the outfit. Since they are simple to make, it is best to cut out several at once, in case it is necessary to mark several fishing spots in one area.

For saltwater markers, a larger, more visible buoy is desirable. One-half- to one-gallon bleach or similar household product plastic bottles serve well for buoys. Clean off any labels, rinse out, and glue the cap in place. If the bottle has a handle, tie the line to it, and then wrap the line around the center of the bottle. (Otherwise tie the cord around the center of the bottle.) Depending upon the depths of water fished, this line may be from 50 to 200 feet in length.

The one disadvantage of this method is that since the bottle is not flat, the entire cord will unwind once the bottle is thrown out of the boat. For this reason, do not make the cord any longer than necessary. However, even with the entire cord unwound, the angle of the cord caused by tides and winds will not be enough to affect the marked spot significantly.

A heavier sinker here might be necessary to hold the bottom on a strong tide. Also, nylon cord is a must to prevent rotting or mildew.

One solution to the problem of the bottle's completely unwinding is to use a flat bottle that will have less of a tendency to turn over once the sinker hits the bottom.

These flat bottles are usually smaller—about 1-quart size—but white ones will still be visible and they will float high enough.

Another solution is to take one of the ½- to 1-gallon round bottles and fill it partially with plaster, concrete, or gravel mixed with glue. Fill the bottle about a quarter full and turn it on its side until the material cures and hardens. Any material like this will not stick to the slick plastic sides, but will tend to keep the bottle from unwinding in the water, since the weight will prevent it from revolving freely.

An alternative is to run several large round-head screws into the side of the bottle and turn the bottle so that these are in the concrete, plaster, or gravel-glue mixture as it hardens. This will hold the weight on the side and prevent the bottle from rolling in the water. However, it also opens the side of the bottle to possible leaks. If using this method, coat the screw heads with several layers of waterproof glue or cover with several layers of plastic waterproof tape.

LEADER STRAIGHTENER

With a small piece of leather and a small sheet of rubber, it's possible to make a simple and effective fly-fishing leader straightener that can be clipped to your fishing vest or clothing.

It has long been known that natural rubber, such as used to be found in automobile tubes, is an excellent leader straightener. The leader is pinched between the folded rubber and pulled under tension, and is almost instantly straightened.

By adding a leather backing for a better grip, it can be greatly improved. A small square of rubber 2 inches by 2 inches, along with a patch of flexible leather the same size and some light rivets or eyelets are all that is needed.

Experiment with the rubber before making the leader straightener. The best I have found is the large squares included in most auto tire patch kits. The backing can be peeled off and the rubber fastened to the leather. Rivets or eyelets in each corner will hold the leader straightener together. Eyelets are perhaps best, since a light cord can be run through one corner to secure the leader straightener to clothing or a fishing vest.

MAKING A BOBBIN

Simple bobbin for winding tails on bucktails and treble hooks can be made from coat hanger and pliers.

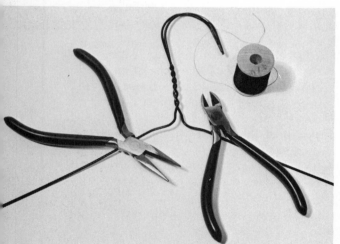

First bend made in coat hanger wire.

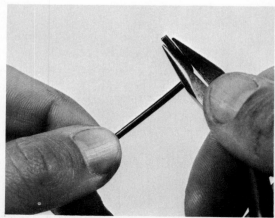

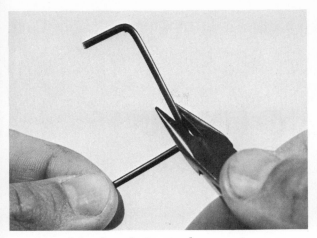

Second bend made in coat hanger wire.

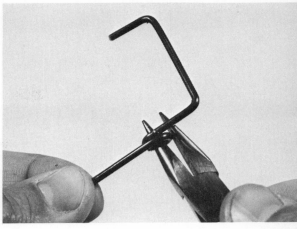

Loop in wire is made for the thread to run through while winding thread on bucktails.

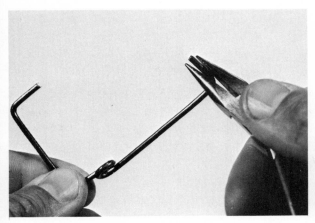

Third bend made in wire.

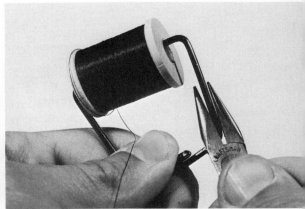

Fourth bend is made in wire with thread spool in place. Tension on spool is adjusted by degree of bend in wire.

Completed bobbin being used to wrap thread.

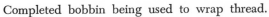

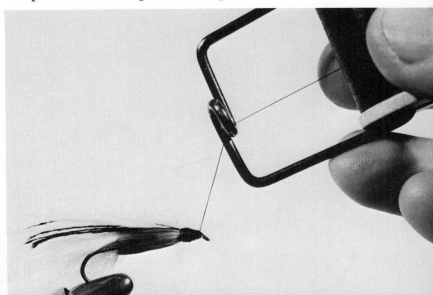

12

PAINTING AND FINISHING

*TOOLS · TYPES OF PAINTS · OTHER FINISHING
MATERIALS · PAINTING METHODS, DIPPING ·
PAINTING METHODS, SPRAYING · PAINTING
METHODS, BRUSHING · PAINTING WOOD PLUGS ·
PAINTING PLASTIC LURES · PREPARATION OF
METAL LURES FOR PAINTING · PAINTING METAL
SPOONS AND SPINNER BLADES · PAINTING
BUCKTAILS · PAINTING PATTERNS AND USING
STENCILS · PAINTING SCALE FINISHES · ADDING
AND PAINTING EYES · BAKING OF PAINTS ·
ELECTROPLATING METAL LURES · ADDITION OF
GLITTER TO LURES · ADDING FLOCKED MATERIALS ·
ADDING TAPES · COLORING PLASTIC WORMS AND
LURES WITH FELT-TIP MARKERS · FINAL LURE
FINISHING · COST · KITS*

BASIC TOOLS	HELPFUL TOOLS
Paint brushes	Masking tape
Scale netting	Embroidery hoop
Finishing nails and pins	Electroplating kit
	Felt-tip markers

∾ It Is Not Enough to Turn Out a Fine Wood Plug, Assemble a
series of plastic lures, cut, bend, and finish spoons, or mold bucktails by the hundred. Before they can be fished, they must be painted or finished. There are

numerous ways of finishing lures, depending upon the lure material, the method used, your choice of colors and patterns, scale finishes, and use of tape and reflective materials.

TOOLS

Very few tools are needed for finishing lures. The best methods involve dipping or spraying the paint, to prevent paint build-up or brush marks on the finished lure. If brushes are to be used, they should be the best obtainable. Small packets of cheap brushes, available for about $1 per pack of 20, are satisfactory for painting glass eyes on plugs or for brushing paints on small spinner and spoon blades; but for anything larger, they generally are a poor choice. The bristles tend to come out, and the nuisance factor, both in time consumed and poor results, make these "cheap" brushes too expensive. They should be thrown away after one use. If brushes are used or desired for some techniques, use the best-grade artist's brush in small sizes. Flat brushes in ¼- to ½-inch widths are best.

Since aerosol spray paints are so popular and readily available today, special air brush devices are unnecessary. In any case, their expense would probably make them an unlikely addition to lure finishing equipment.

If you're planning on more than a solid coat of color on your lures, you'll need masking tape. It is possible to cut out patterns in the tape, tape the pattern on the lure, spray, and remove the tape later. It will also be necessary for spray painting the head of a lure a different color from the body, as in the popular red head/white body plugs.

To add a scale finish to a plug, spoon, or spinner blade, a special netting pattern will be needed. This netting, available from suppliers such as Herter's, Finnysports, and Netcraft, has special hexagonal meshes to simulate the scales of fish. The cost is about $0.50 per square foot, $2.50 per square yard.

There are several ways to use the finishing netting, the handiest of which involves stretching it over an embroidery hoop, so that the lure can be held against the netting and sprayed the scale color. Embroidery hoops come in 4- to 12-inch diameters, and in oval and round shapes. They are available at all sewing, notion, and department stores for $0.50 to $1.00 depending upon size.

Eyes can be painted on lures using simply made tools. These tools are nothing more than several sizes of finishing nails or straight pins pushed into a short wood dowel which serves as a handle. The different-size heads on the pins and nails, when dipped into paint, make different-size eyes and/or pupils.

Since painting can be a messy job, the workbench or work area should be covered with oil cloth, newspapers, or other covering to make clean-up easy. Spraying is especially messy, since the fine paint mist tends to float in the air. If using spray paints, use some sort of "trap" to keep the paint in a confined space. One way to make a trap is to place a cardboard box on its side in back of the lures. A wire, length of pipe strap, or small link chain hung horizontally along the front top edge of the box serves to hang the lures. Even with a box like this, however, some of the spray will bounce back out of the box. One way I have found to prevent this is to line the back of the box with an

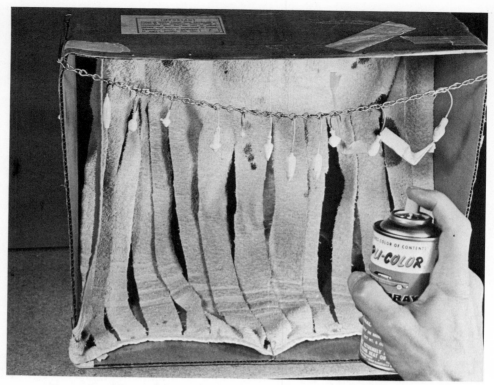

Example of box used to trap excess paint while spray-painting lures.

old turkish towel and hang strips of old toweling in front of this backing. The towel backing and strips trap the mist of paint and prevent it from filling the room.

While using spray paints, it's wise to wear goggles to protect the eyes and a small mask to cover the nose. These are both available from hardware and paint stores for several dollars each. If possible, an exhaust fan should be employed for extensive spray painting, or it should be done outdoors on a *calm* day.

TYPES OF PAINT

Paint comes in two basic ways—in cans and in aerosol sprays. The spray paints are generally more expensive for several reasons. First, packaging the paint with an aerosol propellant adds to the initial cost. A quick look at the net weights and costs of aerosol versus canned paint will show this to be true. Also, because of the spraying technique, much of the paint does not cover the lure, but instead is dispersed into the air. This is particularly true when spraying small items such as lures. For this reason, it's best to use some sort of rack and spray many lures at once to reduce waste as much as possible.

To its advantage, spray painting gives a very good, smooth finish on a lure if done correctly and in light coats. It is also the only way that scale finishes, "feathering" (blending) of two colors, and painting through stencils or masks can be effectively accomplished.

Canned paint can be used with a brush, or to dip lures. If you're dipping, thin the paint to prevent running streaks or the formation of a solidified paint drop at the lower end of the lure. Lure companies using dipping techniques avoid this by employing a mechanized conveyer chain that dips the lure and slowly removes it from the paint trough to prevent solidified drops. This is beyond the scope of the home craftsman, so thinner paint is a must.

Since paints of different types and manufacture can vary greatly as to their viscosity, no definite thinning directions can be given. The best method is to experiment with small quantities of a given paint and the proper thinner until proper results are achieved; keep records, so that the results can be duplicated with other colors or larger quantities.

Another factor to be considered in dipping lures is that larger quantities of paint will be needed than in brushing. Even one-pint cans are seldom deep enough for large lures, and so the paint must be transferred to a taller, thinner container to allow the lure to be completely submerged in the paint. This is not necessary when using brushes; even the small, quarter-ounce bottles of Testor's Pla enamel, available in hobby shops, can be used to paint large salt-water lures.

Both types of paint, canned and aerosol, vary greatly in their properties; some are best for wood lures, some for plastic, and some for metal. Mail-order houses specializing in do-it-yourself fishing supplies often offer different paints for different purposes.

The term "lacquer" can apply to a clear varnish and also to a colored nitrocellulose base paint of thin consistency. Sometimes these color lacquers are called lacquer enamels. They are excellent for painting metal (such as spinner and spoon blades and lead bucktails), and are very fast-drying. Often they are not at all acceptable for plastics, since the solvent in some reacts chemically with the plastic. But they vary widely, and some (such as an Express lacquer currently offered by Finnysports) are advertised as being good for plastics, corks, metal, and wood. Herter's also carries several pearl, radiant color, and fluorescent lacquers that can be used on all lure materials. Prices on lacquers vary from $0.30 per ounce in small bottles to $2.50 per pint.

Automobile touch-up lacquers are excellent for dipping or spraying and they come both ways. Hardware and auto supply stores carry them in the same colors to be found on cars. For metal lures and jigs, they offer about the most durable, toughest finish available.

Enamels are usually heavier, thicker paints, often advertised as "covering in one coat." They can generally be used on any type of lure material, but are not available in the same variety of colors as lacquers and auto touch-up paints. They are also slower-drying than lacquers. Prices are about the same as for lacquers, and they come in bottles, cans, and aerosols.

Alkyd and acrylic enamels are more modern enamels. They are available in small cans from lure suppliers as well as department and paint stores. They can be used on metal, wood, and some but not all plastics.

Epoxy paints, like epoxy glue, come in two parts, which must be mixed. These paints are very tough, but have the disadvantage of a flat finish, rather than the gloss preferred for most lures. But this can be overcome by using a

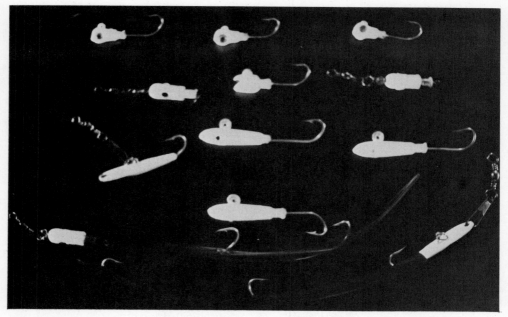

Phosphorescent painted bucktails and jig-heads. This picture was taken in complete darkness with only lures illuminating the photo.

finishing glossy coat of clear lacquer over the epoxy. These paints are available from paint and department stores, and generally come only in half-pint cans or larger containers.

In addition to the standard range of colors in the above paints, there are also special colors and paints that make even more elaborate lures possible. Fluorescent paints in red, orange, pink, yellow, green, blue, and purple are available from some tackle supply houses, such as Finnysports and Herter's. Many times these colors can be found either in cans or aerosols in drug, hobby, department, and stationery stores. Be careful when buying fluorescent paints that they are not water-based colors, designed only for poster work.

For best results, fluorescent colors must be used over a base coat of white; any other color, or painting over bare metal or wood, will not produce the expected bright color.

Phosphorescent paints, which glow in the dark, are also available for lure finishing. In some states or areas they may be illegal on lures, so be sure to check local laws and regulations before using them.

Phosphorescents also come in colors; the most common is a standard yellow or white, but blue and green are also available. These shades refer to the glowing color, not necessarily to the daylight one. Any lure painted phosphorescent will not glow indefinitely, but must be "recharged" with sunlight periodically. Therefore, it works best on lures that are frequently cast or exposed to the sun, rather than used for continued deep-water trolling.

There are also phosphorescent pigments that can be added to regular paints to give an underwater phosphorescent color in addition to a daylight color. Prices for these are about $2 per ounce of pigment material. Any of the above phosphorescent paints should be used over a base coat of white for best results.

Pearl pigments and paints give a lure a shiny, mother-of-pearl look. They can be used on plugs, but are more frequently found on spoons, spinner blades, and bucktails. Prices—about 35 cents per ounce.

Don't neglect to explore other paint possibilities. At Christmastime, I have found special paints normally used for holiday decoration that do well on lures also. Some of these include colored spray paints that contain fine bits of bright metallics to give a base color with a silvery, glittering overcoat.

Paints are also available that, when dry, give a crystal pattern to any lure. These are also sold at Christmastime to simulate the crystal patterns similar to those formed by ice on windowpanes. Their prices are often reasonable, about $2 per 8-ounce can, and they can usually be brought for reduced prices after the season.

OTHER FINISHING ITEMS

Other material for finishing lures can be used in place of paint, or with it. Reflective and colored tape can be used on fishing lures, including plastic and wood plugs, spoons, and spinner blades. Some tapes, such as Luhr Jensen Prism Lite, are shiny, prismlike reflective materials that can be cut to any shape. They have self-adhesive backing and are easy to add to any lure. They come in several different sheet and tape sizes, and in both gold and silver finishes.

Similar red reflective tape, designed as a car bumper reflector, can be used on lures with the same results. Some supply houses, such as Finnysports, carry other tape-finishing materials; one of these is a metallic flake glitter tape, available in 2-inch by 6-inch sizes for about 75 cents each. Colors available include silver, gold, red, and purple. A similar material available from hobby shops is a glitter tape in ½-inch by 6-foot rolls in gold, silver, and red colors, selling for less than $1 per roll.

A reflective tape with microscopic glass beads in silver, blue, white, red, and yellow sells for about $1 per 2- by 6-inch sheet.

Fluorescent colors in red, orange, yellow, blue, aluminum, and gold also come in tape and in 2- by 6-inch sheets, at less than $1 each. Phosphorescent glow-in-the-dark materials in sizes up to 2 by 6 inches sell for less than $1 each.

Pigments and glitter materials make it possible to add flash to any drab or scarred lure, or to design new lures with extra fish-getting flash. Most popular are the glitter materials in gold, red, silver, and green. These are tiny metallic bits that can be glued in place with any clear glue, or with a special clear glitter adhesive. They come in small bottles or plastic tubes and cost about 50 cents per ounce. Flocking material is similar but has a flat, furlike look. It is used principally on surface plugs to simulate the fur of a small animal such as a mouse.

Fluorescent, phosphorescent, and standard color pigments can also be used with lures, by dipping the lures into a clear lacquer or thin adhesive, and rolling or sprinkling the pigments where desired (detailed methods of using these materials will be given later).

Electroplating of spinner and spoon blades is also possible with a small battery operated, Plate-A-Matic electroplating craft set. Complete with all needed parts and gold, silver, and copper electrolyte, the set makes it possible to plate any spoon or to replate older, worn, or scarred spoons. The kits sell for $19.95 in hobby shops; replacement electrolyte refills are available.

> CAUTION: Once beginning to paint any lure, follow through the entire process with paints of the same type. This includes base coats, finish coats, scale finishes, masked sprays, eyes, and clear protective coats. Switching from one type of paint to another, even though the underlying coats are dry, can cause a chemical reaction with the result that the new coat may never dry or might crinkle, wrinkle, peel, crack, or blister. Unless clearly stated that a paint can be used over other types of paint, try to avoid such practices.

PAINTING METHODS—DIPPING

Dipping is perhaps the best method to use, for most lures, to get a base or single-color coat. Wood and plastic lures, spoon and spinner blades (where it is desirable to cover both sides of the blade with paint) can all be dipped, and dipping is ideal for painting bucktails.

The paint must be thinned *with the proper thinner*. It is hard to give exact directions on thinning because of the infinite variety of paints and formulations, but a 1-to-1 ratio is about average. If you're in doubt, experiment with small quantities first.

Since the entire lure must be dipped into the paint, often the paint must be transferred from the original bottle or can into a tall container, and this is especially true with plugs. Cheap juice glasses, olive jars, and similar items are excellent for this. Be sure to cover the work area with old newspapers and to have a rack handy on which to hang the lures to dry. A simple square of wood, with two end supports on which to string wire, chain, or pipe strap, makes a serviceable rack. The pipe strap and chain are ideal for heavy lures, since the hooks or hangers can be slipped into the chain links or pipe-strap holes to keep the lures from sliding together. Make sure that the rack side supports are higher than the length of any lure plus the length of the hooks or hanging wires.

Bucktails and spoons can be hung by the hook. Since plugs must be painted before any hardware is added, it will be necessary to use open-end screw eyes partially turned into the tail or head of the lure or a straight pin pushed into the plug with the shaft turned in a J shape for hanging.

Dip each lure carefully, covering the lure completely, and withdraw it slowly from the paint to minimize running streaks of paint. Once it's completely out of the paint, hold it over the container briefly to allow excess paint to run back into the container.

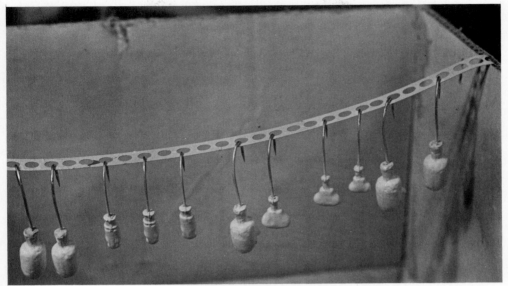

Pipe strap will keep lures separated while they are drying.

It helps to touch the lower part of the lure to the top of the paint surface here, to remove the last drop. If the paint is thin enough, this may be sufficient to prevent a dried droplet of paint on the finished lure. If the paint is not thin enough, it may be necessary to check the drying lures later, touching the lower part of the lure with a rag or absorbent towel to remove any drops of paint. The proper time for this will depend upon the paint's drying time. With lacquers, it may be necessary in a matter of minutes. With slower-drying enamels, it may be possible to wait an hour or longer. Dipping is ideal for base coats on bucktails and plugs.

SPRAYING

Spraying, providing it is done correctly, has the advantage of covering evenly, without streaks or droplets. The spraying should be done lightly, and several coats used to cover if necessary; too heavy a coat will run. Use a spraying box, as previously described, and line up lures as closely as possible to prevent waste of the aerosol paint. Since one spray coat will not cover all sides of a lure, turn the lures for each complete coat. Once the base coat is on the lure, additional secondary coats can be added. In this case each plug will have to be done separately unless "masked"—a technique to be discussed later. This does give good results, since the second coats of color can be "feathered" with the first coat, giving it a professional appearance.

Since the plugs must be held by hand, or with cheap long-nose pliers, to do this, wear rubber or light plastic painting gloves to keep the spray paint off your hands. Rubber gloves are available in houseware departments with the plastic painting gloves at paint stores.

Spraying does have some disadvantages. When spraying the base coat on the lead head of a bucktail (before the tail is tied on), you may get paint on the hook points. Unless the paint is removed, hooking fish becomes more difficult. One way to avoid this is to cover the points with a small bit of masking tape.

Before you put a finishing coat on a bucktail, tie the tail in place. This is done for the specific purpose of covering the thread windings with a protective layer of paint, and so that the lure will have a uniform color—but paint must be kept off the tail. Cover the tail with masking tape if you're spraying instead of dipping.

BRUSHING

Brushing is not generally adviseable for painting lures. It can leave brush marks, and there is a chance that a bristle will come off the brush and stick to the paint. It has no real advantage over either dipping or spraying, except when you are using a fine brush to add fine lines or other delicate work, a technique that also requires some skill. Delicate bars, stripes, spots, and similar markings can also be added by masking with stencils.

PAINTING WOOD PLUGS

Wood plugs should be finished with a fine, 7/0 or 8/0 grade sandpaper in order to get good results when painting. Once it's sanded smooth, the plug should be dipped, sprayed, or brushed with a wood sealer, to seal the pores of the wood and prevent subsequent coats of paint from soaking into the wood. If wood sealer it not used, the paint will soak into the wood in an uneven pattern, depending upon the grain, making several more coats necessary.

Once the wood sealer is dry, rough the surface of the sealer with a fine steel wool to give the sealer some "tooth," so that the subsequent coats of paint will adhere to it. Each subsequent coat of paint, except for the final coat, should also be buffed lightly with steel wool to give it "tooth" for the next coat. Both spraying and dipping work well on wood plugs.

PAINTING PLASTIC LURES

Plastic plugs are painted the same way as wood plugs, except that additional care must be taken in the choice of paint. Some plastics will react chemically with some paints, so the paint being used should be clearly marked as being suitable for plastic. If it's not, test it first on an old plug or a small corner of the one you're painting, to be sure that the paint cures properly without softening the plug or otherwise chemically reacting. Spraying, brushing, and dipping techniques can be used.

PREPARATION OF METAL LURES
FOR PAINTING

Preparation for painting of bucktails, spoons, and spinners is extremely important. All rust, grease, oils, perspiration, and dirt must be removed for proper adherence of the paint: use an acid or metal cleaner, dipping the spoon, spinner blade, or bucktail body into the solution according to directions. Several types of acid cleaners are available from mail-order supply houses. Some are used undiluted, others are diluted with two parts water. Most of these cleaners are of an "inhibited" acid type that will prevent any damage to the surface of the metal.

Because of the acid content of these cleaners, they can be used only in plastic (polyethylene), glass, or crockery containers, since they would attack metal cans. The solutions are irritating to the skin and toxic if breathed in quantity, and are volatile, with low flash points. Handle them with care, *use them with proper ventilation or outdoors*, and *don't smoke* while you're using any product like this. A weak acid, such as white vinegar or acetone, can be used as an alternative to clean and prepare metal lures. These are less dangerous to use, but still should be used with the above same precautions.

Shortly after the metal surface is cleaned it should be painted; waiting will only allow more dirt, oil, and grease to accumulate on spoon or bucktails and prevent good adherence of the paint. Lead lures will oxidize if not painted immediately, and the oxidation prevents the adherence of subsequent coats of paint.

PAINTING METAL SPOONS
AND SPINNER BLADES

Often, spoons and spinners are painted only in a few stripes, dots, or bars, or with a solid color on one side of the blade only. So dipping is seldom used, except in rare cases when it is desirable to cover the entire spoon or spinner with paint.

Spraying is the best way to cover with a single coat, or in a pattern of stripes or bars. Brushing can be used, if aerosols are not available. To spray a solid color on one side of the spoon or spinner blade, lay the blade on old newspapers in front of the spraying box and spray evenly with several light coats. The same technique will work if you use masking tape or stencils to paint stripes, bars, or similar patterns on the spoon. Brushing will also work on metal spoons and spinners but is generally best on a small area, such as one outlined with stencils.

PAINTING BUCKTAILS

Before you apply any base coat, the bucktail head should be dipped into a mild acid, acetone, or vinegar solution, rinsed with water and dried thoroughly. Bucktails can be painted either before or after the tail is tied on. The

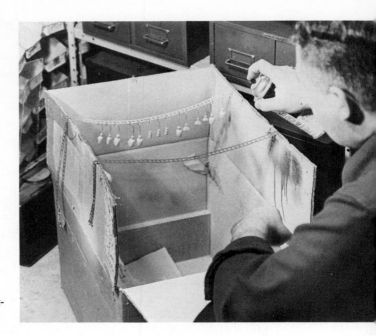

Dick Savage spray-painting bucktails.

advantage of painting before any tying is that the entire paint job can be finished, the tail then tied with a contrasting color thread. This thread is then protected with fly-head cement; by painting it after the tail is wrapped, you can protect the thread with the coat of paint.

Adherence of paint to lead lures is not good, even on commercially made lures. Automotive touch-up lacquer colors adhere best; dip the lures for easy, complete coverage.

PAINTING PATTERNS AND USING STENCILS

It's seldom that a lure is painted one solid color. This is true sometimes with underwater plugs, bucktails, and some spoons, but most lures are given a scale finish, bars, mottled pattern markings, or a similar finish. Stencils and various masks can be used over any base coating of any plug, spoon, or even bucktail.

Stencils and masks are essentially sheets of plastic, masking tape, cardboard, or paper that are cut out with designs. By covering a lure with the stencil and spraying through the cut-outs in the stencil, you can add a sharp, professional pattern to any lure.

Some typical patterns include bars added to the sides of plugs and spoons (as in the popular red and white spoon), dots, mottled patterns, and stripes. Gill slits can also be masked and painted red.

Some plug and spoon kits come with stencils included, like those of Aspen Lures. The best method in using these is to tape one side or end of the stencil to a base of cardboard or old newspaper. Slip the lure under the stencil, position it properly, and lightly tape the other end or side of the stencil to the base. Then the lure can be sprayed, the lightly taped side lifted, and the lure removed. This is not nearly as time-consuming as it sounds, and a number of identical lures can be patterned quickly this way.

Placing mask over spoon. Mask is taped down.

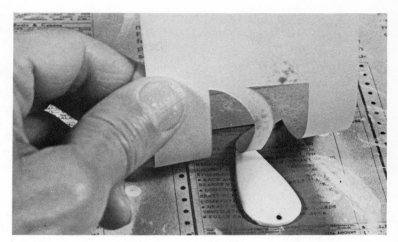

Spraying masked spoon.

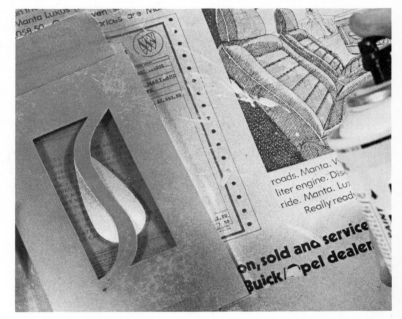

Typical red and white spoon resulting from masked painting.

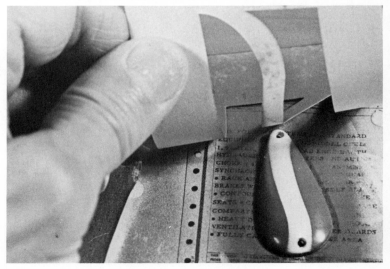

In the case of spoons, this one masking is usually all that is required, since the spoon is usually only painted on the convex side. Plugs and bucktails, however, are patterned on both sides, and the best way to accomplish this is to paint all of the lures on one side, allow them to dry, and then stencil and spray the opposite side.

Masking tape can also be cut out and taped onto lures to be sprayed. It takes a little more time, but works well on small round lures that a flat stencil will not completely cover.

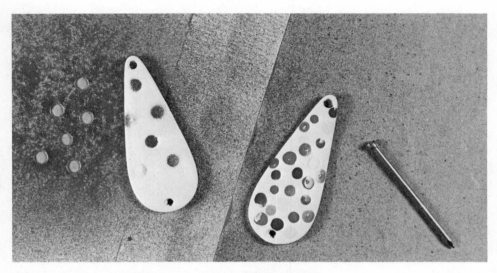

Dots can be added to a lure through a mask (left), or by dotting the lure with the head of a finishing nail dipped in paint.

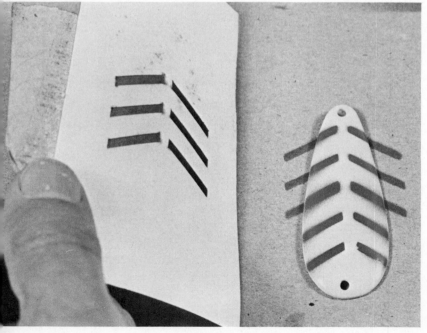

Another type of mask and the result. Note that the spoon has been sprayed twice here and was repositioned after the first spraying to make the five bars on each side.

PAINTING SCALE FINISHES

Scale finishes are added over base coats or over the selected base color of the lure. Where a scale finish is to be added, it's best to use a light color for the base, covering with a darker or contrasting color for visibility.

The scale netting used for these finishes is available from all mail-order outfits specializing in do-it-yourself tackle. It can be used in two different ways. One is to dip the scale netting into a paint or enamel thinner and wrap it tightly around the lure. The paint thinner on the net will have a tendency to cut into the base coat of the lure and make a more pronounced scale finish. Once the scale netting is wrapped on, spray the lure with the chosen finish color and allow to dry. With most spray enamels or lacquers, this will be only a few minutes. Remove the netting and wash it in the thinner again for the next lure. Failure to wash out the netting each time will result in smeared lures, since the paint from the spraying operation will get on the next lure. It's a slow operation, but produces good results.

Better still is the method of using the scale netting in a frame, holding each lure in place behind the netting for spraying. You can build a frame out of wood strips, but an embroidery hoop, available in department stores works just as well. The netting is clamped in the hoop, and the hoop held in a vise or base support to hold it vertically.

In either type of frame, the netting must be loose, since it is necessary

Scale netting held in an embroidery hoop is an ideal way to spray lures. Note painting box in back to trap spray paint.

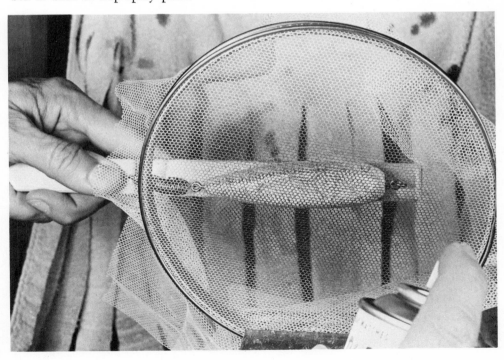

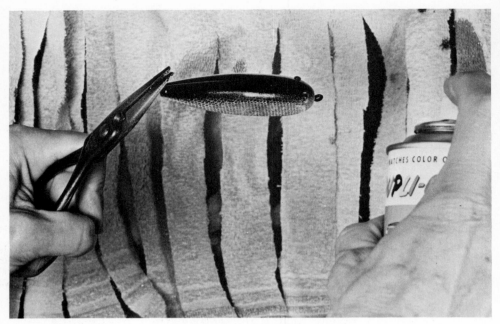

Once plugs are given scale finishes on the side, they are usually painted a dark color on the back, as shown.

to fit the netting tightly against the entire side of the plug or lure. The plug can be held by hand or by a screw eye into one end of the plug, in turn held by a pair of cheap needle-nose pliers. In either case, there is the probability of getting paint on your hands, so invest in a pair of cheap rubber or plastic gloves. Hold the lure tightly against the netting, then spray with one or two even passes with the aerosol paint can.

The usual procedure for painting a plug with the scale finish is to spray or brush the entire plug the chosen light-colored base coat. Then the sides are sprayed through the netting with a darker shade. Finally the top of the plug is sprayed a dark color for contrast. The final effect is very similar to a bait fish—dark on the top, scale finish on the sides, and light or white on the bottom.

Two screw eyes and spring make simple support for holding plugs and spoons to be finished in scale pattern by spraying through hexagonal netting.

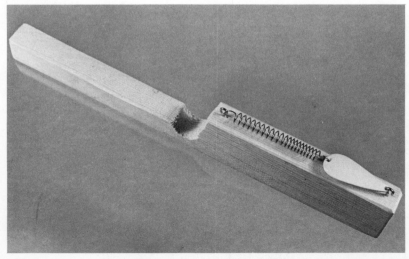

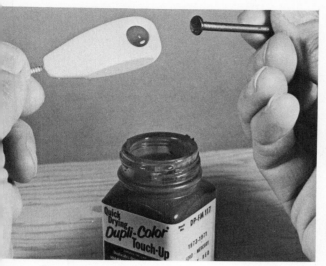

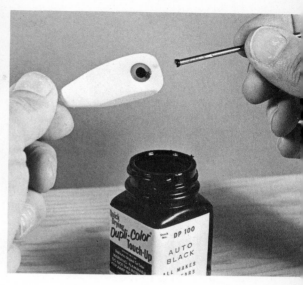

Dotting an eye on a lure.

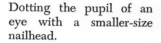

Dotting the pupil of an eye with a smaller-size nailhead.

ADDING AND PAINTING EYES

Eyes can be painted on any plug, bucktail, spoon, or other lure. The "tool" used for adding eyes is nothing more than different-size common nails, finishing nails, and straight pins. Seat the pins in a small dowel or cork, which serves as a handle. Dip the head of the nail or pin into the chosen color of paint and then lightly touch it to the side of the plug. Eyes are added only after all other coats of paint are dry on the lure.

Once the large dot of eye color is dry, a second smaller dot or "pupil" can be added with a smaller pin- or nailhead and contrasting paint; a third eye color can be added with still a smaller pinhead.

In all cases, the dots of eye color are made a contrasting color to the color of the plug. Second and subsequent eye-color dots should contrast with previous ones. Popular colors for eyes include white, yellow, red, and black. Usually white or yellow is used as the first eye color on a dark plug, red or black as the first color on a light plug.

Decal eyes are also available for lures and are added in the way decals are added to car windows.

Glass eyes on wire shafts or special map tacs (used with business graphs) can also be used as eyes. The glass eyes must be painted on their undersurface to contrast with the plug color. The map tacs come in a variety of colors.

In use, the glass eye wires are cut off at about a length of ½ inch, the eye pinned and glued into the wood plug. Map tacs have short pins and are also glued and pinned in place. Because map tacs have round heads (instead of the flat heads of glass eyes) the plug should be countersunk at the spot where the eye is to be added.

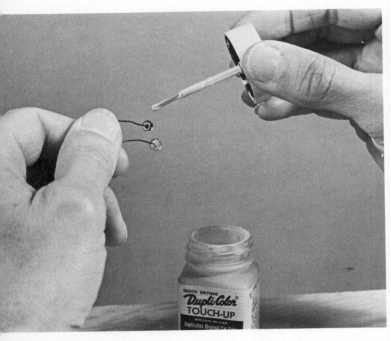

Glass eyes should be painted on their under-surface with the paint a contrasting color to the color of the plug.

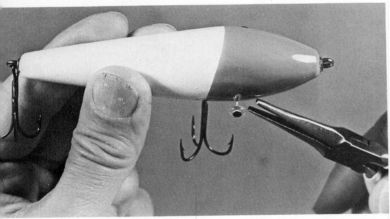

Glass eyes have the shafts cut short and then inserted into a side of the wood plug. Glue also helps to hold them in place.

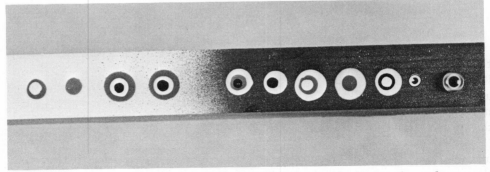

Examples of eyes painted on both light and dark backgrounds. To the right are a decal eye and a glass eye.

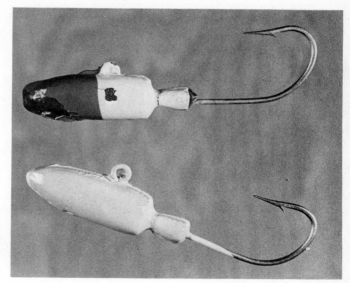

Baking paints will increase their durability. Both lures were hammered identically on a steel anvil, but top lure had not been baked and the paint chipped readily.

BAKING PAINTS

One method of increasing the durability of lure finishes (especially on bucktails) is to bake them in the kitchen oven. This must be done as the paint is drying and curing for maximum durability. Since paints vary widely, baking procedures will vary accordingly.

Experiment with small quantities of lures and paint until the best procedure for a given type and brand of paint is established. As a starting point, try baking paints in a preheated oven at 175 to 200 degrees for about 15 minutes. The result can be the difference between a lure with a fragile finish that chips readily and one that is tough, comparing favorably with those finishes applied to commercial lures. Automotive touch-up paints are especially suitable for baking.

ELECTROPLATING METAL LURES

Until recently it was not possible to electroplate metal lures at home; that was only because a small electroplating kit was not available for the do-it-yourselfer. Now one such kit (the Plate-A-Matic, described earlier) is available, and although primarily advertised as a kit for refinishing old silver spoons, musical instruments, antiques, jewelry, vases, lamps, souvenirs, trophies, and the like, it is equally adaptable for metal fishing tackle.

Some metals cannot be electroplated, such as stainless steel and aluminum, and any metals with painted, chrome, varnished, or coated finishes must have the old finish removed before electroplating.

Gold, silver, or copper can be electroplated directly with any of the

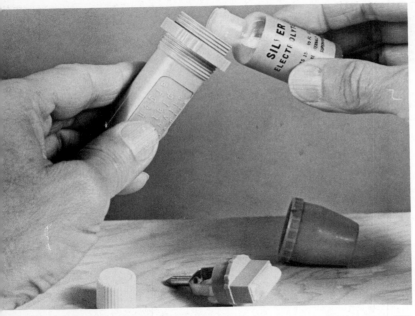

With the Plate-a-Matic electroplating set, silver electrolyte is added to the cartridge gun.

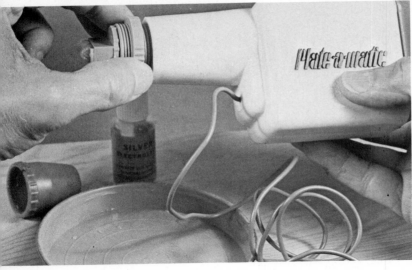

Placing the cartridge in the electroplating gun.

electrolytes furnished in the kit, but other metals give best results with a base coating of copper if a silver or gold finish is desired.

The kit has a battery operated "gun," to which is added a fluid cartridge, previously filled with the chosen electrolyte. The metal lure is polished with a polish provided in the kit, then cleaned thoroughly with running water, followed by cleaning with a special cleaner, also provided.

The electrolyte is poured into the cartridge, the cartridge added to the end of the electroplating gun. An alligator clip running from the gun is attached to the article to be plated, then the pad wet with the electrolyte fluid in the gun cartridge is placed on the lure and brushed lightly back and forth. Since the fluid will leak from the wet pad, small trays are provided to catch the run-off electrolyte fluid, which can be used over again.

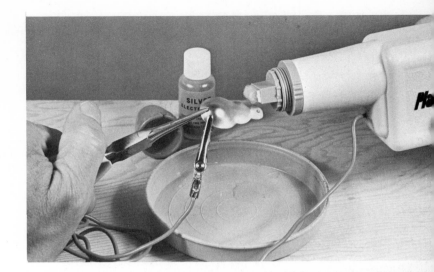

Alligator clip is attached to metal lure and wet pad brushed lightly over the lure. Tray catches excess electrolyte, which can then be re-used.

Electroplated lure will appear dark until it is polished as shown.

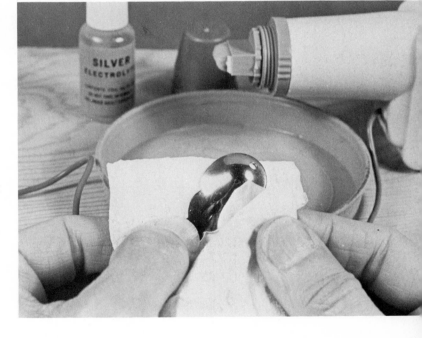

When it's finished, the lure is rinsed and lightly polished with a soft cloth, since the electroplating leaves all metal objects dark until polished. With this simple method, metal spoons and spinner blades can be finished in any of three basic metal finishes.

ADDITION OF GLITTER TO LURES

Metallic glitter flakes can be added to any lure to add to its attractiveness. This metallic glitter is available in silver, gold, green, and red at all hobby and craft shops, as well as drugstores and tackle supply houses.

There are several different ways to add it to a lure, depending upon the

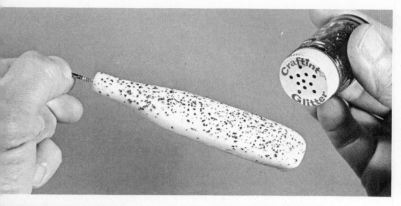

Metallic bits of glitter can be added to any lure painted with a clear adhesive or special glitter cement.

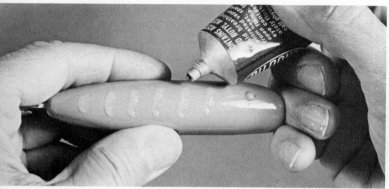

Glitter can also be added selectively by painting glue on only part of a lure.

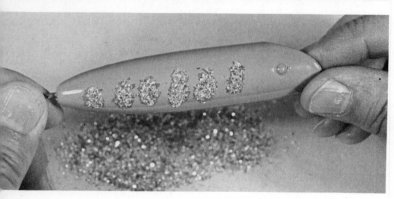

Result of above.

desired effect. For an overall glitter effect, coat the entire lure with special glitter cement (also readily available) or with a clear, adhesive coating. Then shake the glitter out of the bottle over the lure, turning the lure to assure even distribution of the metallic flakes. Most of the glitter comes in shaker jars to make this easy.

If it doesn't come packaged this way, place it in an empty shaker bottle such as is used for packaging minced onion and dried herbs. Salt or pepper shaker holes are usually too small to allow passage of the metalic flakes, but the herb shakers are just about right. Also, be sure to have a newspaper or tray under the glitter during application. Some of the glitter will not stick to the lure, and any excess that falls to the paper or tray can then be collected and returned to the shaker bottle.

Another method of adding glitter is to paint the clear cement or adhesive selectively on parts of the plug (such as the top, sides, or head) and then shake the glitter over these parts. It will not stick elsewhere and the result is glitter placed for maximum effectiveness.

It's also possible to roll the glue-coated plug in the glitter, resulting in a thick coating of glitter all over the lure or in selected bars, stripes, or other patterns if the glue is painted on the lure in this pattern. Once the glue is added to the lure, place the glitter on a clean surface and roll the plug in it. Since the glitter will only stick to those parts covered with glue, attractive patterns are easy to make by this method.

ADDING FLOCKED MATERIALS

The same method described above for adding glitter to lures can be used for adding flocking. Flocking is a flat-finish, fabric type of material that gives the appearance of fur on a lure. It is most often used on surface plugs.

ADDING TAPES

There are a number of tape products that can be added to lures. Some of these are very shiny, such as the Luhr Jensen Prism Lite tape, while others come in bright fluorescent, phosphorescent, or even glitter finishes. All have adhesive backs.

To use, cut the tape to the desired size and shape for the lure, remove the backing, and position over the lure. Since most of the adhesives are permanent upon contact, take care that the tape is properly positioned before contact is made. In the case of large pieces of tape used on large plugs or lures with compound curves, it may be necessary to cut slits into the tape to help it conform to the shape of the lure.

Many taped materials, such as this Luhr Jensen Prism Lite, can be added to lures.

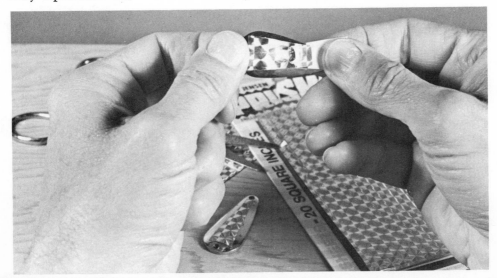

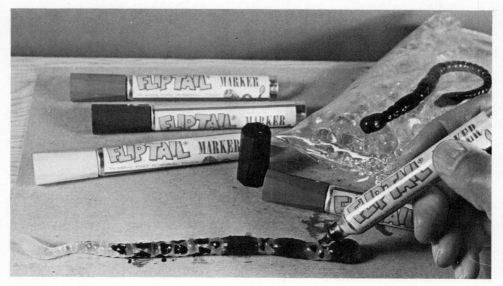

Clear and light-colored plastic worms can be colored with special felt-tip markers. Special ink dries shortly after being applied.

COLORING PLASTIC WORMS AND LURES WITH FELT-TIP MARKERS

Plastic worms are usually molded in the desired color to begin with. Often, however, when out on bass water, the fish may suddenly exhibit a desire for some color worm not in your tackle box; you can then recolor a worm to the desired shade. In fact, Fliptail has a kit of eight colored felt-tip markers just for this purpose. They recommend that light-colored or clear worms be used with the colors, since it is difficult to recolor an already dark worm or plastic lure. Plastic lures can be made a solid color using the markers in this kit, or they can be banded, striped, or otherwise patterned.

Indelibile (nonwashable) felt-tip markers will also work on soft-plastic lures. The same felt-tip markers can be carried in a tackle box and used for last-minute color changes of any lure, plug, spoon, spinner, or bucktail. However, this use is not recommended unless required by fishing conditions, since such a finish cannot be removed at a later date and will permanently mark what is probably a colorful and otherwise effective lure.

FINAL LURE FINISHING

All lures, whether plugs, spoons, spinners, or bucktails, will look better and last longer if several final finishing coats of clear lacquer or varnish are added to protect the paints. These should be added only after all base coats, scale finishes, eyes, tapes, glitter, and other finishing procedures outlined here have been completed.

Examples of finishes on spoons, plugs, and bucktail heads. Lures must be completed and have hooks added after this stage.

Such a clear finishing coat must be chemically compatible with the previous coats used on the lures so as not to cause a reaction with underlying paints. Dipping or spraying is the best method of application.

COSTS

Cost of finishing a lure is hard to compute, since it depends on many variables; the size of the lures, the number of base and finish coats, the addition of scale and masked finishes, and the amount of waste—either in cans or aerosol sprays—vary with the operator.

In general, however, if paints are bought and used wisely, covered after each use to prevent drying out, and used on an assembly line basis, the cost per lure will be less than 5 cents. This may be slightly higher if you use expensive tape finishes, electroplating, glitter finishes, or other additions are included, but it'll still be cheap. The cost of any finish coat, coupled with the basic cost of making the lure, will be well below the cost of a similar lure from a tackle store.

KITS

Painting kits are available and provide an easy way to get the proper colors and finishing materials for lures at minimal cost. Herter's and Netcraft carry painting kits, while a number of other companies, such as Finnysports, Hille, Lure-Craft, Reed Tackle, and others, carry the individual paints in the small-size bottles and sprays needed by lure builders.

13
MOLDS AND SPECIAL TOOLS

*ALUMINUM BUCKTAIL MOLDS • PLASTER BUCKTAIL
MOLDS • MISCELLANEOUS SINKER MOLDS • TIN
SQUID MOLDS • ONE- AND TWO-PIECE PLASTIC
LURE MOLDS • WIRE FORMERS • ANVILS • METAL
FINISHING STAMPS • ELECTRIC ROD WINDERS •
ROD WRAPPERS • ROD-HANDLE GLUING CLAMP •
ROD AND TUBE-BENDING JIGS*

BASIC TOOLS		HELPFUL TOOLS
Aluminum molds	*Anvils*	Wood gouge
Hacksaw	Drill	Sabre saw
Electric drill or router	Router bits	
Routing bits	*Metal-finishing stamp*	
Plaster molds	Files	
Plaster of Paris	*Rod winder*	
Miscellaneous sinker molds	Drill	
Electric drill	Saw	
Wire formers	*Tube bender*	
Hammer	Coping saw	
Hacksaw	Screwdriver	

From Odds and Ends of Scrap Aluminum, Wood, Nails, and Other bits and pieces, it's possible to make a number of special tools and aids that will help in all phases of tackle building. Most take little time, talent, or materials, and can add greatly to the ease with which tackle can be constructed.

ALUMINUM BUCKTAIL MOLDS

The angler with a design for a bucktail for which there is no commercial mold is not lost. You can make bucktail molds yourself, out of aluminum blocks.

Construction of aluminum molds requires block aluminum (¼-inch-thick Reynolds aluminum is suitable for molds of small lures), special drills, rotary files, and routers. A portable drill on a light drill stand, drill press, or rotary grinder is really necessary for machining the cavities in the two aluminum mold halves. This equipment costs about $25.00, so it is hardly a worthwhile investment just for making a few molds, but for those who already have the equipment in their home workshop, the basic technique is as follows:

First, cut out the two blocks of aluminum to the size needed for the bucktail or bucktails. Allow for at least a 1-inch margin on all sides of the jig. Clamp the two blocks together, and drill a ⅛-inch hole through opposite corners of the two blocks, drilling both blocks together. Insert a No. 10 finishing nail (or other stiff, ⅛-inch wire) through the two holes in one block, tapping them firmly in place. Cut the pins flush on the outside of the mold and leave about ¼ inch exposed inside to fit into the holes on the other block. This procedure ensures proper registration of the two mold halves for the rest of the work and for pouring the lead heads once the mold is completed.

Place a sheet of paper between the two halves, and clamp it together so that the two pins (or nails) cut holes into the paper. Outline the block on the paper and then remove it. Draw an outline of the chosen bucktail shape on the center of the paper square. Cut out the outline of the bucktail and place the paper template on the mold. Taking care that the holes in the paper are positioned exactly over the holes or pins of the blocks, scribe the bucktail outline onto each half of the mold.

Using rotary files in a rotary grinder, drill, or drill press, cut out the shape of the bucktail on each half of the mold. Periodically check the shape of the mold by pressing a small piece of beeswax or children's modeling clay between the two mold halves. Continue cutting until the two cavities are symmetrical in the shape desired, with the edges in perfect alignment.

Similarly, rout out a sprue hole. (This is a tapered opening through which the lead is poured into the mold cavities.) Mark the proper position for the jig hook (use the template to get this in exact alignment on both sides of the mold) and cut slots for the shank and holes for the eye, and any other additions desired. Once completed, the mold can be used in the same way as any commercially made mold, following the techniques outlined in Chapter 3. Easy Molds, Inc., sells for $1 detailed instructions on how to make molds out of block aluminum using methods similar to those described above.

PLASTER BUCKTAIL MOLDS

Molds made from plaster are well within the capabilities of any tackle tinkerer, and do not require elaborate tools. Plaster of Paris, small boxes for pouring the plaster, two nails or pins, vaseline or liquid soap, and an example of

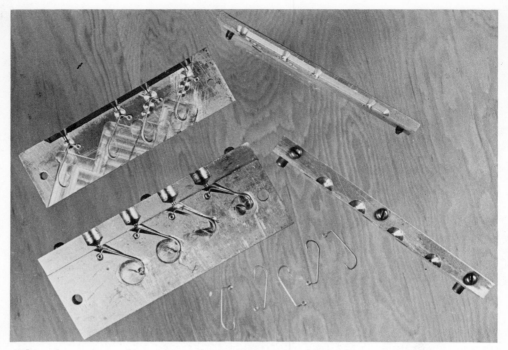

Side and top views of two types of homemade aluminum bucktail molds. Top: ballhead jig mold; bottom: shad dart mold. Note that these are pinned molds.

the bucktail to be molded are all that's needed. If it's an original design, make a body of wood, plastic wood, modeling clay, liquid steel, liquid aluminum, or similar easy-to-work material. If you are using a standard commercial bucktail, strip off all the thread and tail material before proceeding.

Find a suitable small box into which to pour the plaster. A good size for a single-cavity mold of a ½-ounce bucktail would be about 4x3x1½ inches or 2 inches deep. Mix the plaster with water to a consistency resembling thick, smooth pancake batter. However, the plaster should flow, not "drop," into the mold box. Mix only enough to fill half the box, since the mold must be made in two separate parts. It is important to have the plaster as smooth as possible, without air bubbles that could cause defects. (To remove air bubbles, rap the mixing bowl repeatedly on a table or hit it sharply with a spoon or light mallet.)

At this same time, it is also possible to either lengthen the curing time, if the plaster is setting up too rapidly, or to hasten it, if it seems too thin. Add salt to speed up the process of curing; a little vinegar will slow curing. Another tip for using plaster is to mix it in a flexible plastic bowl. That way, any remaining plaster can be allowed to harden and then cracked out by flexing the bowl, to save washing time.

Pour evenly over the bottom of the box, filling half the box with plaster. While the plaster is starting to set, cover the entire bucktail body, hook, and eye with a thin coating of vaseline, to prevent it from sticking to the plaster. Place the bucktail on its side in the plaster. There is a critical time for doing this, since if it is done too early, the bucktail may sink too far into the plaster, while if it is done too late, you may not be able to push it halfway into the plaster. Before the plaster sets, take two short 1- to 1½-inch nails and sink them

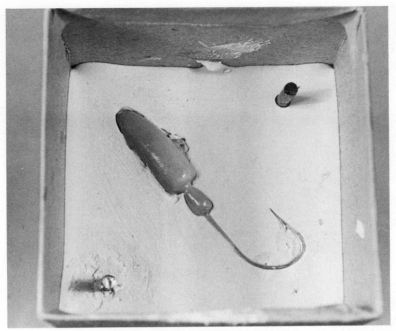

The master bucktail is placed in the box of plaster, with pins placed in opposite corners for proper registration of the second part of the mold.

vertically, head end into the plaster, at opposite corners of the mold. Leave about ¼ inch of the point end extending out of the plaster. These nails serve to ensure proper "register" of the mold in casting. Allow the plaster to set for one-half to one hour, then coat the entire exposed surface of the mold with vaseline.

Mix another batch of plaster and pour evenly over the bucktail and first half of the mold. When the second pouring has set, again in about one hour, break apart the cardboard box and remove the solid block of plaster. Carefully separate the two mold halves, running a knife blade along the joint. Remove the bucktail from the mold and allow the mold to cure and dry thoroughly. Plaster holds a great deal of water for a long time, and the curing cannot be hurried. For average size molds, allow to dry at least two weeks.

CAUTION: Don't ever pour molten lead into a mold that has not been properly cured. The water in the plaster will cause the molten lead to splatter dangerously, and will probably crack and ruin the mold.

During the two-week drying period, finish the mold by carving a sprue hole. Sprue holes, or "gates," allow the molten lead to reach the bucktail cavity. Usually they are placed at either the head or tail end of the bucktail and between the two mold halves. Taper the hole, leaving an opening of about ¼ inch at the entrance to the cavity. It is an advantage to have the sprue hole at the tail end. Then the sprue (excess lead left in the hole from molding) can be cut off with wire cutters, without additional finishing, and the fur or feather tail will hide any slight defects. You can, if you desire, carve slots in the mold for weedless hooking arrangements, spinner bait wire, or similar additions.

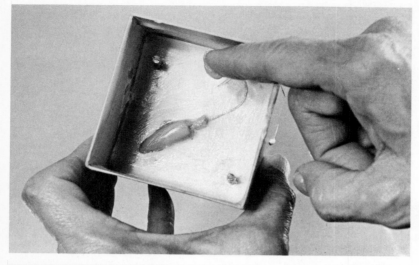

The cured half of the bucktail mold is covered with Vaseline before the second half is poured.

Completed bucktail mold, just opened with a knife.

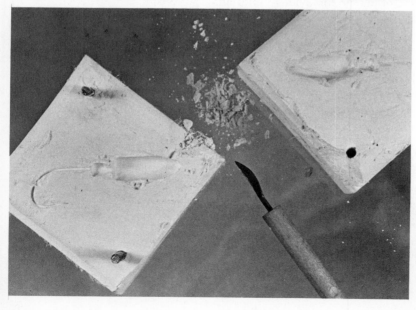

The cured completed plaster bucktail mold must have a sprue hole carved for pouring the molten lead.

Once the mold is completed and cured, place the hook in the mold. Clamp the mold together with wood workers or C-clamps. If you're using C-clamps, clamp them very lightly, since excessive pressure will crack the mold. Plaster molds will not last indefinitely as will iron or aluminum molds, but with care they are usually good for several dozen lures. In time, the mold cavity will start to chip around the edges, causing excessive flash on the molding. Using this method, molds with from one to six cavities can be made.

Some dealers have capitalized on the make-your-own-mold idea. As of this writing, Finnysports has a kit that includes special molding powder, plastic molding clay, jig hooks, one jig pattern, and instructions.

Plaster molds cannot be considered permanent, so a good one or one of a unique or original design jig might be worth taking to a foundry to have a permanent mold made from cast iron, brass, or aluminum. Made by a sand-casting method, the permanent mold usually requires some finishing, particularly on the contact surfaces of the two halves. The cost of a foundry mold is usually less than $10.

The same technique can be used for making sinker molds. Usually these can be used a little longer, since the excess flash on a sinker is less objectionable than on a bucktail.

MISCELLANEOUS SINKER MOLDS

While many sinkers are designed and shaped specifically for a special type of fishing, it is possible to mold a common sinker by drilling or carving holes in a wood block. The results are rough in appearance, but for holding a lake or shore bottom, they will work as well as sinkers bought in a tackle store or made in a commercial mold.

To make a two-piece wood mold, clamp together two pieces of 1- to 2-inch thick wood and drill holes of the appropriate size. Keep the drill centered along the joint of the two pieces. No sprue hole is used. The hole in the two pieces of wood (clamped together for molding) is filled with molten lead, a brass eye held in the center of the sinker with pliers until it cools. Once the sinker has cooled, the two parts of the mold are separated, and the sinker pried out with an awl or pliers. The molding hole in the wood will burn slightly, but many sinkers can be made before the mold has been rendered unusable. The cylindrical sinker in various sizes can be used for many types of fishing.

Similarly, a crude type of egg sinker can be made, using the same method as above, but placing a nail vertically in the center of the mold cavity to form a hole through the center of the sinker.

TIN SQUID MOLDS

Using the techniques outlined above, you can also make one-piece tin squid molds. Tin squids are usually flat on one surface and lend themselves to one-piece molds, even though they are generally available commercially only as two-part molds. Using a tin squid for a model or following a drawing or

Example of open-face plaster tin squid mold showing cavities to be filled.

design pattern, trace an outline on a block of wood or aluminum, carving it out with suitable tools to the shape desired. Plaster blocks can also be carved or a tin squid can be molded in plaster, using the same technique as that for making the first half of a two-piece plaster bucktail mold, previously described.

Take care in using this type of mold, since the mold must be filled completely with tin or lead, without overflowing. A small ladle for pouring the lead helps here.

ONE- AND TWO-PIECE PLASTIC LURE MOLDS

Following the directions given above for making two-piece plaster bucktail and one-piece squid molds, it's possible to make plaster molds for molding plastic lures by the cold mold–hot plastic method, described in Chapter 5.

There are two possible ways to make a one-piece plaster mold, but in both methods a good commercial or homemade worm "master," or model, is a must. One is to lay a plastic lure on a flat sheet of glass. This method is best when using a model lure that sinks or can be glued or stuck to the glass. By this method, it is possible to get a completely flat mold that is very easy to work with. Stick the worm to the glass sheet (an 8- by 10-inch sheet of glass is fine except for extralarge worms or lures) and place over it a cardboard box, open at the top and bottom. The box is only needed to contain the plaster until it sets. Weight the box down or tape by the outside edges to the glass to prevent plaster leakage.

Fill it with plaster, following previous directions. Allow to set overnight, remove the box sides, lift from the glass, and carefully remove the model lure. If you have difficulty in lifting the worm out, stick a pin in one end at an angle and lift carefully. Any small pieces of plaster that may crack off the edges should be shaken or brushed away before using.

In the second method, a box (with bottom) is filled with plaster. The "master" lure is carefully placed in the box, with the flat side up, and the molded portion in the plaster. Take care to push the worm down into the plaster until the flat surface is flush with the top. Allow to dry overnight; remove and clean as before.

Once the mold is cured and dry, it can be used, following the methods described in Chapter 5. However, the plaster will cause the molded lures to have a dull finish. A shiny finish can be achieved by first carefully painting the mold cavity with a gloss or semi-gloss heat-resistant paint. These are readily available in several colors, although the color is not important here. These paints resist heat to 400° and will help protect the mold cavity while giving a shiny finish to the lures.

Using these methods, it is also possible to make molds for worms, spring lizards, and other lures by cutting and combining parts of soft plastic lures. This technique is shown in the photos, where a standard split tail for spinner baits is combined with the tail of a plastic worm to make a spinner bait strip with three tails.

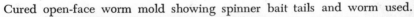

Cured open-face worm mold showing spinner bait tails and worm used.

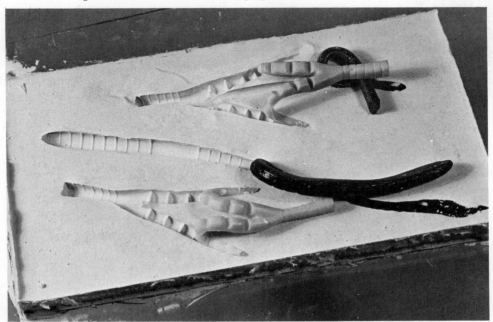

256

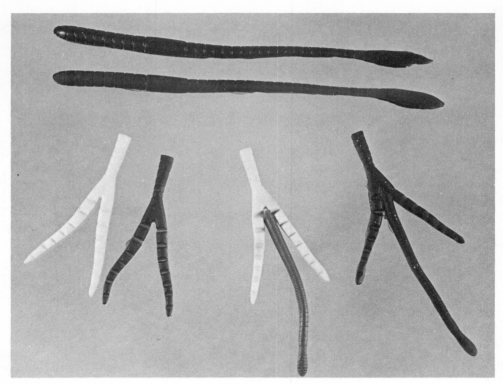

Master and molded examples of spinner bait tails and plastic worm. Note that triple-tailed spinner bait on right has been made from split tail and plastic worm tail.

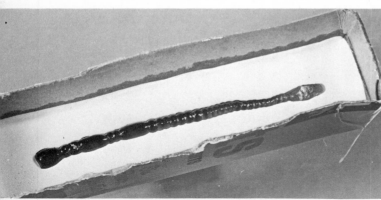
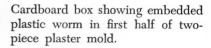

Cardboard box showing embedded plastic worm in first half of two-piece plaster mold.

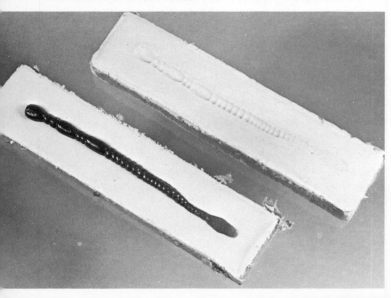

Round-model worm and two-piece plaster worm mold made from it.

Two-piece plaster molds for soft plastic lures can be made, following directions as outlined for making two-piece bucktail molds. A higher box must be used, since the plaster must be thicker than for a one-piece mold, and must be poured in two parts. If making a worm mold, be sure to pick a "master" that is completely round—otherwise, a one-piece flat mold will make worms just as well as with less trouble. And, when placing a round worm in the bottom part of the plaster mold, be sure to position it so that the seam line on the worm is identical with the seam line of the plaster mold. Otherwise resultant molded worms will have two seams—one from the original master worm and the second resulting from the homemade plaster mold.

Once the first part of the mold is partially cured (½ to 1 hour), cover the mold surface and the lure with vaseline and pour the second part. Allow it to cure for about 1 hour, then open the box and run a knife around the mold joint. Carefully open the mold and allow to cure overnight.

At one end of the mold carve a sprue hole through which to pour the molten plastic. If it is a worm mold, place this sprue hole at the head end; for other plastic lures, place the sprue hole at the largest part of the mold cavity. Since the molten plastic is more viscous than the lead used in bucktail molds, the opening from the sprue hole to the mold cavity must be relatively large. If for any reason a mold does not fill completely, carving the sprue hole larger will usually correct the difficulty.

The mold cavity and sprue hole can be painted with heat-resistant paint to give a shiny finish, or it can be left as is.

WIRE FORMERS

While it's certainly desirable to have several types of pliers and wire cutters at hand, these are not necessary to form eyes in wire, make spinner shaft eyes, or for the through-wire construction needed in saltwater plugs. In some cases, as in forming eyes for sinkers, bucktails, or tin squids, it's simpler to use a special homemade wire former than to make the eyes with pliers. This also applies to other wire products where repetitive, consistent results are desired.

Use nails hammered into a wood block to form the bends in the wire. The size of the nail determines the size of the loop eye, or the degree of sharpness of the bend.

Making a wire former is simple. Hammer the nails securely into the wood where bends are needed. Use a dense wood, so that the nails won't loosen or wobble later. Hammering them into end grain is often best. Two nails close together (a little more than the wire width apart) serve to hold the wire shaft while the bend is made around one of the nails. After the nails are hammered in, saw off the nail heads (the wire eyes and loops will not come off, otherwise), and file the nail posts smooth.

While only two nails are needed to make one bend, several nails are needed to make most eyes. For example, when making brass wire eyes for sinkers, I use six nails in the wire former. Two nails can be used for making an eye in a spinner shaft, but a separate longer nail is needed in the same

First step in making homemade wire former is to
hammer large nails into
end of grain wood to form
bends as shown.

Nailheads must be cut off
the homemade wire for-
mer so that any formed
tackle may be removed.

Showing homemade wire
former in use. Note the
two posts on the left that
are needed to make any
round circle or eye in wire.

Depressions for forming the proper curvature in spoons and spinner blades are best made by carving or routing curved depressions in a block of wood.

block so that the wire can be wrapped around the shaft after the eye is formed. Sometimes it is helpful to make the nails in a wire former of different heights to aid in bending the wire around to make some complex bends.

Commercial wire formers are available in hardware and hobby shops, but the steel posts are generally too large and placed too far apart to be useful for bending the small-diameter wires used in tackle building.

ANVILS

Cutting out spoons and spinner blades is one thing; forming the proper curve in them is something else again. A small anvil can be of help, as can special curved depressions into which spoon and spinner blades can be hammered to shape.

Since it is easier to hammer a blade to shape into a concavity than over a convex form, depressions carved into a block of wood are the best solution.

Such concave depressions can be made in any hard wood. I usually use a 2-by-4 piece of lumber, carving with a curved wood gouge the size and depth of curve desired. For those without these tools, an old stainless steel teaspoon or tablespoon, repeatedly heated red hot and burned into the wood, will do just as well. Routers and rotary files on an electric drill also work well.

Carve several depressions of different diameters and depths, so that different curves can be hammered into the blades. Oval as well as round depressions will be useful. For scale and hammered finishes on spoon and spinner blades (described in Chapter 12) it's best to work on some sort of anvil. Without a convex surface on which to work, any curve of the blade will be flattened as the finish is hammered. Of course, the rounded end on machinist's vises and some small hobby anvils are usable, but not as satisfactory as a completely rounded surface that will conform to the curve of the blade.

There are several easy ways to make round anvils just for finishing spoons; one way is to round off the end of a short, 2-inch to 4-inch length dowel with

Stamps for finishing metal spoons and spinner blades made by filing down common nails. Left to right: L-shaped, straight, crescent, and crossed stamps for finishing metal lures.

pocketknife, wood rasp, and sandpaper, and fit the dowel into a hole drilled for the purpose in a block of wood. Half-inch, ¾-inch, 1-inch, and 1½-inch dowels are convenient sizes to work with. A brace and bit or large wood bits for an electric drill will cut the holes needed to hold the dowels in place.

A wood darning egg can be cut down and fitted on a dowel for the same purpose. The darning egg can also be cut lengthwise to give an oblong convex surface for long spoons.

METAL FINISHING STAMPS

In addition to using the nail sets and various punches described in Chapter 6 for the finishing of spoons and spinner blades, it is also possible to make special stamps for special effects. Short, 3-inch lengths of metal rod in ⅛- to ¼-inch diameters will work best, but hardened nails of the type used for fastening wood to cinder block and concrete will also work.

The rod or nail must be cut and filed flat. Then by filing the sides of the end of the bar or nail, you can cut various star, chisel, grooved, and other designs. These stamps are used exactly as are nail sets and punches for creating a stamped finish on a metal lure, as described in Chapter 6.

ELECTRIC ROD WINDERS

It is also possible to make an electric rod winder. There are several on the market, generally designed for use by small manufacturers and tackle stores making custom rods. A unique and simple electric rod winder was shown to me by Mrs. Kitty Lourie, proprietor of the Buxton Sportsmen's Center near Cape Hatteras, on the Outer Banks of North Carolina.

Mrs. Lourie got into the rod-building business about fifteen years ago; she bought a homemade electric rod winder from Joe Scott of Elizabeth City, North Carolina, for $40. Since then she has been building about a hundred rods per year and repairing and rewinding countless others.

Her rod winder consists of a sewing machine motor (although any other type of motor would do) operated by a foot pedal to leave her hands free.

The motor speed is slowed by going through a gearbox, and two universal joints coming out of the gearbox make it unnecessary to have the rod blank lined up exactly with the motor shaft, as would be the case were the rod chucked into an electric drill or lathe.

A rubber rod button bolted to the end of the universal joint holds the

Commercially made electric rod winder complete with foot pedal and rod support. Courtesy: Featherweight Products.

Mrs. Kitty Lourie's homemade electric rod wrapper.

rod butt. The rest of the rod is supported with several tall adjustable stands, cut with a V and lined with leather to protect the blank.

Mrs. Lourie sits on a small stool, to the front of which is clamped a thread holder, along with a special universal joint bracket holding a short section of a rod tip through which the rod winding thread runs. By controlling the rotating speed with the foot pedal and guiding the windings with her finger, Mrs. Lourie is able to turn out good-looking wraps fast and efficiently.

ROD WRAPPERS

I don't use an electric rod winder; I have found that I can make rod winding far simpler and more pleasant by modifying an inexpensive commercially available rod wrapper.

Commercial rod wrappers used by many companies and small tackle stores. Courtesy: Featherweight Products.

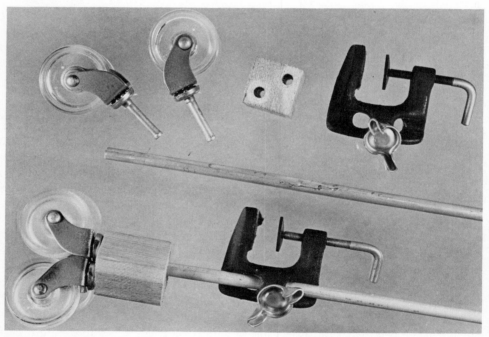

Rod wrapping supports. Top: two tray wheels, wood block, aluminum rod, and fly-tying vise clamp used to make wrapper. Bottom: completed rod wrapper.

This device clamps to a table and has a thumb screw for adjusting the tension on the winding thread. Metal arms fit into the wrapper to support the rod blank. I have found these metal arms to be virtually useless. On most rod winders, they are below the thread spool and too close together to support the rod blank adequately. The low position of the arms usually places the rod too far away for one to see the winding operation well, while the rod has a tendency to "walk" along the arms.

By using a set of four 2-inch diameter tray wheels or casters, you can make an excellent rod blank support in fifteen minutes. Pair two of the wheels facing each other, leaving only a small, ⅛-inch, gap between the wheel edges. Since these wheels are mounted on metal rods designed to fit into tray legs, the best way to rig them is in a 1-inch block of wood, drilled to accept the wheel rod supports. The block of wood can then be mounted on ⅜-inch aluminum or steel rod, to fit into a fly-tying vise clamp. An alternative method is to use longer blocks of wood mounted as pedestals; two such supports should be made.

In use, the rod blank is supported between the two supports, with the rod winder clamped to a bench between them. The wheels support the rod and make turning the blank to wrap guides a real pleasure.

ROD-HANDLE GLUING CLAMP

The angler who makes rods frequently will find a rod-handle gluing clamp a useful addition to his tackle making tools. A gluing clamp makes it easy to clamp the cork rings of a handle together until the glue cures, prior to shaping the grip.

You'll need two 2x1x5-inch strips of wood, two 12-inch threaded rods, six nuts, two wing nuts, and two washers to fit the threaded rods to make a gluing clamp.

Drill a ¾-inch hole in the center of each of the wood strips to accommodate the rod blank. Drill two holes in each side of the wood strips to fit the threaded rod. Using the six nuts, attach one end of the threaded rods to the holes in one of the wood strips, using two nuts on the end of the rod to lock them in to form the base of the gluing clamp.

Ream out the two outer holes in the other wood strip, so that the threaded rods slide easily through the holes. Slip the second wood strip onto the threaded rods; add the washers and the wing nuts.

In use (covered in Chapter 8), the cork rings are added to the blank to build up the rod handle. Then the base of the gluing clamp is slipped over one end of the blank so that the wood strip seats against the cork ring at one end of the handle. Slip the other wood strip (at the end of the gluing clamp) over the rod blank and threaded rods, add the washers and wing nuts, and tighten to draw the cork rings together for curing.

This size rod handle gluing clamp works for fly, spinning, and straight-handle casting rods. A larger and longer clamp can be built for surf and big game rods.

ROD AND TUBE BENDING JIGS

Bending tubing, steel, or aluminum rod for landing net frames requires some sort of jig.

A bending jig is nothing more than a wood frame into which the metal rod or tubing is placed, so that an even pressure will bend the metal into a smooth curve. Basically then, a bending jig is made by cutting a curve of wood the proper radius, fastening it to a base plate, and adding some method of securing the end of the tubing or rod while the bends are being formed. Such bending jigs can be made or modified in several different ways, but the following description will serve as a guide to the basic idea.

Cut an 18-inch square base piece of plywood (½-inch thickness is best).

Separately, cut quarter-circles in radii of 3 inches, 6 inches, 9 inches, 12 inches, and 15 inches from ½ inch plywood. An electric sabre saw is best for this, but a coping or keyhole saw will do the job. Place each of the quarter-circles in turn (starting with the largest) on the base plate, lining up the square corner of the quarter-circle with one corner of the base plate. Each quarter-circle should be glued in place and also screwed down, since pressure will be exerted against them as the tubing and rod are bent. Place the screws so that they will be hidden under each successive smaller quarter-circle so that exposed screw heads (even though flat-head) will not scratch the tubing or rod.

After completing this stage of the tube-bending jig, determine the largest-diameter tubing or rod to be bent (usually ½-inch), and screw down a small block of wood or a spool ½ inch away from the edge of each tier of quarter-circles. Use a heavy, large screw, since severe strain will be placed against this stop. This will serve as a clamp for the end of the tubing or rod and against which the material will be bent around the quarter circles. Where smaller tubing or rod is used, shims of wood can be placed between the stop and the materials.

Once finished the entire frame can be clamped to a workbench top, and tubing or rod of different radii bent for landing nets of different diameters. In case a frame of only one size is needed, the same principle can be used, choosing only one tier of quarter-circle of the proper radius.

14

THE CARE AND REPAIR
OF TACKLE

*TOOLS · ROD CARE · ROD REPAIRS · REEL CARE · REEL
REPAIR · LINE CARE · LINE REPAIR · PLUG CARE · PLUG
REPAIR · SPOON AND SPINNER CARE · SPOON
AND SPINNER REPAIR · SOFT PLASTIC LURE CARE ·
SOFT PLASTIC LURE REPAIR · BUCKTAIL CARE ·
BUCKTAIL REPAIR · MISCELLANEOUS
EQUIPMENT CARE*

CARE OF FISHING TACKLE, WHETHER HOME-BUILT OR COMMERCIALLY made, is important if it is to work well and last long. Occasionally, however, repairs are necessary on any type of tackle. These repairs should be made promptly and properly.

TOOLS

Of absolute importance in care and repair of tackle is the necessity of having the right tools and equipment. Using too large a screwdriver, a pair of pliers instead of a wrench or the wrong-size wrench, will only scratch the tackle, burr screw and bolt heads, and make a reel unsightly if not useless. It can also destroy the plating, exposing tackle to saltwater corrosion. On a somewhat smaller scale, this applies to repairing and caring for plugs, rods, spoons, and all other fishing equipment as well.

For all my fishing, but especially in saltwater, I rely strongly on the moisture-repelling, rust-proofing, spray-on compounds such as WD40, P38, and CRC. These all come in aerosol cans and are colorless, harmless sprays. Reports indicate that they do not hurt the line, and so can be sprayed directly on a reel after a trip. I usually keep large, 12- to 16-ounce, cans, at home as well

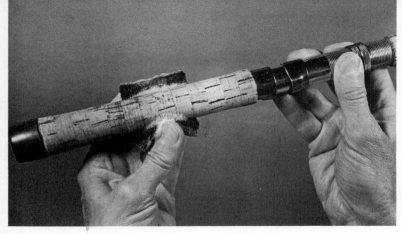

Kitchen cleansers and cleaning pads are ideal for cleaning dirt off cork rod handles.

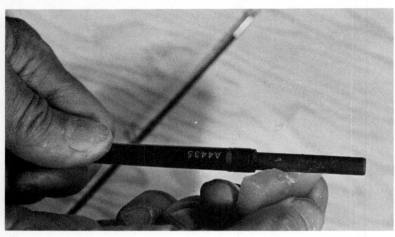

Beeswax on a glass-to-glass ferrule will help tighten the ferrule; parafin on a glass-to-glass ferrule will loosen it.

as in the seventeen-foot center console fishing boat I use for saltwater fishing. I also carry small cans in my tackle boxes for freshwater use.

These compounds are ideal for spraying anything metal that might rust or corrode in either fresh water or salt water. I use them to spray reels, rod guides, and reel seats, hooks on plugs, metal spoons and spinners, and anything else that I think needs it at the time. A quick spray is a small price to pay for the protection that these compounds give to fishing tackle.

Other tools that help in tackle repair include everything from small screwdrivers to crocus cloth (for polishing guides). A kit of four to six small screwdrivers makes it possible to dismantle reels, remove hook hangers on plugs, replace hooks, and accomplish similar tasks. Combination screwdriver-wrenches come with most reels and should be used when dismantling for cleaning or repair.

Additional tackle repair and maintenance items can include, for example, a filed-off football needle (for making nail knots in fly line-to-leader attachments), various glues (including epoxy glues for repair of plastic foam lures), reel oils and grease, ferrule cement (for tip top and ferrule replacement), and thread for rod guide replacement.

While repair and maintenance should be carried out in the home with an eye toward preventive maintenance, tackle failures do sometimes occur on the water. If I'm close to home, I usually carry enough spare tackle to cope with any such failure. On an extended trip, I carry a small fishing tackle repair kit that includes all the items mentioned above, along with fly line cleaners, an assortment of spare guides and tip tops for all types of rods, terminal tackle parts, screw eyes and line connectors for plugs, spare drag washers and other small parts for reels, and a reel tool for every reel I own. This all fits in a small tough *Vlchek* lure box measuring 10½ by 6½ by 1½ inches, with six compartments for separation of the items. It is the best tackle insurance policy I have.

ROD CARE

More rods are broken in car and home screen doors than on fighting fish, and more guides are bent by being stepped on or knocked about than by any other means.

One of the easiest ways to protect rods from accidents is to carry them in cases both to and from fishing trips. Construction of plastic pipe rod cases is covered in Chapter 11, but commercially available aluminum, fiber, or plastic rod cases can be used. While the rod case will protect the rod from hard knocks, it can still rattle around in the case unless placed in a rod bag. Rod bags are commercially available, or they can easily be sewed up at home from a length of flannel cloth. Be sure to make any rod bag large enough for the guides and handle, and make it long enough to overlap at the open end.

Guides on hard-fished rods become dirty, particularly in fishing weedy or algae-filled water. Often algae and bits of weed will become lodged in and around the guide rings and frames. Also, dirt will cling to the rod blank. Salt-water fishermen will always have the problem of corrosion from salt, air, and water. Because of these and similar problems, all fishing rods should be cleaned after each fishing trip.

It's not enough to run the garden hose over the rod and consider the job done. That doesn't clean off the salt and debris around the rod guides. I have found that the best way to clean rods is to stand them in the shower, rinse with warm water for a few minutes, and then individually scrub them with an old washcloth. If dirt adheres under or around the guide frames, a small toothbrush will remove it handily. I also take the corner of a washrag and run it through the ring of the guide to clean it thoroughly. Similarly, the rod blank, ferrules, handle, and reel seat should be washed and rubbed down.

Sometimes a bit of dirt can lodge in a female ferrule. Do *not* try to loosen it with a sharp instrument or by running the male ferrule into the opening. Sometimes, if the ferrule is inverted and tapped lightly, the dirt will fall out. If that doesn't work, blow sharply into the ferrule to loosen and dislodge the dirt. If neither of these methods works, try loosening it with a folded-up pipe cleaner, small-caliber rifle-cleaning brush, typewriter cleaning brush, or child's toothbrush. If the ferrule is small, a mascara brush, cleaned thoroughly first in lighter fluid, may work.

If the ferrule has a deposit of scum or oil on the inside, a twisted handkerchief, pipe cleaner, or small rag dipped in lighter fluid will usually clean it out. The male ferrule can be cleaned by the same means.

The threads, hoods, and other metal parts of reel seats can also be cleaned with the small brushes. Anti-rust proofing agents such as WD40, CRC, and P38

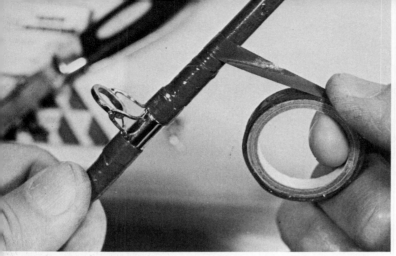

Replacement guides can be temporarily added very easily with adhesive-backed plastic tape.

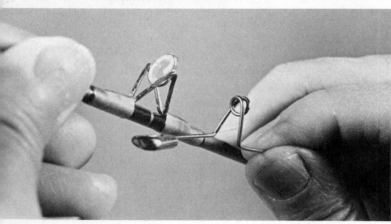

If you lack a replacement guide, make one from a large safety pin as shown.

are excellent both for cleaning metal parts and for spraying cleaned tackle to keep it new-looking.

ROD REPAIRS

Some rod repairs are unavoidable, and might even be considered maintenance instead of repairs. All guides except agate, Carboloy, and aluminum oxide will ultimately groove and must be replaced. Sometimes these grooves are microscopic and difficult to see, yet can still scrape and ultimately ruin line. One way to check for grooved guides is to run a discarded nylon stocking through each guide. If the stocking catches at any point on the guides, it's a cinch that the line will too; the guide should be replaced. Remove the winding, carefully sand any excess color preservative and rod varnish from the rod blank, and replace the guides using the methods outlined in Chapter 8.

Even before guides become grooved, rod varnish and color preservative can chip or wear off the windings, exposing them to the elements. All rod windings should be checked yearly and several additional coats of rod varnish added. Often this simple procedure can mean the difference between a rod with clean strong windings and one with loose or frayed windings. The additional rod varnish should be added in thin coats with the tip of a finger.

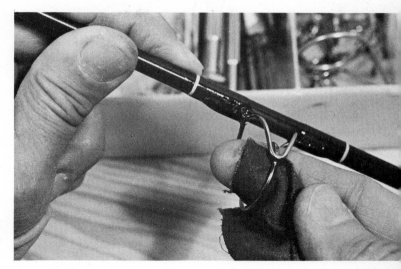

Crocus cloth is ideal for temporary guide repair, in polishing out slight grooves caused by line.

If a ferrule is bent, there's not much that can be done except to remove and replace it, as outlined in Chapter 8. However, if a ferrule is loose, it can sometimes be salvaged, at least for a short time. One way to salvage a loose ferrule is to place the male ferrule in a drill chuck and tighten the chuck gently with the chuck key. The idea here is that when the male ferrule is tightened in the drill chuck, the ferrule will be re-formed from a round cross-section to a slightly triangular shape which will more nearly fit the female ferrule. This must be done in several stages, testing frequently along the way, since tightening the chuck too much will make the male ferrule too large for the female section.

A tight ferrule is easier to correct. Use fine crocus cloth on the male ferrule, polishing it evenly and firmly on all sides. Check frequently for the proper fit. However, make sure first that the ferrule doesn't just need a cleaning.

Occasionally a cork rod handle can become chipped, or cut, requiring replacement of some or all of the cork rings. If the entire handle is ruined, remove the cork grip down to the rod blank. The ideal way to replace a cork grip is to slip the new cork rings over the ferrule end of the rod. But this means that guides, keeper rings, winding checks, and trim windings must also be removed and then later replaced.

There is another way to rebuild a cork grip, by adding cork rings from the butt end—not the best way, but it works as follows:

First remove the cork grip and any glue on the rod blank, being careful not to remove any of the outer skin of glass from the rod blank. Leave the winding check in place. Wrap cotton cord evenly around the rod blank, beginning at the winding check and progressing up and down the rod. The goal is to build the handle portion of the rod blank up to an even diameter equal to that of the butt end of the rod. Since the rod is tapered, there will be more layers of cord at the winding check than at the butt end. Check it with calipers or a simple template. An easily made template can be constructed from a sheet of cardboard cut in a U shape the diameter of the butt end.

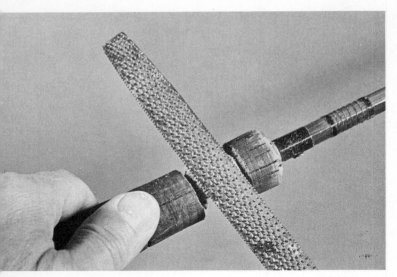

Damaged cork section is removed.

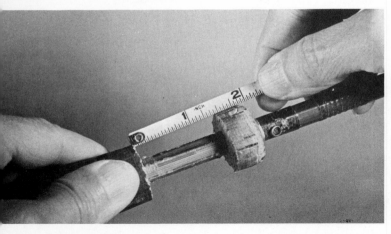

Removed portion must measure in ½-inch increments so that the cork rings that are ½ inch in thickness will fit properly.

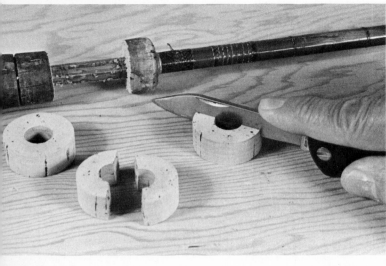

Cork rings are cut in half, reamed to fit rod, and checked for size and placement.

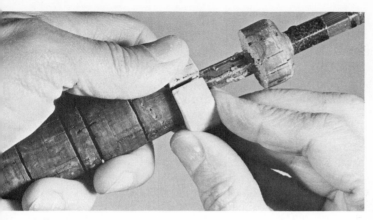

Checking cork ring for placement in damaged rod handle area.

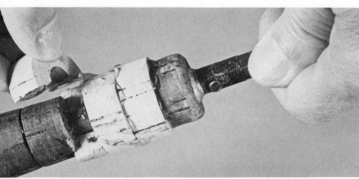

Gluing the cork rings in place in the center of the handle.

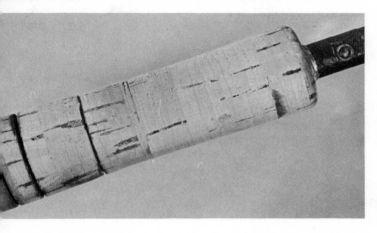

Finished rod handle after being filed and sanded down.

Once this is done, ream out the cork rings to the diameter of the butt end of the rod and prepare to glue in place. Only one cork ring is glued in place at a time. Soak the contact surfaces of the cork ring with glue. Also spread glue on the wrapped rod blank at the point where the cork ring will seat. If a reel seat is to be added, often the fiber or wood bushing that comes off the rod will be impossible to use. The diameter of the wrapped rod blank is now too thick for the bushing. Instead, use cork rings as a replacement, filing and sanding them down when dry to fit under the reel seat. Glue the reel seat in place. Then the aft grip can be completed and the handle sanded to shape. Protect the reel seat from scratching with a taped-on rag.

In case just one or two cork rings in the center of the grip are ruined, the above procedure will not be necessary. In this case, remove the damaged cork section from the rest of the grip, using a wood rasp or coarse file.

Take care not to damage the rod blank. Once the damaged portion is cut away, carefully finish the remaining ends of the cut cork with a fine file. The two cut surfaces must be absolutely flat and at right angles to the plane of the rod blank. Also, the cut-out portion of the grip must have a gap measured in ½-inch increments, i.e., ½-inch, 1-inch, 1½-inches, 2 inches, and so forth. The reason for this is that the cork rings to be fitted into this gap are a standard ½ inch in thickness.

Take the required number of cork rings and slice each of them in half with a razor blade. Ream the hole with a rattail file to fit the rod blank. Take the two halves of each cork ring, soak the contact surfaces with waterproof glue, and fit them around the rod blank next to the cut end of the cork grip. Add the other cork rings the same way, one at a time. If necessary, wrap the rings with cord to hold them in place while the glue dries. Then, remove the cord.

File and sand the new cork rings to the diameter of the rest of the cork grip. If this is done properly, it will be almost impossible to tell where the cork ring halves were glued together. If any pits remain, they can be filled with a glue-cork dust mixture and sanded when dry. If the damage to a cork grip is very slight, this glue-cork dust filler can be used as a repair method to fill in the damaged area.

Broken glass rods were once thought to be irreparable, there being no solution short of replacing the damaged section. More recently, methods of repairing them have been developed that can return a broken stick to full usefulness and almost to its original action. Several methods have been described in some magazine articles, the best by Frank Woolner in the 1966 (sixth) edition of *Fisherman's Digest*. This describes the use of tubular fiberglass plugs inserted into the break, with the break then wrapped with fiberglass.

If the break is clean (not crushed), repair is relatively easy. If it is splintered or crushed, repairs are more difficult, and might result in some loss of rod action. Breaks in large-diameter tubular glass rods are easiest to repair. Fractures in the small-diameter trout fishing and light spinning rods can be repaired by the same means, but the technique is more difficult.

Materials and tools needed for repairing a tubular glass rod include a car or boat fiberglass repair kit, available for $4 and up. An alternative is to buy the glass tape or cloth and small quantities of catalyst and resin separately. You'll also need sandpaper, several cheap brushes, and a tubular section of fiberglass (although rolled-up paper can be used in tip sections and a wood dowel in lower butt sections).

If you're involved in making glass-to-glass ferrules as described in Chapter 8, sections of a rod blank such as the ones used for the ferrule will do. An alternate method is to use rolled-up paper for tip sections or a wood dowel for fractures in the rod butt. The wood dowel insert should be used *only* in the butt, where rod action and flexing are minimal.

Magazine articles have described using everything from solid aluminum rods to thin wire in tip sections and wood dowels in fractures in any part of the rod. I can't recommend these materials. As a rod flexes it becomes elliptical in cross-section rather than round. The stress areas are on the upper and lower surfaces of the rod in line with the flexing. Except for the butt sections where flexing is minimized, any solid plug in a rod will resist this bend into an elliptical cross-section and will create undue stress at each end of the repaired break. Using a solid plug can create the potential of another break just to one side of the first.

Begin glass rod repairs by cleaning the break, and sanding the surface of the glass rod for several inches on either side of the break. If guides are in the way, remove them and clean away any varnish that may have accumulated on the blank around the windings.

If the broken sections will fit together, so much the better. If the rod is crushed, it might take some juggling to match the two parts. In any case, make sure that the remaining guides are lined up properly. Mark the two rod sections to indicate proper guide alignment. Since the fiberglass rod plug should fit tightly, it will be necessary to remove the male ferrule from the tip section or the butt cap from the handle of the butt section to slide the plug into place.

Measure a fiberglass tubing plug or wood dowel (scrap rod sections for this may be available from a tackle dealer for butt sections) to fit the rod. If these are unavailable or if you are working with a light tip section, use a 4-inch length of rolled-up paper. By rolling the paper to a very small diameter, you can insert it into the rod sections and then allow it to unroll to fit the rod blank. Rolled bond paper also has the advantage of matching the rod taper exactly as it expands to fit. Make sure that the rod section, wood dowel, or rolled paper extends 2 inches on each side of the break.

Get someone to help you before this next important step. Mix up the catalyst and resin, following the directions on the can. Take one of the cheap brushes and brush a light coat of resin over the rod break, covering the rod 2 inches to each side of the break. Now wrap the break and the rod for a distance of 2 inches to each side of the break with the glass tape or cloth. If you're using the fiberglass cloth, cut it to a 4-inch width.

If using tape, begin 2 inches from the break, wrap spirally to 2 inches the other side of the break, and then reverse the wrapping direction. While wrapping on the cloth or tape, have your helper liberally coat the wrapping material with the mixed resin. Usually two complete wraps of cloth around the rod, or the tape spiraled in both directions, are enough to strengthen the break. If working on a butt section, however, you may want to add another wrap or two for additional strength. Speed of operation is extremely important in this step, since the resin sets up in minutes.

After cutting off any excess tape or cloth, tie the end of the cloth or tape down with thread. One easy way to do this is to spiral wrap thread over the entire repair area, tying it off at one end with half hitches. If there is a bend, cant, or "dog leg" to the rod, correct it before the resin sets up. Some of the fiberglass strands will probably stick out from the rod blank at this point, but these and the binding thread can be sanded off later.

Curing usually requires about 48 hours. Once cured, sand the repair wrapping with fine 4/0 to 6/0 sandpaper to remove both the excess fiberglass strands

Cutting fiberglass plug so that it can be inserted into broken, hollow fiberglass rod.

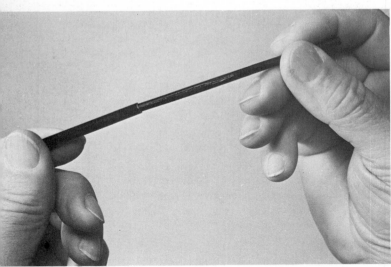

Checking cut fiberglass plug for size in broken rod.

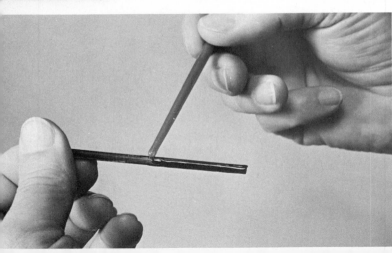

Smear glue on thin end of fiberglass plug and insert in tip portion of broken rod.

Glue is smeared on lower section of fiberglass plug and around the slotted parts of the plug.

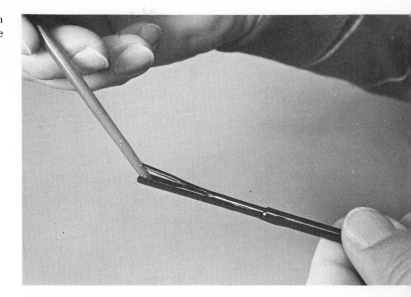

Glue is placed in the butt section of the broken rod.

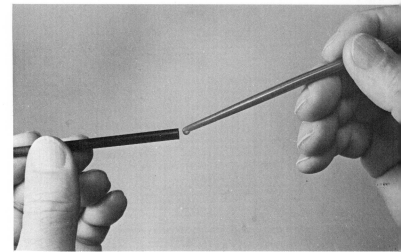

Plug being inserted into butt section of broken rod and the two parts of the rod joined together.

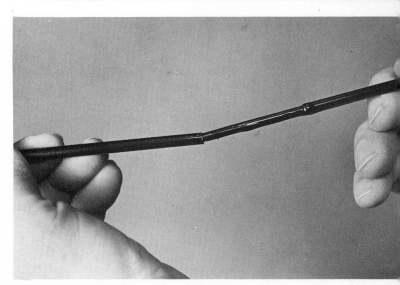

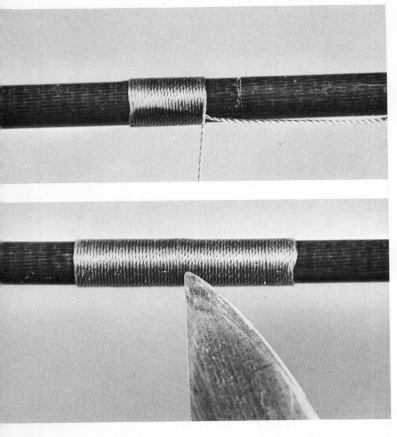

Glued break, being wrapped for additional protection.

Completed wrap; knife points to spot where break occurred.

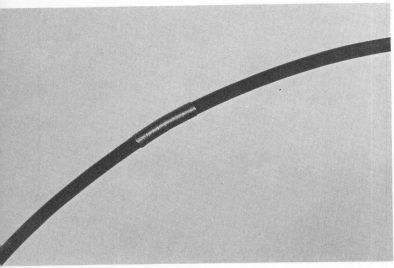

Repaired rod showing degree of bend it can sustain without damage.

and the binding thread. Mix up some more resin-catalyst and coat the repaired section evenly. Allow it to cure again for 48 hours, add any guides that may have been removed, and the rod is ready to be fished. The repair work will be noticeable since the rod will be slightly thicker at this point, but the rod will not really be ugly or sluggish in action. If the rod is a good one, this is an easy way to salvage it.

In collaboration with Irv Swope, I've developed another method. Basically it is a compromise between the method described above and the technique of making glass-to-glass ferrules as outlined in Chapter 8. Its advantage is that it does not require that the rod be partially disassembled for insertion of the glass repair plug.

The basic technique involves insertion of a 4- to 6-inch sleeve of fiberglass rod into the broken section. First clean the break and fit a repair sleeve into the tip section. When it's firmly in place, mark the sleeve at the point of the break and remove. Saw out a repair sleeve 2 to 3 inches on either side of this mark.

Now saw the thicker end of this plug vertically, holding the plug carefully in a vise, protected with a cork stopper or similar cushion to prevent the glass sleeve from being crushed. By sawing two cuts at right angles, you can fit this thicker end of the sleeve into the butt portion of the rod. A single cut may be all that is required for some rods.

Once this thicker sleeve is fitted (check it often during sawing), smear epoxy glue on the *thin* part of the sleeve and seat it securely into the tip section of the broken rod.

Spread glue over and into the cuts in the opposite end of the repair plug. With a fine bodkin or stick, smear glue into the butt section of the broken rod. Join the sleeve (already glued to the tip of the rod) to the broken butt section and check to be sure that the guides are aligned. Allow to cure overnight. Once the glue is cured, sand off any excess glue from the break and wrap the break with thread, extending the wrap 1 inch on either side of the break. Add color preservative and varnish and the rod is ready to use.

This type of repair is obviously less sturdy than the fiberglass wrap repair previously mentioned, but it's adequate for the tip section of most rods. However, with the same technique an outer repair sleeve of fiberglass rod can be added to this so that the rod is reinforced both inside and outside. For this, saw longitudinal cuts in the tip section of outer hollow fiberglass repair sleeve (which also should be 4 to 6 inches long). When the inner repair sleeve is glued into the tip of the broken rod, glue the outer sleeve to the butt section.

Slip the two parts together and align the guides. Wrap thread loosely over the tip portion of the outer repair sleeve until it cures. Sand off any excess glue, wrap as above, and the rod is ready to use. This type of repair should always be used in the butt sections, and in any but clean, sharp breaks.

It's also possible to repair splintered bamboo rods, providing that the rod has a splintering break that does not completely separate the two rod pieces. However, since many bamboo rods are very expensive, it would be advisable to first send any rod to a reliable manufacturer for an estimate of repair costs. Orvis, Dunton, Leonard, and Thomas and Thomas will all repair bamboo rods.

If the rod is inexpensive, or seems unsalvageable, you may still want to try a last-ditch effort. Remove the guides and wrappings from the entire splintered section. Carefully separate the various splinters, being careful not to break any off. Because of the tough outer skin of bamboo, this is a remote possibility anyway.

Using a good flexible cement such as Pliobond, soak all the splintered fibers with the cement. Be sure to work cement well up into all parts of the splintered rod. Because of the way bamboo splinters, this will be well away from the point of the actual break.

When all the splinters are thoroughly soaked with glue, begin to work them back into place in the rod, splinter by splinter, working from the inside to the outer skin. If there are many splinters, it may prove better to soak only the inner section of rod first, working them into place and continuing on out to the skin of the rod. It is not as messy to do this way, and the glue on the outer splinters will not begin to set up before the inner splinters can be worked into place. The trick is to work the splinters back into place in the order in which they belong, which is easier to do than you might think.

Once all the glue-soaked splinters are worked back into place, wrap the broken section tightly with strong cord until the glue sets. This is not unlike the original process of building a split-bamboo rod in which the six strips are bound tightly while the glue sets.

Use strong cord and wrap the rod in a tight spiral. Wrap with as much pressure as possible, but be careful not to exert enough pressure to dislodge some splinters or to force the rod into an elliptical instead of a hexagonal cross-section.

Once the rod is wrapped, tie it down and allow the glue to cure for several days. Remove the cord. Some glue will have oozed out between the splinters and around the cord. This is best removed by carefully scraping the glue from the surface with a flat piece of broken glass. Hold the flat piece of glass at right angles to the rod blank, but take extreme care not to cut into the skin of the bamboo. Once the glue is removed, buff the rod blank with fine steel wool and add a protective coat of varnish.

The easiest way to varnish a complete rod or rod section is to soak an old nylon stocking with rod varnish and rub the rod with the stocking. The result is an even, thin coating, with no bubbles, brush marks, or runny varnish. Once the varnish is dried, replace any guides on the rod. It will also help to add a few additional windings along the rod at the point of repair, to strengthen the splintered break and keep any surface splinters from popping out of place.

Some broken rods can be salvaged in other ways. For example, if a rod tip is broken 2 to 3 inches from the tip top, it would be practically impossible, because of the thinness of the blank, to repair the break. Yet, often the broken portion can be discarded, a new tip top added at the fracture point, and the top few guides repositioned. The result will be a shorter rod and one with perhaps a slightly different action, but it will still be a usable rod.

Sometimes because of the constant flexing of a rod back and forth, the rod will break at the shoulder of the ferrule, on either the male or the female

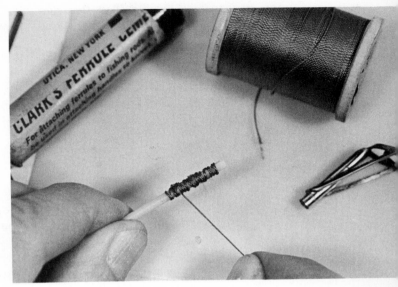

Tip tops in an emergency repair kit may not always fit the rod to be repaired. In this case, use an oversize tip top and build up the rod blanks with thread as shown.

side. Usually it is a clean break. It may be necessary to add a new ferrule to the rod, discarding the broken section still lodged in the ferrule.

It's worthwhile to heat the ferrule holding the broken blank, remove this section, and see if the ferrule will still fit on the rod. If the rod break is at the male ferrule (in the tip section) the ferrule will still fit because of the rod taper. Most likely, though, the ferrule will be a little loose, since the rod, 2 inches up from the break, will be of a smaller diameter. The solution to this is to add thread to the rod blank to build it up as outlined in the section on seating ferrules in Chapter 8.

If the break is on the butt section (at the female ferrule) the ferrule may not fit, because the rod end will be thicker as a result of the taper. Remove the ferrule from the broken rod section to see if the ferrule will fit. Sometimes with a little sanding, the glass blank can be fitted in place. However, be sure to sand it lightly—anything more will invite another similar break at a later date.

If the female ferrule won't fit, buy a new set (male and female) of ferrules that will. It will again be necessary to build up the ferrule end of the tip section of the rod with thread so that the ferrule will fit the rod without a rattle.

If a rod is severely damaged with a long crushing break, such as might result from being slammed in a car trunk or door, it still may be possible to use the remaining lengths. For example, if a long light spinning rod is crushed in the tip section, it may still be possible to use the remainder of the rod to make a shorter medium or heavy action spinning rod, or perhaps use the stripped blank to build a casting rod. If a spinning rod is smashed in the butt section, rod possibilities include an ultra-light short spinning rod or a bantam-sized light fly rod. Broken tip sections can be used for short stubby ice-fishing rods.

Similarly, fly rods smashed at the butt can be converted into shorter light-fly rods, although in the shortened version they will frequently take a fly line one or two sizes heavier than that designed for the original rod. A fly rod smashed at the tip can be converted into a medium-action spinning rod, and so forth.

The procedure in all cases is to remove all the guides and parts, sand off any lumps of varnish, buff the blank with steel wool, finish with a varnish-soaked stocking, and allow to dry. Rebuild the rod, using the directions given in Chapter 8. In cases where the tip is broken (as when a light spinning rod is being converted to a shorter medium-action spinning rod), it will be necessary only to replace and reposition the guides.

REEL CARE

Fishing reels require nothing more than periodic cleaning, with regular oiling and greasing of parts as outlined in the instruction manual that comes with every new reel. An annual overhaul—taking the reel completely apart, removing all grease and oil, checking for and replacing worn parts, and reassembling—will keep any reel running smoothly for years.

However, be sure that you have the parts and instruction book handy before taking any reel apart. If you're not mechanically inclined, send the reel to the factory for its annual overhaul.

Regular cleaning and checking after each fishing trip is necessary to prevent the accumulation of dust, dirt, and grime. And if a reel is used in saltwater, it will be necessary to wash it off in freshwater at home. There are conflicting theories as to the best method of washing the salt off a reel. Unlike a rod, a reel has nooks and crannies that are difficult to reach. One theory favors the use of a forceful stream of water to get into all these places and rinse the salt out. However, opponents to this method argue—and I think I agree with them—that this sometimes forces the salt farther into the reel or into cracks and crevices where it will only cause trouble later.

While there is probably no sure way to get salt out of a reel without a complete dismantling after each trip, I find that soaking the reel in warm water is best. I work over the reel with a rag since just soaking or casual washing will not wash off all the salt.

After it's thoroughly cleaned, remove the reel from the water, shake it dry, and spray with a moisture-repelling agent such as WD40, P38, or CRC. Then oil and grease as per the instructions in the reel manual. Freshwater fishermen can dispense with the long soak and just rinse off the reel to remove algae, loose grit, and grime.

Annually, or sometimes more often, if a reel is used heavily, it should be taken apart, thoroughly cleaned, oiled, and greased, and reassembled.

Spinning, spin-cast, casting, and saltwater reels have many parts, and the manufacturer's disassembly instructions should be followed closely. First, find a good place to work and spread out newspapers to protect the work surface. Since reels have many small parts, it is helpful to use an old egg carton or similarly divided tray to hold the parts and screws *in the order that they are removed from the reel*. Required tools for reel disassembly will include the

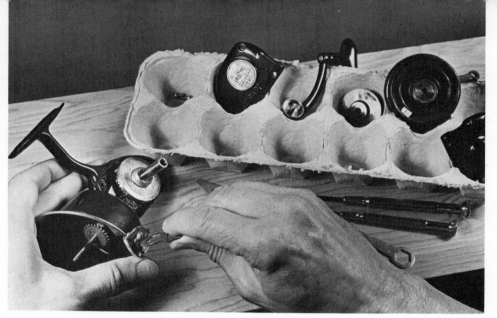

When cleaning reels annually, place all parts in an egg carton in the order in which they are removed from the reel. This makes it easy to replace parts in order when reassembling the reel.

reel tool or tools that come with the reels, small screwdrivers, and small wrenches. Do *not* use pliers or screwdrivers and wrenches of the wrong size.

Take the reel apart according to the manufacturer's instructions, cleaning each major part as it is removed. While gasoline, kerosene, and carbon tetra-chloride are good solvents for removing the old grease, oil, and grime, they cannot be recommended. If used, keep them outside. Gasoline and kero-sene are extremely flammable, and the carbon tetrachloride gives off extremely toxic fumes. Mineral spirits or a similar solvent is recommended. Be careful to clean only the metal parts, since some plastics used in reels may react with the solvent. After dipping the parts in the solvent and cleaning with an old rag, place them in order of removal in the egg carton. When all the parts are clean, reassemble, and oil and grease each part as recommended.

Often it's not necessary to disassemble a reel completely. On fly reels, just taking the spool out of the frame is sufficient for a good cleaning job. It is not necessary to take the screws out of the frame, unless some corrosion demands replacement of a screw or pillar.

Similarly, on spinning reels, several screws will usually remove the side plate from the reel to expose the gears. The gears can be taken out, cleaned, and put back without separating the rotating cup from the gear box. Special attention should be paid to the roller over which the line runs; make sure that it is not grooved or pitted, and that it revolves when replaced. Also check the bail springs, handle, and handle shafts, and other points of wear. Dirt and dust can accumulate here, and dirt on the roller will wear line. Remove these parts, clean thoroughly, and reassemble.

Removing the side plate of a casting or saltwater reel will allow the spool to be removed, and the interior cleaned. Special attention should be given to the level wind, if the reel has one. Because it is heavily lubricated, dirt easily accumulates there. The pawl should be examined for wear and replaced, if necessary.

REEL REPAIR

Usually it is only necessary to replace worn parts on a reel if it has been cleaned carefully and regularly. Parts that most frequently wear out include the pawl and level wind mechanism of casting reels, roller guides and bail springs on spinning reels, and drag washers on all reels. Tackle stores often carry these replacement parts or they can be ordered from the factory, according to the instructions in the reel manual.

Any broken parts can be replaced as needed; carefully follow the disassembly instructions and exploded views in the instruction manual.

LINE CARE

Care of lines will vary, depending upon their type and construction. Lines in use today include monofilament, braided nylon, dacron, Cortland's Micron, lead-core nylon-covered trolling line, and single-strand wire line and the various fly lines.

Monofilament line is best cared for by storing (either on the reel or on bulk storage spools) in a cool, dry, dark place. Sunlight and heat will harm these lines, causing the surface to get a powdery feel as the line begins to break down and lose strength.

Edwin H. Keller, Marketing Manager for Du Pont Stren monofilament fishing line, has over the years come up with other suggestions and tips to ensure that monofilament line lasts as long as is practicably possible. "A premium monofilament line purchased this year should last at least two years if the angler understands the nature of the line and observes a few simple rules about its care," he notes.

Some tips from Keller on care of monofilament line include an easy way to take a set out of line that is left on the reel spool between fishing trips. A "set" in line means that the line has taken the shape of the spool and, when cast or pulled from the spool, comes off in tight loops.

To remove, tie one end of the line to a stationary object and stretch gently. When the line is released and rewound on the reel it will have recovered its original length and will be relatively loop free. When rewinding line after this, do so under slight tension, as is done when line is originally placed on the reel. (Incidentally, the same stretch process can be used to straighten fly lines.)

Keller also suggests that anglers carefully check fishing rod guides and tip tops for wear and nicks. A nick or rough spot in a guide will quickly abrade line and weaken it with repeated casting. Faulty guides should be replaced in the way outlined above.

Another problem in using line is twist, caused by some lures and trolling techniques. A swivel will prevent some twist, but not all. The best method

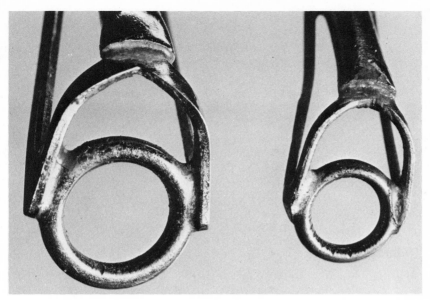

Grooved tip tops or guides such as these should be replaced as soon as possible. Grooved guides will severely chafe and damage line.

of removing twist is to run the line behind a moving boat with no terminal tackle attached and troll the line until it is straight.

Keller emphasizes the importance of winding new line on the reel to prevent both twist and damage. The line should be under some tension and the line should come off the manufacturer's spool in the same direction that it goes on to the reel spool.

This means that in spooling monofilament (or any line for that matter) on a casting or saltwater conventional reel (revolving spool reel), the spool should be placed on a pencil, with the line coming off the top of the spool and onto the reel.

With a spinning reel, the line should come off the end of the spool without the spool turning. But it is important to take the line off the correct end. The line must come off the spool end in the same direction that the line is being laid on the reel spool as the bail, pick-up arm, or roller rotates. Otherwise, excessive twist will result.

Avoiding excessive exposure to the sun is another of Keller's tips for preserving the useful life of mono. Basically this means not buying line that has been displayed in a store window, or leaving tackle in the sun for long periods on car rod racks, in rear windows, or outside. Oil from trolling or fishing in a chum slick or from reel lubricating can be another problem for monofilament, although Keller insists that the oil in itself will not harm the line. The problem is that the oily line will pick up dust and dirt, which as the line moves through the guides will cause it to become rough, abraded, and in time, weakened.

Dacron line, widely used in saltwater fishing, has great resistance to saltwater damage, unlike the linen lines of years ago. It requires little in the way of care, but should be washed on the reel after use in saltwater and stored in a cool dark place. Micron line care is similar.

Lead core and wire line care mainly involves carefully handling the line while fishing to prevent any kinks or twists. A twist or kink in wire line is sure to cause breakage later; the line must be cut at this point and spliced. The best care for wire lines of any type is a roller tip top on a rod to minimize the bend of the line as it leaves the rod.

Most damage to modern fly lines occurs when various insect repellents, sun tan lotions, and gasoline (sometimes on the hands of boat fly rodders) come into contact with the line.

Leon Martuch, president of Scientific Anglers, Inc. (the foremost producer of fly lines), and a chemist by training, explains that most coatings of today's fly lines are made of polyvinyl chloride—commonly called PVC. This is the same tough material used in shower curtains, convertible car tops, plastic water pipe (see Chapter 11), and the like. Surprisingly, some damage comes from line cleaners.

"Some line dressing and cleaners, usually liquids," Martuch says, "contain chlorinated solvents. These extract the plasticizers (which keep the line flexible) from the coating material. Gasoline, insect repellent, and suntan lotions also have the same effect. This results in what we call 'chemical attack.' The coating becomes stiff and brittle and loses its life. Then, when the line is flexed, the coating breaks."

Care also must be exercised in casting fly lines, since too short a pause for the back cast to straighten out results in a "whipcrack" in which the line actually breaks the sound barrier. The effect of this on the line is the equivalent of hitting a brick wall, and the line breaks down quickly.

Proper floating of a fly line requires only that it be kept clean with the manufacturer's dressing or cleaner. If the line is dirty, it will not float and it won't "shoot" properly on a cast. Algae—common in most waters where fish are—also sticks to the line, causing it in turn to pick up more dirt.

LINE REPAIR

About the only repair that can be made on a line is to piece together, or splice, the two broken or cut ends. Even splicing is not recommended, unless absolutely necessary.

Mono and braided nylon lines are best tied with a blood knot. Even this knot, however, makes an awkward bump in the middle of the line, and the line should be replaced as early as possible.

Dacron and Cortland's Micron lines are hollow and can be spliced together with a splicing needle—available at tackle stores or often packaged with bulk spools of the line. This splice results in only a slight increase in the size of the line at the splice, so that it's still fishable.

Wire line that develops a kink must be broken and spliced. To make such a splice the ends of the wire line are overlapped by about 12 inches and held in the middle securely with pliers. One end of the line is wrapped around the standing part at least 25 turns. The second end is wrapped similarly. The two ends of the wraps are cut short and wrapped smoothly around the

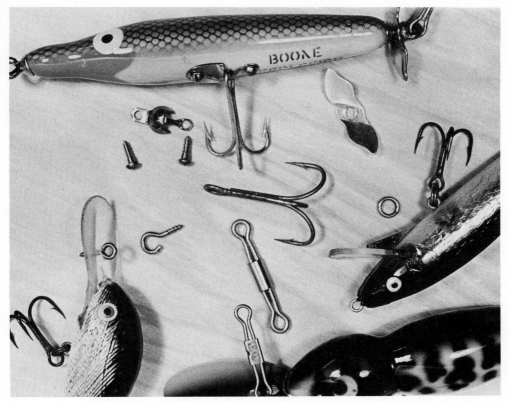

Spare plug parts such as hook hangers, screws, screw eyes, connecting links, split rings, and hooks make it easy to repair most plugs.

standing part of the line. This splice will be flexible and is said to retain up to 80 percent of the original line strength.

PLUG CARE

Proper care of fishing plugs means keeping them separated in the tackle box. Many anglers lump several plugs together in one tray compartment. The disadvantage of this, aside from hooks getting tangled when you want to change lures, is that the plugs will rub together, resulting in scarred finishes. This is more of a danger for wood plugs than for molded plastic lures. It is obvious that plugs should be kept in a tackle box when not tied to the line. Leaving them on a boat seat is inviting disaster to yourself, while they may get stepped on and crushed if left on a boat deck.

If plugs are returned to their trays wet, open the tackle box after each trip so that excess moisture can evaporate. Saltwater plugs should be washed in freshwater after use.

Sharp hooks are extremely important for hooking fish, which is what fishing is ultimately all about. Some curved-point hooks, because of the design of the hook point, are difficult to sharpen successfully. However, straight-point hooks

Old plugs can be revitalized by painting or finishing with glitter as shown here.

can be sharpened easily with a small ignition, wood scraping, or warding file. Sharpen hooks by filing the sides of the point and barb into a sharp wedge shape. This way, no metal is removed from the outside of the hook point. To protect the points of treble hooks, hook bonnets that cover the hook completely are available.

PLUG REPAIR

Not much can happen to plugs that cannot be repaired, unless the plug body is completely shattered by hitting a stump on a cast, or by the strike of a strong saltwater fish. (If fish this strong are the quarry, solid wood or plastic plugs with through-wire construction should be used for just this eventuality.)

If a hook becomes rusted, broken, or bent, replace it by removing the hook hanger or screw eye and adding a new hook. Plugs with through-wire construction usually have the hooks attached by means of a split ring. In this case, remove the old hook from the split ring and add a new one simultaneously. If the hook is wired in place, it may be necessary to cut the hook eye and add the new hook with a split ring.

You can sometimes repair a hollow plug that has cracked by spreading the crack carefully apart with a nail or small screwdriver, filling the crack with an epoxy glue, and clamping it until cured. Clothespins make ideal gluing clamps for plugs.

Plugs with a scratched, faded, worn, or chipped finish must have all the hardware removed for complete refinishing. For refinishing of painted wood plugs, scrape off any chipped paint and sand with fine 7/0 sandpaper or steel wool to give the plug some "tooth" to hold new paint. Spray or dip a coat of sealer or base white and finish or repaint as outlined in Chapter 12.

Some plastics and paints react chemically. If the plug is plastic, use paint designed for plastic or test by dabbing a small inconspicuous part of the plug with the paint. Allow to dry and test for adherence and any reaction before continuing.

A third alternative is to keep the hardware on the plug, spray, or brush with a clear adhesive coat and cover any flaws with glitter, flocking, or sequin finishes. The glitter or flocking can be sprinkled on the plug until the desired effect is achieved.

The adhesive can also be sprayed onto a masked plug to give an appearance of stripes, bars, spots, or similar effects as the glitter is added. Brush-on adhesive can be added selectively for the same results. For a heavier coat, roll the plug in glitter or flocking that has been spread on a sheet of paper. Any excess material can be saved for later use. See Chapter 12 for additional ideas and methods for finishing plugs.

SPOON AND SPINNER CARE

Spoon and spinner care is similar to that of plugs. Because of the shiny polished finish on most metal lures, it is extremely important to keep them separate to avoid scratching of spoon and spinner blades. Special pocket-size tackle and lure boxes that compartmentalize small spoons and spinners are available, and bigger tackle boxes have compartmented trays to separate bigger spoons. Spoon and spinner blades that become scratched can sometimes be polished with silver, copper, or other metal polishes. These polishes are widely available and work well on metal lures. In the field, Brillo, SOS, or even cigarette ashes work well as polishes.

SPOON AND SPINNER REPAIR

Hooks can be replaced on both spoons and spinners. On spinners, the hook may have to be cut off and a new hook added with a split ring, since most hooks are added to an eye, formed on the spinner shaft as the spinner is completed. Most spoons have hooks attached with a split ring, but some bigger spoons have hooks rigged by means of soldered solid rings or soldered split rings. These must be cut off to add a new hook and split ring.

Spoon and spinner blades that are completely tarnished and worn may be painted or electroplated in a silver, copper, or gold finish. Instructions for preparing the metals for paint, the choice of paint, and electroplating instructions are the same as for new spoons, and can be found in Chapter 12. Other alternatives, also discussed in Chapter 12, include the application of glitter, flocking, reflective tapes, and similar materials.

In case a spinner is completely ruined and you cannot salvage it by painting the blade or replacing the hook, parts of it can still be used. Cut the spinner shaft and save any useful parts for building new spinners.

SOFT PLASTIC LURE CARE

Proper care of plastic worms, minnows, frogs, and similar lures consists not so much in protecting them, but in keeping them away from other tackle that they can damage. The soft plastic lures contain chemical plasticizers that can ruin the hard plastics in most old (and some new) tackle boxes, eat into hard plastic plugs, and take the finish off wood lures.

Many modern tackle boxes are labeled "worm proof," and plastic lures can be kept in their trays without damage. Small tackle boxes and single-tray lure boxes designed just for plastic worms are also made. With the current emphasis on plastic worming for bass, most of these have long narrow compartments. However, do not mix soft plastic lures with other lures.

SOFT PLASTIC LURE REPAIR

After a fish gets through chewing on it, a soft plastic lure is not much good. In setting the hook into a bass (or trying to) the hook will pull partially through a worm body, making rehooking and further use difficult. However, these worms should be saved and added to the stock pot of plastic to be melted down and used in molding soft plastic lures, as discussed in Chapter 5.

Since the plastic formulations of different companies may not mix, it is best to stick to one brand of plastic molding material and to remelt only lures made from this material. Since the plastic lures can be used over and over this way, it further reduces the cost of molding soft plastic lures.

It is possible to repair a plastic lure that has been broken or cut in half. Since the plastic becomes molten with heat, melt both ends of the broken lure with a match or other small flame. When the cut ends just approach a liquid state, fuse the two parts together and hold until cool, or drop the repaired lure into a pan of cold water. Similarly, parts of soft plastic lures can be combined to make new and different lures this way.

It is also possible to recolor soft plastic lures, using the Fliptail Marking Kit. This set of eight waterproof felt-tipped markers is designed for adding new colors to lures. While recommended for use on clear plastic worms, it can also be used on white, yellow, and other light-colored soft plastic lures. Colors in the kit are green, brown, purple, red, blue, yellow, orange, and black.

BUCKTAIL CARE

Except when tied to the end of a line, bucktails and jigs should be protected just as are other types of lures. Since the bucktail heads are painted, they should be protected from scratching and scarring by being separated from other lures as much as possible. Since any type of paint chips readily from the soft heads, avoid hitting the lures on anything hard.

If possible, wash after using in saltwater and allow to dry before returning to the tackle box. If any paint comes loose from the thread wrappings, cover with varnish or fly-tying cement, or repaint or wrap with narrow vinyl tape for protection.

BUCKTAIL REPAIR

As with plugs, chipped bucktails can be repainted. Since the tail is already tied in place, dip the bucktail body into a jar of thinned acrylic car touch-up lacquer. Be sure to cover the thread wrappings, so as to protect them and keep them from becoming unraveled. If there are only a few chips on the bucktail head, some glitter, glued on with a clear adhesive or lacquer, will hide them and give the bucktail added flash.

If a fish completely tears up a bucktail, the heads should still be saved to be retied and repainted later. At home, such bucktails should be stripped of all tail material and thread. Sand or buff lightly any remaining paint. If the metal is oxidized, dip in vinegar to etch it, then rinse clean and dry. Dip it several times to give it a smooth base coat. Add tail as outlined in Chapter 3, and finishing coats as discussed in Chapter 12.

MISCELLANEOUS EQUIPMENT CARE

The care of other fishing equipment is mainly a matter of checking it carefully after each trip and putting it away in such fashion that it will be ready for use on the next trip. Wire leaders, wire-rigged lures, and wire-bottom fishing rigs should be handled so as to prevent kinks. Lay them flat in a tackle box. Long leaders should be individually coiled and stored. Tackle boxes should be periodically cleaned and the moving hinges and tray supports lightly oiled. Check rivets on latches and handles periodically to be sure that they are not pulling out. If they are, replace them with pop rivets or other do-it-yourself rivets.

Ice-fishing equipment—rods, tip ups, skimmers, and ice-cutting spuds—should be washed and dried, and all metal parts sprayed with a light coating of WD40, P38, CRC, or a similar rust-proofing and moisture-repelling compound before being stored after the season.

Replacement nets are added by slipping the top meshed loops over the dismantled aluminum frame one at a time.

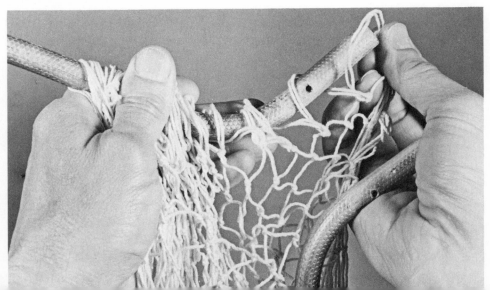

Not all the mesh loops are placed on the frame at once. The net must be pulled around the net frame as shown here, then the additional mesh loops slipped on the end of the frame.

APPENDIX 1

Action. Used to describe the type of bend that a rod makes when casting or fighting a fish; also the degree a rod bends. In the first case, the rod can have a light tip, described as "tip action" or "fast action," or an even bending from tip to butt, known as "parabolic action." The second use describes the stiffness of a rod in relation to the fishing; thus, a freshwater spinning rod could have light, medium, or heavy action, describing the degree of bend against a constant pull. A medium-action freshwater rod would be only a light or very light saltwater rod. Light, heavy, or medium action rod can also be either fast tip or parabolic, since the two terms are not related.

Aetna guide. See Foulproof guide.

Aircraft cable. A very large-diameter twisted leader wire used in big game fishing. Comes in 175- to 800-pound test strengths. Also called airplane cable.

Airplane cable. See Aircraft cable.

Aluminum oxide. A guide ring material. Used in Lew Childre and Sanders guides.

Attractor tubing. Round hollow tubing in bright red, orange, and other colors that is cut into short lengths and added to the shaft of a treble hook to be placed on a spinner. Used to create more attraction for the fish.

Ball-bearing swivel. A swivel in which tiny ball bearings are used for the swiveling surface. Used in big game fishing, and also when line twist is a particular problem, as in fishing spinners, they are more expensive than regular swivels.

Ball-head jig. A lead head jig with a spherical head often used in making crappie lures.

Banjo-eye bucktail. A large bucktail with bulging eyes. Usually the eyes are molded into the lure, but sometimes are made of glass, and glued on later.

Bank sinker. A teardrop-shaped sinker with hexagonal sides, designed to be used in rocky areas. The shape of the sinker resists hanging up on rocks.

Barrel swivel. A simple two-eye swivel in which the central swiveling part resembles a small barrel.

Bass-casting sinker. A pear-shaped sinker with a molded-in swivel eye, also called a dipsy doodle sinker, dipsy sinker, or bell sinker.

Basswood. A wood used to carve out fishing plugs. Other woods often used include cedar and fine-grain clear pine.

Beads. Round or faceted pieces of glass, plastic, and metal, drilled with a central hole, and used for the body of a spinner.

Bell sinker. See Bass casting sinker.

Belmar frame. See Belmar guide.

Belmar guide. A rod guide in which the frame that supports the guide ring is much longer and more extended than in a normal guide. Also called a bridge guide, it is found mostly on big game or trolling rods.

Bib. A small, short type of wiggling plate or lip.

Blade. See Blank, definition 2.

Blank. 1. The fiberglass or bamboo stick used to build a fishing rod. "Blank" here refers to the rod without any of the appointments of the finished rod such as handle, reel seat, guides, ferrules, or windings. 2. An unfinished metal spoon without the addition of the hook or split rings, also called a blade.

Body. 1. The entire part of the female ferrule, excepting the cap onto which the thread windings are wound. 2. The center-drilled solid piece of metal (usually brass or steel), tapered or bullet-shaped, that fits onto the shaft in making spinners, providing the weight.

Box swivel. A simple two-eye swivel in which the center swiveling part resembles the sides of a box; not commonly used today.

Boxing-glove jig. A large bucktail with a head similar in shape to a boxing glove. Used mostly in saltwater fishing.

Brass lure wire. A heavy wire, usually 0.060 inch in thickness, used for making through-wire rigging for plugs, hook lears, and bottom rigs, since it is both strong and easy to form.

Bridge frame. See Belmar guide.

Bridge guide. See Belmar guide.

Bullet-head bucktail. A bucktail with a lead head shaped like a bullet.

Bushing. Most frequently used to describe the cork, fiber, wood, or similar material used to fill up the space between the rod blank and the reel seat on fly, spinning, popping, surf, and similar rods where the reel seat is placed over the rod blank. Special bushings are sold in a variety of inside and outside diameters to fit every rod blank–reel seat combination. Also called reel seat bushing.

Butt cap. A plastic or metal cap that fits over the butt end of the rod handle. Many look like a plastic or rubber chair tip, which may also be substituted in tackle construction. Some lightweight butt plates serve the same purpose as a butt cap and are screwed in place, but most are glued.

Butt ferruled. A term sometimes used to describe a two-piece rod in which the ferrules are in two unequal sections, with the tip section the longer length. As a result, the ferrule is closer to the butt. Often confused with the special butt ferrule applied to the base of casting rod blanks, which fits into a collet in a casting rod handle.

Butt plate. A small lightweight metal plate that is screwed onto the end of the handle of a rod, most often on lightweight tackle in the place of a butt cap.

Butt section. The lower or butt portion of the rod, that which incorporates the rod handle. In a two-piece rod, it is the heavier of the two sections. In a multiple-piece rod, it is the lowest of the several sections.

Calcutta cane. One type of cane used for rods, but not as popular as Tonkin cane. It is no longer used, but was once highly thought of for rod making.

Cap. That part of a male or female ferrule onto which the decorative thread windings are wrapped.

Carboloy guide. Any of a number of types of guides in which the ring is made of tungsten carbide. Carboloy is a trademark of General Electric. Mildrum calls its guides of the same material Mildarbide.

Cedar. The wood principally used for carving plugs. Other good plug woods include basswood and fine-grain pine.

Center. That portion of the male ferrule that fits into the female ferrule.

Center ferruled. Applies to a two-piece rod in which the ferrule is placed in the exact center.

Cigar style grip. See Philippe style grip.

Clamp type mold. A bucktail, sinker, or jig mold in which the two mold halves are completely separate, but in use are clamped together with built-in pinned clamps.

Clevis. The small U-shaped wire or sheet stamped devices used to attach the spinner blade to the spinner shaft. The clevis is run through the eye of the spinner blade, and then the spinner shaft run through the holes in the ends of the clevis. See also Folded clevis and Wire clevis.

Coastlock snap. A very long snap, designed for maximum strength and used extensively in the East.

Coil-spring fastener. The spring used to close and fasten the loop shaft of a spinner.

Collet. The chucklike device at the fore end of a casting or spin-cast rod handle that is tightened on the butt ferrule of the rod to hold it securely.

Color preservative. A thin, watery finishing liquid that must be used over thread wraps before any final protective coats of varnish are added. If color preservative is not used, the varnish will turn white and light colors almost transparent, dark colors almost black. Two coats of color preservative before varnishing are sufficient.

Colorado blade. A tapered spinner blade, rounder than an Indiana blade (see size charts in Appendix).

Connecting link. Looks almost like a very long link of a chain with a sliding locking bar in the center, to keep the ends from springing apart. Since it can be taken apart and yet locked securely for high strength, it is often used as the attachment for line at the metal lip of plug.

Core pin. See Core rod.

Core rod. A brass or steel rod placed in a sinker mold to form a hole in egg sinker molds, plastic worm slip sinker molds, and molds for spinner bodies. Also called a core pin.

Cork grip. The handle material of most rods with the grip formed of round, ½-inch-thick center-drilled rings.

Cork rings. The round, drilled, ½-inch-long rings used to build up a handle on a fishing rod. They come in two types of cork—species and mustard cork—and in several outside diameters and a number of inside diameters to fit any rod blank.

Crimping pliers. Specially made pliers, with jaws for crimping different sizes of leader sleeves. Some also have a built-in wire cutter.

Cross-line swivel. A swivel with three eyes, in which two of the eyes are in a single plane with the third at right angles—almost like a T. Used for hanging drop sinkers in trolling.

Cup washers. Small cupped washers, about ⅛ inch in diameter, used under a screw eye in a plug both for a finished appearance and also to limit the movement of the hooks to prevent tangling. The deeper washers, used principally under screw eyes holding hooks, are often called derby washers.

Dart jig. A small tapered jig with a flat face. Also called a quill dart jig or shad dart.

Decal eyes. Fishing plug eyes that come on decal sheets. They are usually sold fifty to the sheet. They are placed on the finished plug as regular decals are, and covered with a clear coat of varnish.

Decorative windings. See Windings.

Derby washer. Similar to a cup washer but deeper. Designed to go under the screw eye holding the hook on a plug, these deeper washers limit the movement of a hook to prevent it from scarring the plug finish or tangling with other hooks or the line.

Dipsy doodle sinker. See Bass-casting sinker.

Down gate. See Sprue hole.

Drail. A heavy large L-shaped sinker used in deep trolling.

Dry fly action. A fly rod action in which the tip does most of the bending. Designed for fly fishing years ago, when the fast action was needed to dry out a fly between casts. (The opposite of wet fly action, an action extending well down into or toward the grip.) Today, rods are seldom characterized by the type of fishing even though different rod actions are available.

Double snap swivel. A standard snap swivel to which a second snap is attached to the free eye of the swivel.

Duo-lock snap. A simple, single wire snap made by Gladding in which the construction makes it possible to unhook the snap at either end. It has a double-locking arrangement that makes it especially strong, but does not swivel.

Ear-grip sinker. See Pinch-on sinker.

Egg sinker. A round or torpedo-shaped sinker with a hole running through its long axis. Designed for bottom fishing, the line running through the sinker prevents the fish from detecting the sinker weight while mouthing or running with the bait.

Eyed shaft. A spinner shaft that comes with the closed eye for line attachment already formed in one end. Available in several lengths, it's the most popular spinner shaft for making spinners.

Faceted beads. Beads that have flat surfaces to reflect light, sometimes used in place of round beads in a spinner body.

Fast tip. A rod action in which the tip bends sharply while the butt is stiff. See also Action.

Female ferrule. That half of a ferrule set that is a hollow center into which the male ferrule fits. In a set of metal ferrules, the female ferrule is fitted to the butt section of the rod, while in a glass ferrule the female is fitted or built into the tip section of the rod. The difference in the ferrule arrangement is because of the rod tapers that require the glass ferrule arrangement.

Ferrule. The metal or built-in glass parts of a two- or multiple-piece rod that hold the rod sections together for fishing. Metal ferrules are cemented to the rod and come in male and female parts. Glass ferrules are often built into the rod as in the popular Fenwick rods, although tip and butt section glass ferrules can be built by the home craftsman.

Ferrule cement. A resin-based cement in stick form that must be heated to be used. It can be used easily to glue ferrules and tip tops to a rod blank, and gives secure bonding. If replacement of ferrules or tip tops is ever necessary, they can be removed by reheating the cement.

Figure-eight attachment. Just what it sounds like—a figure-eight-shaped piece of wire attached to the metal wiggle lip of a plug and by which the line is tied to the plug.

Flash. The excess lead, lead alloy, or tin that leaks out along the joint of two mold halves from the mold cavity during the pouring of a lead or tin bucktail head, squid, or sinker. It is attached to the center plane of the lure or sinker. It must be removed from the lure by cutting or filing, but will not interfere with the use of sinkers.

Flat sinker. A sinker design of several shapes—all flat—designed to be snagless. Shaped much like a spinner blade.

Folded clevis. A clevis stamped from sheet metal in the shape of an O, and folded over to make a U-shaped clevis. See Clevis.

Foregrip. That part of a cork or wood handle that is in front of or above the reel seat. Casting rod handles come with or without a foregrip, while all spinning rod and boat rod handles have a foregrip of some type.

Foulproof guide. A flexible guide made from a single strand of wire, made by Aetna and sold by Gudebrod. It comes in fly rod, spinning rod, casting rod, spin cast, and heavy-duty sets and sizes.

French type blade. Used in popular spinners, in which the blade has an egg-shaped raised surface on the convex side of the blade.

Full Wells style grip. Used on fly rods. A grip with a cigar-shaped swollen center that narrows before flaring out at both ends. See chart in Appendix.

Gimbal. A heavy, solid butt cap for fighting rods in which the bottom is slotted (or double slotted as in an X) so as to fit onto a bar placed in the gimbal socket of a fighting chair or belt filled with a gimbal socket. Usually made of heavily chromed brass. Also called a knock.

Glass eyes. Glass eyes come paired on a long wire, and are used to finish wood fishing plugs. The wire is cut off ½ inch from the eye and the short wire inserted with pliers into the wood plug body. An advantage of these eyes is that they can be underpainted any desired color around the black pupil.

Gordon style grip. A fly rod handle similar to the Phillippe tapered style grip, except that the rear part of the grip flares out instead of remaining straight. See chart in Appendix.

Grip check. See Winding check.

Half Wells style grip. A fly rod grip design, almost a reversed Hardy grip in which the front is flared, followed by a swelling, then tapered at the rear of the grip. See chart in Appendix.

Hammered blade. A spinner blade which has been hammered or given a hammered finish. Can apply to any shape of blade.

Hammerhead jig. A bucktail with protruding eyes on each side of the head, much like a hammerhead shark, thus the name.

Handle. The part of the rod held in the hand as the rod is used. Fly rods have the handle above the reel seat, spinning rod handles incorporate reel seats of sliding rings, while casting rod handles are separate from the rod and have the reel seat above the grip. Boat and trolling rod handles are larger and longer and also incorporate the reel seat. "Handle" usually implies that the reel seat is also included, while "grip" refers only to the wood, cork, or plastic part meant to be held in the hand.

Handled mold. A bucktail, jig, or lead head mold that is hinged on one side, with handles on the other side of each of the two halves. It has the advantage of making lead molding a quick and easy operation.

Hardy style grip. A modified cigar or Phillippe style handle used on fly rods, in which the rear part of the grip flares out slightly. See chart in Appendix.

Hold-down clamp. The small flat piece of metal found on the reel seat of some casting or spin cast handles, to hold the foot of the reel.

Hook hanger. A small metal device, shaped like a bent garden trowel, by which hooks are added to a plug. These are fastened to the plug with very small round-head screws. The advantage of these over-screw eyes is that hook hangers limit the forward movement of the hook to prevent tangling of the hook with the line or other hooks.

Hook hanger spreader. A small wire device, first popularized by the Helin Flatfish, designed to hang two hooks out from the body of the lure, with the hook hanger spreader hanging from a single screw eye.

Hook keeper. See Keeper ring.

Hosel. A large, usually plastic device designed to serve the same purpose as a winding check. Center drilled, they fit over the rod blank and up against the rod handle, and are primarily decorative.

Ice tong snap. A special type of terminal rigging snap, the end of which looks like a pair of ice tongs. Often used in attaching sinkers with bottom rigs for saltwater. Preferred mainly on the West Coast. Also called a McMahon snap.

Indiana blade. A pear-shaped spinner blade. (See size and shape charts in Appendix.)

Ingot mold. A mold for making ingots or bars of lead for future use. Most molds usually make four bars of about one to two pounds.

Jig. (1) Another name for a bucktail or bucktail head; (2) A device used for forming or bending tubing or rod as in making a landing net frame. This term could also be used for a wire former of thin wire used in making terminal tackle.

Jig hook. A special hook designed to be used in molding jigs and bucktails. It has a right-angle bend near the eye of the hook, and the eye is in the same plane as the shank, rather than at right angles to it, as with regular hooks.

Jointed plug. See Two-part plug.

Jump ring. A small open ring sometimes used to attach hooks or swivels to spoons and spinners. In use, the parts to be attached are placed in the ring, and the ring closed with pliers, but it is strongest when soldered closed.

June Bug spinner. A spinner that uses a blade with a cut-out central portion that forms a leg that also attaches to the spinner shaft. The leg running from the center of the blade holds the blade at a constant angle from the spinner shaft. June Bug spinners are often used in conjunction with bait.

Keeper ring. A small metal device, almost like a small snake guide, wrapped to the rod just ahead of the handle or grip. It is used to hold a hook or lure to keep it from swinging when you are moving from one fishing spot to the next. Also called hook keeper.

Knock. See Gimbal.

Lead dipper. A small, deeply cupped, specialized pouring ladle (see Pouring ladle).

Lead pot. A large cast-iron pot for melting lead. Lead is not poured into the mold from these pots, but transferred to a smaller long-handled pouring ladle. Capacity of the pots varies from about 5 to 15 pounds of lead.

Leader sleeves. Small metallic cylinders used to fit over doubled twisted leader wire to form loops and make leaders. They come in different sizes for use with different-size wire, but cannot be used with single-strand wire. Also called sleeve fasteners.

Loop shaft. A shaft for spinners that comes with a loop eye formed in one end. Used to make some types of spinners (such as the French spinner) with the hook added to the loop shaft, followed by the body and other parts, with the eye for line attachment formed last. Also used in conjunction with a coil-spring closure on spinners so that the hook can be changed at will.

McMahon snap. See Ice tong snap.

Male ferrule. The ferrule which has a solid center that fits into the female ferrule. With metal ferrules, the male ferrule is fitted to the tip section. In a glass ferrule, the male ferrule is fitted to the butt section of the rod. The difference is due to the rod taper that requires the male ferrule at the butt end on glass ferruled rods.

Mandrel. The steel tapered rod used as the core when making hollow glass fishing rod blanks. The glass cloth is wrapped around the mandrel and baked, then the mandrel is removed.

Mask. A term used in finishing in which the lure is painted selectively with dots, streaks, stripes, or similar patterns. A "mask" of paper, tape, or similar materials prevents the sprayed-on paint from hitting other parts of the plug. It can also refer to the materials used for the masking process.

Mesh gauge. A gauge used to measure the size of the meshes in landing and fishing nets. Gauge sizes range from ½ inch to 3 inches, although any long, rectangular piece of plastic, metal, wood, or stiff cardboard can serve as a gauge for meshes larger or smaller. Use is covered in Chapter 11.

Mildarbide. Trademark of Mildrum, for tungsten carbide guide material.

Mold furnace. A special furnace used mostly by bullet casters. Costing about $15 to $30, these have the advantage of a thermostatic control for melting lead, plus a gravity feed pot that makes completely filled molds almost a sure thing, while assuring the absence of slag, which floats to the surface.

Multiple-cavity mold. A bucktail, jig, sinker, or worm mold with anywhere from two to eight cavities for molding several lead heads, sinkers, or worms at one time.

Mustard cork. A lower grade of cork used in cork rings or handles on cheaper rods. The natural pits in the cork run at right angles to the plane of the hole in the cork ring. In specie cork the pits and the hole are parallel. The disadvantage of mustard cork is that often a large pit will be uncovered as the cork handle is being turned down to finished size.

Net wheel. A round wire frame wheel, which clamps to a tabletop, used for making landing nets without seams. The frame includes forty clips to which the first loops of a landing net are secured. Additional rows of meshes are added with the netting knot.

Netting knot. A sheet bend, used to knot together the rows of meshes used in landing and fishing nets.

Node. 1. The swollen part of a bamboo pole. In making split-bamboo fishing rods, these nodes are planed down and staggered along the rod blank so that the nodes will not all be at the same point, since the node is slightly weaker than the rest of the bamboo. 2. As a rod is rapidly shaken, that point where the two curves of the shaken rod intersect is called a "nodal point."

Nylon-coated leader wire. Twisted leader wire coated with nylon for easy handling.

Off-center ferruled rod. A two-piece rod in which the two sections are cut in unequal lengths the butt section is always shorter, the tip always longer. The reasoning is that the action will be less adversely affected with the ferrule toward the butt. A disadvantage is that the rod will need a longer rod case than for an equal-length center-ferruled rod. Also called butt-ferruled.

Open-face mold. A one-piece mold for making tin squids or plastic worms and lures, in which the molten metal or liquid plastic is poured into the open side of the mold. Because the mold is one piece, the squid, plastic worm, or lure is molded on one side only, the other side being flat. Also called a one-piece mold.

Open screw eye. An open screw eye used in plug construction so that a treble hook can be added to the eye. The screw is then closed with pliers before being screwed into the plug body.

Pack rod. A rod, usually spinning, fly, or casting, which by means of multiple sections and ferrules, breaks down for easy packing for a backpack or horse pack-in trip. They are also useful for short business trips where much tackle cannot be taken. Usual breakdown length is between 18 and 22 inches.

Parabolic action. Rod action in which the rod bends evenly from the tip to the handle. This is the best type of action for most rods. See also Wet fly action.

Payne style grip. A fly rod grip similar to the cigar or Phillippe style grip, except that the rear of the grip has straight parallel sides. Only the front is tapered like a cigar. See chart in Appendix.

Phillippe style grip. A round fly rod grip, large in the middle and smaller at both ends, similar to a fat cigar. See chart in Appendix.

Phillippe tapered-style grip. A tapered fly rod grip with straight sides, the forward end of the grip thicker than the rear diameter.

Pinch-on sinker. A long tapered sinker with a slot cut in the long axis for the line and small ears at each end to clamp the sinker on the line.

Pistol grip. A large heavy grip used on casting and spin cast rods, used primarily in bass fishing. Usually made of plastic or wood, sometimes of cork, sometimes called a comfort grip, or bass grip.

Plastic foam. A tough solid plastic used in many saltwater plugs, where it is especially adaptable for commercial through-wire construction molding.

Pompanette snap. A very long snap, usually made in extra-heavy wire, and designed primarily for big game use. Comes in large sizes only, with 100-pound test the minimum size.

Pouring ladle. A long-handled ladle, usually of cast iron, used for pouring molten lead into jig and sinker molds. It comes in various sizes with capacities from one to about six pounds.

Propeller blades. Similar to a plane propeller in which the two blades are joined to the spinner shaft by a centrally placed hole.

Quill dart jig. See Dart jig.

Reel bands. See Spinning rod rings.

Reel seat. A tubular device fitted with hoods to hold the reel foot and locking threaded rings to hold the hoods in place. They come in a number of sizes, colors, and styles, for the fly, spinning, casting, spin-cast, surf, boat, and big game rods. Big game and trolling rod reel seats often incorporate a ferrule as well. Lightweight skeletal reel seats are sometimes used on fly rods, while sliding rings serve the same purpose on some spinning rods.

Reel seat bushing. See Bushing.

Ripple blade. A blade with a rippled surface almost like the surface of corrugated cardboard.

Rod hosel. See Hosel.

Rod tip. The upper section of a two-piece rod or the uppermost section of a multiple-piece rod. Can also mean the uppermost portion of any rod.

Rod winding check. See Winding check.

Roller guide. A big game rod guide in which the guide is fitted with a smooth roller over which the line runs. The advantage of roller guides in big game fishing is that the roller will prevent line wear during strong fast runs of a large fish.

Ruby lip bucktail. A bucktail or jig with pronounced lips molded in. Usually the lips of the finished lure are painted bright red, thus the name.

Safety snap. A small snap that closes and locks almost like a safety pin. Used for attaching lures to line.

Scale finish netting. A small-mesh, hexagonal-hole netting designed especially for painting the scale finishes on lures and plugs. The lure is painted a base color, held tightly against the netting, and sprayed with a finishing color. The base color shows through the finish color as scales. For details see Chapter 12.

Scoop. A term sometimes used for a large type of wiggle plate or lip that causes a lure to dive deeply.

Screw eyes. Either open or closed small wire screw eyes used in plug construction. The closed screw eyes are used for the head of the plug (where the line is tied on) while open screw eyes are used where the hooks are to be added to the lure. Both styles come in several different wire thicknesses and several lengths.

Self-lock snap shaft. A type of spinner shaft in which the open loop end of the eye can be closed in a manner similar to fastening a safety pin. It makes the use of coil-spring fasteners on a loop-eye shaft unnecessary, while still allowing the option of changing hooks.

Shoulder. That part of a male ferrule extending from the center portion (that fits into the female ferrule) to the cap. The cap is the tapered end onto which the thread windings are wrapped. No longer a widely used term.

Shuttle. The plastic device used to hold net-making twine, so that it can be passed easily through the net while making rows of net meshes. They come in different sizes for use with different-size net twine and for different-size net meshes.

Single-cavity mold. A bucktail or jig mold which makes only one lure at a time. This type of mold is usually found only in the more expensive and highly finished professional type molds that mold lures with no flash. It can also apply to an open-face worm mold that has only one cavity for making one worm at a time.

Slag. The waste materials found in most lead and lead alloys used for molding lead-head lures and sinkers. It floats to the surface of the molten lead and can be skimmed off before the lead is poured into any mold.

Slip sinker. A bullet-shaped sinker used in fishing plastic worms. Also see Egg sinker.

Snake guide. A small guide used on fly rods that is made from a single piece of wire and looks almost like a twisted snake. It comes in different sizes and finishes.

Solid brass rings. Small solid brass rings used in lure and terminal riggings when a high degree of strength for size is needed.

Specie cork. The better of the two types of cork used in rod handles. In specie cork, the natural pits in the cork run parallel to the central hole drilled in the cork ring. It sometimes comes in two grades, Extra Select and Select, the Extra Select rare but better since it has fewer pits. See also Mustard cork.

Spinner bait jig. A lead head molded on a wire or safety pin for finishing as a spinner bait.

Spinner bearing. A small bead used between the clevis and the body of the spinner for frictionless rotation of the spinner blade. Without a spinner bearing the clevis will have a tendency to bind on the spinner body. Also called a uni-spin or unie.

Spinner body. A small, usually tapered body with a hole through the long axis, used as the body in building spinners. Commercially available in brass and other metals, as well as painted lead. Molds for making these bodies out of lead are available as well.

Spinning guide. A guide with a large-diameter ring to be used on spinning rods and with spinning reels. The theory of the large ring is that the rod will cast better since the line is coming off the spinning reel in large loops. One theory claims that the first or butt guide should be two-thirds the diameter of the spinning reel spool. The guide rings decrease in size toward the tip top.

Spinning-rod rings. These are rings placed over the spinning rod handle to hold the reel in place when a fixed reel seat is not used. The two rings fit snugly on the cork handle and are usually tapered or swaged to hold the foot of the reel.

Split-ring pliers. Made by the Worth Company, these small inexpensive pliers have a tooth at the end of one jaw for opening a split ring in making spinners and spoons. Indispensable for the spoon and spinner maker.

Split rings. Like miniature key rings, these round rings make possible easy attachment of hooks, swivels, and other fittings to the body of a spoon or spinner. Also used to attach hooks to some plugs and to make other terminal riggings.

Sprue hole. The funnel-shaped opening into a two-piece mold cavity through which the molten metal or liquid plastic is poured to mold sinkers, bucktails, and plastic lures. Also called a gate or down gate.

Stainless steel leader wire. Single-strand leader wire made from stainless steel. Used in saltwater.

Straddle mounting. Mounting the guide by wrapping the guide feet at the side, not the top, of the rod. A special type of four-footed guide must be used to straddle the rod blank. Used mainly in big game rods.

Stripping guide. The lowest or butt guide on a fly rod, this guide is not a snake guide (such as is used on the rest of the rod) but instead a lightweight small ring spinning or spin-cast guide. Also called a butt guide.

Swivel shaft. A spinner shaft in which half of a swivel is built into the end used for line attachment. Helps prevent line twist.

Swing blade. A narrow elliptical tapered spinner blade used in popular types of spinners.

Tail tags. Small bright pieces of plastic drilled with a hole at one end and attached to the eye of a spinner shaft along with the treble hook. Used to make the spinner more attractive to fish.

Template. A paper, cardboard, steel, or plastic sheet with the outline shape of a plug, spoon, spinner blade, rod handle, or similar item. The template makes it easy to duplicate a number of identical tackle items.

Tenite. A tough plastic often used in injection molding of plastic fishing lures. Most plug bodies sold to tackle tinkerers are of this material.

Thread windings. See Windings.

Three-way swivel. A swivel with three eyes for tying line, all three at equidistant points around the central ring that holds the eyes.

Through-wire construction. A method by which all the hooks of a plug as well as the eye to which the line is tied are connected together through the center of the plug with a heavy wire. Used primarily on saltwater plugs, where the chance is greater that a fish may shatter a plug on a strike. The two methods of through-wire construction are outlined in Chapter 7.

Tip action. Rod action in which most of the bending is in the tip of the rod. See also Dry fly action.

Tip top. Sometimes called the top guide or top eye, it is the topmost line guide. It is mounted on a metal tube which in turn is fitted onto the top of the rod. There are spinning rod, casting rod, spin casting, trolling, and big game roller guide styles. Also called top guide.

Tonkin cane. Comes from the Tonkin province of China, and is the best cane available for making split-bamboo rods.

Top guide. See Tip top.

Top rod mounting. Refers to the type of guide foot and how it is mounted on the rod. In this type of mounting, the guide foot sits directly on top of the rod and is wrapped in place. See also Straddle mounting.

Trim windings. See Windings.

Trolling sinker. A sinker made specifically for trolling. These can be crescent-shaped, torpedo-shaped, or keeled. The crescent and keeled shapes precent line twist, while the torpedo-shaped sinker is usually molded with swivels in each end (or added later) to minimize twist.

Tungsten carbide guide. Guide in which the rings of the guide are made of tungsten carbide, a very hard tough slightly brittle material. Called Carboloy, a trademark of General Electric, or Mildarbide, a trademark of the same material by Mildrum.

Twisted leader wire. Leader wire made from a number of smaller strands. Used with leader sleeves for making leaders and terminal riggings.

Two-part plug. 1. A plug in two halves, joined in the middle by two screw eyes. These plugs wiggle more under water and presumably are more lifelike. Also called jointed plugs. 2. Plastic plug blanks which come in two halves and must be glued together before finishing or using.

Two-piece mold. A mold for making sinkers, bucktails, or plastic lures in which two halves of the mold are joined so as to make a round finished lure. The two mold halves are either hinged and handled, locked by clamps, or pinned together to assure proper register of the two half-mold cavities. The molten metal or liquid plastic is poured into the mold cavity through a gate or sprue hole.

U frame guide. Spinning, casting, or spin-cast guide in which the frame holding the guide ring is of a U shape when viewed from the end of the guide. See V frame guide.

Under-wrapping. A thread wrapping placed on the rod before a guide is seated. Not often used on light rods, under-wrapping helps protect the finish of the rod blank under the strain of fighting a big fish.

Unie. See Spinner bearing.

Unispin. See Spinner bearing.

V frame guide. Spinning, casting or spin-cast guide in which the frame holding the guide ring is shaped like a V when viewed from the end. See U frame guide.

Varnish. A clear protective finish for rods and especially rod wrappings. The best is a special rod varnish or a spar varnish, placed on the rod or windings in thin coatings. Color preservative must be used over thread wrappings before varnishing or the varnish will change the color of the thread.

Vinyl skirt. A soft flexible skirt of plastic strands that can be attached to a plug, spinner, bucktail, or other lure, either as the primary skirt or as an additional attraction. They come in several sizes and many colors. Also called rubber skirt.

Weed guard. A wire device that extends over the hook to prevent it from catching weeds while being retrieved. Both single and double wire weed guards are used and can be wrapped, soldered, or wired to the hook shank.

Welt. The thicker, outer lip of a female ferrule designed to protect the lip from expanding with the strain of flexing the rod.

Wet fly action. A slow type of fly rod action in which the bend of the rod is well down into or toward the grip. Named because it was desired for wet fly fishing years ago in contrast to the fast tip action of a dry fly rod. Rods today are seldom characterized by the type of fishing, even though different actions are available.

Wiggle eye. A small plastic bubble with a flat back (to be glued to a plug) and a loose dark central pupil. Because the pupil is loose in the plastic bubble, it rolls around as the lure moves through the water.

Wiggle lips. Metal lips, screwed to the head of a plug, and designed to make it dive under water. They come in a wide variety of shapes and sizes, to fit all plugs and to vary the diving depth of the plug. Also called a wiggle plate.

Wiggle plate. See Wiggle lips.

Willow leaf blade. A long thin spinner blade, similar in shape to a willow leaf, used most often in spinners, placed in front of a trolled bait or other lures.

Winding check. A small round dish-shaped metal plate, center drilled and designed to fit over the rod and tight against the upper rod handle. Primarily decorative. Also called grip check. A larger plastic fitting with the same function is called a rod hosel. See Hosel.

Windings. The wraps of thread that are used to hold the guides of a rod in place and are used also as decoration at other points on the rod. There are a number of types of windings, such as single wrap, double wrap, underwrap, spiral wrap, spiral wrap over Mylar, etc. Decorative wraps, also called "trim" wraps, are also placed at the ferrules, tip top, and the winding check or rod hosel. These wraps serve no purpose other than decoration. Windings are usually made with silk or nylon thread, but monofilament line and stainless steel wire can also be used.

Wire clevis. A clevis formed from round wire with the ends flattened and drilled for the holes. (See also Clevis.)

Wire former. A tool used for bending or forming wire. They come in two basic sizes. The large size is used by the tackle tinkerer to bend wire for making eyes for sinkers and tin squids, hook lears, bottom rigs, trolling sinkers, and similar wire devices. Wire formers for handling small wire are used for making closed, loop, and self-locking snap eyes in spinner shaft wire. There are several commercial wire formers for handling the small diameter wire, but a homemade wire former can be used for the larger tackle items.

Wrappings. See Windings.

APPENDIX 2

CHARTS AND TABLES

SIZE CHARTS

⟞ The Following Charts Will Be Useful in Determining the Size of many of the tackle components described in the text of the book. In all cases, where there is any doubt as to the proper size of hooks, ferrules, guides, tip tops, plug hardware, spinner blades, and the like, refer to the following. In addition, there is a chart listing suggestive guide spacing for a number of types of fly, spinning, spin-cast, and casting rods.

HOW TO SIZE GUIDES

Mildrum guide sizes are designated by the outside diameter of the guide rings. This measurement is expressed in millimeters. The printed circles below are in true dimension and will enable you to select Mildrum guides properly.

SIZE CHART FOR TOP ROD GUIDES OR TIP TOPS

Mildrum tops are designated by the inside diameter of the tube expressed in 64ths of an inch. Printed circles are in true dimension and will enable you to correctly size tops for any rod (see following page).

> NOTE: Guides of other manufacturers may be measured by the inside diameter instead of the outside diameter as are Mildrum guides. Check to be sure before buying guides.

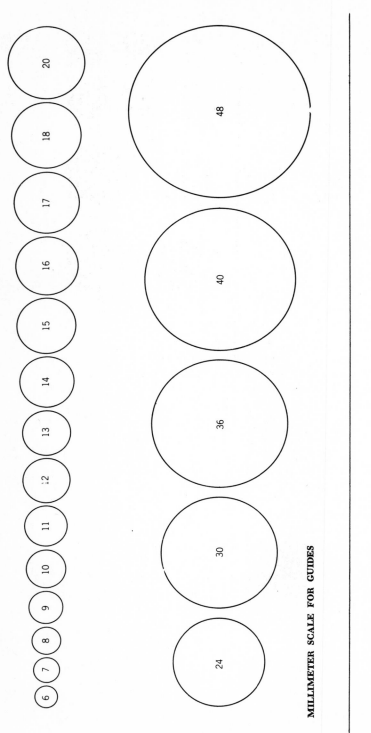

MILLIMETER SCALE FOR GUIDES

64THS OF AN INCH SCALE FOR TOPS

Courtesy: Mildrum Manufacturing Company

FERRULE SIZE CHART

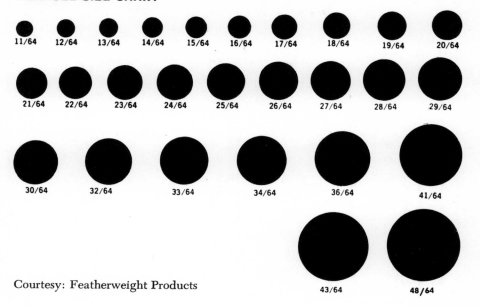

Courtesy: Featherweight Products

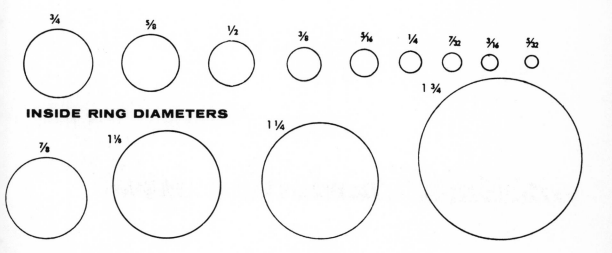

INSIDE RING DIAMETERS

Courtesy: Gudebrod Bros. Silk Company, Inc.

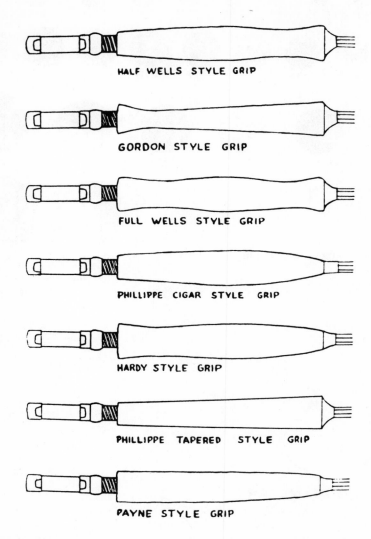

HALF WELLS STYLE GRIP

GORDON STYLE GRIP

FULL WELLS STYLE GRIP

PHILLIPPE CIGAR STYLE GRIP

HARDY STYLE GRIP

PHILLIPPE TAPERED STYLE GRIP

PAYNE STYLE GRIP

Fly rod grip shape chart from *Professional Glass and Split-Bamboo Rod Building Manual and Manufacturers Guide,* by George Leonard Herter.

GUIDE SPACING CHART

All measurements are from the tip of the rod down. Figures indicate measurement at the guide ring.

CASTING OR SPIN-CASTING RODS	1st	2nd	3rd	4th	5th	6th	7th	8th
5 1/2′ light action	4½	12	23	36				
6′ medium-light action	4	10	18	28	40			
6′ wide range taper, medium action	4	8¼	13	18	24½	32⅛	42	
6′ wide range taper, medium-heavy action	3½	7½	12	17⅜	23⅝	31⅞	42½	
6′ 4″ hairline rod, very light	4	10	18½	28½	41			
6′ 4″ tournament rod, 3/8 ounce	4	10	18½	28½	41			
6′ 4″ light action, some butt power	4	10	18½	28½	41			
6′ 4″ reserve power, 1/4 to 5/8 ounce	4	10	18½	28½	41			
FLY RODS								
5′ 5″ ultra-light flea rod	5	13	25	40				
6′ fly rod	3	7½	12	17¾	25	33	42½	
7′ 6″ fast-action dry fly	6	13	21	30	41½	60		
7′ 8″ lightest dry fly	6	13	21	30	43	62		
8′ all-around trout	6	13	21	30	41	52	66	
8′ dry fly	6	13	21	30	40	53	66	
8′ light bass bug action	6	13	21	30	41	53	66	
8′ 6″ medium-weight dry fly	6	13	21	30	40	56	73	
8′ 6″ power butt, sensitive tip	6	13	21	30	40	56	73	
9′ featherweight	5	11	18	26	35	45	58½	73
9′ bass or salmon	5	11	18	26	35	45	58½	73
10′ saltwater or salmon	6	13	22	32	43	54½	66½	80½
PARABOLIC ACTION FLY RODS								
7′ full parabolic action	5½	12	19¾	28½	38	55		
7′ 6″ full parabolic	5½	12	19½	28	41	59		
8′ full parabolic action	6	13	21	30	41	52	66	
SPINNING RODS								
4′ 6″ ultra light	5	11¾	19¾	29				
5′ ultra light	5	11	18	25½	34			
6′ featherweight, lures to 1/4 ounce	5½	15½	27½	40½				
6′ ultra light, 4 pound line	3½	10	19	29¼	41½			
6′ 6″ light action, lures to 1/4 ounce	3½	8½	15	23	33	46		
6′ 6″ medium-light action	3½	8½	15	23	33	46		
6′ 6″ wide-range taper, lures 1/8 to 1 ounce	5	10⅜	16⅜	23⅜	31⅞	44		
6′ 6″ wide-range taper	5	10⅜	16⅜	23⅜	31⅞	44		
6′ 6″ medium action, lures 1/8 to 3/8 ounce	3½	8½	15	23	33	46		
7′ combination spinning and fly	4	10	18	27½	38½	52½		
7′ light action, lures 1/16 to 3/8 ounce	4	10	18	27½	38½	52½		
6′ 6″ heavy action, lures to 5/8 ounce	3½	8½	15	23	33	46		
7′ heavy fresh or light saltwater action	4	10	18	27½	38	51		

NOTE: Chart is courtesy of Reed Tackle, Caldwell, N.J., and is based on the rods listed in their catalog. Notations as to the action of the rods have been abbreviated by the author from a fuller description in the Reed catalog. While these guide spacings are adequate for most rods, they should only be considered a guide—some changes and adjustments may be necessary to achieve proper results and action on rods of other suppliers and manufacturers.

SIZE CHARTS—PLUG HARDWARE

Screw Eyes

Style

1   2

D2   D1   C1   B1   A1   1A

Actual Size

Plug Propellers

Actual Size

"S" Connectors

S S S

Actual Size

Courtesy: Herter's, Inc.

Solid Connectors

1

2   3

Slide Link Connectors

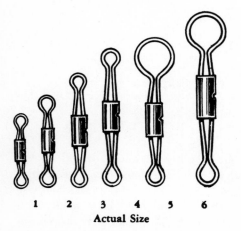

1   2   3   4   5   6

Actual Size

Courtesy: Herter's, Inc.

Plug Propellers

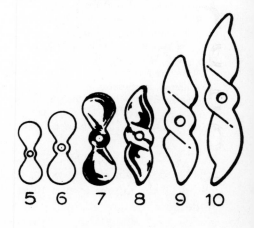

5   6   7   8   9   10

Courtesy: Finnysports

SNAP AND SWIVEL SIZE CHART

Snaps

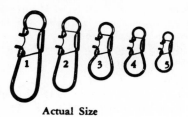

Actual Size

Snaps—Swivels

Actual Size

Swivels

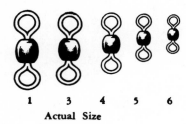

Actual Size

Duo-Lock Snaps

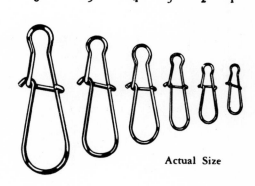

Actual Size

Three-way Swivels

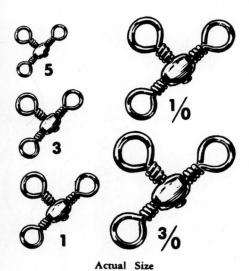

Actual Size

Courtesy: Herter's, Inc.

FRESH WATER SERIES

General usage: nos. 1 and 2, light spin fishing; no. 2, casting also; no. 3, spinning, casting and trolling; no. 4, casting and trolling; no. 5, heavy casting and trolling; no. 6, extra heavy trolling.

The pound designation figure below each number indicates swivel test.

SALT WATER SERIES

Designed for use in all types of salt water fishing. Different riggings are available for local fishing requirements and preferences.

The pound designation figure below each number indicates swivel test.

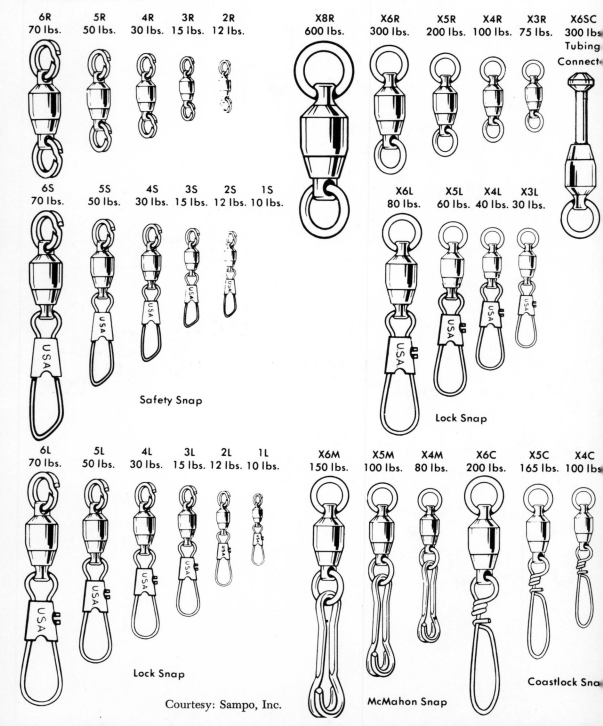

Safety Snap

Lock Snap

Lock Snap

Lock Snap

McMahon Snap

Coastlock Sna

SIZE CHART FOR BEAD CHAIN SWIVELS

SWIVELS

ITEM NO.	LBS. TEST

PLAIN

21	25
61	35
101	75
131	175

SINGLE SNAP

22	25
32	30
62	35
645	45
102	75
132	120

DOUBLE SNAP

63	35
103	75
133	120

Pat. Pend.

LOCK TYPE SNAP

62L	35
102L	75
132L	150

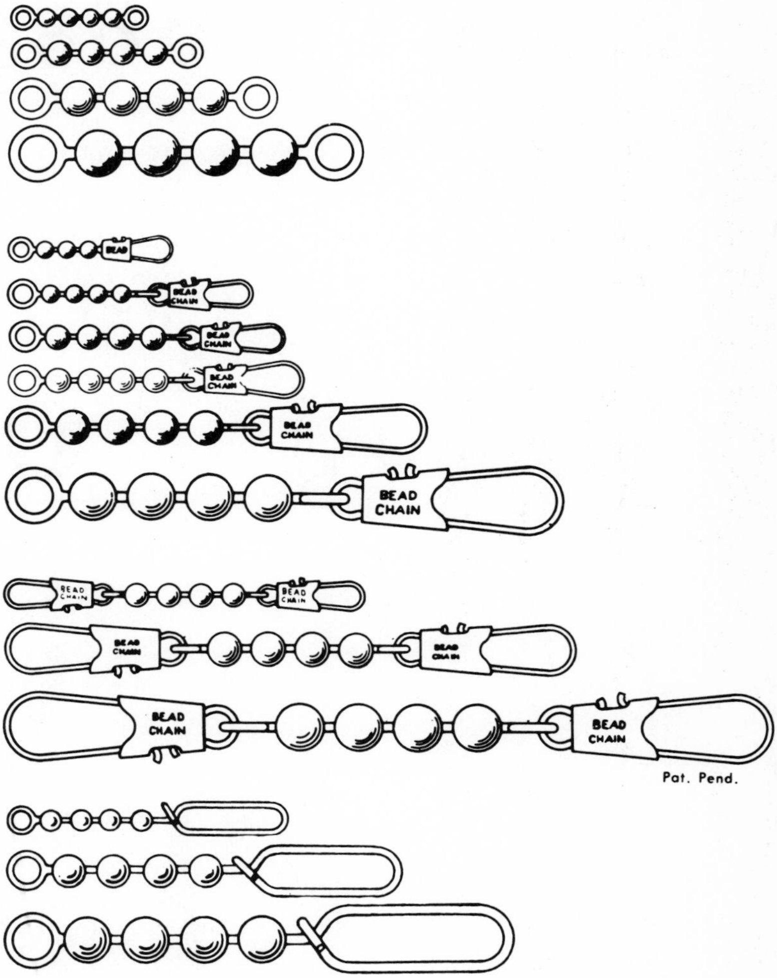

Courtesy: Bead Chain Company

SIZE CHARTS—SPINNER PARTS

Swivel Shank Spinner Shafts

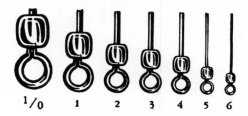

1/0   1   2   3   4   5   6

Courtesy: Herter's, Inc.

Clevises

Folded

1W   2W   3W

Stamped

CL-0   CL-1   CL-3

Wire

1   2   3

Courtesy: Finnysports

Split Rings

7   8   9   10   11   12

WORTH

Above are Actual Sizes of Split Rings

Courtesy: The Worth Company

SIZE CHARTS—SPINNER BLADES

Hoosier Blades

Actual Size

Fluted Trolling Blades

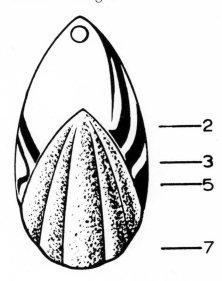

—— 2

—— 3

—— 5

—— 7

Courtesy: Finnysports

Courtesy: Finnysports

Doc Shelton Trolling Blades

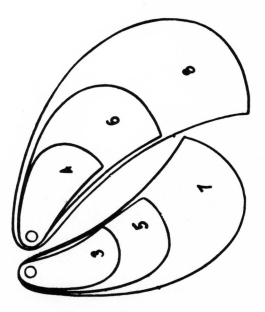

Car Fender Trolling Blades

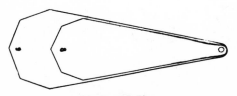

½ Actual Size

Courtesy: Herter's

Courtesy: Finnysports

SIZE CHARTS—SPINNER BLADES

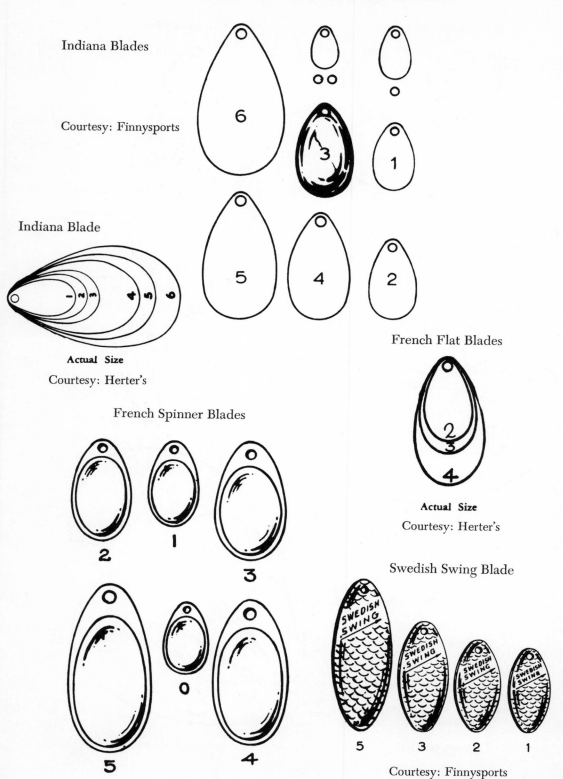

Indiana Blades

Courtesy: Finnysports

Indiana Blade

Actual Size

Courtesy: Herter's

French Spinner Blades

French Flat Blades

Actual Size

Courtesy: Herter's

Swedish Swing Blade

Courtesy: Finnysports

SIZE CHARTS—SPINNER BLADES

Jet Spinners

Courtesy: Finnysports

Bar Bell Propellers

Courtesy: Finnysports

Colorado Blades

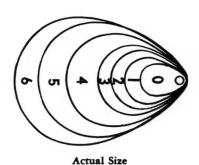

Actual Size

Courtesy: Herter's

Willow Leaf Blades

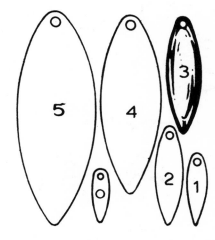

Courtesy: Finnysports

Mother-of-Pearl Blades

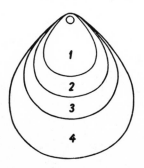

**Willow
Leaf
Actual Size**

**Indiana
Actual Size**

Courtesy: Herter's, Inc.

SIZE CHARTS—SPINNER BLADES

Lobo Blade

Silver City Blades

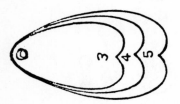

Courtesy: Herter's

Rhythm Blades

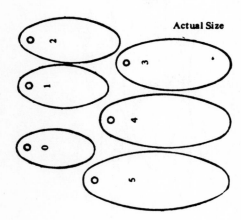

Actual Size

Courtesy: Finnysports

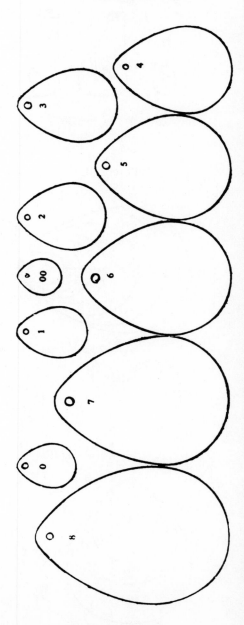

Courtesy: Finnysports

SIZE CHART FOR PLASTIC WORM HOOKS
EAGLE CLAW WORM MASTER

**SOUTHERN SPROAT
WORM HOLDER
KINKED SHANK**

295JB BRONZE FINISH
295JBL BLUED FINISH
295JW NICKEL PLATED

APPROXIMATE SIZE

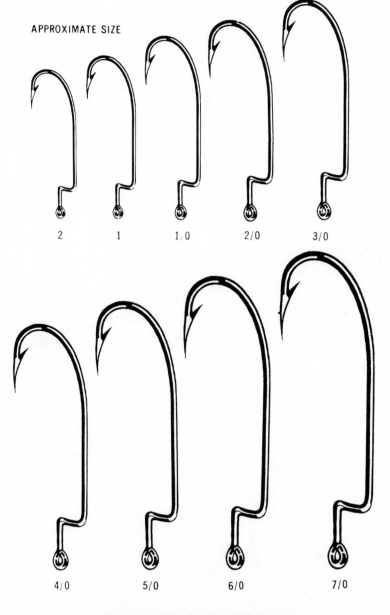

2   1   1/0   2/0   3/0

4/0   5/0   6/0   7/0

Courtesy: Wright & McGill Company

SIZE CHART FOR PLASTIC WORM HOOKS
EAGLE CLAW WORM MASTER

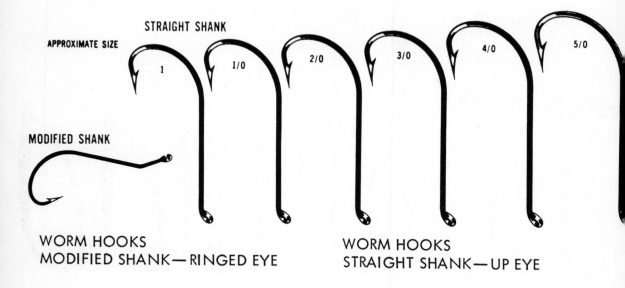

STRAIGHT SHANK

APPROXIMATE SIZE

1   1/0   2/0   3/0   4/0   5/0

MODIFIED SHANK

WORM HOOKS
MODIFIED SHANK—RINGED EYE

WORM HOOKS
STRAIGHT SHANK—UP EYE

WEEDLESS "Nylon Bonded"
Pat.

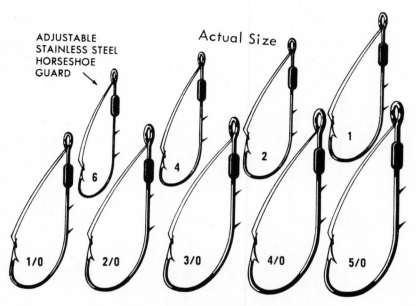

ADJUSTABLE
STAINLESS STEEL
HORSESHOE
GUARD

Actual Size

6   4   2   1

1/0   2/0   3/0   4/0   5/0

Courtesy: Wright & McGill Company

SIZE CHART FOR EAGLE CLAW
WEIGHTED WEEDLESS WORM HOOKS

WEIGHTED WEEDLESS

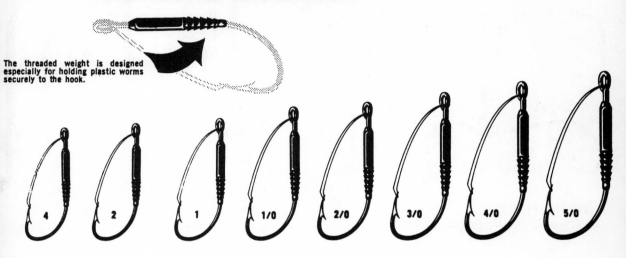

The threaded weight is designed especially for holding plastic worms securely to the hook.

4   2   1   1/0   2/0   3/0   4/0   5/0

Courtesy: Wright & McGill Company

SIZE CHART FOR JIG HOOKS

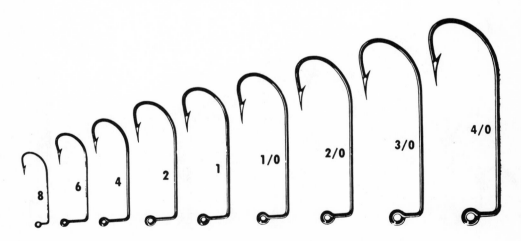

8   6   4   2   1   1/0   2/0   3/0   4/0

Courtesy: Wright & McGill Company

SIZE CHART—OPEN EYE SIWASH HOOKS

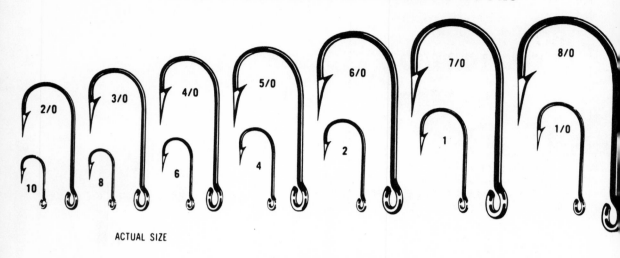

ACTUAL SIZE

Courtesy: Wright & McGill Company

SIZE CHART FOR TREBLE HOOKS

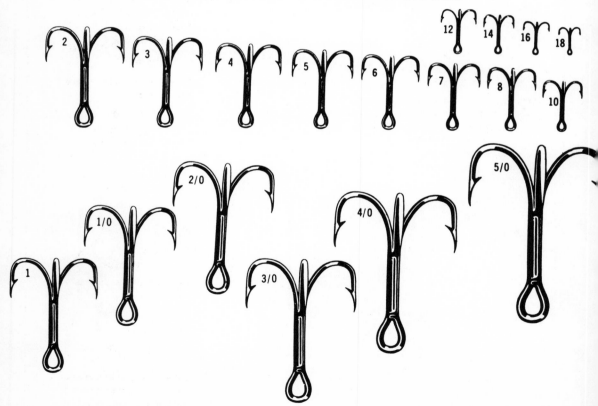

Courtesy: Wright & McGill Company

HOW TO MAKE A PROPER CRIMP

1
Thread end of leader material through sleeve forming a loop, do not allow end to protrude. To avoid the possibility of slippage, be certain to use the proper size sleeve.

2
Hold the loop in a horizontal position - be careful not to cross wire inside sleeve - apply the crimping tool in a horizontal position to the sleeve, and crimp in one or more places depending on the length of the sleeve.

3
NOTICE HOW FIRMLY AND COMPLETELY The Sleeve Strand Swadges Around All Strands Of The Wire!
IMPORTANT
We recommend the use of two sleeves spaced one inch apart on the 90 - 400 lb. test leader material.

TO GAIN A STRONGER LOOP WHEN APPLYING SLEEVES TO SEVALON AND DURATEST

1
Thread Sevalon thru sleeve and hook eye.

2
Make overhand knot.

3
Go thru hook a second time.

4
Make second overhand knot thru sleeve, draw up loop and crimp twice.

Courtesy: Fenwick

English-Metric Conversion Table

Inches Dec.	mm	Inches Dec.	mm	Inches Frac.	Dec.	mm	Inches Frac.	Dec.	mm
0.01	0.2540	0.51	12.9540						
0.02	0.5080	0.52	13.2080	1/64	0.015625	0.3969	33/64	0.515625	13.0969
0.03	0.7620	0.53	13.4620	1/32	0.031250	0.7938	17/32	0.531250	13.4938
0.04	1.0160	0.54	13.7160	3/64	0.046875	1.1906	35/64	0.546875	13.8906
0.05	1.2700	0.55	13.9700						
0.06	1.5240	0.56	14.2240	1/16	0.062500	1.5875	9/16	0.562500	14.2875
0.07	1.7780	0.57	14.4780	5/64	0.078125	1.9844	37/64	0.578125	14.6844
0.08	2.0320	0.58	14.7320	3/32	0.093750	2.3812	19/32	0.593750	15.0812
0.09	2.2860	0.59	14.9860	7/64	0.109375	2.7781	39/64	0.609375	15.4781
0.10	2.5400	0.60	15.2400						
0.11	2.7940	0.61	15.4940	1/8	0.125000	3.1750	5/8	0.625000	15.8750
0.12	3.0480	0.62	15.7480						
0.13	3.3020	0.63	16.0020	9/64	0.140625	3.5719	41/64	0.640625	16.2719
0.14	3.5560	0.64	16.2560	5/32	0.156250	3.9688	21/32	0.656250	16.6688
0.15	3.8100	0.65	16.5100	11/64	0.171875	4.3656	43/64	0.671875	17.0656
0.16	4.0640	0.66	16.7640						
0.17	4.3180	0.67	17.0180	3/16	0.187500	4.7625	11/16	0.687500	17.4625
0.18	4.5720	0.68	17.2720	13/64	0.203125	5.1594	45/64	0.703125	17.8594
0.19	4.8260	0.69	17.5260	7/32	0.218750	5.5562	23/32	0.718750	18.2562
0.20	5.0800	0.70	17.7800	15/64	0.234375	5.9531	47/64	0.734375	18.6531
0.21	5.3340	0.71	18.0340						
0.22	5.5880	0.72	18.2880	1/4	0.250000	6.3500	3/4	0.750000	19.0500
0.23	5.8420	0.73	18.5420	17/64	0.265625	6.7469	49/64	0.765625	19.4469
0.24	6.0960	0.74	18.7960	9/32	0.281250	7.1438	25/32	0.781250	19.8437
0.25	6.3500	0.75	19.0500	19/64	0.296875	7.5406	51/64	0.796875	20.2406
0.26	6.6040	0.76	19.3040						
0.27	6.8580	0.77	19.5580	5/16	0.312500	7.9375	13/16	0.812500	20.6375
0.28	7.1120	0.78	19.8120	21/64	0.328125	8.3344	53/64	0.828125	21.0344
0.29	7.3660	0.79	20.0660	11/32	0.343750	8.7312	27/32	0.843750	21.4312
0.30	7.6200	0.80	20.3200	23/64	0.359375	9.1281	55/64	0.859375	21.8281
0.31	7.8740	0.81	20.5740						
0.32	8.1280	0.82	20.8280	3/8	0.375000	9.5250	7/8	0.875000	22.2250
0.33	8.3820	0.83	21.0820						
0.34	8.6360	0.84	21.3360	25/64	0.390625	9.9219	57/64	0.890625	22.6219
0.35	8.8900	0.85	21.5900	13/32	0.406250	10.3188	29/32	0.906250	23.0188
0.36	9.1440	0.86	21.8440	27/64	0.421875	10.7156	59/64	0.921875	23.4156
0.37	9.3980	0.87	22.0980						
0.38	9.6520	0.88	22.3520	7/16	0.437500	11.1125	15/16	0.937500	23.8125
0.39	9.9060	0.89	22.6060	29/64	0.453125	11.5094	61/64	0.953125	24.2094
0.40	10.1600	0.90	22.8600	15/32	0.468750	11.9062	31/32	0.968750	24.6062
0.41	10.4140	0.91	23.1140	31/64	0.484375	12.3031	63/64	0.984375	25.0031
0.42	10.6680	0.92	23.3680						
0.43	10.9220	0.93	23.6220	1/2	0.500000	12.7000	1	1.000000	25.4000
0.44	11.1760	0.94	23.8760						
0.45	11.4300	0.95	24.1300						
0.46	11.6840	0.96	24.3840						
0.47	11.9380	0.97	24.6380						
0.48	12.1920	0.98	24.8920						
0.49	12.4460	0.99	25.1460						
0.50	12.7000	1.00	25.4000						

For converting decimal-inches in "thousandths," move decimal point in both columns to left.

Courtesy: The L. S. Starrett Company

Metric-English Conversion Table

mm	Inches	mm	Inches	mm	Inches	mm	Inches	mm	Inches
0.01	.00039	0.41	.01614	0.81	.03189	21	.82677	61	2.40157
0.02	.00079	0.42	.01654	0.82	.03228	22	.86614	62	2.44094
0.03	.00118	0.43	.01693	0.83	.03268	23	.90551	63	2.48031
0.04	.00157	0.44	.01732	0.84	.03307	24	.94488	64	2.51968
0.05	.00197	0.45	.01772	0.85	.03346	25	.98425	65	2.55905
0.06	.00236	0.46	.01811	0.86	.03386	26	1.02362	66	2.59842
0.07	.00276	0.47	.01850	0.87	.03425	27	1.06299	67	2.63779
0.08	.00315	0.48	.01890	0.88	.03465	28	1.10236	68	2.67716
0.09	.00354	0.49	.01929	0.89	.03504	29	1.14173	69	2.71653
0.10	.00394	0.50	.01969	0.90	.03543	30	1.18110	70	2.75590
0.11	.00433	0.51	.02008	0.91	.03583	31	1.22047	71	2.79527
0.12	.00472	0.52	.02047	0.92	.03622	32	1.25984	72	2.83464
0.13	.00512	0.53	.02087	0.93	.03661	33	1.29921	73	2.87401
0.14	.00551	0.54	.02126	0.94	.03701	34	1.33858	74	2.91338
0.15	.00591	0.55	.02165	0.95	.03740	35	1.37795	75	2.95275
0.16	.00630	0.56	.02205	0.96	.03780	36	1.41732	76	2.99212
0.17	.00669	0.57	.02244	0.97	.03819	37	1.45669	77	3.03149
0.18	.00709	0.58	.02283	0.98	.03858	38	1.49606	78	3.07086
0.19	.00748	0.59	.02323	0.99	.03898	39	1.53543	79	3.11023
0.20	.00787	0.60	.02362	1.00	.03937	40	1.57480	80	3.14960
0.21	.00827	0.61	.02402	1	.03937	41	1.61417	81	3.18897
0.22	.00866	0.62	.02441	2	.07874	42	1.65354	82	3.22834
0.23	.00906	0.63	.02480	3	.11811	43	1.69291	83	3.26771
0.24	.00945	0.64	.02520	4	.15748	44	1.73228	84	3.30708
0.25	.00984	0.65	.02559	5	.19685	45	1.77165	85	3.34645
0.26	.01024	0.66	.02598	6	.23622	46	1.81102	86	3.38582
0.27	.01063	0.67	.02638	7	.27559	47	1.85039	87	3.42519
0.28	.01102	0.68	.02677	8	.31496	48	1.88976	88	3.46456
0.29	.01142	0.69	.02717	9	.35433	49	1.92913	89	3.50393
0.30	.01181	0.70	.02756	10	.39370	50	1.96850	90	3.54330
0.31	.01220	0.71	.02795	11	.43307	51	2.00787	91	3.58267
0.32	.01260	0.72	.02835	12	.47244	52	2.04724	92	3.62204
0.33	.01299	0.73	.02874	13	.51181	53	2.08661	93	3.66141
0.34	.01339	0.74	.02913	14	.55118	54	2.12598	94	3.70078
0.35	.01378	0.75	.02953	15	.59055	55	2.16535	95	3.74015
0.36	.01417	0.76	.02992	16	.62992	56	2.20472	96	3.77952
0.37	.01457	0.77	.03032	17	.66929	57	2.24409	97	3.81889
0.38	.01496	0.78	.03071	18	.70866	58	2.28346	98	3.85826
0.39	.01535	0.79	.03110	19	.74803	59	2.32283	99	3.89763
0.40	.01575	0.80	.03150	20	.78740	60	2.36220	100	3.93700

For converting millimetres in "thousandths" move decimal point in both columns to left.

APPENDIX 3

LIST OF SUPPLIERS

This list has been made as complete as possible, and compiled from all available sources of mail-order dealers and major manufacturers of tackle component items. Also check in the classified ads of the major outdoor magazines for additional or new listings. Fly-tying supply houses, not listed here, carry fur, feathers, thread, and sometimes other components used in building the tackle items mentioned in this book. Many of the following carry extensive general fish tackle other than the do-it-yourself components mentioned here.

Ace Cast Metal Products Company
2525 Monroe Avenue
Sta. "A," Box 2087
Cleveland, Ohio 44113

Manufacturers and dealers of sinker molds. Catalog sheet.

Allan Manufacturing Company
325 Duffy Avenue
Hicksville, New York 11801

Manufacturer of guides, fishing rod hardware, and parts. See dealers. Catalog.

Ament Mold Company
402 Capelle
Grain Valley, Missouri 64029

Manufacturer and mail-order distributor of bucktail and sinker molds. Catalog.

Anglers Pro Shop
Box 35
Springfield, Ohio 45501

Mail-order dealer of rod-building parts, blanks, and materials. Catalog.

Aspen Lures
Box 2918
Aspen, Colorado 81611

Mail-order distributor and manufacturer of spinner and spoon kits. Catalog.

Bead Chain Tackle Company
110 Mountain Grove Street
Bridgeport, Connecticut 06605

Manufacturer of bead chain terminal tackle. See dealers.

Berkley and Company, Inc.
Highway 9 and 71
Spirit Lake, Iowa 51360

Manufacturer of terminal tackle products, rods, reels, etc. See dealers. Catalog.

Best Bet Lures
7009 Pleasant Oak Circle
Charlotte, North Carolina 28214

Mail-order dealer of plastic lure molds and terminal tackle. Catalog.

Brookstone Company
12 Brookstone Building
Peterborough, New Hampshire 03458

Mail-order dealer of hard-to-find tools, including many of use to the tackle tinkerer. Catalog.

Cabela's, Inc.
Box 199
812 13th Avenue
Sidney, Nebraska 69162

Mail-order dealer in bucktail molds, plastic lure molds, rod blanks, and parts, etc. Catalog.

Carver Plastisols, Inc.
Box 432
Minden, Louisiana 71055

Worm kits, molds, and plastics for soft plastic lures. Catalog.

Lew Childre and Sanders, Inc.
Box 535
Foley, Alabama 36535

Manufacturer of rods, blanks, speed guides that can be added to blanks without thread wrappings. See dealers. Catalog.

DDD Tackle, Inc.
136 Boone Trail
Severna Park, Maryland 21146

Mail-order dealer of terminal tackle, surgical eel lure supplies. Catalog.

Sewell N. Dunton and Son, Inc.
4 Fiske Avenue
Greenefield, Massachusetts 01301

Manufacturer and dealer of split-bamboo fly and spinning rod kits. Catalog.

Easy Molds, Inc.
Box 64
Converse, Louisiana 71109

Detailed instructions on making bucktail molds from block aluminum.

Edmund Scientific Co.
300 Edscorp Building
Barrington, New Jersey 08007

Scientific supplies, carries small motors for rod wrapping, other tools, foil for lure use. Catalog.

Fairfield Sporting Goods Company
1275 Bloomfield Avenue
Fairfield, New Jersey 07006

Mail-order dealer of rod-building parts.

Featherweight Products
3454–58 Ocean View Blvd.
Glendale, California 91208

Manufacturer of rod blanks, popular rod-building handles, components, and ferrules. See dealers.

Fenwick/Sevenstrand Tackle Mfg. Co.
14799 Chestnut Street
Westminster, California 92683

Manufacturer of rod blanks, wire products, vinyl trolling skirts. Catalog; see dealers.

Finnysports
2910 Glanzman Road
Toledo, Ohio 43614

Large mail-order dealer of tackle, spinner, spoon, jig, sinker, plastic lure, rod building, and other do-it-yourself components. Catalog.

Fireside Angler, Inc.
Box 823
Melville, New York 11746

Mail-order dealer of fly materials, with some rod building also. Catalog.

Fish-it
Box 1033
Torrington, Connecticut 06790

Makes multi-action variable design do-it-yourself lures and plugs.

Fishin' World
5509 West Lovers Lane
Dallas, Texas 75209

Mail-order dealer in plastic worm kits, rod building parts, etc. Catalog.

Gladding–South Bend Tackle Company
Box 260
Syracuse, New York 13201

Manufacturer of terminal products. See dealers. Catalog.

Gudebrod Brothers Silk Company, Inc.
12 South 12th Street
Philadelphia, Pennsylvania 19107

Manufacturer of rod winding thread and Aetna guides. See dealers. Catalog.

Gene Bullard Custom Rods
10139 Shoreview Road
Dallas, Texas 75238

Rod blanks, handles, grips, guides, reel seats, similar materials for rod building. Catalog.

H & L Distributing Co., Inc.
Route 1
Finger, Tennessee 38334

Injection molding machines for molding soft plastic lures. Catalog.

Herter's, Inc.
Waseca, Minnesota 56093

Large mail-order dealer and manufacturer of tackle, spinner, spoon, plug, rod, plastic lure, sinker and bucktail parts, tools, and materials. Catalog.

E. Hille
815 Railway Street
Williamsport, Pennsylvania 17701

Mail-order dealer of rod, spinner, plug, and other tackle components. Catalog.

Horrocks-Ibbotson Company
20 Whitesboro Street Terminal
Utica, New York 13502

Manufacturer of general tackle including terminal snaps, swivels, etc. See dealers.

Ike's Fly Shop
23461 Norwood
Oak Park, Michigan 48237

Mail-order dealer of fly-tying equipment, but also carries rod-building parts. Catalog.

Joe's Custom Rods
5827 Hinckley Court
Dayton, Ohio 45424

Rod blanks, handles, grips, guides, similar materials for rod building. Catalog.

Lectrochem Company, Inc.
Box 319
Lake Bluff, Illinois 60044

Manufacturer of electroplating kit. See dealers.

H. L. Leonard Rod Company
25 Cottage Street
Midland Park, New Jersey 07432

Dealer of fine tackle, including rod building parts. Catalog.

Limit Manufacturing Corporation
515 Melody Lane
Richardson, Texas 75080

Mail-order dealer of kits, parts, and materials for plastic lure molding. Catalog.

Luhr Jensen and Sons, Inc.
West May
Hood River, Oregon 97031

Tackle manufacturer, including Prism Lite tape material for lures. Catalog.

Lure-Craft
Box 1418
Bloomington, Indiana 47401

Mail-order dealer of worm materials and molds. Catalog.

Lure Kits
2617 Franklinville Road
Joppa, Maryland 21085

Manufacturer and dealer in kits of lures made from nylon rope.

M-F Manufacturing Co., Inc.
Box 13442
Fort Worth, Texas 76118

Plastic worm kit, molds, and plastics for soft lures. Catalog. See dealers.

Maumelle Plastics Company
Box 5965
North Little Rock, Arkansas 72119

Mail-order dealer and manufacturer of plastic lure-molding supplies. Catalog.

Midland Tackle Company
66 Route 17
Sloatsburg, New York 10974

Mail-order dealer of sinker and jig molds, net twine, spoon and spinner blades and parts, rod-building parts, and surge lure tubing. Catalog.

Mildrum Manufacturing Company
230 Berlin Street
East Berlin, Connecticut 06023

Manufacturer of fishing rod guides. See dealers. Catalog.

O. Mustad and Son (USA), Inc.
Box 396
42 Washington Street
Auburn, New York 13021

Manufacturer of fish hooks. See dealers. Catalog.

Netcraft Company
3101 Sylvania
Toledo, Ohio 43613

Mail-order dealer of tackle, spinner, spoon, plug, rod, bucktail, sinker, plastic lure, and other tackle components. Catalog.

The Orvis Company
Manchester, Vermont 05254

Mail-order dealer of fine tackle, including rod-building parts. Catalog.

Ottawa Supply Company
Box 110
Miami, Oklahoma 74354

Soft plastic lure supplies, including molds, plastics. Catalog.

Palmer Manufacturing Company
Plummer School Road
West Newton, Pennsylvania 15089

Manufacturer and distributor of jig and sinker molds. Catalog.

Phillipson Rod Company
2705 High Street
Denver, Colorado 80205

Manufacturer of rod blanks, rod-building components. Catalog.

Reading Instrument Company
Box 78
Reading, Pennsylvania 19603

Manufacturer and mail-order dealer of sinker and squid molds. Catalog.

Reed Tackle
Box 390
Caldwell, New Jersey 07006

Mail-order dealer of rod, spinner, spoon, jig, and other supplies. Catalog.

Reinke Brothers
3144 West Greenfield Avenue
Milwaukee, Wisconsin 53215

Mail-order dealer of rod blanks, parts, and bucktail jigs, other do-it-yourself tackle.

Reynolds Metals Company
Richmond, Virginia 23261

Manufacturer of aluminum tubing, rod, sheet, etc. See dealers.

Rodmaker's Supply Catalog
3875 Lake Harbor Road
Muskegon, Michigan 49441

Mail-order dealer of rod-building blanks and parts. Catalog.

Sampo, Inc.
North Street
Barneveld, New York 13304

Manufacturer of ball-bearing and other swivels and terminal gear. See dealers. Catalog.

Santee Lure & Tackle Company, Inc.
730 East Trade Street
Charlotte, North Carolina 28202

Manufacturer and distributor of plastic worm kits that include the solid block plastic.

Shoff's Sporting Goods
406 West Meeker Street
Kent, Washington 98031

Mail-order dealer of rod-building supplies. Catalog.

Stembridge Products, Inc.
Box 90756
East Point, Georgia 30344

Manufacturer of plastic worms and felt-tip worm markers. See dealers. Catalog.

Super-Sport
Box 696
Bishop, California 93514

Worm Maker Kit, supplies, plastics, and two-piece molds. Catalog.

Tack-L-Tyers
939 Chicago Avenue
Evanston, Illinois 60202

Manufacturers of spinning lure and jig kits. See dealers.

Tackle-Craft
Box 489
Chippewa Falls, Wisconsin 54729

Mail-order dealer of plastic lure molds, other tackle. Catalog.

Tackle Shop
2406 Hancock Street
Bellevue, Nebraska 68005

Mail-order dealer of fly supplies but also jig molds and materials. Catalog.

Thomas and Thomas
4 Fiske Avenue
Greenfield, Massachusetts 01301

Manufacturer and dealer of rods, rod blanks, bamboo and glass. Catalog.

Toledo Manufacturing Company
Box 4042
Richardson, Texas 75080

Plastic worm kits, molds, and materials for soft plastic lures. Catalog.

Varmac Manufacturing Company, Inc.
4201 Redwood Avenue
Los Angeles, California 90066

Manufacturer of big game rod parts and guides. See dealers. Catalog.

Weber Tackle Company
Stevens Point, Wisconsin 54481

Manufacturer of terminal tackle parts. See dealers. Catalog.

Erwin Weller Company
2105 Clark Street
Sioux City, Iowa 51102

Manufacturer of terminal tackle items, general tackle. Catalog. See dealers.

The Worth Company
Box 88
Stevens Point, Wisconsin 54481

Manufacturer of split-ring pliers, terminal tackle, lure and jig kits. See dealers.

Wright and McGill Company
4245 East 46th Street
Denver, Colorado 80216

Manufacturer of tackle including Eagle Claw hooks. Catalog. See dealers.

SELECTED BIBLIOGRAPHY

There has been little comprehensive information in the past on tackle building, with most books covering only one or a few aspects of the field. A list of those that have appeared in past years include:

Bait Makers Bible, from Finnysports, Toledo, Ohio.

The Bamboo Rod and How to Build It, by Claude M. Kreider, The Macmillan Company, 1951. Out of print, but available in libraries for details on making split-bamboo rod blanks.

Fiberglass Rod-Making, by Dale P. Clemmens, Winchester Press, 1974.

Fisherman's Knots and Nets, by Raoul Graumont and Elmer Wenstrom, Cornell Maritime Press, Cambridge, Maryland, 1948.

How to Make Fishing Lures, by Vlad Evanoff, Ronald Press Company. Out of print, available at some libraries.

Popular Netcraft, by H. T. Ludgate, Netcraft Co. Details on all types of nets and techniques for making them.

Practical Fishing Knots, by Lefty Kreh and Mark Sosin, Crown Publishers. First book on fishing knots.

Professional Fly Tying, Spinning, and Tackle Making Manual and Manufacturer's Guide, by George Leonard Herter, Herter's, Inc., Waseca, Minn. Mostly on fly-tying, some on other lures.

Professional Glass and Split-Bamboo Rod Building Manual and Manufacturer's Guide, by George Leonard Herter, Herter's, Inc., Waseca, Minn. Out of print.

Rods—How to Make Them, by J. B. Walker, Herbert Jenkins Ltd., London, England. Not readily available.

Salt Water Fishing Tackle, by Harlan Major, Funk and Wagnalls Company. Out of print, but good information on tackle design.

Tackle Tinkering, by H. G. Tapply, A. S. Barnes and Company, N.Y., 1946. Out of print but available in libraries.

Tackle Tricks with Wire, by H. T. Ludgate, The Netcraft Company. Details on wire formers, fishing tackle made with wire.

332

Index